Film Review

1996-7

James Cameron-Wilson became a committed film buff when he moved to London at the age of seventeen. After a stint at the Webber Douglas Academy of Dramatic Art he joined *What's On In London* and took over from F. Maurice Speed as cinema editor. Later, he edited the trade newspaper *Showbiz*, became commissioning editor for *Film Review*, was the consultant and quizmaster for *The Movie Show* on BSkyB, and a frequent presenter on the Radio 2 *Arts Programme*. He is also the author of the books *Young Hollywood* and *The Cinema of Robert De Niro*. He currently writes for *Film Review*, *Flicks* and *The Times*, is syndicated in the *What's On* magazines and is the cinema correspondent for BBC Worldwide Television.

Film Review

1996-7

Including Video Releases

James Cameron-Wilson

Founding father: F. Maurice Speed

TO MY DAUGHTER JULIET,
WHOSE ENTHUSIASM FOR THE
CINEMA KEEPS MY OWN LOVE
ALIVE.

Acknowledgement

The author would like to express his
undying gratitude to the following,
without whom this book would not
have been possible (or at least damn
difficult): Charles Bacon, Ewen
Brownrigg, Christopher Cameron,
Sarah Clark, Joel and Ethan Coen (for
inspiration), Ian Gilchrist, Annabel
Hutton, Karen Krizanovich, Nigel
Mulock, my mother, Frances Palmer,
Virginia Palmer, Simon Rose, Mansel
Stimpson and David White. Till next
year...

First published in Great Britain in 1996 by
VIRGIN BOOKS
an imprint of Virgin Publishing Ltd
332 Ladbroke Grove, London W10 5AH

*A catalogue record for this book is available
from the British Library*

ISBN 0 7535 0012 4

Designed and typeset by Fred Price

Printed in Great Britain by
Butler & Tanner Ltd

Contents

Introduction	6
Top Twenty Box-Office Hits	8
Top Ten Box-Office Stars	10
Releases of the Year	12
Video Releases	135
Movie Quotations of the Year	147
Faces of the Year	152
Film World Diary	159
Film Soundtracks	165
Bookshelf	168
In Memoriam	173
Awards and Festivals	181
Index	187

Introduction

James
Cameron-Wilson

This, the 52nd edition of the world's longest-running film annual, is an historic one. Historic, because it is the last that its founder, F. Maurice Speed, will contribute to. At the respectable age of 85, Maurice (if I may call him that, although I still think of him as Mr Speed) has decided that enough is enough. I can't even begin to calculate how many films he has sat through in his celluloid-wrapped life, but the number must be mind numbing. They say that by the age of 80 the human brain holds enough data to fill 7,142,857, 142,860,000 floppy disks. Well, with the cinematic images that have gilded Maurice's imagination over the decades, he'd probably need a few trillion CD-ROMs as well.

He started the annual in 1944, the year of *Double Indemnity*, *Meet Me in St Louis*, *National Velvet* and D-Day. It was also the year that Danny DeVito, Michael Douglas, George Lucas and Alan Parker entered this world and Harry Langdon departed it.

Thirty-two years later I entered Maurice Speed's life as a callow clerk for *What's On In London*, the listings magazine he then edited alongside his duties on *Film Review*. While I harboured aspirations to

F. Maurice Speed enjoying a good read

become an actor, I was so bewitched by the world of journalism that I took an abrupt career-switch, a change of heart that landed me with the job of cinema editor before the year was out. To this day I remember one word of advice Maurice bestowed on me, which was *never* to refuse work when it was offered (even if it meant staying up all night on some occasions).

I can't say I've followed this counsel to the letter, but I've done my best to type my fingers to the bone, writing my first feature for *Film Review* – on the phenomenon of the *Emmanuelle* films! – for the 1978-9 edition. Since then my responsibilities on the annual have grown, leading up to my 'official' solo editorship this year.

Movies have changed dramatically since the inception of this book and we have tried to adapt accordingly. Not everything will be to Maurice's taste, but then cinemagoers' appetites have altered significantly. Speaking for myself, I still love the medium. And I know it is love that has sustained Maurice's commitment to *Film Review*.

Top Twenty Box-Office Hits

(for the period July 1995–June 1996)

1   Toy Story
2   Batman Forever
3   Seven
4   Babe
5   Goldeneye
6   Casper
7   Jumanji
8   Sense and Sensibility
9   Braveheart
10   Apollo 13
11   Trainspotting
12   Pocahontas
13   Ace Ventura: When Nature Calls
14   Die Hard With a Vengeance
15   Heat
16   Waterworld
17   Muriel's Wedding
18   Judge Dredd
19   While You Were Sleeping
20   The Santa Clause

Woody and Buzz Lightyear issue in the computer age of cinema with Disney's *Toy Story*

Morgan Freeman and Brad Pitt listen to the voice of lunacy in David Fincher's stylishly made *Seven*

Fly and Babe discuss the box-office figures of the year's biggest surprise hit, *Babe*

Val Kilmer flexes his streamlined rubber in Joel Schumacher's inexplicably successful *Batman Forever*

Pierce Brosnan and Gottfried John exorcise their aggression in Martin Campbell's *Goldeneye*, the biggest Bond

Top Ten Box-Office Stars

For only the second time in the history of this poll, one star has managed to take the number one position twice. And two years running, at that. No wonder Columbia Pictures paid Jim Carrey a record $20 million to star in *The Cable Guy*. Since then, of course, Arnold Schwarzenegger has eclipsed that figure with his share of the back-end profits and merchandising from *Batman and Robin*, on top of his fee of $20-25m (depending on which source you trust).

Intriguing, too, to see the disparity between UK and US box-office performance. For instance, in North America *The Santa Clause* grossed $110.1 million *more* than *Judge Dredd*. Yet in Britain the comedy was outclassed by the Sly sci-fier to the tune of £1.2m. Also interesting is that the triumphant triumvirate of *Crimson Tide*, *Dangerous Minds* and *Bad Boys* – from the producing team of Don Simpson and Jerry Bruckheimer – didn't make it into the British top twenty (although the films did enter the list at 22nd, 23rd and 24th, respectively).

Also, I found it enormously encouraging that such excellent foreign titles as *The Horseman on the Roof* and *The City of Lost Children* did so well in Britain – even if they failed to compete with the more obviously commercial *Get Shorty* and *The Birdcage* (ranked 25th and 26th). Anyway, the runners up in the annual chart of box-office stars include Al Pacino, Robert De Niro, John Travolta, Val Kilmer, Michelle Pfeiffer, Hugh Grant, Bill Pullman and Tim Allen.

2 Tom Hanks

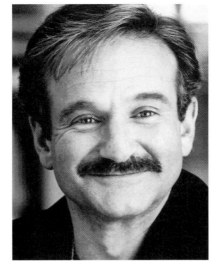

3 Robin Williams

4 Brad Pitt

5 Emma Thompson

6 Mel Gibson

7 Bruce Willis

8 Kevin Costner

9 Sylvester Stallone

10 Sandra Bullock

Releases of the Year

In this section you will find details of all the films released in Great Britain from 1 July 1995 to the end of June 1996 – the period covered by all the reference features in the book.

The normal abbreviations operate as follows: Dir – for Director; Pro – for Producer; Assoc Pro – for Associate Producer; Ex Pro – for Executive Producer; Pro Ex – for Production Executive; Pro Sup – for Production Supervisor; Co-Pro – for Co-Producer; Pro Co-Ord – for Production Co-Ordinator; Ph – for Photographer; Ed – for Editor; Art – for Art Director; Pro Des – for Production Designer; M – for Music; and a few others which will be obvious.

Abbreviations for the names of film companies are also pretty obvious when used, such as Fox for 20th Century-Fox, Rank for Rank Film Distributors, and UIP for Universal International Pictures. Where known, the actual production company is given first, the releasing company last.

All films reviewed by James Cameron-Wilson unless otherwise specified. Additional contributors: Charles Bacon, Ewen Brownrigg, Jeremy Clarke, Karen Krizanovich, Nigel Mulock, Simon Rose, Mansel Stimpson and Derek Winnert.

Ace Ventura: When Nature Calls

Mourning the death of a favoured quadruped in a Tibetan ashram, the pet detective is lured to Africa to locate a stolen sacred bat. Love him or hate him, Jim Carrey outdoes even his own excesses here, adding a whole new gallery of facial tics to his manic persona (watch those eyebrows, admire those ears). Kicking off with an hilarious parody of the opening scene from *Cliffhanger*, *Ace Ventura* quickly slides into Carrey's solo performance art, buoying a weak script poorly realised by first-time director Oedekerk (who, uncredited, helped pen the first film). While many of the set pieces are truly inspired (notably the scene in which a rhinoceros gives birth to Ventura), there are not enough to carry the feeble plot. Performances, photography, production design and locations (South Carolina doubling for Africa) are all exceptionally dismal.

Cast: Jim Carrey (Ace Ventura), Ian McNeice (Fulton Greenwall), Simon Callow (Vincent Cadby), Maynard Eziashi (Ouda), Bob Gunton (Burton Quinn), Sophie Okonedo (The Princess), Tommy Davidson (Tiny Warrior), Adewale, Danny D. Daniels, Sam Motoana Phillips, Damon Standifer, Andrew Steel, Bruce Spence, Thomas Grunke, Arsenio 'Sonny' Trinidad, Kristen Norton, Michael Reid MacKay.

   Dir and Screenplay: Steve Oedekerk. Pro: James G. Robinson. Ex Pro: Gary Barber. Co-Pro: Andrew G. La Marca. Ph: Donald E. Thorin. Ed: Malcolm Campbell. Pro Des: Steven J. Lineweaver. M: Robert Folk; 'Spirits In The Material World' sung by Pato Banton and Sting. Costumes: Elsa Zamparelli. (Morgan Creek–Warner.) Rel: 26 December 1995. 93 mins. Cert PG. USA. 1995.

All Men are Mortal

Rouen/Paris; the late 1940s. A successful and beautiful stage actress, Regina observes that she lives in a time when 'everything had to be new – we were obsessed with the idea to be different'. Yet as France heals its post-war wounds with jazz, philosophy and sartorial innovation, Regina craves something deeper, something greater – something that will last. Then she encounters the strange and eccentric Fosca, a man for whom life has no meaning because, he claims, he is immortal... A truly abysmal adaptation of Simone de Beauvoir's 1946 novel *Tous les Hommes sont Mortels*, this falls down on virtually every level. Poorly dubbed, randomly directed and feebly acted, it defies description. As for the passion between Irene Jacob and Stephen Rea, there's more chemistry in a cup of tea. Then what is one to expect when the director of *Highway to Hell* and *Drop Dead Fred* tackles the existential complexities of de Beauvoir? Filmed in Budapest and Amsterdam.

Cast: Stephen Rea (Fosca), Irene Jacob (Regina), Colin Salmon (Chas), Marianne Sagebrecht (Annie), Maggie O'Neill (Florence), Steve Nicolson (Laforet), Chiara Mastroianni (Francoise), Jango Edwards, Derek De Lint, John Nettles, Miranda Forbes, Jane Wymark, Ewan Bailey, David Healy.

   Dir: Ate de Jong. Pro: Rudolf Wichmann, Matthijs van Heijningen and Jean Gontier. Ex Pro: Frederic Golchan. Line Pro: Trevor Ingman. Screenplay: De Jong, Steven Gaydos and Olwen Wymark. Ph: Bruno de Keyzer. Pro Des: Ben van Os. Ed: Nicolas Gaster. M: Klaus Doldinger; 'Paris, Paris,' performed by Catherine Deneuve, Malcolm McLaren, Nicole Amovin, Joelle Esso and Tracy Ackerman. Costumes: Jany Temime. (Sigma Pictures/Nova Films–Warner.) Rel: 5 January 1996. 91 mins. Cert 15. UK/Netherlands/ France. 1995.

The American President

As scenarist Aaron Sorkin points out, 'most stories deal with putting an

No asparagus spared: Jim Carrey goes into his routine as the potty detective in Steve Oedekerk's lunatic Ace Ventura: When Nature Calls *(from Warner)*

White House whitewash: Michael Douglas and Annette Bening in the romance of the century – in Rob Reiner's The American President *(from UIP)*

ordinary man in extraordinary circumstances'. So, in collaboration with director Rob Reiner, Sorkin set about concocting a scenario in which an extraordinary man – the most powerful in the world – has to deal with everyday situations. It's one thing for the US president to send planes to bomb Libya, it's another to discreetly engineer a date with a good-looking woman. The permutations are endless, and Andrew Shepherd – the world's most eligible bachelor – is finding it impossible to order flowers from a local florist. While coating the presidency in a gauze of candyfloss, Sorkin's screenplay does hit some bullseyes. The parallels between Shepherd and Bill Clinton are there for the picking (Shepherd struggling with the issue of character versus politician), and when Sydney Wade (Annette Bening) tells the president that she makes more money than he does, it's staggering to think that in real life the actress made far more for this film than Clinton will have in his first term of office. FYI: Robert Redford was the first choice for the role of Shepherd, but backed out due to the film's 'political edge'.

Cast: Michael Douglas (Andrew Shepherd), Annette Bening (Sydney Ellen Wade), Martin Sheen (A.J. MacInerney), David Paymer (Leon Kodak), Samantha Mathis (Janie Basdin), Michael J. Fox (Lewis Rothschild), Anne Deavere Smith (Robin McCall), Shawna Waldron (Lucy Shepherd), Richard Dreyfuss (Senator Bob Rumson), Nina Siemaszko (Beth Wade), Wendie Malick (Susan Sloan), John Mahoney (Leo Solomon), Anne Haney, Beau Billingslea, Gail Strickland, Joshua Malina, Clement Von Franckenstein, Taylor Nichols, Jordan Lund, Kamilah Martin, George Murdock, Jack Gilroy, Matthew Saks, Googy Gress, Ron Canada, Aaron Sorkin.

Dir and Pro: Rob Reiner. Ex Pro: Charles Newirth and Jeffrey Stott. Screenplay: Aaron Sorkin. Ph: John Seale. Ed: Robert Leighton. Pro Des: Lilly Kilvert. M: Marc Shaiman. Costumes: Gloria Gresham. State Dinner Consultant: Laurie G. Firestone. (Universal/Castle Rock/Wildwood Enterprises–UIP.) Rel: 8 December 1995. 113 mins. Cert 15. USA. 1995.

Angel Baby

Harry and Kate are a couple of schizophrenics who meet and fall in love, each taking strength from the other in their battle to live their own way against the disapproval of family and society. When Kate becomes pregnant, Harry insists that they throw away their calming drugs so that the baby can have a chance of growing up normally. But Harry's callous boss fires him from his computer job, precipitating a crisis ... *Angel Baby* comes to Britain trailing honours as winner of seven Australian Film Institute awards, including best film and two for writer-director Michael Rymer, who must take credit for the marvellously compelling script and surefooted, steady handling of a difficult subject. Unsettling, but profoundly moving, the film is lifted high by a pair of triumphant (award-winning) performances from John Lynch and Jacqueline McKenzie. [*Derek Winnert*]

Cast: John Lynch (Harry), Jacqueline McKenzie (Kate), Colin Friels (Morris), Deborra-Lee Furness (Louise), Robyn Nevin, Daniel Daperis, David Argue, Geoff Brooks, Humphrey Bower, Jane Menelaus.

Dir and Screenplay: Michael Rymer. Pro:

The etymology of entomology and other metaphors: Kristin Scott Thomas and Mark Rylance are busy bees in Philip Haas' intelligent Angels and Insects *(from Film Four)*

Timothy White and Jonathan Shteinman. Ph: Ellery Ryan. Pro Des: Chris Kennedy. Ed: Dany Cooper. M: John Clifford White. Costumes: Kerri Mazzocco. (Stamen/Meridian Films–AFC/Barbican.) Rel: 2 February 1996. 100 mins. Cert 15. Australia. 1995.

Angels and Insects

Shipwrecked on his return from the Amazon, the naturalist William Adamson is welcomed into the home of the affluent, aristocratic Reverend Harald Alabaster, an amateur insect collector. There, Adamson falls for the physical charms of the Reverend's daughter, Eugenia, who agrees to marry him in spite of his lower social standing. But darker forces are at work as Adamson attempts an ambitious study of unknown insect species, creatures every bit as socially complex as Adamson's benefactors. With a remarkable appreciation for his material, director Philip Haas (*The Music of Chance*) paints a scenario of affected refinement and suppressed sexuality, his discreet camera moves tracing the gentility of a hypocrisy embalmed in porcelain and lace. Furthermore, the parallels of ant behaviour and that of Victorian high society is never pushed too far. Elegantly adapted by Haas and his wife Belinda from A.S. Byatt's novella *Morpho Eugenia*, the film projects a depth, intelligence and subtlety that intoxicates the intellect, while the perfectly modulated performances of Mark Rylance and Kristin Scott Thomas add considerable distinction.

Cast: Mark Rylance (William Adamson), Kristin Scott Thomas (Matty Crompton), Patsy Kensit (Eugenia Alabaster), Jeremy Kemp (Sir Harald Alabaster), Douglas Henshall (Edgar Alabaster), Annette Badland (Lady Alabaster), Saskia Wickham (Rowena Alabaster), Anna Massey (Miss Mead), Chris Larkin (Robin), Lindsay Thomas, Michelle Sylvester, Clare Lovell, Jenny Lovell, Oona Haas, Angus Hodder, Paul Ready, Naomi Gudge, John Jenkins, Clare Redman.

Dir: Philip Haas. Pro: Joyce Herlihy and Belinda Haas. Ex Pro: Lindsay Law. Screenplay: Belinda and Philip Haas. Ph: Bernard Zitzerman. Ed: Belinda Haas. Pro Des: Jennifer Kernke. M: Alexander Balanescu; Maro Refosco. Costumes: Paul Brown. (Playhouse International/Samuel Goldwyn–Film Four.) Rel: 8 December 1995. 117 mins. Cert 15. UK/USA. 1995.

Angus

Avid scientist and awkward school fat boy Angus is voted king of the freshman Winter Ball as a joke. To make matters worse, he has a crush on Melissa, the ball's popular and blandly beautiful queen. This dilemma launches the touching, truthful yet slightly too triumphant examination of what it's like to 'be different' in a high school in the American Midwest. Shot in Minnesota and nimbly directed by Patrick Read Johnson (*Baby's Day Out*), *Angus* benefits from strong if truncated performances from Kathy Bates as Angus's truck-drivin' mum and George C. Scott as his wise if curmudgeonly grandfather. Newcomer Charlie Talbert (supposedly discovered in a burger joint queue) nails the central character with conviction, making this film a soothing poultice for the social wounds of all childhood outcasts. [*Karen Krizanovich*]

Cast: Charlie Talbert (Angus Bethune), George C. Scott (Grandpa Ivan), Kathy Bates (Meg Bethune), Ariana Richards

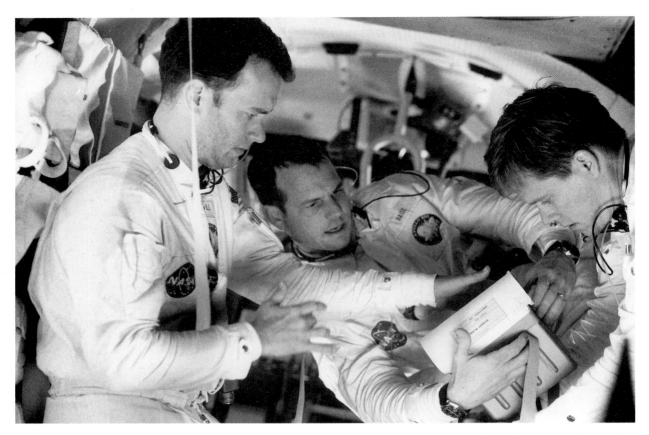

Inside the Vomit Comet: Tom Hanks, Bill Paxton and Kevin Bacon have a problem in Ron Howard's proficient Apollo 13 *(from UIP)*

(Melissa Lefevre), Chris Owen (Troy), James Van Der Beek (Rick Sanford), Lawrence Pressman (Principal Metcalf), Rita Moreno (Madame Rulenska), Robert Curtis-Brown, Kevin Connolly, Salim Grant, Epatha Harris, James Keane, Irvin Kershner, Wesley Mann, Monty O'Grady, Bethany Richards, Anna Thomson.

Dir: Patrick Read Johnson. Pro: Dawn Steel and Charles Roven. Ex Pro: Robert Cavallo, Gary Levinson and Susan B. Landau. Screenplay: Jill Gordon, based on a short story by Chris Crutcher. Ph: Alexander Grusynski. Pro Des: Larry Miller. Ed: Janice Hampton. M: David Russo; numbers performed by Love Spit Love, Squeeze, Goo Goo Dolls, Ash, Tilt, Green Day, Smoking Popes, The Muffs, Dance Hall Crashers, Mazzy Star, Pansy Division, Squeeze Box!, Buster Poindexter, Peter Gabriel, etc. Costumes: Jill Ohanneson. (Turner Pictures/Atlas Entertainment–Entertainment.) Rel: 24 May 1996. 90 mins. Cert 12. USA. 1995.

Apollo 13

Outer space; 1970. The understated announcement 'Houston, we have a problem' – voiced by Captain James A. Lovell Jr on April 13, 1970 – set in motion the most ambitious rescue mission in the history of mankind. Faced with suffocation, carbon dioxide poisoning, starvation, refrigeration and/or incineration, Lovell, Fred Haise and Jack Swigert, the astronauts a stone's throw from the moon, were forced to fly their crippled craft back to earth in the space of four days. In spite of all the impressive technology and narrative irony (Apollo 13 was launched at 13:13 military time), the film displays an anodyne predictability due, perhaps, to the story's foregone conclusion and lack of any human conflict. Apart from a brief set-to between Haise and Swigert, the drama rests solely on the discomfort of three historical figures aided by the sketchiest of characterisations. Still, the recreation of the rocket launch, the breathtaking views of the earth and moon from space and in particular the conditions of weightlessness (filmed on board NASA's gravity-defying KC-135 jet) are to be seen to be believed.

Cast: Tom Hanks (Captain James A. Lovell), Kevin Bacon (Jack Swigert), Bill Paxton (Fred Haise), Gary Sinise (Ken Mattingly), Ed Harris (Gene Kranz), Kathleen Quinlan (Marilyn Lovell), Jean Speegle Howard (Blanch Lovell), Tracy Reiner (Mary Haise), David Andrews (Pete Conrad), Xander Berkeley (Henry Hurt), Clint Howard (EECOM White), Loren Dean (EECOM Arthur), Mark Wheeler (Neil Armstrong), Larry Williams (Buzz Aldrin), Mary Kate Schellhardt, Emily Ann Lloyd, Miko Hughes, Max Elliott Slade, Michelle Little, Chris Ellis, Joe Spano, Marc McClure, Ben Marley, Tom Wood, Googy Gress, Patrick Mickler, Ray McKinnon, Max Grodenchik, Christian Clemenson, Brett Cullen, Ned Vaughn, Geoffrey Blake, Wayne Duvall, Joseph Culp, Karen Martin, Austin O'Brien, Rance Howard, Todd Hallowell, Roger Corman.

Dir: Ron Howard. Pro: Brian Grazer. Ex Pro: Todd Hallowell. Screenplay: William Broyles Jr and Al Reinert, based on the book *Lost Moon* by Jim Lovell and Jeffrey Kluger. Ph: Dean Cundey. Ed: Mike Hill and Dan Hanley. Pro Des: Michael Corenblith. M: James Horner; numbers performed by Annie Lennox, Santana, James Brown, Bobby Darin, The Rascals, Grace Slick, Peter Townshend, Steppenwolf, The Jimmy Hendrix Experience, Norman Greenbaum, Trini Lopez, Hank Williams, and The Mavericks. Costumes: Rita Ryack. (Imagine/Universal–UIP.) Rel: 22 September 1995. 140 mins. Cert PG. USA. 1995.

Assassins

Just as he's about to retire, conscience-stricken, world-class assassin Robert Rath (pronounced 'wrath') is handed an assignment he can't refuse: the termination of four Dutchmen and a female hacker for a cool $2 million. However, Rath's hit misfires when a rival assassin moves in on his contract. The stakes then increase to $20m as Rath finds himself pitted against an adversary with an uncanny knowledge of his own tricks of the trade. Can Rath's years of experience make up for the deadly ambition of the new kid on the block? Cold, calculating and slick, *Assassins* displays the proficiency of a computer game, although its formulaic moves strip the film of the suspense it could have packed. FYI: The role of Rath was previously earmarked for Wesley Snipes and Mel Gibson. Previously known as *Day of Reckoning*.

Cast: Sylvester Stallone (Robert 'Joseph' Rath), Antonio Banderas (Miguel Bain), Julianne Moore (Electra), Kelly Rowan (Jennifer), Anatoly Davydov, Muse Watson, Stephen Kahan, Reed Diamond, Kai Wulff, Pearl the Cat.
Dir: Richard Donner. Pro: Donner, Joel Silver, Bruce Evans, Raynold Gideon, Andrew Lazar and Jim Van Wyck. Ex Pro: Lauren Shuler-Donner and Dino De

Killing for a living: Sylvester Stallone cosies up to his 'mark' (Julianne Moore) in Richard Donner's Assassins *(from Warner)*

Hamming it up: Babe takes control of the situation in Chris Noonan's bewitching Babe *(from UIP)*

Laurenttis. Co-Pro: Richard Solomon, Alexander Collett and Dan Cracchiolo. Screenplay: Andy Wachowski, Larry Wachowski and Brian Helgeland. Ph: Vilmos Zsigmond. Ed: Richard Marks. Pro Des: Tom Sanders. M: Mark Mancina; 'Like A Rolling Stone' performed by The Rolling Stones. Costumes: Elizabeth McBride. (Silver Pictures/Donner/Shuler-Donner–Warner.) Rel: 6 October 1995. 125 mins. Cert 15. USA. 1995.

Asterix Conquers America

50 B.C. France/the US. When a camp centurion (straight out of *Fellini Satyricon*) dispatches the druid Getafix beyond the edge of the world, Asterix and Obelix follow – and discover the New World. There they find a land overrun with savage Native Americans (quick, contact the PC brigade) and struggle to overcome a ruthless witch doctor and a welter of outdated clichés. Crude animation, clumsy plot devices and some poor vocal interpretations add to the gloom. However, some light word play may keep older viewers (aged 8-12) awake. Seventh in the series based on Goscinny and Uderzo's comic strip and the first made in Germany.

Voices: John Rye (narrator), Craig Charles (Asterix), Howard Lew Lewis (Obelix), Geoffrey Bayldon (Getafix), Henry McGee (Caesar), Christopher Biggins (Lucullus), Robin Lyons, Andrew Offiler, Bill Speers.
Dir: Gerhard Hahn. Pro: Jurgen Wohlrabe. Line Pro: Christa Kistner. Screenplay: Thomas Platt and Rhett Rooster, based on an idea by Albert Uderzo and Pierre Tchernia. Ed: Ulrich Steinvorth. M: Harold Faltermeyer; numbers performed by Aswad, Bonnie Tyler, Wild Kit, and Right Said Fred. Animation director: Bill Speers. (Extrafilm Prods/Berlin Film Fund–Fox.) Rel: 11 August 1995. 84 mins. Cert U. Germany. 1994.

Babe

Southern Highlands, New South Wales; today. Saved from the abattoir by being chosen as a fairground attraction, the Pig With No Name has his weight guessed correctly by laconic sheep farmer Arthur Hoggett and ends up as the sole pig at Hoggett's Farm. There his porcine identity is challenged by his friendship with various farmyard critters and, like Wilbur in *Charlotte's Webb*, he is forced to establish his own uniqueness in order to save his bacon. By being polite to the sheep, 'Babe' soon becomes as efficient a drill sergeant as his canine colleagues and wins the respect and wonder of his keeper. Some pig. Adapted from Dick King-Smith's children's book *The Sheep-Pig*, Chris Noonan's *Babe* takes the unprecedented step of putting words into the animals' mouths, aided by animatronic wizardry. It's virtually impossi-

Coming clean: Marie Gillian (left) confesses the worst to bathmate Marie Ravel in Bertrand Tavernier's disturbing The Bait *(from Artificial Eye/Mayfair Film)*

ble to distinguish between the puppets and the real thing, giving this absorbing, ingenious family film a credibility that never detracts from the charm or fun. Beguiling, touching, funny and a total original. FYI: In the US, pork sales slumped by twenty per cent after the film's release.

Cast: James Cromwell (Arthur Hoggett), Magda Szubanski (Esme Hoggett). Voices of: Christine Cavanaugh (Babe), Miriam Margolyes (Fly), Danny Mann (Ferdinand), Hugo Weaving (Rex), Miriam Flynn (Maa), Russie Taylor (Cat), Evelyn Krape (Old Ewe), Michael Edward-Stevens (Horse), Charles Bartlett (Cow), Paul Livingston (Rooster), Roscoe Lee Browne (narrator), Zoe Burton, Paul Goddard.
   Dir: Chris Noonan. Pro: George Miller, Doug Mitchell and Bill Miller. Screenplay: Miller and Noonan. Ph: Andrew Lesnie. Pro Des: Roger Ford. Ed: Marcus D'Arcy and Jay Friedkin. M: Nigel Westlake; Camille Saint-Saens, Leo Delibes, Grieg, Rodgers & Hart, Bizet and Fauré. Costumes: Roger Ford. Animatronic Characters: Jim Henson's Creature Shop. Sheep: John Cox and Robotechnology. Animation and Visual Effects: Rhythm & Hues. (Universal/Kennedy Miller–UIP.) Rel: 15 December 1995. 92 mins. Cert U. Australia. 1995.

The Bait - L'Appat

A shop assistant-cum-model, Nathalie, 18, moonlights as an escort girl and shares her cramped Paris apartment with her boyfriend, Eric. Both come from privileged backgrounds, so their horrific descent into crime seems all the more baffling (commanding sensational headlines in France). Based on real events, *The Bait* not only sheds fascinating and disturbing light on the teenage psyche, but reveals the influence of the rest of the world (par-

All work and no sleigh: Balto *competes with* Steele *(left) to lead the husky train in Simon Wells' gripping cartoon (from UIP)*

ticularly America) on contemporary France. At one point a policeman even reprimands Nathalie for 'watching too many American TV movies'. By employing quick cutting and fluid camerawork, director Tavernier wires the concentration, while rewarding us with some outstanding performances from his young cast. Marie Gillain, who played Gerard Depardieu's daughter in *Mon Pére, Ce Heros*, is a future star if ever there was one, but then all of Tavernier's characters are deeply shaded.

Cast: Marie Gillain (Nathalie), Olivier Sitruk (Eric), Bruno Putzulu (Bruno), Richard Berry (Alain), Philippe Duclos (Antoine), Marie Ravel (Karine), Clotilde Courau (Patricia), Jean-Louis Richard, Christophe Odent, Jean-Paul Comart, Jacky Nercessian, Alain Sarde, Philippe Torreton, Francois Berleand, Jeanne Goupil.
   Dir: Bertrand Tavernier. Pro: Rene Cleitman and Frederic Bourboulon. Screenplay: Tavernier and Colo Tavernier O'Hagan, from the book by Morgan Sportès. Ph: Alain Choquart. Ed: Luce Grunenwaldt. Set Des: Emile Ghigo. M: Philippe Haim; numbers performed by Us 3, Jane Birkin, Inner City, Soul II Soul, Lenny Kravitz, The Faith Healers, Peter Gabriel, Iggy Pop, Eddy Mitchell, etc. Costumes: Marpessa Djian. (Hachette Premiere/Little Bear/France 2 Cinema/M6 Films/Canal Plus–Artificial Eye/Mayfair Film.) Rel: 22 September 1995. 115 mins. Cert 18. France. 1995.

Balto

Alaska; 1925. Due to his jumbled pedigree, the half-wolf/half-husky Balto is rejected by his canine colleagues and shirked by the human population of Nome, Alaska. Only the

beautiful husky Jenna and the grouchy but pragmatic Boris, a Russian goose, accept Balto for who he is. While desperate to prove his worth as a sled dog, Balto is repeatedly undermined by the vicious, proud husky leader Steele and fails to win a place on the team. Then, following an outbreak of diphtheria among the children of Nome, a shipment of vital antitoxin is needed to be transported from Nenana 674 miles away. When Steele leads the sled team astray, Balto at last has a chance to prove his heroism... Drawing on all the crucial elements of a classic animated film – action, romance, drama, humour, suspense, spectacular scenery and a struggle against the odds – *Balto* delivers in spades. From the richly realised characters to the heart-tugging story to the visual spectacle, *Balto* serves as a model of its kind. Only Steven Spielberg, who previously executive-produced *An American Tail*, *The Land Before Time* and *Who Framed Roger Rabbit*, seems able to compete with the technical expertise and emotional canvas of Disney. *Balto*, incidentally, is loosely based on a true story – with a statue of the heroic husky in Central Park, New York, to prove it.

Cast: Miriam Margolyes (Grandma Rosy), Lola Bates-Campbell (granddaughter). Voices: Kevin Bacon (Balto), Bob Hoskins (Boris), Bridget Fonda (Jenna), Jim Cummings (Steele), Phil Collins (the polar bears Muk and Luk), Jack Angel (Nikki), Juliette Brewer (Rosy), Danny Mann, Robbie Rist, Sandra Searles Dickinson, Donald Sinden, William Roberts, Mike McShane, Miriam Margolyes, Reed Martin.
   Dir: Simon Wells. Pro: Steve Hickner. Ex Pro: Steven Spielberg, Kathleen Kennedy and Bonne Radford. Screenplay: Cliff Ruby, Elana Lesser, David Steven Cohen and Roger S.H. Schulman. Pro Des: Hans Bacher. Ed: Nick Fletcher and Sim Evan-Jones. M: James Horner; 'Reach For The Light' performed by Steve Winwood. Dir of Technology: Lem Davis. (Universal/Amblin Entertainment–UIP.) Rel: 29 March 1996. 78 mins. Cert U. USA/UK. 1995.

Barb Wire

In the year 2017 the USA has become divided by civil war and Barb Wire, the cynical owner of the Hammerhead Bar and Grille nightclub, finds her establishment constantly frequented by Nazis. Still, she has an understanding with the local chief of police, a shaky alliance that just about keeps her chin

Pamela Anderson Lee shows off her pair of magnificent shooters in David Hogan's excruciating Barb Wire *(from PolyGram)*

above water. Then, of all the gin joints in all the towns in all the world Barb's ex-lover walks into hers. He is now married and although Barb still holds a flame for him she knows she must do the honourable thing... Like *The Mask*, *Barb Wire* is a creation of Dark Horse Comics and for want of a better story line the producers have seen fit to build an update of *Casablanca* around her. Having said that, it's pretty hard to follow what's actually going on as the film seems to have been cut together by a chainsaw on amphetamines. Pounding heavy metal music, flash MTV lighting, cardboard villains and a leading lady out of kilter with her material all add to the misery. And, yes, you do get to see those famous breasts (albeit briefly).

Cast: Pamela Anderson Lee (Barb Wire), Temuera Morrison (Axel Hood), Victoria Rowell (Cora D), Jack Noseworthy (Charlie Kopetski), Xander Berkeley (Alexander Willis), Udo Kier (Curly), Steve Railsback (Colonel Pryzer), Andre Rosey Brown (Big Fatso), Clint Howard (Schmitz), Jennifer Banko, Tony Bill, Shelly Desai, Tiny 'Zeus' Lister, Marshal Manesh, Mary Anna Reyes, Loren Rubin, Michael Russo, Teo, Nicholas Worth, Salvator Xuereb.
   Dir: David Hogan. Pro: Brad Wymany,

Mike Richardson and Todd Moyer. Ex Pro: Peter Heller. Line Pro: Robert Del Valle. Screenplay: Chuck Pfarrer and Ilene Chaiken. Ph: Rick Bota. Pro Des: Jean-Philippe Carp. Ed: Peter Schink. M: Michel Colombier; numbers performed by Gun, Michael Hutchence, Hagfish, Die Cheerleader, Mr Ed Jumps the Gun, Marion, Jack Johnson, Tommy Lee, Shampoo, etc. Costumes: Rosanna Norton. (Propaganda/ Dark Horse Entertainment-PolyGram.) Rel: 3 May 1996. 94 mins. Cert 15. USA. 1996.

Barnabo of the Mountains – Barnabo Delle Montagne

Exquisitely photographed, leisurely paced tale of a young forest ranger whose moment of cowardice in the line of duty haunts him forever. Drenched in atmosphere and glowing in detail, *Barnabo* is not about plot or dramatic showdowns but is a contemplative observation of a man's maturation in harmony with his natural surroundings. Whether registering the unblinking stare of a peasant or dwelling on the intoxicating mountain scenery, the film elevates cinema as an art form.

Cast: Marco Pauletti (Barnabo), Duilio Fontana, Carlo Caserotti, Antonio Vecellio, Angelo Chiesura, Alessandra Milan, Marco Tonin, Mario Da Pra, Gianni Bailo.
   Dir: Mario Brenta. Pro: Tommaso Dazzi and Gabriella Lazzoni. Screenplay: Brenta, Angelo Pasquini, Francesco Alberti and Enrico Soci, from the novel by Dino Buzzati. Ph: Vincenzo Marano. Ed: Roberto Mis-

Figures in a landscape: forest rangers take to the hills in Mario Brenta's remarkable Barnabo of the Mountains *(from Artificial Eye)*

siroli. Pro Des: Giorgio Bertolini. M: Stefano Caprioli. Costumes: Paolo Rossetti. (Nautilus Film SRL/Les Films Number One/Flach Film/RAI-Radio Televisione Italiana–Artificial Eye.) Rel: 28 July 1995. 124 mins. Cert 12. France/Italy/Switzerland. 1994.

The Basketball Diaries

A frighteningly pertinent film for today's youth, *The Basketball Diaries* – based on Jim Carroll's autobiography set in the late 1960s – injects its way into the drug culture of New York with the precision of a hypodermic needle. Leonardo DiCaprio, the most authentic and charismatic talent of his generation, plays Carroll himself, the poet and musician who confronted some pretty powerful demons in his youth. The scenes in which he and his neighbourhood cronies goof off (and shoot up) are fresh and dynamic, but it is the interaction between Jim and his mother (Lorraine Bracco) that bruises the heart. FYI: Marks the feature film debut of Scott Kalvert, the music video director (Rod Stewart, LL Cool J, Marky Mark, etc).

Cast: Leonardo DiCaprio (Jim Carroll), Bruno Kirby (Swifty), Lorraine Bracco (Jim's mother), Ernie Hudson (Reggie Porter), James Madio (Pedro), Patrick Mc-Gaw (Neutron), James Dennis Carroll (Frankie Pinewater), Mark Wahlberg (Mickey), Michael Imperioli (Bobby), Juliette Lewis (Diane Moody), Marilyn Sokol, Roy Cooper, Jimmy Papiris, Josh Mostel, Manny Alfaro, Cynthia Daniel, Brittany Daniel, Michael Rapaport.
  Dir: Scott Kalvert. Pro: Liz Heller and John Bard Manulis. Ex Pro: Chris Blackwell and Dan Genetti. Line Pro: Kathie Hersch. Screenplay: Brian Goluboff. Ph: David Phillips. Ed: Dana Congdon. Pro Des: Christopher Nowak. M: Graeme Revell; numbers performed by Jim Carroll and Pearl Jam, P.J. Harvey, The Doors, Massive Internal Complications, The Posies, Soundgarden, The Cult, Flea, etc. Costumes: David C. Robinson. Sound: Victor Iorillo. Rain Effects: J.C. Brotherhood. (Island Pictures–First Independent.) Rel: 24 November 1995. 97 mins. Cert 18. USA. 1995.

Needle in a haystack: Leonardo DiCaprio records his drug habit in Scott Kalvert's numbing The Basketball Diaries *(from First Independent)*

Double trouble: Tommy Lee Jones as the grotesque Harvey Two-Face plotting with Jim Carrey's Riddler to destroy the Caped Crusader – in Joel Schumacher's Batman Forever *(from Warner)*

Batman Forever

With a budget of close to $100 million, a handsome new Batman and the cinema's hottest comic as The Riddler (Jim Carrey, replacing Robin Williams for a mere $5m), one hoped for something better than this celluloid headache. In what is definitely a case of more is less, Batman finds himself pitched against the two-timing Harvey Two-Face, an acid-scarred, vengeful district attorney, and Ed Nygma, a scientific genius with the capacity to manipulate the nation's brain waves. Throw in a romantic tangle straight out of *Superman* (in which Nicole Kidman favours Batman over Bruce Wayne), add Robin, and you have an action-packed behemoth that ends up chasing its own tail – to diminishing returns. Directed like a two-hour music video (Joel Schumacher taking over the viewfinder from Tim Burton), *Batman Forever* is an incoherent, over-edited, over-scored shambles. Not so much a movie, more a merchandising frenzy.

Cast: Val Kilmer (Batman/Bruce Wayne), Tommy Lee Jones (Harvey Two-Face/Harvey Dent), Jim Carrey (The Riddler/Edward Nygma), Nicole Kidman (Dr Chase Meridian), Chris O'Donnell (Robin/Dick Grayson), Michael Gough (Alfred Pennyworth), Pat Hingle (Commissioner Gordon), Drew Barrymore (Sugar), Debi Mazar (Spice), Rene Auberjonois (Dr Burton), Elizabeth Sanders, Joe Grifasi, Philip Moon, Dennis Paladino, Kimberly Scott, Michael Paul Chan, Don 'The Dragon' Wilson.

Dir: Joel Schumacher. Pro: Tim Burton and Peter MacGregor-Scott. Ex Pro: Benjamin Melniker and Michael E. Uslan. Screenplay: Lee Batchler, Janet Scott Batchler and Akiva Goldsman. Ph: Stephen Goldblatt. Ed: Dennis Virkler. Pro Des: Barbara Ling. M: Elliot Goldenthal; numbers performed by U2, Seal, The Offspring, The Flaming Lips, and Brandy. Costumes: Bob Ringwood and Ingrid Ferrin. Make-Up: Rick Baker. (Warner.) Rel: 14 July 1995. 122 mins. Cert PG. USA. 1995.

Beautiful Thing

Jamie Gangel is picked on at school, Ste Pearce is bullied by his father and older brother. Next door neighbours on the dilapidated Thamesmead housing estate in South London, the boys form a tenuous attachment that, in the face of ignorance and the pervading lager culture, blossoms into something else ... Walking the sticky path between the naturalism of Ken Loach and the earthy caricature of Mike Leigh, *Beautiful Thing* is a remarkably successful adaptation of Jonathan Harvey's play dealing with gay puppy love. A spunky unknown cast (led magnificently by Linda Henry) makes every moment count, while the play's theatrical origins are all but swept away by the deft direction of Hettie Macdonald. Interestingly, several gay critics took exception to the film, while heterosexual scribes embraced it. True, it does propagate some myths of gay life (Jamie's love of musicals and dislike of football, for instance), but its entertaining plea for tolerance cannot be more heartily applauded.

Cast: Linda Henry (Sandra Gangel), Glen Berry (Jamie Gangel), Scott Neal (Ste Pearce), Ben Daniels (Tony), Tameka Empson (Leah), Jeillo Edwards (Rose), Daniel Bowers (Trevor Pearce), Meera Syal, Martin Walsh, Julie Smith, Anna

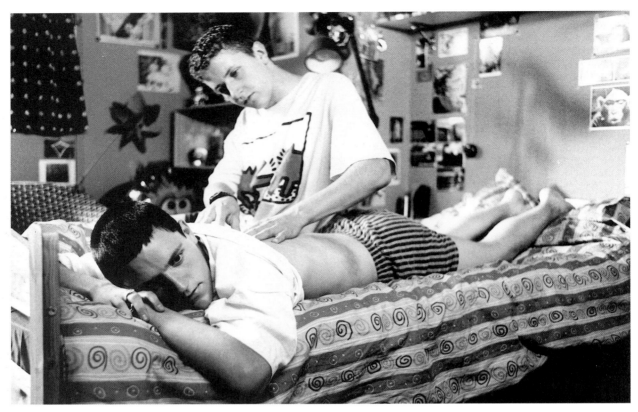

Bermondsey Dreamin': Scott Neal and Glen Berry in Hettie Macdonald's spunky Beautiful Thing *(from Film Four)*

Karen, Garry Cooper, Terry Duggan, Sophie Stanton, John Benfield, Davyd Harries, Beth Goddard, Dave Lynn.

Dir: Hettie Macdonald. Pro: Tony Garnett and Bill Shapter. Screenplay: Jonathan Harvey. Ph: Chris Seager. Pro Des: Mark Stevenson. Ed: Don Fairservice. M: John Altman; numbers performed largely by The Mamas & the Papas. Costumes: Pam Tait. (Channel Four/World Prods–Film Four Dist.) Rel: 14 June 1966. 91 mins. Cert 15. UK. 1995.

Bed of Roses

New York; now. An investment banker escaping from a loveless childhood, Lisa Walker has no time for romance. 'I work for a living,' she tells her best friend and confidante, Kim, 'and I live on a little island called Reality.' However, when she receives a magnificent arrangement of flowers from an anonymous admirer, Lisa becomes obsessed with unmasking the identity of the sender. As it happens, he's a complete stranger, a young man who spotted Lisa crying at her balcony window one night and who decided to brighten up her day. It could be the

start of something special... A simple, straightforward story of unlikely souls finding happiness together, *Bed of Roses* may prove too sweet and gentle for its own good but should accelerate business at Interflora. Performances are all top-notch (Pamela Segall is a

Bloomin' love: Mary Stuart Masterson and Christian Slater in Michael Goldenberg's fragrant Bed of Roses *(from Entertainment)*

gem as Lisa's girlfriend), but the story lacks motivation and begs for a kick up the ass. Still, romantics will eat it up with a trowel. Previously known as *Amelia and the King of Plants*.

Cast: Christian Slater (Lewis Farrell), Mary Stuart Masterson (Lisa Walker), Pamela Segall (Kim), Josh Brolin (Danny), Ally Walker (Wendy), Brian Tarantina, Debra Monk, Mary Alice, Kenneth Cranham, Anne Pitoniak, R.M. Haley, Cass Morgan,

Gina Torres, Nick Tate, Victor Sierra, Claire Mari Jacobs, S.A. Griffin.

Dir and Screenplay: Michael Goldenberg. Pro: Allan Mindel and Denise Shaw. Co-Pro: Michael Haley. Ex Pro: Joseph Hartwick and Lynn Harris. Ph: Adam Kimmel. Pro Des: Stephen McCabe. Ed: Jane Kurson. M: Michael Convertino; numbers performed by Eddi Reader, Scarlet, The Borrowers, Matthew Sweet, Jann Arden, Daniel O'Brien, Sarah McLachlan, etc. Costumes: Cynthia Flynt. Floral Design: Chris Bassett. Product Placement: Tony Hoffman. (Mindel/Shaw–Entertainment.) Rel: 16 February 1996. 88 mins. Cert PG. USA. 1995.

Before and After

Small-town Massachusetts; today. Before the incident, the Ryans were a close, happy and ideal family. Then, one fateful February afternoon, their American dream crumbles in a maelstrom of confusion, distrust and suspicion. A single, random episode throws their very future into uncertainty as each member of the family struggles to do what they believe is right, in their own way. But can Ben and Carolyn's teenage son, Jacob Ryan, really have murdered his girlfriend? Once in a while a film comes along which, in spite of bursting with good intentions and talent, is so fatally flawed that you wonder how it got made. Scripted by Ted Tally (fresh from his Oscar for *The*

Cycle of death: Labina Mitevska caught in the crossfire in Milcho Manchevski's powerful Before the Rain *(from Electric)*

Silence of the Lambs), *Before and After* suffers from clumsy plotting, inane dialogue and the most stupid character to appear on screen since Jim Carrey's moron in *Dumb and Dumber*. Yet as Liam Neeson's doltish father stumbles around in emotional turmoil, other

characters are not much more convincing, while Alfred Molina's miscasting as a wily American lawyer is nothing short of an embarrassment. Howard Shore's meddlesome music doesn't help.

Cast: Meryl Streep (Dr Carolyn Ryan), Liam Neeson (Ben Ryan), Edward Furlong (Jacob Ryan), Alfred Molina (Panos Demeris), Julia Weldon (Judith Ryan), Daniel Von Bargen (Fran Conklin), John Heard (Wendell Bye), Alison Folland (Martha Taverner), Ann Magnuson, Kaiulani Lee, Larry Pine, Wesley Addy, Pamela Blair, John Wylie, John Webber.

Dir: Barbet Schroeder. Pro: Schroeder and Susan Hoffman. Ex Pro: Roger Birnbaum and Joe Roth. Screenplay: Ted Tally, based on the book by Rosellen Brown. Ph: Luciano Tovoli. Pro Des: Stuart Wurtzel. Ed: Lee Percy. M: Howard Shore; Beethoven. Costumes: Ann Roth. (Hollywood Pictures/Caravan Pictures-Buena Vista.) Rel: 19 April 1996. 108 mins. Cert 12. USA. 1995.

Before the Rain

Macedonia/London. Haunting, powerful drama divided into three chapters: Words, Faces and Pictures, each offering an ironic twist to its title. In the first, a young Greek Orthodox monk has taken a vow of silence. Thus, he

Family indigestion: Meryl Streep and Liam Neeson confront their son, Edward Furlong, in Barbet Schroeder's leaden Before and After *(from Buena Vista)*

Changing their spots: Robin Williams (right) gives his lover, Nathan Lane, some lessons in masculinity, in Mike Nichols' enormously successful The Birdcage *(from UIP)*

cannot verbally express his love for an Albanian runaway, whom he harbours. In London, a picture editor is forced to choose between her boring husband and a Macedonian Pulitzer Prize-winning photographer, the former losing face both figuratively and literally. Then, back in the Balkans, the photographer tears up his pictures in an act of humanitarian defiance – before all three stories are united in a startling narrative curve. While the film – the first to be produced in the new republic of Macedonia – is technically accomplished on all fronts, it is the photography (emphatic close-ups, spectacular landscapes) that carves a place in the memory. Nominated for an Oscar for best foreign film.

Cast: Katrin Cartlidge (Anne), Rade Serbedzija (Aleksander), Gregoire Colin (Kiril), Labina Mitevska (Zamira), Jay Villiers (Nick), Silva Stojanovska, Phyllida Law, Josif Josifovski, Kiril Ristoski, Petar Mircevski, Ljupco Bresliski, Igor Madzirov, Ilko Stefanovski, Suzana Kirandziska, Peter Needham, Meto Jovanoski.
Dir and Screenplay: Milcho Manchevski. Pro: Judy Counihan, Cedomir Kolar, Samantha Taylor and Cat Villiers. Ph: Manuel Teran. Ed: Nicholas Gaster. Pro Des: Sharon Lamofsky and David Munns. M: Anastasia. Costumes: Caroline Harris and Sue Yelland. (Aim Productions/Noe Productions/Vardar Film/ British Screen/ European Co-Production Fund/PolyGram Audiovisuel/The Ministry of Culture for the Republic of Macedonia–Electric.) Rel: 11 August 1995. 116 mins. Cert 15. UK/ France/Macedonia. 1994.

The Birdcage

Miami; today. A middle-aged homosexual couple, Armand and Albert, are forced to compromise their behaviour for one night when Armand's grown-up son gets engaged to the daughter of the co-founder of the Coalition For Moral Order... *La Cage Aux Folles* was a great play, but after the French film version, its two sequels and the Broadway stage musical, the premise is wearing a bit thin. Now, in the wake of *The Adventures of Priscilla*, *To Wong Foo* and *Stonewall*, comes the straight American remake. Of course, straight is hardly the word to describe Albert, the screaming queen who performs Sondheim at the drag club of the title. Nathan Lane, who previously played the Sondheim-loving gay priest in *Jeffrey* (qv), minces marvellously as Albert, allowing Robin Williams – as his 'straight' lover – to take a back seat for once. Gene Hackman works equally hard to remind us that this is a comedy, although his later scenes do pay off handsomely. Yet in spite of a terrific opening shot and contemporary jokes made at the expense of Robert Dole and John Major, *The Birdcage* feels incredibly dated. Previously known as *Birds of a Feather*.

Cast: Robin Williams (Armand Goldman), Gene Hackman (Senator Keeley), Nathan Lane (Albert), Dianne Wiest (Louise Keeley), Dan Futterman (Val Goldman), Calista Flockhart (Barbara Keeley), Hank Azaria (Agador), Christine Baranski (Katharine), Tom McGowan, Grant Heslov, Kirby Mitchell, James Lally, Luca Tommassini, Ann Cusack, Dorothy Constantine, Trina McGee-Davis.
Dir and Pro: Mike Nichols. Ex Pro: Neil Machlis and Marcello Danon. Assoc Pro: Michele Imperato. Screenplay: Elaine May, based on the stage play *La Cage Aux Folles* by Jean Poiret and the script by Poiret, Francis Veber, Edouard Molinaro and Marcello Danon. Ph: Emmanuel Lubezki. Pro Des: Bo Welch. Ed: Arthur Schmidt. Music arranged and adapted by: Jonathan Tunick. Costumes: Ann Roth. Choreography: Vincent Paterson. (United Artists–UIP.) Rel: 26 April 1996. 119 mins. Cert 15. USA. 1996.

Blue in the Face

Jim Jarmusch shares his final cigarette with Auggie Wren, the proprietor of The Brooklyn Cigar Company store. A local man explains his 'fascinating and fun' hobby of retrieving plastic bags from trees. Lou Reed stares at the camera and pronounces, 'I get scared in Sweden. Everything works.' Yes, it's another day on the planet Brooklyn, one of the most culturally diverse yet community-conscious locations in the world. A series of improvised skits spotlighting the ethnic colour and idiosyncrasies of New York's fabled borough (interspersed with newsreel footage and interviews with Brooklyn natives), *Blue in the Face* is a priceless, engaging oddity. Gathering together some of the actors from their previous movie *Smoke*, director Wayne Wang and scenarist Paul Auster hit on the idea of shooting an instant extension of their just completed film. With a minimal budget and less than one week at their disposal, Wang and Auster collaborated with their eclectic cast, building on a series of ideas they more or less dreamed up on the spot. Innately cultish and spontaneous, *Blue in the Face* quickly attracted the attention of other talent who showed up on set to join in the experiment. Short, sharp and recherché.

Cast: Harvey Keitel (Auggie Wren), Roseanne (Dot), Michael J. Fox (Peter Malone), Mel Gorham (Violet), Giancarlo Esposito (Tommy), Jared Harris (Jimmy Rose), Victor Argo (Vinnie), Jim Jarmusch, Lou Reed, Lily Tomlin, Malik Yoba, Mira

Mad Mac: William Wallace masses his troops in Mel Gibson's invigorating Braveheart *(from Fox)*

Sorvino, Keith David, RuPaul, Jose Zuniga, Stephen Gevedon, The John Lurie National Orchestra, Sharif Rashed, Peggy Gormley.

Dir: Wayne Wang and Paul Auster. Pro: Greg Johnson, Peter Newman and Diana Phillips. Ex Pro: Harvey Keitel, Bob Weinstein and Harvey Weinstein. Co-Pro: Hisami Kuriowa. Screenplay: Wang and Auster in collaboration with the actors. Ph: Adam Holender. Pro Des: Kalina Ivanov. Ed: Christopher Tellefsen. M: John Lurie, Calvin Weston and Billy Martin; numbers

White water dogs: Sean Pertwee, Steven Mackintosh, Peter Gunn and Ewan McGregor in Carl Prechezer's idiosyncratic Blue Juice *(from Film Four Distribution)*

performed by David Byrne and Selina, Louis Prima, Soul Coughing, The John Lurie National Orchestra, Celia Cruz, La Casa, Victor Argo, Cabo Verde, Mel Gorham, Bongo Joe, Lou Reed, etc. Costumes: Claudia Brown. Choreography: Linda Talcott. (Miramax/NDF/Euro Space/Blue In the Face–Artificial Eye.) Rel: 17 May 1996. 84 mins. Cert 15. USA. 1995.

Blue Juice

A ragbag of hip characters hurtling towards thirty find themselves in a picturesque corner of coastal Cornwall. With the local shaman Shaper (Heathcote Williams, author of *Whale Nation* and sometime actor) predicting the arrival of an epic wave, 29-year-old 'J.C.' must choose between upholding his reputation as Cornwall's Old Spice champion or making a domestic commitment to the most beautiful girl west of the Tamar. Other characters struggle with alternative crises of identity, most of them wildly improbable. A cross between *Big Wednesday* and *Brookside*, *Blue Juice* exudes a certain charm but ends up being too schematic for its own good. Still, it's probably the best British comedy about surfing ever made.

Cast: Sean Pertwee (JC), Catherine Zeta Jones (Chloe), Steven Mackintosh (Josh Tambini), Ewan McGregor (Dean Raymond), Peter Gunn (Terry Colcott), Heathcote Williams (Shaper), Colette Brown (Junior Sands), Michelle Chadwick (Sarah), Keith Allen, Robin Soans, Jenny Agutter, Guy Leverton, Mark Frost, Paul Reynolds, Edwin Starr.

Dir: Carl Prechezer. Pro: Peter Salmi and Simon Relph. Screenplay: Prechezer and Salmi, from an idea by Salmi, Prechezer and Tim Veglio. Ph: Richard Greatrex. Ed: Michael Ellis. Pro Des: Mark Tildesley. M: Simon Davison; numbers performed by Edwin Starr, Heavy Stereo, T-Rex, Ride, Jamiroquai, Swervedriver, Sam Dees, Apollo 440, Gillian Wisdom, etc. Costumes: Linda Alderson. Northern Soul advisor: Lee Vowles. (Film Four International/ Pandora Cinema/Skreba–Film Four Distribution.) Rel: 15 September 1995. 98 mins. Cert 15. UK. 1995.

Braveheart

Scotland; 1280-1305. Truly epic, bloody, passionate and extremely grim slice of history following Sir William Wallace's rebellion against the English. While some events have been enhanced for dramatic effect, the

Making his day: Meryl Streep shares a brief encounter with Clint Eastwood in the latter's tasteful The Bridges of Madison County *(from Warner)*

bones of the plot are for real (the murder of Wallace's young wife, the battle of Stirling Bridge, the defeat at Falkirk), bringing considerable colour and vitality to the dusty pages of history. With his flowing hair, rippling torso and muddied face, Mel Gibson makes a credible figure as Mad Mac and has a commendable crack at his Scottish accent (putting Kevin Costner's Robin Hood to shame). This is a hero we can believe in, a man of the people determined to right the wrongs of the English and to bring Scotland freedom: at *any* cost. Patrick McGoohan makes a wonderful villain out of Edward I, a delicious mix of regal dignity and sustained rage, while Sophie Marceau and Catherine McCormack are exceptionally striking as the women who steer Wallace's heart. Battle scenes, photography and production design are all of the highest order.

Cast: Mel Gibson (William Wallace), Sophie Marceau (Princess Isabelle), Patrick McGoohan ('Longshanks' King Edward I), Catherine McCormack (Murron), Brendan Gleeson (Hamish), James Cosmo (Campbell), David O'Hara (Stephen), Alun Armstrong (Mornay), Angus McFadyen (Robert the Bruce), Peter Hanly (Prince Edward), James Robinson (young William), Ian Bannen, Sean Lawlor, Sandy Nelson, Sean McGinley, Alan Tall, Brian Cox, Stephen Billington, Barry McGovern, John Kavanagh, Tommy Flanagan, Julie Austin, Alex Norton, Rupert Vansittart, Michael Byrne, Malcolm Tierney, Donal Gibson, Jeanne Marine, Martin Dunne, Jimmy Chisholm, John Murtagh, Bernard Horsfall, Richard Leaf, David Gant.

Dir: Mel Gibson. Pro: Gibson, Alan Ladd Jr. and Bruce Davey. Ex Pro: Stephen McEveety. Screenplay: Randall Wallace. Ph: John Toll. Ed: Steven Rosenblum. Pro Des: Tom Sanders. M: James Horner. Costumes: Charles Knode. Sword Master: Nick Powell. (Icon Prods/Ladd Company–Fox.) Rel: 8 September 1995. 177 mins. Cert 15. USA. 1995.

The Bridges of Madison County

Madison County, Iowa; 1965/1995. Dedicated to caring for her husband and two teenage children, Francesca Johnson, formerly from Italy, leads à life of unremarkable blandness in the rural wasteland of Iowa. Then, when the family is away visiting the Illinois State Fair, Francesca is approached by a stranger seeking directions to a nearby covered bridge. Tall, rugged and polite, the stranger, Robert Kincaid, is drawn to Francesca's coquettish charm, and she to his gallantry and sense of worldliness. Soon, both housewife and stranger start to feel things they've never dreamed possible... Terribly tasteful, long-winded adaptation of North America's record-selling hardback novel, lovingly and sensitively brought to the screen by director-producer-star Clint Eastwood. Carefully avoiding the pitfalls of heavy-handed emotional manipulation, Clint has produced a good-looking, heartfelt drama from Richard LaGravenese's literate, well crafted adaptation. But with Clint and Meryl Streep in the roles of the bewildered lovers it's hard to forget that they're Clint and Meryl. Maybe it is this fact that stems the flow of tears. So you can't win really, can you?

Cast: Clint Eastwood (Robert Kincaid), Meryl Streep (Francesca Johnson), Annie Corley (Carolyn), Victor Slezak (Michael), Jim Haynie (Richard), Sarah Kathryn Schmitt, Christopher Kroon, Phyllis Lyons, Debra Monk, Richard Lage, Michelle Benes, James Rivers.

Dir: Clint Eastwood. Pro: Eastwood and Kathleen Kennedy. Screenplay: Richard LaGravenese, based upon the novel by Robert James Waller. Ph: Jack N. Green. Ed: Joel Cox. Pro Des: Jeannine Oppewall. M: Lennie Niehaus; 'Doe Eyes' composed by Niehaus and Eastwood; numbers performed by Ahmad Jamal, Maria Callas, The Shangri-Las, Dinah Washington,

James Rivers, Johnny Hartman, etc. Costumes: Colleen Kelsall. (Amblin/Malpaso–Warner.) Rel: 15 September 1995. 94 mins. Cert 12. USA. 1995.

Broken Arrow

While feigning an 'older brother' attachment to his young colleague, Riley Hale, crack pilot Vic Deakins is not all he appears to be. When the daring duo are entrusted with the mission of flying a top-secret B-3 stealth bomber on a test run, Deakins reveals his true colours. A ruthless terrorist, he intends to steal the plane's nuclear warheads for his own nefarious ends. But then Riley Hale is also more than meets the eye... Featuring the pyrotechnic direction of John Woo, a script from the writer of *Speed* and John Travolta in his first role as an out-and-out villain, *Broken Arrow* is an action-thriller of pedigree and promise. Indeed, the film is bursting with Woo's traditional explosions (nuclear, no less), balletic stunts and showers of shrapnel, but it does disappoint on other levels. Graham Yost's screenplay lacks the originality, leanness and ingenuity of *Speed* and Christian Slater looks too young to carry off the film's heroics with conviction. Still, *Broken Arrow* does boast the uncommon distinction of flaunting a villain more likeable than its hero.

Cast: John Travolta (Vic Deakins), Christian Slater (Riley Hale), Samantha Mathis (Terry Carmichael), Delroy Lindo (Colonel Max Wilkins), Bob Gunton (Pritchett), Frank Whaley (Giles Prentice), Howie Long (Kelly), Kurtwood Smith (Secretary of Defense Baird), Daniel von Bargen (Air Force General Creely), Vondie Curtis-Hall, Jack Thompson, Vyto Ruginis, Ousaun Elam, Shaun Toub, Jim Palmer, Chris Mulkey.

Dir: John Woo. Pro: Mark Gordon, Bill Badalato and Terence Chang. Ex Pro: Christopher Godsick and Dwight Little. Co-Pro: Allison Lyon Segan. Screenplay: Graham Yost. Ph: Peter Levy. Pro Des: Holger Gross. Ed: John Wright, Steve Mirkovich and Joe Hutshing. M: Hans Zimmer. Costumes: Mary Malin. (Mark Gordon/WCG Entertainment–Fox.) Rel: 12 April 1996. 109 mins. Cert 15. USA. 1996.

The Brothers McMullen

Long Island, New York; today. For Jack, Barry and Patrick McMullen, being Catholic means different things. Patrick, the youngest, is convinced he's going to hell for getting his girlfriend pregnant. Jack, the solid, emo-

Look who's shootin': John Travolta gets nasty in John Woo's top-grossing Broken Arrow *(from Fox)*

tional anchor of the trio, finds himself drawn into an adulterous affair. And Barry, forever the cynical realist, refuses to believe that he's falling in love. The miracle of this micro-budgeted first-time movie (shot on weekends over a period of eight months) is that the performances are so well honed and the script so dense. Nonetheless, the wit could have done with some sharpening (Whit Stillman would've had a field day with this material), while a familiarity with New York Irish Catholicism would help to appreciate the story's ironies. Edward Burns, a

In the Name of the Brother: Mike McGlone, Edward Burns and Jack Mulcahy confront their differences in Burns' The Brothers McMullen *(from Fox)*

An idyll husband: Actor/director Nikita Mikhalkov with his own daughter Nadia Mikhalkov and celluloid wife Ingeborga Dapkounaite in Burnt by the Sun *(from Guild)*

former production assistant on TV's *Entertainment Tonight*, not only directed, scripted and co-produced the film, but plays the role of Barry McMullen because, he says, 'it was one less mouth to feed.' It was also the best role in the movie.

Cast: Jack Mulcahy (Jack McMullen), Mike McGlone (Patrick McMullen), Edward Burns (Barry McMullen), Shari Albert (Susan), Maxine Bahns (Audry), Catharine Bolz (Mrs McMullen), Connie Britton (Molly McMullen), Peter Johansen (Marty), Jennifer Jostyn (Leslie), Elizabeth P. McKay (Ann).

Dir and Screenplay: Edward Burns. Pro: Burns and Dick Fisher. Ex Pro: Edward J. Burns, Ted Hope and James Schamus. Ph and Ed: Fisher. M: Seamus Egan. (Marlboro Road Gang/ Videography/Good Machine/Fox Searchlight Pictures–Fox.) Rel: 8 December 1995. 98 mins. Cert 15. USA. 1995.

Burnt by the Sun - Utomlennye Solntsem

On a perfect summer's day in 1936, a hero of the Bolshevik revolution enjoys 24 hours off with his family and friends. In spite of the brief intrusion of a battalion of tanks – which the colonel sends packing – the day is full of music, swimming, dancing and laughter. Only the unannounced arrival of 'Uncle Mitia', a former lover of the colonel's young wife, casts seeds of dissonance. While conjuring up a rich, voluptuous tapestry of dacha life in the tradition of Chekhov, *Burnt by the Sun* imperceptibly discloses cracks in the social plaster, hinted at by a glance here, a veiled remark there. Only Nadia, the colonel's carefree six-year-old daughter, seems oblivious to the unseen shadows closing in. With director Nikita Mikhalkov leading the way as the charismatic, robust Kotov, and with his own daughter delightful as Nadia, *Burnt by the Sun* is a film of many cinematic pleasures. Sensual, hypnotic and thought-provoking.

Winner of the 1995 Oscar for Best Foreign Language Film.

Cast: Nikita Mikhalkov (Serguei Petrovitch Kotov), Oleg Menchikov (Mitia), Ingeborga Dapkounaite (Maroussia), Nadia Mikhalkov (Nadia), Andre Oumansky, Viatcheslav Tikhonov, Svetlan Krioutchkova, Vladimir Ilyine, Alla Kazanskaia.

Dir: Nikita Mikhalkov. Pro: Mikhalkov and Michel Seydoux. Ex Pro: Leonid Verechtchaguine, Jean-Louis Piel and Vladimir Sedov. Screenplay: Mikhalkov and Roustam Ibraguimbekov. Ph: Vilen Kaluta. Ed: Enzo Meniconi. Art: Vladimir Aronin and Alexandre Samulekine. M: Edouard Artemiev; Shostakovich, etc. Costumes: Natalia Ivanova. (Studio Trite/ Camera One/Canal Plus–Guild.) Rel: 18 August 1995. 134 mins. Cert 15. Russia/ France. 1994.

Bushwhacked
See *French Twist*.

Butterfly Kiss

On the windswept motorways of Lancashire a psychotic nymphomaniac and a mousy simpleton meet up and kick-start a tug-of-war between good and evil, love and lust, dependence and liberty. A deeply unpleasant and one-note odyssey, *Butterfly Kiss* fails to equal the imagination of *Heavenly Creatures* or the sheer exuberance of *Thelma & Louise*, two films it resembles. The fundamental problem is the character of Eunice, played with abrasive, selfless commitment by Amanda Plummer with a thick northern accent. A nice addition to her c.v., no doubt, Plummer's role is merely the latest in a string of showy weirdos. It is Saskia Reeves, however, who – as Eunice's simple, bewildered companion – reveals new depths as an actress.

Cast: Amanda Plummer (Eunice), Saskia Reeves (Miriam), Kathy Jamieson, Des McAleer, Lisa Jane Riley, Freda Dowie, Paul Bown, Ricky Tomlinson, Katy Murphy.

Dir: Michael Winterbottom. Pro: Julie Baines. Assoc Pro: Sarah Daniel. Screenplay: Frank Cottrell Boyce, from an idea by Boyce and Winterbottom. Ph: Seamus McGarvey. Ed: Trevor Waite. Art: Rupert Miles. M: John Harle; numbers performed by Helen Shapiro, Gloria Gaynor, The Cranberries, The New Seekers, Patsy Cline, Bjork, Shakespears Sister, P.J. Harvey, New Order, etc. Costumes: Rachel Fleming. (British Screen/ Merseyside Film Production Fund/ Dan Films–Electric Pictures.)

Rel: 18 August 1995. 88 mins. Cert 18. UK. 1994.

Canadian Bacon

With the Cold War over, the US president no longer has a suitable enemy to shoulder the blame for his country's woes. The Ayatollah, Mao Tse-tung and Ho Chi Minh are all dead, Russia is in a shambles and the invasion of Grenada was too fleeting. What the US needs is a big, fat, helpless opponent, a country that flouts the old-fashioned (opposite to metric) system, produces undistinguished beer and dispatches such contemptible foreign ambassadors as Anne Murray, Neil Young and Michael J. Fox. Echoing the well-informed, satirical precision of his heralded documentary *Roger & Me*, Michael Moore's fictional debut, *Canadian Bacon*, starts off very promisingly indeed. But no sooner has the director fired off his advance rockets than the film deteriorates into undisciplined farce. Had Moore reined in the histrionics and come up with a decent story, he might've pulled off a *Dr Strangelove* for the nineties.

Cast: John Candy (Bud B. Boomer), Alan Alda (The President of the United States), Rhea Perlman (Deputy Honey), Kevin Pollak (Stuart Smiley), Rip Torn (General Dick Panzer), Kevin J. O'Connor (Roy Boy), Bill Nunn (Kabral), G.D. Spradlin (R.J. Hacker), Brad Sullivan, Steven Wright, James Belushi, Wallace Shawn, Stanley Anderson, Michael Moore, Ben Hamper, Michael Copeman, Bruce Hunter, Richard Council, Dan Aykroyd.
    Dir and Screenplay: Michael Moore. Pro: Moore, David Brown, Ron Rotholz and Steve Golin. Co-Pro and Costumes: Kathleen Glynn. Ex Pro: Freddy Demann and Joni Sighvatsson. Ph: Haskell Wexler. Ed: Geraldine Peroni and Wendey Stanzler. Pro Des: Carol Spier. M: Elmer Bernstein; numbers performed by Tex Ritter, Life In a Blender, R.E.M., Barry Sadler, Bobby Goldsboro, Anne Murray, etc. (PolyGram/Propaganda Films/Maverick–Rank.) Rel: 20 October 1995. 95 mins. Cert PG. USA. 1995.

Candyman 2: Farewell to the Flesh

They will never learn, will they? Repeat his name five times and the spectre of the eponymous serial killer will appear to claim your soul. This time he's nipped down to picturesque New Orleans to join in the Mardi Gras celebrations. Losing the claustrophobic

Fuelling the hate: Amanda Plummer lays on the gas in Michael Winterbottom's dismal Butterfly Kiss *(from Electric)*

inner-city setting of the first film, the sequel compensates with colourful Louisiana detail and first-rate production values. The script though – based on a story by Clive Barker – leaves a lot to be desired and most of the cast aren't up to the task of salvaging it. [*Charles Bacon*]

Cast: Tony Todd (Candyman), Kelly Rowan (Annie Tarrant), Timothy Carhart (Paul McKeever), Veronica Cartwright (Octavia Tarrant), William O'Leary (Ethan Tarrant), Fay Hauser (Pam Carver), Joshua Gibran Mayweather (Matthew), Bill Nunn (Reverend Ellis), Matt Clark, David Gianopoulos, Caroline Barclay, Michael

Bergeron, Michael Culkin, Stephen Dunn.
    Dir: Bill Condon. Pro: Sigurjon Sighvatsson and Gregg D. Fienberg. Ex Pro: Clive Barker. Screenplay: Rand Ravich and Mark Kruger. Ed: Virginia Katz. Ph: Tobias Schliessler. Pro Des: Barry Robinson. M: Philip Glass. Costumes: Bruce Finlayson. Sound: Ben Wilkins. (Propaganda Films–PolyGram.) Rel: 1 December 1995. 95 mins. Cert 18. USA. 1995.

Carrington

For Dora Carrington living was more important than her art – she only painted because she wanted to. However, when she died her pictures

Maple syrup: John Candy and Rhea Perlman out to kick ass in Michael Moore's lamentable Canadian Bacon *(from PolyGram)*

A conspiracy of friendship: Jonathan Pryce and Emma Thompson as Lytton Strachey and Dora Carrington (from PolyGram)

brought her a fame she never realised during her lifetime. On the other hand, for Lytton Strachey writing was an enormous effort, but he lived to see his books transform the art of biography into a new realm. Strachey was also a homosexual, and when he met Carrington, she was a virgin. Yet over the next 17 years they formed a unique friendship that transcended the merely carnal: theirs was a love that suffered no compromise ... Although a little hard to follow at times and hampered by a somewhat static narrative framework (the film is divided into neat little chapters), this is a work of enormous grace and heart. Jonathan Pryce in particular is wonderful as Strachey, and strode off with the best actor award at the 1995 Cannes festival. FYI: Hampton, who penned his original screenplay in 1976, took over the directorial reins at the eleventh minute when Mike Newell accepted a juicier offer from Hollywood.

Cast: Emma Thompson (Dora Carrington), Jonathan Pryce (Lytton Strachey), Steven Waddington (Ralph Partridge), Rufus Sewell (Mark Gertler), Samuel West (Gerald Brenan), Penelope Wilton (Lady Ottoline Morrell), Janet McTeer (Vanessa Bell), Jeremy Northam (Beacus Penrose), Richard Clifford (Clive Bell), Peter Blythe, Alex Kingston, Sebastian Harcombe, David Ryall, Stephen Boxer, Annabel Mullion.

Dir and Screenplay: Christopher Hampton, from the book *Lytton Strachey* by Michael Holroyd. Pro: Ronald Shedlo and John McGrath. Ex Pro: Francis Boespflug, Philippe Carcassone and Fabienne Vonier. Ph: Denis Lenoir. Ed: George Akers. Pro Des: Caroline Amies. M: Michael Nyman. Costumes: Penny Rose. Fight Arranger: William Hobbs. (Freeway/Shedlo/Cinea & Orsans/Canal Plus–PolyGram Film Entertainment.) Rel: 22 September 1995. 122 mins. Cert 18. UK. 1995.

Casino

Before Las Vegas became a Disney attraction for the rich, the town was run by ruthless men who peddled dreams for hard cash. Anything was possible, so long as you had the money. Sam 'Ace' Rothstein had an uncanny nose for a win, and when he was put in charge of the Tangiers casino by the Mob (without a gaming licence), his dream was complete. Then his childhood friend and fellow mobster Nicky Santoro decided he wanted a piece of the action ... Following the wildly misconceived *The Age of Innocence*, Martin Scorsese returns to familiar territory with this sweeping, profane, violent and magnificently crafted gangster epic. Yet by duplicating the operatic style and structure of *Good-Fellas* (reflective voice-over, period songs) Scorsese is simply recycling stale celluloid. Even Robert De Niro and Joe Pesci return to play their old roles (dignified gangster, parasitic psychopath), while the supporting cast looks all too familiar. Only Sharon Stone, in a horrific part, brings a sense of fresh vitality and despair. The year's most unpleasant movie giftwrapped to perfection.

Cast: Robert De Niro (Sam 'Ace' Rothstein), Sharon Stone (Ginger McKenna), Joe Pesci (Nicky Santoro), James Woods (Lester Diamond), Don Rickles (Billy Sherbert), Alan King (Andy Stone), Kevin Pollak (Phillip Green), L.Q. Jones (Pat Webb), Frank Vincent (Frank Marino), Dick Smothers, John Bloom, Pasquale Cajano, Melissa Prophet, Bill Allison, Vinny Vella,

Oscar Goodman, Catherine Scorsese, Phillip Suriano, Erika Von Tagen, Frankie Avalon, Steve Allen, Jayne Meadows, Jerry Vale, Catherine T. Scorsese, Paul Herman, Graig Vincent, Clem Caserta, Richard Riehle, Alfred Nittoli, J. Charles Thompson, Claudia Haro, Haven Earle Haley.

Dir: Martin Scorsese. Pro: Barbara De Fina. Screenplay: Scorsese and Nicholas Pileggi, based on Pileggi's book. Ph: Robert Richardson. Pro Des: Dante Ferretti. Ed: Thelma Schoonmaker. M: J.S. Bach, Richard Strauss, Georges Delerue; numbers performed by Louis Prima, Dean Martin, Muddy Waters, Ottis Redding, The Rolling Stones, Ramsey Lewis, Little Richard, Roxy Music, Ray Charles, Jeff Beck, Dinah Washington, The Staple Singers, Jerry Vale, Emmylou Harris, The Velvetones, The Moody Blues, DEVO, Fleetwood Mac, B.B. King, Tony Bennett, The Animals, etc. Costumes: Rita Ryack and John Dunn. Title sequence: Elaine and Saul Bass. (Universal Pictures/Syalis D.A. & Legende Enterprises/De Fina/Cappa-UIP.) Rel: 23 February 1996. 178 mins. Cert 18. USA. 1995.

And let there be neon: Joe Pesci and Robert De Niro conspire in Martin Scorsese's disappointing Casino *(from UIP)*

Casper

Dr James Harvey specialises in 'after-life therapy', i.e. ridding haunted houses of their 'living impaired' occupants. However, when he moves into Whipstaff Manor in the town of Friendship, Maine, he meets his match

Ghost of a chance: Christina Ricci gets spooked by Casper *(from UIP)*

in a trio of mischievous spooks called Stretch, Stinkie and Fatso. But, luckily for Dr Harvey, the ghostly trio's genial little nephew, Casper, has a crush on the exorcist's 12-year-old daughter ... Casper, the friendly ghost of *Harvey Comics* fame, gets the big screen treatment in this unashamedly over-the-top ectoplasmic cross between *E.T.* and *Ghostbusters.* Steven Spielberg

executive produced, so expect extravagant special effects (which are amazing) and a high sugar content.

Cast: Christina Ricci (Kat Harvey), Bill Pullman (Dr James Harvey), Cathy Moriarty (Carrigan Crittenden), Eric Idle (Dibs), Malachi Pearson (the voice of Casper), Joe Nipote (Stretch), Joe Alaskey (Stinkie), Brad Garrett (Fatso), Garette Ratliff Henson (Vic), Jessica Wesson (Amber), Amy Brenneman (Amelia), Ben Stein, Don Novello, Mr Rogers, Terry Murphy, Ernestine Mercer, Rodney Dangerfield, Wesley Thompson, Devon Sawa, Dan Aykroyd, Clint Eastwood, Mel Gibson.

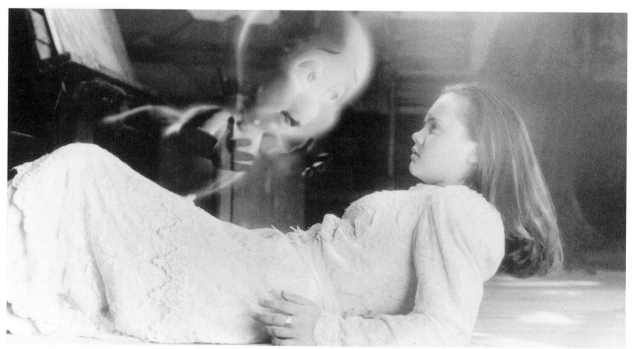

Service with a smile: Isabelle Huppert and Sandrine Bonnaire act up in Claude Chabrol's La Cérémonie *(from Gala Film)*

Dir: Brad Silberling. Pro: Colin Wilson. Ex Pro: Steven Spielberg, Gerald R. Molen and Jeffrey A. Montgomery. Screenplay: Sherri Stoner and Deanna Oliver, based on *Casper the Friendly Ghost* by Joseph Oriolo. Ph: Dean Cundey. Ed: Michael Kahn. Pro Des: Leslie Dilley. M: James Horner; numbers performed by Little Richard, Frank Sinatra, Digital Underground, Jordan Hill, etc. Costumes: Rosanna Norton. (Universal/Amblin/Harvey Entertainment–UIP.) Rel: 28 July 1995. 100 mins. Cert PG. USA. 1995.

La Cérémonie

Hired as the housekeeper of the large country home of the Lelievre family, Sophie strives hard to be liked, whipping up wonderful meals, keeping the house spotless and maintaining a low profile. But Sophie's friendship with a rebellious woman from the local post office and her obsessive desire to conceal her illiteracy is beginning to tarnish her perfection ... A drama exploring the uncomfortable divide between domestic and employer, *La Cérémonie* is every bit as disturbing as Joseph Losey's *The Servant*. A psychological drama in the true sense of the word (distinct from such simplistic fare as *The Juror*), *La Cérémonie* is a fascinating look at the ambiguous ripples generated by calm waters, perfectly embodied by Sandrine Bonnaire in an unflinching, barely off-centred performance. The film's chilling conclusion is made all the harder to bear due to the distracted bonhomie of the affluent, loving Lelievre family. Adapted from the novel *A Judgement in Stone* by Ruth Rendell.

Cast: Isabelle Huppert (Jeanne), Sandrine Bonnaire (Sophie), Jacqueline Bisset (Catherine Lelievre), Jean-Pierre Cassel (Georges Lelievre), Virginie Ledoyen (Melinda Lelievre), Valentin Merlet (Gilles Lelievre), Julien Rochefort (Jeremie), Dominique Frot, Jean-Francois Perrier, Yves Verhoeven, Pierre Godard.
Dir: Claude Chabrol. Pro: Marin Karmitz. Screenplay: Chabrol and Caroline Eliacheff. Ph: Bernard Zitzermann. Pro Des: Daniel Mercier. Ed: Monique Fardoulis. M: Matthieu Chabrol. Costumes: Corinne Jorry. (MK2/France 3 Cinema/Prokino Filmproduction/Olga-Film/ZDF/Canal Plus–Gala Film.) Rel: 8 March 1996. 112 mins. Cert 15. France. 1995.

Chungking Express – Chongqing Senlin

Laying two stories on top of each other – loosely linked by the all-night Chungking Express cafe – Wong Kar-Wai reveals a bustling Hong Kong swept by rain, lit by neon and charged with unrequited love. In the first story a young policeman, cop #223, takes to purchasing tins of pineapple chunks with a May 1 expiry date: the time of his anticipated reconciliation with his girlfriend. In the second, cop #663 laments the loss of his love with his cuddly toys, threadbare towel and soap. Idiosyncratic, aurally audacious and visually hypnotic, *Chungking Express* makes up for the turgid pretension of Wong's last film released here, *Days of Being Wild*. And newcomer Faye Wang (a Chinese update of a young Jane Birkin) is irresistible as the waif who surreptitiously haunts 663's flat. FYI: Quentin Tarantino selected this for the first release on his new video label.

Cast: Brigitte Lin (blonde woman), Kaneshiro Takeshi (He Qiwo, cop #223), Faye Wang (Faye), Tony Leung (cop #663), Valerie Chow (air hostess), 'Piggy' Chan (manager of Midnight Express).
Dir and Screenplay: Wong Kar-Wai. Pro: Chan Yi-Kan. Ex Pro: Chan Pui-Wah. Ph: Christopher Doyle and Lau Wai-Keung. Ed: William Chang, Hai Kit-Wai and Kwong Chi-Leung. Pro Des: William Chang. M: Frankie Chan and Roel A. Garcia; 'California Dreamin'' performed by The Mamas and the Papas. Costumes: Yao Huiming. (Jet Tone–ICA Projects.) Rel: 15 September 1995. 97 mins. Cert 12. Hong Kong. 1994.

City Hall

New York; now. Both a homage to New York and a thriller about political corruption, *City Hall* follows the aftermath of a shooting that downs a cop, a drug dealer and a six-year-old boy. With one eye on the needs of his people and another on electoral opportunity, New York mayor John Pappas (Pacino) navigates the stormy waters of imminent scandal with the help of his sharp-witted, silver-tongued deputy (Cusack in James Carville mode). With a screenplay concocted by the estimable team of Paul Schrader (*Taxi Driver*), Nicholas Pileggi (*Goodfellas*) and Bo Goldman (*One Flew Over the Cuckoo's Nest*) – based on Ken Lipper's original draft – *City Hall*

Post-coital fun with toy aeroplanes: Valerie Chow and Tony Leung in Wong Kar-Wai's weird and winsome Chungking Express *(from ICA Projects)*

wears its pedigree on its sleeve. Yet in spite of all the great lines and rhetoric ('a man's stature is determined by his enemies, not by his friends'), it's hard to believe people saying these things. Still, Harold Becker's dexterous, fast-paced direction is a model of camouflaged narrative skill (take note De Palma and Oliver Stone) and Al Pacino's charismatic performance (a secondary role to John Cusack's) is masterly.

Cast: Al Pacino (Mayor John Pappas), John Cusack (Kevin Calhoun), Bridget Fonda (Marybeth Cogan), Danny Aiello (Frank Anselmo), Martin Landau (Judge Walter Stern), David Paymer (Abe Goodman), Tony Franciosa (Pauly Zapatti), Richard Schiff (Larry Schwartz), Lindsay Duncan (Sydney Pappas), Nestor Serrano, Mel Winkler, Lauren Velez, Chloe Morris, Ian Quinlan, Roberta Peters, Rob LaBelle, Mark Lonow, Richard Gant.
   Dir: Harold Becker. Pro: Becker, Edward R. Pressman, Ken Lipper and Charles Mulvehill. Screenplay: Lipper, Paul Schrader & Nicholas Pileggi, and Bo Goldman. Ph:

Michael Seresin. Pro Des: Jane Musky. Ed: Robert C. Jones and David Bretherton. M: Jerry Goldsmith. Costumes: Richard Hornung. John Cusack's Dialect Coach: Robert Easton. (Castle Rock–Rank.) Rel: 12 April 1996. 112 mins. Cert 15. USA. 1996.

And justice for all? Al Pacino (right) points the way to John Cusack in Harold Becker's City Hall *(from Rank)*

The City of Lost Children - La Cite des Enfants Perdus
Unable to dream, Krank, a Max Schreck lookalike, is ageing beyond his years and needs the sweet dreams of children to stall the march of time. Aided by high technology, a team of clones, a dwarf and a disembodied brain, Krank secures a constant supply

Visions of hate: Judith Vittet and Ron Perlman cower in the water in Jean-Pierre Jeunet and Marc Caro's extraordinary The City of Lost Children *(from Entertainment)*

of young children kidnapped by a grotesque force of electronically-operated Cyclops. Then, one foggy night, the Cyclops make the mistake of abducting the younger brother of One, a child with the body of a circus strongman ... Artfully conjuring up a surreal world streaked with cruelty and dark humour, director Jean-Pierre Jeunet and art director Marc Caro, the makers of *Delicatessen*, have produced one of the most imaginative, creative, disturbing and consummately realised films in aeons. Imagine Terry Gilliam paying homage to F.W. Murnau via

Hieronymous Bosch and Jules Verne and you have a rough idea of what you're letting yourself in for. A masterpiece of the macabre.

Cast: Ron Perlman (One), Daniel Emilfork (Krank), Judith Vittet (Miette), Dominique Pinon (the clones/the diver), Jean-Claude Dreyfus (Marcello the flea tamer), Genevieve Brunet and Odile Mallet (Zette and Line, 'The Octopus'), Mireille Mosse (Miss Bismuth), Serge Merlin, Francois Hadji-Lazaro, Rufus, Ticky Holgado, Dominique Bettenfeld, Marc Caro, Jean-Louis Trintignant (the voice of Irvin).
Dir: Jean-Pierre Jeunet and Marc Caro. Pro: Claudie Ossard. Line Pro: Daniel Szuster. Screenplay: Jeunet, Caro and Gilles Adrein. Ph: Darius Khondji. Ed: Herve Schneid. Art: Caro. M: Angelo Badalamenti; 'Who Will Take Your Dreams Away' written and performed by Marianne Faithfull. Costumes: Jean Paul Gaultier. (Constellation/Lumiere/Canal Plus/France 3 Cinema–Entertainment.) Rel: 1 September 1995. 112 mins. Cert 15. France. 1995.

Clockers

'A clocker', clarifies co-scenarist Richard Price (on whose novel this is based), 'is slang for the lowest level of drug dealer. He's called a clocker because he's out there around the clock.' Returning to the well-worn territory of racially-torn and crack-infested Brooklyn, writer-director Spike Lee lays on the pretension with a shovel, utilising a variety of colour styles, film stocks and sharp zooms, while feverishly jostling, tilting and juggling his camera. Opening with the close-up of a bullet wound, Lee quickly gets down to brass tacks, pummelling home the message that crack cocaine is bad for you, bad for your society and bad for tourism. Here, two brothers struggle to keep their heads above water, the good one holding down two jobs but barely scraping together a living, the bad one creaming off $3,500 from every shipment of cocaine he handles. Then, when a local drug dealer is shot dead on the street, the good bro' confesses to the murder. Enter scumball cop Harvey Keitel, who's hell-bent on ripping a confession from the other sibling. Of course, all and sundry will pay dearly. Depressing, to say the least.

Cast: Harvey Keitel (Rocco Klein), John Turturro (Larry Mazilli), Delroy Lindo (Rodney Little), Mekhi Phifer (Ronald 'Strike' Dunham), Isaiah Washington (Victor Dunham), Keith David (Andre the Giant), Pee Wee Love (Tyrone), Tom Byrd (Errol Barnes), Michael Imperioli (Jo-Jo), Steve White (Darryl Adams), Regina Taylor, Sticky Fingaz, Fredro, E.O. Nolasco, Lawrence B. Adisa, Hassan Johnson, Frances Foster, Paul Calderon, Brendan Kelly, Mike Starr, Spike Lee, Harry Lennix, Leonard Thomas, Ricky Aiello.
Dir: Spike Lee. Pro: Lee, Martin Scorsese and Jon Kilik. Ex Pro: Rosalie Swedlin and Monty Ross. Co-Pro: Richard Price. Screenplay: Price and Lee. Ph: Malik Hassan Sayeed. Pro Des: Andrew McAlpine. Ed: Sam Pollard. M: Terence Blanchard; numbers performed by Marc Dorsey, Crooklyn Dodgers '95, Philip Bailey, Seal, Des'ree, Rebelz of Authority, Chaka Khan and Bruce Hornsby, KRS-One, etc. Costumes: Ruth Carter. (Universal/40 Acres/Mule Filmworks–UIP.) Rel: 9 February 1996. 128 mins. Cert 18. USA. 1995.

Clueless

Totally cool satire on contemporary American high school mores, focusing on the social machinations and shopping of Cher, the fifteen-year-old major babe of Beverly Hills High. However, Cher, with all her designer clothes and many friends, is not as clued in as she'd like to think she is. She may know Versace from Armani, but she thinks Tony Curtis starred in an epic called *Sporadicus* and – worse – she is still hymenally challenged! An effervescent screenplay, ebullient direction and game performances steer this to laugh heaven. And it's way in tune.

Cast: Alicia Silverstone (Cher Hamilton), Stacey Dash (Dionne), Brittany Murphy (Tai), Paul Rudd (Josh), Donald Faison (Murray), Breckin Meyer (Travis Berkenstock), Jeremy Sisto (Elton), Justin Walker (Christian), Dan Hedaya (Mel Hamilton), Wallace Shawn (Mr Hall), Twink Caplan (Miss Geist), Aida Linares, Elisa Donovan, Julie Brown, Jace Alexander, Ron Orbach, Carl Gottlieb.

Dir and Screenplay: Amy Heckerling. Pro: Scott Rudin and Robert Lawrence. Co-Pro: Adam Schroeder and Barry Berg. Assoc Pro: Twink Caplan. Ph: Bill Pope. Ed: Debra Chiate. Pro Des: Steven Jordan. M: David Kitay; numbers performed by The Muffs, David Bowie, No Doubt, Salt-N-Pepa, Radiohead, Cracker, Lightning Seeds, Supergrass, Coolio, Domino, The Cranberries, The Choclate Hippies, Counting Crows, Velocity Girl, World Party, Spin, Billie Holiday, The Mighty Mighty Bosstones, Jewel, Beastie Boys, General Public, Smoking Popes, etc. Costumes: Mona May. (Paramount–UIP.) Rel: 20 October 1995. 98 mins. Cert 12. USA. 1995.

Major babes: Alicia Silverstone, Brittany Murphy and Stacey Dash tune into the big picture in Amy Heckerling's monster Clueless *(from UIP)*

Cobb

Tyrus Raymond Cobb was the greatest baseball player of his time. With a record-breaking 4,190 hits to his name, he single-handedly changed baseball from a light-hearted entertainment into a serious, high-stakes national obsession. Yet while respected for his skill with a bat, Cobb was reviled for his brutal conduct on the diamond and, by his own admission, sent twelve players to hospital in one season. Indeed, such was his disfavour that police marksmen were recruited to guard the stadium when he played. Ron Shelton, the writer-director of *Bull Durham* and *White Men Can't Jump* (about baseball and basketball respectively) adds more warts to the legend, revealing that Cobb, a misogynist and racist, once pistol-whipped a man to death, beat his wife

and was alienated from his children. Tommy Lee Jones, playing 'The Georgia Peach' in his declining years, chews the scenery with gusto, giving enormous presence to a hateful man. But for all its insights into the dichotomy of 'greatness' – reminiscent of Robert De Niro's monstrous Jake LaMotta in *Raging Bull* – *Cobb* is a hard film to like.

Cast: Tommy Lee Jones (Tyrus Cobb), Robert Wuhl (Al Stump), Lolita Davidovich (Ramona), Ned Bellamy (Ray), Scott Burkholder (Jimmy), Allan Malamud (Mud), Bill Caplan (Bill), Tyler Logan Cobb (young Ty Cobb), Jeff Fellenzer, Doug Krikorian, Lou Myers, J. Kenneth Campbell, Paula Rudy, Stephen Mendillo, Rath Shelton, Jim Shelton, Stacy Keach Sr, Lawrence 'Crash' Davis, Tracy Keehn-Dashnaw, Jimmy Buffett, Bradley Whitford, Don Hood.

Dir and Screenplay: Ron Shelton. Pro: David Lester. Ex Pro: Arnon Milchan. Ph: Russell Boyd. Ed: Paul Seydor and Kim-

berly Ray. Pro Des: Armin Ganz and Scott F. Ritenour. M: Elliot Goldenthal; 'Visit To The Wreckage' from *Alien 3*; numbers performed by Louis Prima and Keely Smith,

A hard man is good to find: Tommy Lee Jones in Ron Shelton's exhausting Cobb *(from Warner)*

Frozen assets: Masatoshi Nagase and Gisli Halldorsson in Fridrik Thor Fridriksson's bizarre Cold Fever *(from Theatrical Experience)*

The Jaguars, Hoagy Carmichael, Sister Wynona Carr, etc. Costumes: Ruth E. Carter. (Regency Enterprises/Alcor Films-Warner.) Rel: 7 July 1995. 128 mins. Cert 18. USA. 1994.

Cold Fever

In Iceland they eat rams' testicles, sheep's heads and fermented shark, are superstitious enough to build highways round giant rocks ('angel stones') and boast the greatest number of Miss Worlds per capita. All these facts and more are revealed in this bizarre, picturesque travelogue of Iceland produced by the iconoclastic Jim Stark (*Down by Law, Mystery Train, Night on Earth*). Anticipating a sunny vacation in Hawaii, Atsushi Hirata, a successful young employee of a Tokyo fish company, instead finds tradition steering him across the snowy wastes of Iceland in deep winter – to conduct a cathartic ceremony at the site of his parents' death. Jim Jarmusch would approve.

Cast: Masatoshi Nagase (Atsushi Hirata), Lili Taylor (Jill), Fisher Stevens (Jack), Gisli Halldorsson (Siggi), Laura Hughes (Laura), Seijun Suzuki (grandfather), Hiro-masa Shimada (Suzuki), Ari Matthiasson, Magnus Olafsson, Katrin Olafsdottir.

Dir: Fridrik Thor Fridriksson. Pro: Jim Stark. Ex Pro: Fridriksson, Christa Saredi, Reinhard Brundig and Peter Aalbaek Jensen. Co-Pro: George Gund III. Line Pro and Ph: Ari Kristinsson. Screenplay: Stark and Fridriksson. Ed: Steingrimur Karlsson. Pro Des: Arni Poll Johansson. M: Hilmar Orn Hilmarsson. Costumes: Maria Olafsdottir. (Icicle Films/Icelandic Film Corporation/Film Fonds Hamburg/Sunrise AG/Pandora Film/Zentropa/Alta Films–Theatrical Experience.) Rel: 29 September 1995. 107 mins. Cert 15. Iceland/Germany/Switzerland/USA. 1994.

The Confessional – Le Confessionnal

Quebec City; 1952/1989. Alfred Hitchcock is filming *I Confess* in Quebec City; Pierre, a painter, returns to Canada after years of studying art in China; a 16-year-old girl is pregnant, but will not reveal the identity of the father; Marc, a rent boy, is spotted in the hotel bedroom of a prominent politician; and, in the background, there is the bloodshed in Tiananmen Square, a foretaste of a more personal tragedy to follow in the Far East ... Utilising both visual and verbal metaphor, *The Confessional* unfolds its complex, gripping story with masterly flair, gradually stepping up the momentum as it slips between time frames. Thus, when Hitchcock yells 'Cut!' in 1952, the film cuts to 1989 to reveal a literal, bloody manifestation of the word, then cuts away again to the freshly painted wall of Pierre's apartment, representing the latter's final exorcism from the ghosts of his past. A fascinating journey into the warped contours of family history (slyly linked with the whole filmmaking process, both actual and contrived), *The Confessional* is one of the great films of French-Canadian cinema.

Cast: Lothaire Bluteau (Pierre Lamontagne), Patrick Goyette (Marc Lamontagne), Kristin Scott Thomas (assistant to Alfred Hitchcock), Jean-Louis Millette (Raymond Massicotte), Ron Burrage (Alfred Hitchcock), Richard Frechette (Andre), Francois Papineau (Paul-Emile Lamontagne), Marie Gignac (Francoise Lamontagne), Normand Daneua (Massicotte, the young priest), Anne-Marie Cadieux (Manon), Suzanne Clement (Rachel), Lynda Lepage-Beaulieu (Jeanne d'Arc), Billy Merasty (Moose), Pascal Rollin, Paul Herbert, Andreanne Lepage-Beaulieu.

Dir and Screenplay: Robert Lepage. Pro: Denise Robert, David Puttnam and Philippe Carcassonne. Co-Pro: Steve Norris. Assoc Pro: Daniel Louis. Ph: Alain Dostie. Pro Des: Francois Laplante. Ed: Emmanuelle Castro. M: Sacha Puttnam; Mozart; numbers performed by Portishead, Depeche Mode, Tricky, Sarah Vaughan, Count Basie, etc. Costumes: Barbara Kidd. (Cinemaginaire/Confessional/Enigma Films/Cinea/Telefilm Canada/Channel Four– Artificial Eye/Mayfair.) Rel: 7 June 1996. 101 mins. Cert 15. Canada/UK/ France. 1995.

Copycat

Nine out of ten serial killers are white, male and aged between 20 and 35. And, in the United States, there are 35 on the loose at any given time. Thus expounds star criminal psychologist Helen Hudson, whose interest in and knowledge of her subject attracts the attention of not one, but two, serial psychos. Acidly remarking, 'I'm their damn pin-up girl,' Helen is reduced to chronic agoraphobia after a nasty incident in a ladies' loo. But, sequestered in her palatial San Francisco apartment listening to opera, Helen cannot keep her nose out of a new case, harassing the police department with anonymous phone calls. Realising the insight that Helen can bring to the investigation, homicide detective M.J.

Playing the game: Lothaire Bluteau indulges in a bit of alcoholic chess in Robert Lepage's masterly The Confessional *(from Artificial Eye/Mayfair)*

Monahan tracks her down and the pair start to unravel the case of a killer who gets his kicks reenacting famous murder scenes... Flawlessly directed by Jon Amiel (*Aunt Julia and the Scriptwriter*, *Sommersby*) and smartly scripted by Ann Biderman and David Madsen, this is a shining model of a well-blooded genre. Performances, music and photography are all first-rate. FYI: The original love story was jettisoned by Amiel for being in bad taste; a wise move if ever I heard one.

Cast: Sigourney Weaver (Helen Hudson), Holly Hunter (M.J. Monahan), Dermot Mulroney (Ruben Goetz), William McNamara (Peter Foley), Harry Connick Jr (Daryll Lee Cullum), J.E. Freeman (Lt Thomas Quinn), Will Patton (Nicoletti), John Rothman (Andy), Shannon O'Hurley, Bob Greene, Tony Haney.

Dir: Jon Amiel. Pro: Arnon Milchan and Mark Tarlov. Ex Pro: Michael Nathanson and John Fielder. Co-Pro: Joe Caracciolo. Screenplay: Ann Biderman and David Madsen. Ph: Laszlo Kovacs. Pro Des: Jim

Clay. Ed: Alan Heim and Jim Clark. M: Christopher Young; Rossini, Fauré, Puccini; numbers performed by Steven Ray, The Four Tops, New World Beat, The Partridge Family, The Police, David Bowie, Silksid, etc. Costumes: Claudia Brown. Ant

Psycho pin-up: Sigourney Weaver defends her statistics in Jon Amiel's gripping Copycat *(from Warner)*

wrangler: Steve Kutcher. Holly Hunter's Dialect Coach: Francie Brown. (New Regency/Monarch Enterprises-Warner.) Rel: 3 May 1996. 123 mins. Cert 18. USA. 1995.

Country Life

Adapted from *Uncle Vanya*, *Country Life* is a sprightly drawing room comedy transported to the spectacular

Ire down below: Gene Hackman (on inter-com), George Dzundza (in front, out of fo-cus) and Denzel Washington (centre) on red alert in Tony Scott's thrilling Crimson Tide *(from Buena Vista)*

Illicit passions: Greta Scacchi and Sam Neill exchange bodily fluids in Michael Blakemore's beguiling Country Life *(from Metro Tartan)*

Australian bush. There, at a remote sheep station, the arrival of the 62-year-old Alexander Voysey creates a terrific stir. It has been 22 years since Alexander left Australia to pursue a career as a theatre critic in London and in the intervening period his reputation has become the stuff of legend. How-ever, his new airs and his striking English wife turn the household of his brother-in-law and daughter on its head. Michael Blakemore, who not only directs his own screenplay but plays the key character of Voysey, him-self left Australia to undertake a career in the English theatre. Happily, though, his return to his roots is entirely more propitious. A most engaging frolic.

Cast: Sam Neill (Max Askey), Greta Scac-chi (Deborah Voysey), John Hargreaves (Jack Dickens), Kerry Fox (Sally Voysey), Michael Blakemore (Alexander Voysey), Googie Withers (Hannah), Robyn Cruze (Violet), Patricia Kennedy (Maud Dick-ens), Ron Blanchard (Wally Wells), Ian Bliss (David Archdale), Maurie Fields, Bryan Marshall, Tony Barry, Terry Brady, Tom Long.
  Dir and Screenplay: Michael Blakemore. Pro: Robin Dalton. Line Pro: Adrienne Read. Ph: Stephen Windon. Ed: Nicholas Beauman. Pro Des: Laurence Eastwood. M: Peter Best; 'Don Cesar De Bazan' per-formed by Dame Nellie Melba. Costumes: Wendy Chuck. (Australian Film Finance Corporation–Metro Tartan.) Rel: 14 July 1995. 114 mins. Cert 12. Australia. 1994.

Crimson Tide

When a megalomaniac Russian leader and his rebel army seize control of a nuclear missile base, there is no reason to disbelieve his threats of catastrophic retaliation. Thus President Clinton is compelled to activate the USS Alabama, a nuclear submarine with enough firepower to melt a cold war. But when push comes to shove, the two men on board with the authority to detonate World War III find they have opposing moral perspectives. According to Lieutenant Commander Ron Hunter 'a true enemy cannot be destroyed. In the nuclear world the true enemy is war itself.' But gung-ho, war-embattled Captain Frank Ramsey isn't taking any chances with a volatile enemy barking up his ass ... Loading a tactical nightmare with a human dimension, *Crimson Tide* comes bursting to the surface with all guns blazing. But it is far more than a grade-A reworking of *The Hunt for Red October*. Charged with state-of-the-art special effects, the film cross-breeds political panic with human friction, stoking a gut-churning, mind-blowing ride. Denzel Washington and Gene Hackman fuel the human suspense with flesh-and-blood performances of dramatic subtlety, while Tony Scott's breathless direction lubricates the action. Music, camerawork, editing and an erudite script (with pop-cultural references supplied by Quentin Tarantino) all add to the pedigree.

Cast: Denzel Washington (Lieutenant Commander Ron Hunter), Gene Hackman (Captain Frank Ramsey), George Dzundza (Cob), Viggo Mortensen (Lt. Peter 'Weps' Ince), James Gandolfini (Lt. Bobby Dougherty), Matt Craven (Lt. Roy Zimmer), Rocky Carroll (Lt. Darik Westerguard), Lillo Brancato Jr. (Russell 'Scotty' Vossler), Vanessa Bell Calloway (Julia Hunter), Daniel Von Bargen (Vladimir Radchenko), Jason Robards (Admiral Anderson), Jaime P. Gomez, Michael Milhoan, Scott Burkholder, Danny Nucci, Eric Bruskotter, Rick Schroder, Steve Zahn, Richard Valeriani, Scott Grimes, Henry Mortensen.
Dir: Tony Scott. Pro: Don Simpson and Jerry Bruckheimer. Ex Pro: Bill Unger, Lucas Foster and Mike Moder. Screenplay: Michael Schiffer and (uncredited) Quentin Tarantino. Ph: Dariusz Wolski. Ed: Chris Lebenzon. Pro Des: Michael White. M: Hans Zimmer; Beethoven, Schubert; numbers performed by Martha Reeves and the Vandellas, Lynyrd Skynyrd, The Gathering, and Miriam Gauci. Costumes: George L. Little. (Hollywood Pictures.) Rel: 3 November 1995. 116 mins. Cert 15. USA. 1995.

Medicine boys: Joseph Mazzello and Brad Renfro find life in the shadow of death in Peter Horton's touching The Cure *(from PolyGram)*

The Cure

Stillwater, Minnesota; now. Branded 'a faggot' by his school mates for living next door to a little boy with Aids, Erik takes out his anger and frustration on his frail neighbour. Gradually, however, curiosity gets the better of him and a tenuous friendship develops between the two boys as they search for a cure to the disease ... Sensitively directed by Peter Horton, *The Cure* brings a welcome intelligence and heart to the spectre of Aids for a younger audience. Part road movie and part rites-of-passage, the film hits its marks with restraint and a straightforwardness that is startlingly moving. The film's stars – Mazzello, Renfro, Sciorra and Davison – are all outstanding, while the scenes between Mazzello and Renfro are particularly extraordinary in their ability to capture the natural interaction of two 11-year-olds.

Cast: Joseph Mazzello (Dexter), Brad Renfro (Erik), Annabella Sciorra (Linda), Bruce Davison (Dr Stevens), Diana Scarwid (Gail), Nicky Katt (Pony), Renee Humphrey (Angle), Aeryk Egan, Craig Gierl, Laurie A. Sinclair, Shirley Venard, Mary McCusker, Peter Moore.
Dir: Peter Horton. Pro: Mark Burg and Eric Eisner. Ex Pro: Todd Baker and William Borden. Screenplay: Robert Kuhn. Ph: Andrew Dintenfass. Pro Des: Armin Ganz. Ed: Anthony Sherin. M: Dave Grusin. Costumes: Louise Frogley. (Island Pictures/Universal–PolyGram.) Rel: 14 June 1996. 98 mins. Cert 12. USA. 1995.

CutThroat Island

1668; Jamaica. The strapping daughter of a notorious pirate competes with the British army and her villainous uncle to find a hidden hoard of treasure ... The most catastrophic box-office disaster of 1995 (costing over $100m, earning $2.3m in its flagship opening weekend), *CutThroat Island* attempts to be the most authentic pirate picture ever made. Besides containing the traditional ingredients of the genre – imposing galleons, cannons, cutlasses, skeletons, taverns, heaving cleavages, elaborately scarred faces and treasure – the film ups its ante with sensational stunts, gruesome sound effects and spectacular visuals. While the dialogue leaves a lot to be desired ('I'm all at sea when it comes to things nautical') and the improbabilities outweigh the logic, the breathless pacing and impressive sets make this a

Voyage of the damned: The Morning Star and The Reaper come to bows in Renny Harlin's box-office catastrophe, CutThroat Island *(from Guild)*

worthy contemporary successor to *Captain Blood* and *The Sea Hawk* (and, unlike *Waterworld*, all the money is on screen). Matthew Modine, who plays the swashbuckling male lead with considerable wile and athleticism, replaced Michael Douglas when the latter jumped ship. Filmed in Malta and Thailand.

Cast: Geena Davis (Morgan Adams), Matthew Modine (William Shaw), Frank Langella (Captain Dawg Brown), Maury Chaykin (John Reed), Patrick Malahide (Ainslee), Stan Shaw (Glasspoole), Rex Linn (Mr Blair), Paul Dillon (Snelgrave), Chris Masterson (Bowen), Jimmy F. Skaggs (Mr Scully), Harris Yulin (Black Harry Adams), Angus Wright (Captain Trotter), Carl Chase, Peter Geeves, Ken Bones, Mary Pegler, Mary Peach, George Murcell, Christopher Halliday, Rupert Vansittart, Nick Bartlett, Chris Adamson.
  Dir: Renny Harlin. Pro: Harlin, Joel B. Michaels, Laurence Mark and James Gorman. Ex Pro: Mario Kassar. Assoc Pro: Jane Bartelme. Screenplay: Robert King and Marc Norman, from a story by Gorman, Michael Frost Beckner, Bruce A. Evans and

Raynold Gideon. Ph: Peter Levy. Pro Des: Norman Garwood. Ed: Frank J. Urioste and Ralph E. Winters. M: John Debney. Costumes: Enrico Sabatini. Digital & Visual Effects: Jeffrey A. Okun. (CutThroat Prods/Carolco/Forge/Canal Plus/Tele Communications–Guild.) Rel: 29 March 1996. 125 mins. Cert PG. USA. 1995.

Bicycle thieves: Le Van Loc on his bike in Tran Anh Hung's Cyclo *(from Entertainment)*

Cyclo - Xich Lo

Hô Chi Minh City; now. A young cyclo, a driver of the ubiquitous bicycle taxis of Vietnam, becomes a target of a rival cyclo gang and is soon caught up in the cycle of blood and death that is destroying the fabric of his country ... Following his award-winning first film *The Scent of Green Papaya* – which, although set in Saigon, was filmed entirely on a sound stage in France – the Vietnamese-born, French-educated filmmaker Tran Anh Hung returns to his roots with a vengeance, utilising natural light and a hand-held camera to capture the raw energy of contemporary Vietnam. On the one hand, *Cyclo* is a vivid and compelling picture of Hô Chi Minh City, technically and artistically every bit as exciting as a Vietnamese *Mean Streets*. On the other, it is a confusing, gratuitously violent mess tenuously connected by one-dimensional characters. No doubt the former Saigon is a city exhausted by history, but its human spirit is missing here.

Cast: Le Van Loc (the cyclo), Tony Leung-Chiu Wai (the poet), Tran Nu Yen Khe (the sister), Nguyen Nhu Quynh (the madam), Bjuhoang Huy (the crazy son), Nguyen Hoang Phuc, Ngo Vu Quang Hai, Vo Vinh Phuc, Le Dinh Huy, Pham Ngoc Lieu.
  Dir and Screenplay: Tran Anh Hung.

Pro: Christophe Rossignon. Dialogue: Tran and Nguyen Trung Bing. Ph: Benoit Delhomme. Pro Des: Benoit Barouh. Ed: Nicole Dedieu and Claude Ronzeau. M: Ton That Tiet; 'Just Like You' performed by Rollins Band. Costumes: Henriette Raz. (Les Productions Lazennec/La Sept Cinema/Cofimage 5 & 6/Canal Plus/Salon Films/Gai Phonh Film Studio–Entertainment.) Rel: 22 March 1996. 129 mins. Cert 18. France/Vietnam. 1995.

Dangerous Minds

Considering that Michelle Pfeiffer is the last person you'd expect to be an ex-Marine teaching in a ghetto classroom, the actress gives a creditable and heartfelt performance as the real-life LouAnne Johnson, a woman with an altruistic agenda. Like *Blackboard Jungle*, *To Sir With Love*, *Stand and Deliver*, *Dead Poets Society*, *Lean On Me* and *Renaissance Man* before it, this is the scenario in which the virtues of education vie with the malaise of social apathy. A surprise hit in the States (due in part to the success of its best-selling soundtrack), *Dangerous Minds* applies an MTV sensibility to some pressing issues. Predictable to be sure, but a well-rounded drama that hits all the right buttons. Previously known as *My Posse Don't Do Homework*. FYI: John N. Smith, the Canadian director of the award-winning TV series *The Boys of St Vincent*, makes his American film debut.

Cast: Michelle Pfeiffer (LouAnne Johnson), George Dzundza (Hal Griffith), Courtney B. Vance (George Grandey), Robin Bartlett (Carla Nichols), John Neville (waiter), Renoly Santiago (Raul Sanchero), Wade Dominquez (Emilio Ramirex), Bruklin Harris (Callie Roberts), Beatrice Winde, Lorraine Toussaint, Marcello Thedford, Roberto Alvarez, Richard Grant, Marisela Gonzales, Toni Nichelle Buzhardt, Norris Young, Rahman Ibraheem, Raymond Grant, Skye Bassett, Cynthia Avila, Roman J. Cisneros.
  Dir: John N. Smith. Pro: Don Simpson and Jerry Bruckheimer. Ex Pro: Sandra Rabins and Lucas Foster. Screenplay: Ronald Bass, from the book *My Posse Don't Do Homework*, by LouAnne Johnson. Ph: Pierre Letarte. Pro Des: Donald Graham Burt. Ed: Tom Rolf. M: Wendy & Lisa; numbers performed by Bob Dylan, Wendy & Lisa, Coolio and L.V., Rappin' 4-Tay, Immature, Big Mike, Tre Black, Mr Dalvin & Static, De Vante, 24-K, Aaron Hall, and Sista and Craig Mac. Costumes: Bobbie Read. (Hollywood Pictures/Via Rosa Prods–Buena Vista.) Rel: 19 January 1996. 100 mins. Cert 15. USA. 1995.

Blackboard wilderness: Wade Dominquez (right) confides in Michelle Pfeiffer in John N. Smith's Dangerous Minds *(from Buena Vista)*

D'Artagnan's Daughter

The South of France/Paris; 1654. When Eloise, a guest at a rural convent, witnesses the murder of the Mother Superior at the hands of ruthless guardsmen, she sets off to Paris to enlist the help of her father, D'Artagnan, to avenge the crime. Stretching the legend of Alexander Dumas's *The Three Musketeers* to embrace a spirited heroine, Tavernier's swashbuckling romp arrives mired in too much talk

Dastardly deeds: Charlotte Kady (right) points out the options to Sophie Marceau in Bertrand Tavernier's bloated romp, D'Artagnan's Daughter *(from Artificial Eye)*

A nun's story: Susan Sarandon ponders on the question of good and evil in her Oscar-winning performance, in Tim Robbins' Dead Man Walking (from PolyGram)

and endless scenes filmed in virtual blackness. Thus, what should have been a rollicking adventure turns up looking like a Rembrandt painting in good need of a clean with jokey captions. Still, Sophie Marceau is a delectable heroine, Philippe Noiret an engaging D'Artagnan and the English subtitles exceptionally in tune with their material. Tavernier, incidentally, took over the directorial reins from Riccardo Freda a week before filming.

Cast: Sophie Marceau (Eloise D'Artagnan), Philippe Noiret (D'Artagnan), Claude Rich (Duc de Crassac), Sami Frey (Aramis), Raoul Billerey (Porthos), Jean-Luc Bideau (Athos), Nils Tavernier (Quentin La Misere), Charlotte Kady (La Femme Rouge), Jean-Paul Roussillon (Planchet), Luigi Proietti (Cardinal Mazarin), Pascale Roberts (Mother Superior), Stephane Legros (Louis XIV), Emmanuelle Bataille, Christine Pignet, Josselin Siassia.
   Dir: Bertrand Tavernier. Ex Pro: Frédéric Bourboulon. Screenplay: Michel Leviant and Jean Cosmos, based on an idea

by Riccardo Freda and Eric Poindron. Ph: Patrick Blossier. Ed: Ariane Boeglin. Art: Geoffroy Larcher. M: Philippe Sarde. Costumes: Jacqueline Moreau. (CIBY 2000/Little Bear/TF1 Films/BNP Images/Canal Plus–Artificial Eye.) Rel: 7 July 1995. 136 mins. Cert 15. France. 1994.

Dead Man Walking

Louisiana; 1981. Dedicated to helping the poor of New Orleans, Sister Helen Prejean responds to a letter from a convict on Death Row and agrees to meet him. Over the ensuing weeks the nun and the profane white-trash killer find themselves irrevocably drawn to each other as they await the outcome of the latter's appeal. Based on Sister Helen Prejean's 1993 book of the same name, *Dead Man Walking* is extraordinarily compassionate and unsentimental, both a profoundly disturbing and affecting drama that probes the contentious issues surrounding the debate on capital punishment. Sean Penn, in arguably his most accomplished performance to date, plays the killer (a composite of real-life Death Row inmates Patrick Sonnier and Robert

Willy) with unassailable conviction and feeling, while Susan Sarandon, as Helen, proves yet again why she is America's premier screen actress. Although the film's momentum slumps in its third quarter, the final chapter will be hard to erase from the memory.

Cast: Susan Sarandon (Sister Helen Prejean), Sean Penn (Matthew Poncelet), Robert Prosky (Hilton Barber), Raymond J. Barry (Earl Delacroix), R. Lee Ermey (Clyde Percy), Scott Wilson (Chaplain Farley), Celia Weston (Mary Beth Percy), Lois Smith (Helen's mother), Roberta Maxwell (Lucille Poncelet), Margo Martindale (Sister Colleen), Barton Heyman, Steve Boles, Nesbitt Blaisdell, Ray Aranha, Larry Pine, Gil Robbins, Kevin Cooney, Clancy Brown, Adele Robbins, Michael Cullen, Peter Sarsgaard, Jack Blacks, Jon Abrahams, Jack Henry Robbins, Mary Robbins, Miles Guthrie Robbins.
   Dir and Screenplay: Tim Robbins. Pro: Robbins, Jon Kilik and Rudd Simmons. Ex Pro: Tim Bevan and Eric Fellner. Ph: Roger A. Deakins. Pro Des: Richard Hoover. Ed: Lisa Zeno Churgin. M: David Robbins; numbers performed by Bruce Springsteen, Nusrat Fateh Ali Kahn, Eddie Vedder, Ry Cooder, Johnny Cash, Susan Sarandon, etc. Costumes: Renee Ehrlich Kalfus. (Working Title/Havoc Prods–PolyGram.) Rel: 29 March 1996. 122 mins. Cert 15. USA. 1995.

Desperado

He is the tallest Mexican you have ever seen, his face deflects the light and he carries a guitar case. He is El Mariachi. And he is desperate for revenge. Taking the spirit of *El Mariachi* (the film he allegedly made for $7,000), upping the firepower and stocking his cast with hip cameos from Steve Buscemi, Cheech Marin and Quentin Tarantino (the last named relating a hilarious joke before losing his brains, literally), Robert Rodriguez has whipped up an impressive sequel. With his bravura, cliché-routing style unleashed on a $3.1m budget (splattered with nods to Sergio Leone and John Woo), Rodriguez piles action on to action, buoyed by a terrific electric guitar score. Even the sex scene is edited like a shoot-out. Talk about delivering the goods.

Cast: Antonio Banderas (El Mariachi), Salma Hayek (Carolina), Joaquim De Almeida (Bucho), Cheech Marin (Short bartender), Steve Buscemi (Buscemi), Carlos Gallardo (Campa), Carlos Gomez, Quentin Tarantino, Tito Larriva, Angel

Aviles, Danny Trejo, Abraham Verduzco, Peter Marquardt, Consuelo Gomez, Jaime De Hoyos, Elizabeth Rodriguez.

Dir, Screenplay and Ed: Robert Rodriguez. Pro: Rodriguez and Bill Borden. Co-Pro: Elizabeth Avellan and Carlos Gallardo. Ph: Guillermo Navarro. Pro Des: Cecilia Montiel. M: Los Lobos; numbers performed by Dire Straits, Link Wray & His Ray Men, Los Lobos, Antonio Banderas, Roger & The Gypsies, Latin Playboys, Tito & Tarantula, Santana, Salma Hayek, etc. Costumes: Graciela Mazon. (Los Hooligans Prods–Columbia TriStar.) Rel: 9 February 1996. 105 mins. Cert 18. USA. 1995.

Devil in a Blue Dress

1948; Los Angeles. Easy Rawlins is one of the few black folk in town who owns his own house, but when you've lost your job and are two months behind on your mortgage, life can be far from easy. Working against his instincts, the war veteran accepts a profitable invitation to trace the whereabouts of Daphne Monet, who's into 'jazz and dark meat' and is the mistress of a local millionaire. Inevitably, matters prove more complicated than at first perceived and soon Easy finds himself a prime suspect for murder ... Dripping atmosphere from every button hole and boasting a plot every bit as preposterous and twisted as *The Big Sleep*, this is film noir of the highest order. It's a shame that much of the dialogue is unintelligible, and the casual violence may alienate some viewers, but the evocation of time and place (and genre) is spot on.

Cast: Denzel Washington (Easy Rawlins), Tom Sizemore (Dewitt Albright), Jennifer Beals (Daphne Monet), Don Cheadle (Mouse), Maury Chaykin (Matthew Terell), Terry Kinney (Todd Carter), Mel Winkler (Joppy), Lisa Nicole Carson (Coretta James), David Wolos-Fonteno (Junior Fornay), Albert Hall, Jernard Burks, John Roselius, Beau Starr, Steven Randazzo, Scott Lincoln, L. Scott Caldwell, Barry Shabaka Henley, Joseph Latimore, Renee Humphrey, Peggy Rea.

Dir and Screenplay: Carl Franklin, from the book by Walter Mosley. Pro: Jesse Beaton and Gary Goetzman. Ex Pro: Jonathan Demme and Edward Saxon. Ph: Tak Fujimoto. Pro Des: Gary Frutkoff. Ed: Carole Kravetz. M: Elmer Bernstein; numbers performed by T-Bone Walker, Jimmy Witherspoon, Duke Ellington, Roy Milton, Brian O'Neill, Pee Wee Crayton, Joan Shaw, Thelonious Monk, Memphis Slim, Lloyd Glenn, etc. Costumes: Sharen Davis. Title Design: Pablo Ferro. (TriStar Pic-

Dual-barrelled escapism: Antonio Banderas blasts his way to international stardom in Robert Rodriguez' dynamic Desperado *(from Columbia TriStar)*

Post-war blues: Denzel Washington lights up the screen in Carl Franklin's powerfully moody Devil in a Blue Dress *(from Columbia*

Having a bad day: Bruce Willis does what Simon says in John McTiernan's exhilarating Die Hard With a Vengeance *(from Buena Vista)*

tures/Clinica Estetico/Muddy Lane Entertainment–Columbia TriStar.) Rel: 12 January 1996. 101 mins. Cert 15. USA. 1995.

Die Hard With a Vengeance

On a typical summer's day in New York half a street block blows up. For his next trick, criminal mastermind Jeremy Irons announces that he has planted a bomb in a school somewhere in the greater metropolitan area. The good news is that the NYPD has three hours and 15 minutes to locate the device, the bad is that should any school be evacuated Irons will detonate the explosion by remote control. Scrambling to save their city, the boys in blue desert the core of the Big Apple – Wall Street – leaving the city's Federal Reserve Bank and its contents ($140 billion worth of gold bars) un-policed ... Opening with a bang and building to a crescendo, the third *Die Hard* reunites director John McTiernan and Bruce Willis from the original and manages to sustain the heart-pounding, jaw-sagging standard of the first two films. Ingenious plotting, ferocious editing and unbelievable stunts ignite the entertainment factor. Jeremy Irons – in his first action role – lends a shot of class, although Willis himself (paid a staggering $15m) is frequently caught sleepwalking. None the less, this is probably the best action movie of 1995. FYI: The original script, called *Simon Says*, was once earmarked as the foundation for a *Lethal Weapon* sequel.

Cast: Bruce Willis (John McClane), Jeremy Irons (Simon), Samuel L. Jackson (Zeus Carver), Graham Greene (Joe Lambert), Colleen Camp (Connie Kowalski), Larry Bryggman (Walter Cobb), Sam Phillips (Katya), Kevin Chamberlin (Charles Weiss), Anthony Peck, Nick Wyman, Sharon Washington, Stephen Pearlman, Michael Alexander Jackson, Aldis Hodge, Rob Sedgwick, Michael Cristofer, John McTiernan Sr., Richard Council.

Dir: John McTiernan. Pro: McTiernan and Michael Tadross. Co-Pro: Carmine Zozzora. Ex Pro: Andrew G. Vajna, Buzz Feitshans and Robert Lawrence. Screenplay: Jonathan Hensleigh. Ph: Peter Menzies. Ed: John Wright. Pro Des: Jackson DeGovia. M: Michael Kamen; numbers performed by The Lovin' Spoonful, Thelonious Monk, Mark Mangini, etc. Costumes: Joseph G. Aulisi. (Cinergi/Fox–Buena Vista.) Rel: 18 August 1995. 128 mins. Cert 15. US. 1995.

Dolores Claiborne

Following the traditionally bleak vista of Maine in winter, this nth Stephen King adaptation opens on a note of hysteria – and spends the rest of the movie trying to recapture it. Dolores Claiborne, the laughing stock of Little Tall Island, is arrested for the murder of her elderly, wealthy employer. Selena St George, Dolores's daughter and a top New York reporter, relinquishes a hot story to see her mother for the first time in 15 years. It's about time Selena found out how her father died ... A sombre, grey movie encumbered by flashbacks, *Dolores Claiborne* is no fun. It's not until the final ten minutes that the film comes into its own, but by then it's decidedly too late. Still, Kathy Bates is on excellent form, whether confronting her despair or barking out sarcastic asides. Of course, the actress won an Oscar on similar ground – as the murderess in Stephen King's *Misery*.

Cast: Kathy Bates (Dolores Claiborne), Jennifer Jason Leigh (Selena St George), David Strathairn (Joe St George), Judy Parfitt (Vera Donovan), John C. Reilly (Frank Stamshaw), Eric Bogosian (Peter), Christopher Plummer (Det John Mackey), Bob Gunton (Mr Pease), Ellen Muth (young Selena), Roy Cooper, Wayne Robson, Ruth Marshall.

Dir: Taylor Hackford. Pro: Hackford and Charles Mulvehill. Assoc Pro: Gina Blumenfeld. Screenplay: Tony Gilroy. Ph: Gabriel Beristain. Ed: Mark Warner. Pro Des: Bruno Rubeo. M: Danny Elfman. Costumes: Shay Cunliffe. (Castle Rock– Rank.) Rel: 8 September 1995. 131 mins. Cert 18. USA. 1995.

Down Periscope

Hoping to run his own state-of-the-art nuclear submarine, maverick Navy Lt. Commander Thomas Dodge finds himself landed with a creaky diesel-powered sub left over from the Second World War. Worse, his crew look like they've escaped from the local sanatorium ... Superimposing the comic ingenuity of the *Police Academy* series on to the genre popularised by *Crimson Tide* and *The Hunt for Red October* (whose fabulous sets are re-used here), *Down Periscope* misfires on most cylinders. Kelsey Grammer, in his first feature starring role, is OK, although the part would have worked better with some edge. [*Charles Bacon*]

Cast: Kelsey Grammer (Lt. Commander Thomas Dodge), Lauren Holly (Lt. Emily Lake), Bruce Dern (Admiral Yancy Graham), Rob Schneider (Executive Officer Lt. Marty Pascal), Rip Torn (Admiral Dean Winslow), Harry Dean Stanton (Howard), William H. Macy, Ken Hudson Campbell, Toby Huss, Duane Martin, Jonathan Penner.

Dir: David S. Ward. Pro: Robert Lawrence. Ex Pro: Jack Cummins. Co-Pro: Stanley Wilson. Screenplay: Hugh Wilson, Andrew Kurtzman and Eliot Wald. Ph: Victor Hammer. Pro Des: Michael Corenblith. Ed: William Anderson and Armen Minasian. M: Randy Edelman; 'In The Navy' sung by The Village People. Costumes: Luke Reichle. (Fox.) Rel: 28 June 1996. 92 mins. Cert PG. USA. 1996.

Dr Jekyll & Ms Hyde

New York; today. When commercial scientist Richard Jacks inherits his

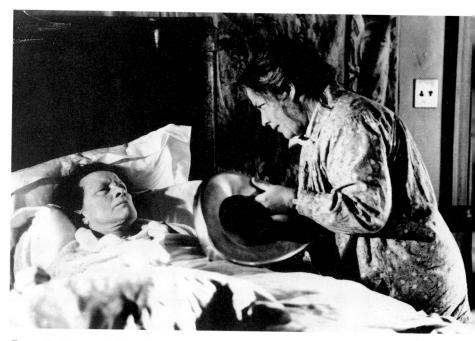

From a dead man to a bedpan, Kathy Bates exercises the chills (seen here with Judy Parfitt, in bed) in Taylor Hackford's lugubrious Dolores Claiborne *(from Rank)*

great-grandfather's old notebooks, he cannot resist combining his forebear's great insights with his knowledge of modern science. The result, with a little tinkering, is that Jacks is periodically transformed into a predatory, sexy woman who is determined to rid herself of the man within. Arguably the year's unfunniest comedy, *Dr Jekyll & Ms Hyde* is a disarray of missed opportunities in spite of valiant playing from Tim Daly as the modern-day Jekyll and Jeremy Piven as his horny colleague. The nudge-nudge give-us-a-laugh music doesn't help.

Cast: Sean Young (Helen Hyde), Tim Daly (Richard Jacks), Lysette Anthony (Sarah Carver), Stephen Tobolowsky (Oliver Mintz), Harvey Fierstein (Yves DuBois), Thea Vidale (Valerie), Jeremy Piven (Pete), Polly Bergen (Mrs Unterveldt), Sheena Larkin, John Franklyn-Robbins, Aron Tager, Robert Wuhl.

Dir: David F. Price. Pro: Robert Shapiro and Jerry Leider. Ex Pro: John Morrissey. Screenplay: Tim John, Oliver Butcher, William Davies and William Osborne, from a story by Price. Ph: Tom Priestley. Ed: Tony Lombardo. Pro Des: Gregory Melton. M: Mark McKenzie; numbers performed by Jean McClain, Devo, Patricia Swanson, etc. Costumes: Molly Maginnis. Make-Up Effects: Kevin Yagher. (Savoy Pictures–Rank.) Rel: 8 December 1995. 90 mins. Cert 12. USA. 1995.

Dunston Checks In

Dunston, as it happens, is an orangutan on the run from his ne'er-do-well partner, jewel thief Rupert Everett. With nowhere to turn, Dunston checks into the plush Majestic Hotel in Los Angeles and, inevitably, wreaks havoc ... Needless to say this monkey business sounds absolutely dire, but thanks to a strong cast and some pacey direction from Ken Swapis the film manages to raise a number of laughs. It's even quite charming. [*Ewen Brownrigg*]

Cast: Jason Alexander (Robert Grant), Faye Dunaway (Mrs Dubrow), Eric Lloyd (Kyle Grant), Rupert Everett (Lord Rutledge), Graham Sack (Brian Grant), Paul Reubens (La Farge), Glenn Shadix (Lionel Spalding), Dunston (Sam), Nathan Davis, Jennifer Bassey, Judith Scott.

Dir: Ken Swapis. Pro: Todd Black and Joe Wizan. Ex Pro: Rodney Liber. Co-Pro: Jason Blumenthal. Screenplay: John Hopkins and Bruce Graham. Ph: Peter Collister. Pro Des: Rusty Smith. Ed: Jon Poll. M: Miles Goodman. Costumes: Alina Panova. (Fox.) Rel: 29 March 1996. 88 mins. Cert PG. USA. 1996.

Eclipse

Yet another splinter in the *La Ronde/Chain of Desire* cycle of lust-ins, in which a variety of seedy characters pass their bodily fluids from one to the

Everything to go: Anthony LaPaglia, Johnny Whitworth and Liv Tyler in Allan Moyle's exuberant Empire Records *(from Warner)*

other until the circuit is completed. This one hangs its flimsy premise on the fact that people act crazy before an eclipse, so various denizens of Toronto strip off and get down to some tiresome coupling. A little biased towards the guys, here, with the sole three women ending up with gays or bisexuals. Shot in various grades of monochrome, the film lays on the pretension by presenting everything in opposites and negatives (e.g. documentary footage is shown in colour).

Fille Fatale: Vanessa Paradis contemplates her future in Jean Becker's disturbing Elisa *(from Gala Films)*

Cast: Von Flores (Henry), John Gilbert (Brian), Pascale Montpetit (Sylvie), Manuel Aranguiz (Gabriel), Maria Del Mar (Sarah), Greg Ellwand (Norman), Matthew Ferguson (Angelo), Earl Pastko (Michael), Daniel MacIvor (Jim), Kirsten Johnson (Carlotta).

Dir and Screenplay: Jeremy Podeswa. Pro: Podeswa and Camelia Frieberg. Ex Pro: Wolfram Tichy. Assoc Pro: Regine Schmid. Ph: Miroslaw Baszak. Ed: Susan Maggi. Art: Tamara Deverell. M: Ernie Tollar. (Fire Dog Films/TiMe Medienvertieb/Telefilm Canada–Pagemedia). Rel: 14 July 1995. 95 mins. Cert 18. Canada/Germany. 1994.

Elisa

After lifting her three-year-old daughter, Marie, into her arms and lighting the candles on the Christmas tree, Elisa Desmoulin suffocates her daughter with a pillow. Then she blows her own head off. Following this extremely upsetting prelude, *Elisa* introduces us to Marie at 17 who, like her compatriots in *La Petite Voleuse* and *The Bait*, is beautiful, sexy and detestable. Dabbling in petty theft and extortion, Marie leads a life of selfish irresponsibility, mocking the elderly and unattractive and exposing the hypocrisy of everyone she encounters. A victim of her own past, Marie has become a social monster and is due for a showdown – if and when she meets someone who can stand up to her (and resist her physical charms). As it happens, Marie has been searching for that person all her life ... Creating decidedly mixed feelings in the viewer, *Elisa* confronts a number of painful moral issues in a fast-paced sexy package, with Vanessa Paradis as coquettish as they come. Compelling viewing, anyhow, vividly directed by the 62-year-old Jean Becker.

Cast: Vanessa Paradis (Marie Desmoulin), Gerard Depardieu (Jacques 'Lebovitch' Desmoulin), Clothilde Courau (Solange), Sekkou Sall (Ahmed), Florence Thomassin (Elisa Desmoulin), Michel Bouquet (Samuel), Philippe Leotard, Catherine Rouvel, Melvil Poupaud, Olivier Saladin, Bernard Verley, Reine Barteve, Andre Julien, Gerard Chaillou, Jose Garcia, Claudine Regnier, Dominique Bluzet, Isabelle Hachmann-Peralt, Jane Becker.

Dir: Jean Becker. Pro: Christian Fechner. Ex Pro: Herve Truffaut and Didier Pain. Screenplay: Becker and Fabrice Carazo. Ph: Etienne Becker. Ed: Jacques Witta. Pro Des: Therese Ripaud. M: Zbigniew Preisner, Serge Gainsbourg and Michel Colombier; 'Elisa' sung by Gainsbourg. Costumes: Arianne Phillips, Juliette Menager, Marie-Francoise Perochon and Gil Noir. (Solo Productions/TF1 Films/Canal Plus/BNP Images 2–Gala Films.) Rel: 1 December 1995. 115 mins. Cert 15. France. 1994.

Empire Records

Wrightsville, Delaware; now. A twin-tiered music emporium that has flourished since 1959 (the year Elvis Presley recorded 'A Big Hunk O' Love'), Empire Records is threatened by a takeover bid from the almighty Music Town chain. Besides homogenising the local music scene, the takeover would require the Empire's staff to tone down their individuality. Over a 24-hour period the shop's beleaguered manager, Joe, attempts to orchestrate his young staff's emotional ups-and-downs while determining how to pull out of financial disaster ... Capturing all the exuberance and fickle heartache of youth, *Empire Records* is a feel-good blast that showcases a radiant cast of newcomers and a driving, eclectic soundtrack. Not only slickly and passionately realised, the film is positively touching in its good-natured naiveté. Of the younger cast, Robin Tunney (as a placid, shaven-headed rebel) and Johnny Whitworth (in early Christian Slater mode) display the greatest promise. Join the party.

Making a molehill: Hugh Grant moving mountains in Christopher Monger's enchanting The Englishman Who Went Up a Hill, but Came Down a Mountain *(from Buena Vista)*

Cast: Anthony LaPaglia (Joe), Maxwell Caulfield (Rex Manning), Debi Mazar (Jane), Rory Cochrane (Lucas), Johnny Whitworth (A.J.), Robin Tunney (Debra), Renee Zellweger (Gina), Ethan Embry (formerly Ethan Randall) (Mark), Brendan Sexton (Warren Beatty), Liv Tyler (Corey), Ben Bode (Mitchell Beck), Coyote Shivers, James 'Kimo' Wills, Melissa Caulfield.

Dir: Allan Moyle. Pro: Arnon Milchan, Michael Nathanson, Alan Riche and Tony Ludwig. Co-Pro: Paul Kurta. Screenplay: Carol Heikkinen. Ph: Walt Lloyd. Pro Des: Peter Jamison. Ed: Michael Chandler. Music Supervisor: Mitchell Leib; numbers performed by Gin Blossoms, The Dirt Clods, Ape Hangers, Queen Sarah Saturday, Maxwell Caulfield, Lustre, Suicidal Tendencies, The Buggles, Cracker, AC/DC, Toad the Wet Sprocket, Dire Straits, Evan Dando, The Cranberries, Edwyn Collins, Gwar, Mouth Music, Coyote Shivers, The The, etc. Costumes: Susan Lyall. (Regency Enterprises/New Regency–Warner.) Rel: 28 June 1996. 90 mins. Cert 12. USA. 1995.

The Englishman Who Went Up a Hill, but Came Down a Mountain

South-East Wales; 1917. In the remote, picturesque village of Ffynnon Garw, two Englishmen, representing Her Majesty's Ordnance Survey, arrive to measure the local hillside. It is their mission to determine whether the village's prized outcrop is a mountain or hill. Falling 16 feet short of the required 1,000ft, the projection is duly classified as the latter. Incensed by the demotion of their local landmark, the villagers decide to build a mound on top of Ffynnon Garw to qualify it as a mountain. The problem is how to detain the Englishmen – so that the crop can be re-measured – while the elevation is augmented ... Deliciously eccentric and brimming with charm, *The Englishman Who ...* kindles a satisfying glow. It's a slim premise, to be sure, but there's wit to spare.

Cast: Hugh Grant (Reginald Anson), Tara Fitzgerald (Betty of Cardiff), Colm Meaney (Morgan the Goat), Ian McNeice (George Garrad), Ian Hart (Johnny Shellshocked), Kenneth Griffith (Reverend Robert Jones), Robert Pugh (Williams the Petroleum), Robert Blythe (Ivor the Grocer), Garfield Morgan (Davies the School), Tudor Vaughn, Hugh Vaughn, Lisa Palfrey, Dafydd Wyn Roberts, Iuean Rhys, Anwen Williams, David Lloyd Meredith, Howell Evans, Maisie McNeice.

Dir and Screenplay: Christopher Monger. Pro: Sarah Curtis. Ex Pro: Sally Hibbin, Robert Jones, Bob Weinstein and Harvey Weinstein. Ph: Vernon Layton. Ed: David Martin. Pro Des: Charles Garrad. M: Stephen Endelman. Costumes: Janty Yates. (Parallax Pictures/Miramax–Buena Vista.) Rel: 4 August 1995. 95 mins. Cert PG. UK. 1995.

Defending the infidel: Halle Berry and Kurt Russell find themselves up against impossible odds in Stuart Baird's buttock-clenching Executive Decision *(from Warner)*

Executive Decision

All-over-the-place; today. We all know that Islamic extremists are willing to die for Allah. And we know that they view America as the cursed infidel. And we know that rebel factions have access to inconceivably destructive weaponry. But how often do we question our impunity in the chill twilight of the Cold War? Dr David Grant, an anti-terrorist consultant, is thrown in at the deep end when he finds himself on a hijacked plane heading for Washington with a cargo of deadly DZ-5 nerve gas... Shame about the uninspiring title. Shame about the unimaginative casting. Shame about the dopey prologue. A shame, because *Executive Decision* came this close to being the most perfect action-thriller since *Die Hard*. As it is, it is the most suspenseful in aeons, but with Kurt Russell thrown into the fray as reluctant hero the movie loses some of its credibility. We know Kurt can cut the mustard. He's

got the build, he's got the jawline and he's already exercised his brawn in *Escape from New York*, *The Thing*, *Tango & Cash* and *Stargate*. A genuine Joe Average, like Tom Hanks, would have really grabbed our undying empathy. And what's with Steven Seagal? A cardboard cut-out with his reputation merely detracts from the intelligence this movie so desperately calls out for. Still, with David Suchet downplaying his psychotic mastermind to chilling effect and with more edge-of-your-seat thrills than a Bruno-Tyson rematch, *Executive Decision* is a helluva ride.

Cast: Kurt Russell (David Grant), Steven Seagal (Lt Colonel Austin Travis), Halle Berry (Jean), John Leguizamo (Rat), Oliver Platt (Cahill), Joe Morton (Cappy), David Suchet (Nagi Hassan), B.D. Wong (Louie), Len Cariou (Charles White), Whip Hubley, Andreas Katsulas, Mary Ellen Trainor, Marla Maples Trump, J.T. Walsh, Ingo Neuhaus, William James Jones, Paul Collins, Nicholas Pryor, Stanley Grover, Eugene Roche, Ken Jenkins, Charles Hallahan, Dey Young, Richard Riehle, Chris Maher, Ray Baker, Michael Milhoan, Yvonne Zima, Juan Fernandez.

Dir: Stuart Baird. Pro: Joel Silver, Jim

Thomas and John Thomas. Ex Pro: Steve Perry. Co-Pro: Karyn Fields. Screenplay: Jim Thomas and John Thomas. Ph: Alex Thomson. Pro Des: Terence Marsh. Ed: Baird, Dallas Puett and Frank J. Urioste. M: Jerry Goldsmith; 'It's Nice To Go Trav'ling' sung by Frank Sinatra. Costumes: Louise Frogley. (Warner/Silver Pictures–Warner.) Rel: 10 May 1996. 133 mins. Cert 15. USA. 1996.

Exit to Eden

What a great idea. Get Garry (*Pretty Woman*) Marshall to direct a script based on Anne (*The Vampire Chronicles*) Rice's bestseller. Cast comedy stalwart Dan Aykroyd, wild woman Rosie O'Donnell and *Strictly Ballroom* star Paul Mercurio (in his first big Hollywood role). Then, for good measure, get the gorgeous Dana Delany to prance around semi-naked for most of the movie. Good so far. The plot? Well, roughly it involves O'Donnell and Aykroyd travelling to Delany's island of sand, sea and sex on the trail of Mercurio's 'valuable evidence', and carries on from there. Needless to say, *Exit to Eden* was a flop. Critically and commercially it stunk. Flat, awkward and contrived though it is, the film does abound with good-looking, partially-clad people and O'Donnell and Aykroyd are genuinely funny in one or two scenes. So *Exit to Eden* isn't as bad as you've heard, provided you treat it as a real pizza-and-beer see-it-on-video kind of thing. Almost so bad it's good. [*Karen Krizanovich*]

Cast: Dana Delany (Lisa Emerson), Paul Mercurio (Elliot Slater), Rosie O'Donnell (Sheila Kingston), Dan Aykroyd (Fred Lavery), Hector Elizondo (Martin Halifax), Stuart Wilson (Omar), Iman (Nina), Sean O'Bryan, Stephanie Niznik, Phil Redrow, Allison Moir, Deborah Lacey, Lucinda Crosby, Rosemary Forsyth, Shannon Wilcox, Diana Kent, Alex Rose, Kathleen Marshall, Frank Campanella, Dr Joyce Brothers, Donna Dixon, Lori Marshall, Don Hood, John Schneider.

Dir: Garry Marshall. Pro: Marshall and Alexandra Rose. Ex Pro: Edward K. Milkis and Nick Abdo. Screenplay: Deborah Amelon and Bob Brunner. Ph: Theo Van De Sande. Ed: David Finfer. Pro Des: Peter Jamison. M: Patrick Doyle; numbers performed by Gene Miller, Enigma, Dr John, Bryan Ferry, Annie Lennox, Ministry, James Patrick Dunne, New World Beat, etc. Costumes: Ellen Mirojnick. (Savoy Pictures–Guild.) Rel: 7 July 1995. 115 mins. Cert 18. USA. 1994.

Exquisite Tenderness

Not quite the fuzzy Franco Zeffirelli romance one might expect from the title, but a one-note hospital thriller with more needles than a fir tree. The 'tenderness' in question is medical jargon for the highest state of pain before blackout, reinforcing the theory that doctors revel in black humour. However, only unintentional jocularity plagues this shocker, a singularly unpleasant exercise that stitches together the worst excesses of *ER* with the frenzied hysteria of *Halloween*. Playing on our natural aversion to hypodermics and surgical saws, the film plumbs for the gross factor while leaving the more precise art of suspense in the waiting room. Still, Charles Dance's accent, careening from London to Texas via Maine, is good for a laugh. For the record, the story concerns a crazed doctor who, empowered by new scientific knowledge aiding the regeneration of bone and tissue, exacts a terrible revenge on a city hospital. Quick, nurse, pass the sick bowl.

Cast: Isabel Glasser (Dr Theresa McCann), James Remar (Dr Benjamin Hendricks), Sean Haberle (Dr Julian Matar), Charles Dance (Dr Ed Mittlesbay), Peter Boyle (Dr Daryl McEllwain), Malcolm McDowell (Dr Roger Stein), Beverly Todd (Nurse Burns), Charles Bailey-Gates (Sgt. Ross), Gregory West (Tommy Beaton), Juliette Jeffers (Lisa Wilson), Walter Olkewicz, Mother Love, Nancy Banks, Kim Robillard, Bernie Coulsen.

   Dir: Carl Schenkel. Pro: Alan Beattie, Chris Chesser and Willi Baer. Ex Pro: Rolf Deyhle and David Korda. Co-Pro: Dennis E. Jones. Screenplay: Patrick Cirillo, based on the screenplay by Bernard Sloane. Ph: Tom Burstyn. Ed: Jimmy B. Frazier. Pro Des: Douglas Higgins. M: Christopher Franke; 'Lollipop' performed by The Chordettes. Costumes: Ushi Zech and Debbie Geaghan. Sound: John Fasal. Special Effects: Steve Johnson. (Connexion Film–Guild.) Rel: 3 November 1995. 100 mins. Cert 18. USA/Germany. 1994.

Eye for an Eye

On the day of her daughter's sixth birthday party, Karen McCann is locked in a traffic jam and, completely helpless, listens on the car phone to her older daughter being raped and murdered. Then, when the DNA in the assailant's sperm is matched up, the case would appear to be closed.

The leggy lawyer: Cindy Crawford gets physical in Andrew Sipes' fast-paced Fair Game *(from Warner)*

But Karen's lawyers forget to turn the evidence over to the defence and so it is dismissed as inadmissible. The killer is out ... A glossy, superficial treatment of a horrendously serious subject, *Eye for an Eye* condones vigilante retribution while condemning the law for its impotency. True, the law is far too lenient on killers and rapists, but it's a trifle more sophisticated than portrayed here. Sally Field, looking great in a rare physical role, gives the film a strong human face, although Kiefer Sutherland is constricted by a one-dimensional part as the white-trash murder suspect who pours hot coffee on stray dogs and urinates in the street. Of course, in real life a killer looks like the man next door, which *is* scary. John Schlesinger guides things along smoothly enough, although James Newton Howard's score is decidedly uninspired.

Cast: Sally Field (Karen McCann), Kiefer Sutherland (Doob), Ed Harris (Mack McCann), Beverly D'Angelo (Dolly Green), Joe Mantegna (Detective Sergeant Joe Denillo), Charlayne Woodard (Angel Kosinsky), Olivia Burnette (Julie McCann), Alexandra Kyle (Megan McCann), Philip Baker Hall (Sidney Hughes), Keith David (Martin), Darrell Larson, Wanda Acuna, Geoffrey Rivas, Armin Shimerman, Natalija Nogulich, Stella Garcia, Justine Johnston, Wayne Pere, Cynthia Rothrock, Tom Lillard, Angela Paton.

   Dir: John Schlesinger. Pro: Michael I. Levy. Co-Pro: Michael Polaire. Screenplay: Amanda Silver and Rick Jaffa, based on the novel by Erika Holzer. Ph: Amir M. Mokri. Pro Des: Stephen Hendrickson. Ed: Peter Honess. M: James Newton Howard; Mozart. Costumes: Bobbie Read. (Paramount–UIP.) Rel: 21 June 1996. 101 mins. Cert 18. USA. 1995.

Fair Game

A gang of ex-KGB Navy seals from Cuba are about to launch an ingenious multi-billion dollar bank heist, aided by the most sophisticated technology in the universe. The only drawback is that their floating, high-tec headquarters (on board a 157-foot freighter) is about to be repossessed thanks to a family attorney in Miami. Killing her sounded like an easy option – until a stubborn homicide detective decides

'What did you say about my haircut?'
Stephen Baldwin (centre) gets rough and
ready with Jonah Blechman and David
Arquette in Paul Warner's moody Fall Time
(from PolyGram)

to protect her to the death ... A civil lawyer as gorgeous as Cindy Crawford is one thing. Nowhere does it say that lawyers can't look great (ever seen *L.A. Law*?). But for an attorney to ask, 'What *is* semtex, officer?' is a stretch. But then nobody should look for logic in a Joel Silver film. What they will find are impossibly attractive leads, death-defying stunts, rapid-fire pacing, state-of-the-art machinery and a villain you love to hate. Cindy doesn't look half bad, either, although she fails to strike any sparks off William Baldwin. FYI: The film is based on the novel which previously spawned the 1986 Sylvester Stallone vehicle *Cobra*.

Cast: William Baldwin (Max Kirkpatrick), Cindy Crawford (Kate McQuean), Steven Berkoff (Kazak), Christopher McDonald (Lt. Mayerson), Miguel Sandoval (Juantorena), Johann Carlo (Jodi), Salma Hayek (Rita), John Bedford Lloyd (Louis), Olek Krupa (Zhukov), Scott Michael Campbell (Adam), Dan Hedaya (Walter), Jenette Goldstein, Marc Macaulay, Sonny Carl Davis, Paul Dillon.
Dir: Andrew Sipes. Pro: Joel Silver. Ex Pro: Thomas M. Hammel. Screenplay: Charlie Fletcher, from the novel by Paula Gosling. Ph: Richard Bowen. Pro Des: James Spencer. Ed: David Finfer, Christian Wagner and Steven Kemper. M: Mark

Mancina. Costumes: Louise Frogley. Ms Crawford's Make-Up: Ronnie Spector, Marietta Carter-Narcisse and Jeni Lee Dinkel. Ms Crawford's Hair: Barbara Lorenz and Kathe Swanson. Ms Crawford's Vocal Consultant: Carla Meyer. Ms Crawford's Dialogue Coach: Leonard Peters. Ms Crawford's Assistant: Lisa Paravano. Ms Crawford's Advisor: Richard Gere. (Silver Pictures–Warner.) Rel: 19 January 1996. 91 mins. Cert 15. USA. 1995.

Fall Time

The American Midwest; 1957. Three recent high school graduates decide to get themselves on the local news by faking a kidnap right outside their high street bank. The plan is that David will borrow his father's Cadillac, Tim will loiter outside the bank, David and Joe will screech to a halt in front of him, fire a round of blanks, scoop Tim up and deposit him in the boot of the car. Then getaway! However, the plan backfires when Tim is shooed away by a real bank robber and David and Joe abduct the wrong man. Neither the abductee nor the bank robber left behind are willing to believe the boys' hair-brained story and want to know the truth ... While eliciting comparisons to everything from *Blood Simple* to *Reservoir Dogs*, Paul Warner's *Fall Time* can neither sustain the tension nor arrest the eye to the same degree, but it does keep us guessing – and interested – until the final denouement.

Cast: Stephen Baldwin (Leon), Sheryl Lee (Patty/Carol), Jason London (Tim), David

Arquette (David), Jonah Blechman (Joe Phillips), Mickey Rourke (Florence), Jeff Gardner (Ken), Steve Alden, Michael Edelstein, Tom Hull, J. Michael Hunter, Sammy Kershaw, Richard K. Olsen, Amy Parrish, Paul Skemp, Suellen Yates, Edward Bates.
Dir: Paul Warner. Pro: Edward Bates. Ex Pro: Jay Cohen. Screenplay: Steve Alden and Paul Skemp. Ph: Mark J. Gordon. Ed: Steve Nevius. Pro Des: Andrew Precht. M: Hummie Mann; numbers performed by Dewey Terry, Paul Gutierrez, In Vitro, Pet, etc. Costumes: Elena Baranova. Mickey Rourke's Bus: Startrax Celebrity Coaches. (Capitol Films/Bates Entertainment–PolyGram.) Rel: 21 July 1995. 84 mins. Cert 18. USA. 1994.

Fargo

Brainerd/Minneapolis, Minnesota; North Dakota; 1987. Up to his neck in debt, affable car salesman Jerry Lundegaard embarks on a bizarre plan to have his own wife kidnapped so that he can collect the ransom money from his moneyed father-in-law. Of course, Jerry's plan goes terribly, terribly wrong ... Drawing on the quirky comedy of *Raising Arizona* and the chilling menace of *Blood Simple*, the Coen brothers return to the small-town, modestly budgeted milieu that made their name, this time filming in their own backyard (Minnesota). Rigidly sticking to the sequence of actual events ('out of respect for the dead,' so a caption reads), *Fargo* is a real-life thriller that looks simply wonderful. And the affectionate, wry treatment of the backwoods people of the upper Midwest is to be applauded. While these folk may be simple, they are by no means the stereotypical dumb hicks that Hollywood so loves to portray. These rustics are funny, but they are also wise. Above all they are human and this makes the film even more credible, touching and disturbing.

Cast: Frances McDormand (Marge Gunderson), Steve Buscemi (Carl Showalter), Peter Stormare (Gaear Grimsrud), William H. Macy (Jerry Lundegaard), Kristin Rudrud (Jean Lundegaard), Harve Presnell (Wade Gustafson), Tony Denman (Scotty Lundegaard), Steven Reevis (Shep Proudfoot), John Carroll Lynch (Norm Gunderson), Larry Brandenberg (Stan Grossman), Steve Park (Mike Yanagita), Gary Houston, Larissa Kokernot, Melissa Peterman, Warren Keith, Bruce Bohne, Cliff Rakerd, Jose Feliciano.
Dir: Joel Coen. Pro: Ethan Coen. Ex Pro: Tim Bevan and Eric Fellner. Line Pro: John

Death in the boondocks: Steve Buscemi makes his point in Joel and Ethan Coen's masterpiece, Fargo *(from PolyGram)*

Cameron. Screenplay: Ethan and Joel Coen. Ph: Roger Deakins. Pro Des: Rick Heinrichs. Ed: Roderick Jaynes. M: Carter Burwell; numbers performed by Chuck Mangione, Merle Haggard and Boy George. Costumes: Mary Zophres. Sound: Skip Lievsay. (Working Title–PolyGram.) Rel: 31 May 1996. 97 mins. Cert 18. USA. 1995.

Farinelli Il Castrato

1722-1740; Madrid/Naples/London. The castrato singer Carlo Broschi, nicknamed 'The Divine Farinelli', was said to be able to produce 250 notes in a single breath and sustain a note for more than one minute. One of the most acclaimed singers of the 18th century, Farinelli was feted across Europe, his unique talent courted by everybody from Handel to King Philip V of Spain. However, his relationship with his older brother, Riccardo, who

Vocal accord: Stefano Dionisi sings a dove story in Gerard Corbiau's sumptuous Farinelli Il Castrato *(from Guild)*

All right on the knight: Richard Gere swings into action in Jerry Zucker's hearty First Knight *(from Columbia TriStar)*

nurtured his career and shared his sexual conquests, was to cast a shadow over Farinelli's success. It's easy to understand Corbiau's fascination with his subject, and the director has created an opulent biography that both seduces the ear and eye. None the less, the womanising, drinking and opium stupors – and the odd sibling tiff – is not enough to sustain the interest for two hours. The singing, though, is wonderful, a digital fusion of the countertenor and soprano voices of Derek Lee Ragin and Ewa Mallas Godlewska. Nominated for an Oscar for Best Foreign Language Film.

Cast: Stefano Dionisi (Carlo 'Farinelli' Broschi), Enrico Lo Verso (Riccardo Broschi), Elsa Zylberstein (Alexandra), Caroline Cellier (Margaret Hunter), Jacques Boudet (Philip V), Graham Valentine (The Prince of Wales), Omero Antonutti (Niccola Antonio Porpora), Jeroen Krabbe (Georg Frederick Handel), Marianne Basler, Renaud Du Peloux De Saint Romain.

Father of the Bride Part II
Now that George Stanley Banks has finally paid off his daughter's wedding, he's looking forward to years of free time to do 'anything I like'. Then his daughter announces her pregnancy, his house develops termites and a leaking roof and Mrs Banks discovers a particularly unexpected surprise up her dress. Can George recover his sense of responsibility to save the day? After establishing its premise and double twist, this remake of the 1951 sequel *Father's Little Dividend* quickly runs out of steam and displaces the laughs with overwhelming sentimen-

Dir: Gerard Corbiau. Pro: Vera Belmont. Ex Pro: Linda Gutenberg, Aldo Lado, Dominique Janne and Stephane Thenoz. Screenplay: Marcel Beaulieu, Andree Corbiau and Gerard Corbiau. Ph: Walther Vanden Ende. Ed: Joelle Hache. Pro Des: Gianni Quaranta. M: Broschi, Handel, Hasse, Pergolesi, and Porpora. Costumes: Olga Berlutti and Anne De Laugardiere. Sound Des: Richard Schorr. (Stephan Films/ Alinea/Canal Plus, etc–Guild.) Rel: 3 November 1995. 110 mins. Cert 15. Italy/ Belgium. 1994.

tality. Funny, it was George who earlier in the movie cracked, 'What are we, the Schmaltz Family?' Still, everybody's on top form and Steve Martin in particular is never less than watchable.

Cast: Steve Martin (George Stanley Banks), Diane Keaton (Nina Banks), Martin Short (Franck Eggelhoffer), Kimberly Williams (Annie Banks-MacKenzie), George Newbern (Bryan MacKenzie), Kieran Culkin (Matty Banks), B.D. Wong (Howard Weinstein), Peter Michael Goetz (John Mackenzie), Kate McGregor Stewart (Joanna MacKenzie), Jane Adams (Dr Megan Eisenberg), Eugene Levy (Mr Habib), Hallie Meyers-Shyer, Jay Wolpert, Sandra Silvestri, Annie Meyers-Shyer.

Dir: Charles Shyer. Pro: Nancy Meyers. Co-Pro: Cindy Williams and Bruce A. Block. Ex Pro: Sandy Gallin and Carol Baum. Co-Ex Pro: James Orr and Jim Cruickshank. Screenplay: Shyer and Meyers, based on the screenplay *Father's Little Dividend* by Albert Hackett and Frances Goodrich. Ph: William A. Fraker. Pro Des: Linda DeScenna. Ed: Stephen A. Rotter. M: Alan Silvestri; numbers performed by Steve Tyrell, Fats Domino, Etta James, and Phillip Ingram. Costumes: Enid Harris. (Touchstone Pictures–Buena Vista.) Rel: 2 February 1996. 107 mins. Cert PG. USA. 1995.

Une Femme Francaise

France/Berlin/Damascus; 1939-1974. When his father collapses outside the church in Nancy, Louis disrupts the wedding of his brother and falls for his prospective sister-in-law in the process. Nine months later Louis and his brother marry the sisters in a joint wedding and Louis discovers the true meaning of 'for better for worse ...' In Claude Chabrol's 1993 *L'Enfer*, Emmanuelle Beart played a beautiful young wife suspected of infidelity by her increasingly paranoid husband. Here, she plays a beautiful young wife who cannot get enough of the other while her husband, usually away fighting wars, prefers to turn a blind eye. It's a wearying business, with plenty of impassioned showdowns and tear-stained cheeks beautifully lit by Francois Catonne and sumptuously scored by Patrick Doyle. Personally, I could watch Mlle Beart until *les vaches* come home, but the self-centred bitch she plays here is hard to spend time with. Incidentally, Beart and Daniel Auteuil are married in real life. P.S: The script is based on the memories director Regis Wargnier has of his own mother.

Cast: Emmanuelle Beart (Jeanne), Daniel Auteuil (Louis), Gabriel Barylli (Mathias Behrens), Jean-Claude Brialy (Arnoult), Genevieve Casile (Solange), Michel Etcheverry (Charles), Jean-Noel Broute (Marc), Laurence Masliah (Helen), Isabelle Guiard, Francois Caron, Maria Fitzi, Samuel Le Bihan, Heinz Bennent.

Dir: Regis Wargnier. Pro: Yves Marmion. Ex Pro: Ingrid Windisch and Gerard Crosnier. Assoc Pro: Fondation Osmane Aidi and Volker Schlondorff. Screenplay: Wargnier and Alain Le Henry. Ph: Francois Catonne. Pro Des: Jacques Bufnoir. Ed: Genevieve Winding and Agnes Schwab. M: Patrick Doyle; Beethoven, Prokofiev. Costumes: Jacques Fonteray. (UGC Images/TF1 Films/DA Films/ Recorded Pictures Company/Canal Plus/ British Screen-Guild.) Rel: 24 May 1996. 99 mins. Cert 18. France/UK/Germany. 1994.

First Knight

It's not so much a case of will King Arthur or will Lancelot win the heart of Guinevere (we know that), but which of the noble knights will slay the dastardly Ben Cross? Dumping the songs and banishing the magic, *First Knight* concentrates on the romance in this cleaned-up, naturalistic and handsome $75m take on the Arthurian legend. However, with Richard Gere's lank tresses dyed dark brown and Sean Connery bestowed with a first-rate toupee, veracity is swept aside to make way for *Indiana Jones* heroism and some sublimely photogenic battle sequences. A well-paced, efficiently guided romp for a quiet Saturday night, this is no *Braveheart* or *Rob Roy*. Top honours go to William Nicholson's erudite script.

Cast: Sean Connery (King Arthur), Richard Gere (Lancelot), Julia Ormond (Guinevere), Ben Cross (Malagant), Liam Cunningham (Sir Agravaine), John Gielgud (Oswald), Paul Kynman (Mark), Robert Gwyn Davin (Sir Gawaine), Christopher Villiers, Valentine Pelka, Colin McCormack, Ralph Ineson, Jane Robbins, Tom Lucy, Mark Ryan, Susannah Corbett, Kate Zucker, Bob Zucker, Charlotte Zucker, Burt Zucker.

Dir: Jerry Zucker. Pro: Jerry Zucker and Hunt Lowry. Ex Pro: Gil Netter, Eric Rattray and Janet Zucker. Screenplay: William Nicholson, from a story by Nicholson, Lorne Cameron and David Hoselton. Ph: Adam Greenberg. Ed: Walter Murch. Pro Des: John Box. M: Jerry Goldsmith. Costumes: Nana Cecchi. Sword Master: Bob Anderson. Armourer: Terry English. (Zucker Brothers–Columbia TriStar.) Rel: 7 July 1995. 120 mins. Cert PG. USA. 1995.

A Fistful of Fingers

Admitting that it 'makes *Waterworld* look like the most expensive film ever made', this £10,000 western spoof sets its own limits with a smile. The hero, aping the dialogue and vocal nuance of Clint Eastwood's *Man With No Name*, looks too young to shave and is forced to ride a hobbyhorse through the wintry gorse of Somerset. His foe, 'Squint', can be no older (not helped by a false moustache), while the rest of the cast looks hurriedly assembled from the ranks of a *Bugsy Malone* sequel. Ultimately, the film works best as an extremely inventive home movie and should be treated as such. While much of its humour is asinine and embarrassing, there are, however, plenty of unexpected giggles. Twenty-year-old director Edgar Wright is a talent to watch. P.S. The film is dedicated to Sergio Leone, Clint Eastwood and Derek Griffiths.

Cast: Graham Low (Walter Marshall), Martin Curtis (Running Sore), Oliver Evans (The Squint), Quentin Green (Jimmy James), William Cornes, Edward Scotland, Stuart Low, Edgar Wright, David Scotland, Neil Mullarkey, Nicola Stapleton, Jeremy Beadle, Henry Scotland, George Scotland.

Dir, Assoc Pro and Screenplay: Edgar Wright. Pro: Daniel Figuero. Ex Pro: Michael Mathias, Zygi Kamasa and Tom McCabe. Co-Ex Pro: Gareth Owen. Ph: Alvin Leong. Pro Des: Simon Bowles. Ed: Giles Harding. M: Francoise Evans. Costumes: Sam Pine. Animation: Oscar Wright. Horse Design: Annie Scotland. (Wrightstuff Pictures–Blue Dolphin.) Rel: 24 November 1995. 81 mins. Cert 15. UK. 1995.

The Flower of My Secret - La Flor De Mi Secreto

Madrid; today. Leo Macias is the Barbara Cartland of Spain and doesn't want anybody to find out. However, her disintegrating marriage (to a NATO official stationed in Brussels) is having an injurious effect on her purple prose and she is deteriorating into a serious writer. Worse, the amorous editor of the cultural supplement of Spain's leading newspaper wants her to write a denunciation of her alter ego's work ... Pedro Almodovar's story is, in itself, a fascinating and compassionate tale of middle-age crisis, tinged with humour and insight. Furthermore, the film marks a new direction for Spain's enfant terrible, who seems to have exorcised his need to shock for shock's sake. Having said that, Almodovar still designs his scenes for cinematic effect, employing irritating narrative devices that ultimately rob his characters and situations of the immediacy – and authenticity – they deserve.

Cast: Marisa Parades (Leo Macias/Amanda Gris), Angel (Juan Echanove), Imanol Arias (Paco Macias), Carmen Elias (Betty), Rossy De Palma (Rosa), Chus Lampreave (Mother), Joaquin Cortes (Antonio), Manuela Vargas (Blanca), Kiti Manver, Gloria Munoz.

Dir and Screenplay: Pedro Almodovar. Pro: Esther Garcia. Ex Pro: Agustin Almodovar. Ph: Affonso Beato. Pro Des: Wolfgang Burmann. Ed: Jose Salcedo. M: Alberto Iglesias. Costumes: Hugo Mezcua. (CiBy 2000/El Deseo SA–Electric.) Rel: 26 January 1996. 110 mins. Cert 15. Spain/France. 1995.

Forget Paris

Mickey Gordon is funny, gutsy and charming and is one of the leading basketball referees in the NBA. Ellen

French miss: Debra Winger introduces Billy Crystal to the Eiffel Tower in Crystal's inconclusive Forget Paris *(from Rank)*

Andrews is funny, bright and gorgeous and is a successful airline executive living in Paris. Together they're magic, but apart their lives are going in opposite directions. Mickey loves Ellen, but he also loves his job, and his job is who he is. However, continually touring the States precludes him from spending time with Ellen … A romantic comedy anchored in a recognisable reality, *Forget Paris* is very funny and very romantic but fails to solve the questions it sets out for itself. Thus, while many of the lines rings true, one can't help but suspect foul play in the plotting. A case of having your cake and going hungry.

Cast: Billy Crystal (Mickey Gordon), Debra Winger (Ellen Andrews), Joe Mantegna (Andy), Cynthia Stevenson (Liz), Richard Masur (Craig), Julie Kavner (Lucy), William Hickey (Arthur), Robert Costanzo (waiter), John Spencer (Jack), Cathy Moriarty (Lois), Tom Wright, Johnny Williams, Marv Albert, Bill Walton, Charles Barkley, David Robinson, Kareem Abdul-Jabbar, Reggie Miller, Charles Oakley, Isiah Thomas, Spud Webb, Marcus Johnson, Rush Limbaugh, David Sanborn, Deb Lacusta, Clint Howard.

Dir and Pro: Billy Crystal. Ex Pro: Peter Schindler. Screenplay: Crystal, Lowell Ganz and Babaloo Mandel. Ph: Don Burgess. Ed: Kent Beyda. Pro Des: Terence Marsh. M: Marc Shaiman; numbers performed by Billie Holiday, Gene Kelly, Louis Prima, John Pizzarelli, Ella Fitzgerald and Louis Armstrong, Anita Baker and James Ingram, etc. Costumes: Judy Ruskin. (Castle Rock/Face–Rank.) Rel: 29 September 1995. 101 mins. Cert 12. USA. 1995.

Four Rooms

Over drinks at a film festival, this four-in-one portmanteau movie must have sounded a laugh. Not for the audience, it isn't. Tim Roth – acting like Jimmy Durante on speed – is a hotel bellhop, having to look after a witch's coven needing his sperm (Allison Anders' segment), a jealous man and his bound wife (Alexandre Rockwell's), two mischievous children (Robert Rodriguez') and a group of Hollywood buddies recreating a famously dangerous Hitchcock TV moment (Tarantino's). Only Rodriguez' section shows any spark of life. If the others had made anything this smug and self-indulgent as their debut, they'd still be in obscurity. Too many kooky directors spoil this broth. This is not a hotel you should check in to. [*Simon Rose*]

Cast: Tim Roth (Ted, the bellhop). *The Missing Ingredient*: Sammi Davis (Jezebel), Amanda de Cadenet (Diana), Valeria Golino (Athena), Madonna (Elspeth), Ione Skye (Eva), Lili Taylor (Raven), Alicia Witt (Kiva). *The Wrong Man*: Jennifer Beals (Angela), David Proval (Sigfried). *The Misbehavers*: Antonio Banderas (man), Lana McKissack (Sarah), Tamlyn Tomita (wife), Patrick Vonne Rodriguez, Danny Verduzco. *The Man From Hollywood*: Jennifer Beals (Angela), Paul Calderon (Norman), Quentin Tarantino (Chester), Marisa Tomei (Margaret), Lawrence Bender (long hair Yuppie scum), Kathy Griffin, Paul Hellerman, Quinn Thomas Hellerman, Marc Lawrence, Unruly Julie McClean.

Dir and Screenplay: Allison Anders (*The Missing Ingredient*), Alexandre Rockwell (*The Wrong Man*), Robert Rodriguez (*The Misbehavers*) and Quentin Tarantino (*The Man From Hollywood*). Pro: Lawrence Bender. Ex Pro: Rockwell and Tarantino. Co-Pro: Paul Hellerman, Heidi Vogel and Scott Lambert. Ph: Rodrigo Garcia, Guillermo Navarro, Phil Parmet and Andrzej Sekula. Pro Des: Gary Frutkoff. Ed: Margie Goodspeed, Elena Maganini, Sally Menke and Rodriguez. M: Combustible Edison. Costumes: Susan L. Bertram and Mary Claire Hannan. (Miramax–Buena Vista.) Rel: 5 January 1996. 97 mins. Cert 18. USA. 1995.

Frankie Starlight

France/Dublin/Texas; 1946-95. An Irish dwarf finds his life transformed when his autobiographical novel is accepted by Penguin. The product of a terminally morose French woman and an absent American GI, Frankie Starlight has less going for him than most. But his love of the stars and the quality of beauty sustains his optimism … Flatly directed by Michael Lindsay-Hogg, *Frankie Starlight* cries out for a touch of style and magic, but is dragged down by a lifeless performance from Anne Parillaud and a totally unconvincing one from Matt Dillon (who's supposed to be a charismatic Texan). Only the Irish sculptor Corban Walker, as the eponymous hybrid (his first acting role), seems to have his heart in it.

Cast: Anne Parillaud (Bernadette Bois), Matt Dillon (Terry Klout), Gabriel Byrne (Jack Kelly), Rudi Davies (Emma Kelly), Georgina Cates (young Emma Kelly), Corban Walker (Frank Bois), Niall Toibin

(Handy Paige), Dearbhla Molloy (Effa Kelly), Alan Pentony (young Frank Bois), Jean Claude Frissung, Victoria Begeja, Barbara Alyn Woods, Ulrich Funke, Julian Negulesco, Elizabeth Keller, Aisling Leyne.

Dir: Michael Lindsay-Hogg. Pro: Noel Pearson. Line Pro: Seamus Byrne. Screenplay: Chet Raymo and Ronan O'Leary, based on the novel by Raymo. Ph: Paul Laufer. Pro Des: Frank Conway. Ed: Ruth Foster. M: Elmer Bernstein. Costumes: Joan Bergin. (Film Four Distributors-Film Four/NFT.) Rel: 17 May 1996. 102 mins. Cert 15. UK. 1996.

Free Willy 2

Willy, the three-and-a-half ton, 22-foot-long killer whale, is back with his family, and Jesse, now 14, has a disagreeable half-brother to deal with. All they need is a menacing oil slick to threaten the local wildlife and to strengthen those family bonds. With a bigger budget and a stronger story, *Free Willy 2* is an exceptionally fine sequel to the 1993 splash hit, even though Keiko – the original Willy – has been replaced by animatronic knowhow. Not that you'd notice through the welling of salt tears. The photography, music and environment-friendly message are all on the nose.

Cast: Jason James Richter (Jesse), August Schellenberg (Randolph Johnson), Jayne Atkinson (Annie Greenwood), Jon Tenney (John Milner), Elizabeth Pena (Dr Kate Haley), Michael Madsen (Glen Greenwood), Francis Capra (Elvis), Mary Kate Schellhardt (Nadine), Mykelti Williamson (Dwight), Paul Tuerpe, M. Emmet Walsh, John Considine, Steve Kahan, Julie Inouye, Basil Wallace, Marguerite Moreau, Chanel Capra.

Dir: Dwight Little. Pro: Lauren Shuler-Donner and Jennie Lew Tugend. Co-Pro: Richard Solomon. Ex Pro: Richard Donner, Arnon Milchan and Jim Van Wyck. Screenplay: Karen Janszen, Corey Blechman and John Mattson. Ph: Laszlo Kovacs. Ed: Robert Brown and Dallas Puett. Pro Des: Paul Sylbert. M: Basil Poledouris; numbers performed by Michael Jackson, Pretenders, Rebbie Jackson, Expose, Nathan Caveleri Band, etc. Costumes: Erica Edell Phillips. (Canal Plus/Regency Enterprises/Alcor Films–Warner.) Rel: 4 August 1995. 98 mins. Cert U. USA. 1995.

French Kiss

Kate is getting her life together. She's engaged to the man she loves, her nest egg can cover the down payment on her dream house and her Canadian citizenship papers are coming through.

Two for the price of one: Willy introduces his brother to Jason James Richter in Dwight Little's agreeable Free Willy 2 *(from Warner)*

Then, when her fiancé visits Paris on business, he meets the love of his life, 'like in a sonnet, like in a movie'. So, combating her terror of aeroplanes, Kate flies to Paris to save her marriage ... A charming romantic fantasy produced by Meg Ryan, *French Kiss* arrived in the slipstream of the similar *Only You* and *While You Were Sleeping*, which somewhat knocked the breath out if its sails. Nevertheless, this is a

While You Were Dating: Kevin Kline and Meg Ryan, the garlic and babycham of romantic comedy, lock horns in Lawrence Kasdan's French Kiss *(PolyGram)*

delightful tale smartly scripted by Adam Brooks, splendidly lit by Owen Roizman and skilfully directed by Lawrence Kasdan. Meg Ryan has never been more lovely or funny as the dizzy blonde out of her depth, although Kevin Kline's 'hygiene-deficient, nicotine-saturated' Frenchman could've been made a little more sympathetic to aid the chemistry.

Cast: Meg Ryan (Kate), Kevin Kline (Luc Teyssier), Timothy Hutton (Charlie), Jean Reno (Jean-Paul), Francois Cluzet (Bob), Susan Anbeh (Juliette), Renee Humphrey (Lilly), Michael Riley (Campbell), Laurent Spielvogel (concierge), Victor Garrivier (Octave), Elizabeth Commelin, Julie Liebowitch, Miquel Brown, Louise Deschamps, Jerry Harte, Adam Brooks (perfect passenger).

Plugging the dyke: Josiane Balasko, Victoria Abril and Alain Chabat fight for domestic harmony in Balasko's hilarious French Twist *(from Guild)*

Dir: Lawrence Kasdan. Pro: Tim Bevan, Eric Fellner, Meg Ryan and Kathryn F. Galan. Ex Pro: Charles Okun. Screenplay: Adam Brooks. Ph: Owen Roizman. Ed: Joe Hutshing. Pro Des: Jon Hutman. M: James Newton Howard; numbers performed by

Plattshtick: Oliver Platt rehearses his dog of an act in Peter Chesholm's Funny Bones *(from Buena Vista)*

Les Negresses Vertes, Charles Trenet, Beautiful South, Louis Armstrong, Kevin Kline, Van Morrison, etc. Costumes: Joanna Johnston. (Fox/PolyGram/Working Title/Prufrock Pictures–PolyGram.) Rel: 3 November 1995. 111 mins. Cert 12. USA. 1995.

French Twist - Gazon Maudit

Loli leads an idyllic existence in a beautiful house in the South of France with her two young children and handsome, successful husband. But then the happy housewife doesn't know what a selfish, lying, hypocritical, intolerant, two-faced, arrogant, sexist swine her husband really is. When Loli discovers her old man's true colours, her revenge takes a most unorthodox trajectory when she jumps into the ample arms of a tough-talking, decidedly masculine lesbian. Creating some media mileage (and *controverse*) in its native France, *Gazon Maudit* is actually a very sweet and charming comedy of manners with a twist. Josiane Balasko (who played Gerard Depardieu's overweight mistress in *Trop Belle pour Toi*) brings a refreshing integrity to her role of the butch seductress, poking fun at the stereotyping of female homosexuality – before turning the screws. A thought-provoking treat. Original US title: *Bushwhacked.*

Cast: Victoria Abril (Loli), Josiane Balasko (Marijo), Alain Chabat (Laurent), Ticky Holgado (Antoine), Miguel Bose (Diego), Catherine Hiegel (Dany), Catherine Lachens (Sopha), Catherine Samie, Michele Bernier, Telsche Boorman, Katrine Boorman, Veronique Barrault.
Dir and Screenplay: Josiane Balasko. Pro: Claude Berri. Ex Pro: Pierre Grunstein. Ph: Gerard de Battista. Pro Des: Carlos Conti. Ed: Claudine Merlin. M: Manuel Malou. Costumes: Fabienne Katany. (Renn Prods/TF1 Films/Les Films Flam/Canal Plus–Guild.) Rel: 1 March 1996. 107 mins. Cert 18. France. 1995.

From Dusk Till Dawn

Following a particularly violent crime spree (gleefully documented by TV reporter Kelly Preston), two bad-ass brothers hole up a dingy motel in the desert. There they kidnap a local preacher and his two teenage kids and, with the minister driving them in his mobile home at gunpoint, they all head for the Mexican border and sanctuary. Yet what awaits them on the other side is something else entirely... The problem with *From Dusk Till Dawn* is that the beginning is so dynamic and stylish, the characters of the Gecko brothers so brilliantly and deftly drawn and the casting of Harvey Keitel (as the solid, paternal pastor) so surprising, that you want the film to continue as it is. Thus, when it changes gear so dramatically halfway through, one is grudgingly torn from a Tarantino movie and plonked into the more questionable arena of a George A. Romero or Peter Jackson gore fest. Still, there's plenty of dark humour to

savour, tons of in-jokes and some stomach-churning special effects. And George Clooney, in his first starring role in a feature, is dynamite. FYI: Tarantino wrote this two years before Keitel produced *Reservoir Dogs*.

Cast: Harvey Keitel (Jacob Fuller), George Clooney (Seth Gecko), Quentin Tarantino (Richard Gecko), Juliette Lewis (Kate Fuller), Cheech Marin (border guard/Chet Pussy/Carlos), Fred Williamson (Frost), Salma Hayek (Santanico Pandemonium), Tom Savini (Sex Machine), Ernest Liu (Scott Fuller), John Hawkes (Pete Bottoms), Marc Lawrence, Michael Parks, Kelly Preston, John Saxon, Danny Trejo, Tito Larriva.

Dir and Ed: Robert Rodriguez. Pro: Gianni Nunnari and Meir Teper. Ex Pro: Rodriguez, Quentin Tarantino and Lawrence Bender. Co-Pro: Elizabeth Avellan, Paul Hellerman, Robert Kurtzman and John Esposito. Screenplay: Tarantino, from a story by Kurtzman. Ph: Guillermo Navarro. Pro Des: Cecilia Montiel. M: Graeme Revell; numbers performed by The Blasters, ZZ Top, Jon Wayne, The Mavericks, Jimmie Vaughan, The Leftovers, Tito & Tarantula, and Stevie Ray Vaughan & Double Trouble. Costumes: Graciela Mazon. (Los Hooligans/A Band Apart–Buena Vista.) Rel: 31 May 1996. 107 mins. Cert 18. USA. 1995.

Funny Bones

You've either got it or you haven't. To be really funny, you shouldn't need other people's jokes to prop you up. Tommy Fawkes, son of the legendary jokemeister George Fawkes, hasn't got what it takes. So, after a disastrous opening night in Las Vegas, Tommy returns to his roots in Blackpool to buy the perfect act. There he encounters Jack Parker, an extraordinarily funny guy with more to him than meets the eye ... *Funny Bones* is such a weird, eccentric film that few are likely to tune into its unique mindscape, although there is much to enjoy. Lee Evans, like a surreal Norman Wisdom, is quite mesmerising, and George Carl and Freddie Davies as his uncle and father are priceless. While there are flashes of genuine humour (the auditions are a hoot), too often the film's whimsy and charm feel forced. Still, to see Jerry Lewis and Oliver Reed on screen at the same time – in Blackpool, of all places – is something.

Cast: Oliver Platt (Tommy Fawkes), Jerry Lewis (George Fawkes), Lee Evans (Jack Parker), Leslie Caron (Katie Parker), Richard Griffiths (Jim Minty), Oliver Reed

Out to lunch: Gene Hackman and Danny DeVito discuss high concept in Barry Sonnenfeld's highly agreeable Get Shorty *(from UIP)*

(Dolly Hopkins), George Carl (Thomas Parker), Freddie Davies (Bruno Parker), Ian McNeice (Stanley Sharkey), Christopher Greet (Lawrence Berger), Terence Rigby (Billy Mann), Ruta Lee (Laura Fawkes), Peter Gunn, Gavin Millar, William Hootkins, Peter Pamela Rose, Ticky Holgado, Olivier Fry, Peter McNamara, Richard Platt, Francois Domange, Phil Kelly, Harold Nicholas, George Khan, Ian Rowe, Ruth Kettlewell, Chris Luby, Fred Evans, Paula Wilcox, Jeremy Clarke, Anita Scott.

Dir: Peter Chelsom. Pro: Chelsom and Simon Field. Ex Pro: Nicholas Frye. Assoc Pro: Peter McMillan. Line Pro: Laurie Borg. Screenplay: Chelsom and Peter Flannery. Ph: Eduardo Serra. Ed: Martin Walsh. Pro Des: Caroline Hanania. M: John Altman; numbers performed by Charles Trenet, John Lee Hooker, Willie Dixon, Washboard Sam, Eartha Kitt, Nina Simone, Duke Ellington, Glen Miller, etc. Costumes: Lindy Hemming. (Hollywood Pictures–Buena Vista.) Rel: 29 September 1995. 128 mins. Cert 15. USA/UK. 1994.

Gazon Maudit

See *French Twist*.

Get Shorty

Miami/New York/Las Vegas/ but mainly Hollywood; today. In spite of his name, Chili Palmer has a cool head, a perfect appliance for a loan shark. Sent to Hollywood to collect from a third-rate producer (whose credits include *Slime Creatures II* and *I Married a Ghoul From Outer Space*), Palmer finds that his strong-arm tactics and knowledge of movies is a perfect combination to get into the business ... Some would say Hollywood is already crawling with crooks, so the thuggery depicted in *Get Shorty* will be nothing new. None the less, the idea of blending a gangster movie with a behind-the-scenes comedy proves to be a heady compound. Working from a strong story – based on the novel by Elmore Leonard – director Sonnenfeld takes a leisurely pace, relying on the effortless charisma of his actors to carry the show. Indeed, this is a character-driven piece, with the humour emerging from the increasingly ludicrous attempts of a variety of

Magna-tic: Guns, girls and gadgets in Mamoru Oshii's Ghost in the Shell *(from Starlight)*

heavyweights to muscle in on an old screenplay. Exceedingly amiable. FYI: Producer Danny DeVito was originally supposed to play Chili Palmer.

Cast: John Travolta (Chili Palmer), Gene Hackman (Harry Zimm), Rene Russo (Karen Flores), Danny DeVito (Martin Weir), Dennis Farina (Ray 'Bones' Barboni), Delroy Lindo (Bo Catlett), James Gandolfini (Bear), Jon Gries (Ronnie

Phone groan: Theresa Randle steams up the switchboard in Spike Lee's Girl 6 *(from Fox)*

Wingate), Renee Props (Nicki), David Paymer (Leo Devoe), Miguel Sandoval (Mr Escobar), Jacob Vargas (Yayo Portillo), Martin Ferrero, Linda Hart, Bobby Slayton, John Cothran Jr., Big Daddy Wayne, Carlease Burke, Vito Scotti, Harry Victor, Barry Sonnenfeld, Ernest 'Chili' Palmer, Bette Midler, Harvey Keitel, Penny Marshall.

Dir and Ex Pro: Barry Sonnenfeld. Pro: Danny DeVito, Michael Shamberg and Stacey Sher. Co-Pro: Graham Place. Screenplay: Scott Frank. Ph: Don Peterman. Pro Des: Peter Larkin. Ed: Jim Miller. M: John Lurie; numbers performed by Booker T. & the MGs, Count Basie and Tony Bennett, Morphine, Us3, Lee Morgan, Greyboy, etc. Costumes: Betsy Heimann. (MGM/Jersey Films–UIP.) Rel: 15 March 1996. 110 mins. Cert 15. USA. 1995.

Ghost in the Shell – Kokaku Kidotai

Tokyo; 2029. Cybernetically rebuilt female agent Kusanagi and her male sidekick Bateau pursue a mysterious computer hacker known as The Puppet Master, who resides in the cyborg shell of the title ... The animation varies from lavish Akira quality to impressive computer generated work to comparatively cheap. The first *anime* feature jointly financed by America, Japan and Britain. [*Jeremy Clarke*]

Voices: Richard George (Bateau), Mimi Woods (Major Kusanagi), William Frederick (Aramaki), Abe Lasser (The Puppet Master), Christopher Joyce (Togusa), Mike Sorich (Ishikawa), Ben Isaacson (Nakamura).

Dir: Mamoru Oshii. Pro: Yoshimasa Mizuo, Ken Matsumoto, Ken Iyadomi and Mitsuhisa Ishikawa. Ex Pro: Teruo Miyahara, Shigeru Watanabe and Andy Frain. Screenplay: Kazunori Ito, based on the graphic novel by Shirow [Shiro] Masamune. Ph: Hisao Shirai. Ed: Shuichi Kakesu. Art: Hiromasa Ogura. M: Kenji Kawai. Animation Director: Toshihiko Nishikubo. Character Designs: Hiroyuki Okiura. (Kodansha/Bandai Visual/Manga Entertainment–Starlight.) Rel: 8 December 1995. 83 mins. Cert 15. Japan/UK. 1995.

Girl 6

Unable to compromise herself even to advance her career as an actress, a nameless New York woman turns to phone sex to pay her bills. Encountering nothing but outraged disbelief from her neighbour, Jimmy, and her kleptomaniac ex-boyfriend, the newly nicknamed 'Girl 6' perseveres and discovers a liking for her new vocation ... Employing his characteristic in-your-face style of filmmaking, Spike Lee infuses his film with considerable vigour, almost saving what is basically a series of inconclusive sketches. However, by assaulting the ears with a continuous drone of Prince songs, the director undermines his narrative which, in the end, comes off like an extended music video. Various spoofs of black cultural phenomenons such as *Carmen Jones*, *Foxy Brown* and TV's *The Jeffersons* are haphazardly inserted into the film, further draining the patience. Ultimately, then, one has to ask what is the point of this superficial, disjointed and not even very shocking diversion? The subject of phone sex was handled with much more conviction in *Short Cuts*.

Deadlier than the male: Famke Janssen, as Xenia Onatopp, lives up to her name – to the detriment of Pierce Brosnan – in Goldeneye *(from UIP)*

Cast: Theresa Randle (Girl 6), Isaiah Washington (shoplifter), Spike Lee (Jimmy), Debi Mazar (Girl 39), Jenifer Lewis (Lil), John Turturro (Murray), Susan Batson (acting coach), Madonna, Quentin Tarantino, Naomi Campbell, Rolanda Watts, Halle Berry, Peter Berg, Richard Belzer, Ron Silver, Desi Moreno, Michael Imperioli, Larry Pine, Mica Hughes, Leonard Thomas, Joie Lee, Ranjit Chowdhry, Rita Wolf, John Cameron Mitchell.

Dir and Pro: Spike Lee. Ex Pro: Jon Kilik. Assoc Pro: Cirri Nottage. Screenplay: Suzan-Lori Parks. Ph: Malik Hassan Sayeed. Pro Des: Ina Mayhew. Ed: Sam Pollard. Songs: Prince. Costumes: Sandra Hernandez. (Fox Searchlight Pictures/40 Acres and a Mule Filmworks–Fox.) Rel: 7 June 1996. 108 mins. Cert 18. USA. 1996.

Goldeneye

Siberia/Monte Carlo/London/St Petersburg/ the Caribbean; now. The Cold War may be over, but a renegade Russian general is heating up a new one – with the help of some state-of-the-art technology. Looming like the *QE2* out of dry dock, the 17th official James Bond film opens with a terrific prologue, follows with a spectacular credit sequence (designed by Daniel Kleinman) and then trumps its ace by re-inventing its own clichés. M, the head of MI6, is now a woman (Dame Judi Dench), and is a tougher match than her predecessor (calling 007 'a sexist, misogynistic dinosaur'). There's also a memorable henchwoman in Famke Janssen's deadly nymphomaniac (for whom killing acts as an aphrodisiac), and some queasy stunt work. Furthermore, the new Bond, the Irish-born Pierce Brosnan, is the most devastatingly handsome of the lot, even if he fails to buoy the feeble one-liners. On the downside, Sean Bean is an exceptionally weak villain, the plot is incomprehensible and the leaps in logic frequently inexcusable (not least when Bond miraculously overtakes a speeding train in a tank). So, after a promising start, this most expensive Bond to date ($42,750,000 by one account) deteriorates into an undisciplined blast of excess. To date, *True Lies* remains the best Bond film ever made.

Cast: Pierce Brosnan (James Bond), Sean Bean (Alec Trevelyan), Izabella Scorupco (Natalya Simonova), Famke Janssen (Xenia Onatopp), Joe Don Baker (Jack Wade), Judi Dench (M), Robbie Coltrane (Valentin Zukovsky), Tcheky Karyo (Dimitri Mishkin), Gottfried John (General Ourumov), Alan Cumming (Boris Grishenko), Desmond Llewelyn (Q), Samantha Bond (Miss Moneypenny), Michael Kitchen (Bill Tanner), Minnie Driver (Irina), Serena Gordon, Simon Kunz, Pavel Douglas, Constantine Gregory, Michelle Arthur.

Dir: Martin Campbell. Pro: Michael G. Wilson and Barbara Broccoli. Ex Pro: Tom Pevsner. Screenplay: Jeffrey Caine and Bruce Feirstein, from a story by Michael France. Ph: Phil Meheux. Ed: Terry Rawlings. Pro Des: Peter Lamont. M: Eric Serra; 'Goldeneye' performed by Tina Turner. Costumes: Lindy Hemming. Second Unit Director: Ian Sharp. (United Artists–UIP.) Rel: 24 November 1995. 130 mins. Cert 12. USA. 1995.

In the name of the father: Jasmine Russell cowers from her husband in Gerard Stembridge's forceful Guiltrip *(from Starlight)*

The Grotesque

Rural England; 1949. Sliding into a state of emotional stagnation, the radical amateur palaeontologist Sir Hugo Coal and his bored, rich American wife, find their lives dramatically transformed with the arrival of the new butler, Fledge, and his hard-drinking missus ... From Boris Karloff in *The Old Dark House* to Sandrine Bonnaire in *La Cérémonie* (via Dirk Bogarde in *The Servant*), domestic helps have been up to no good in the cinema, so it's no surprise when Fledge starts taking things into his own hands. The trouble with *The Grotesque* is that, in spite of the odd chuckle, the film is neither hugely funny nor remotely gripping. Worse, it frequently reminds one of an extended episode from TV's *Tales of the Unexpected*.

Cast: Alan Bates (Sir Hugo Coal), Theresa Russell (Lady Harriet Coal), Sting (Fledge), Trudie Styler (Doris Fledge), Lena Headey (Cleo Coal), Steven Mackintosh (Sidney Giblet), Anna Massey (Mrs Giblet), Maria Aitken (Lavinia Freebody), Jim Carter (George Lecky), Chris Barnes (Little John Lecky), James Fleet (Inspector Limp), John Mills, Timothy Kightley, Annette Badland, Jeffrey Wickham.
   Dir: John Paul Davidson. Pro: Trudie Styler. Screenplay: Patrick McGrath, from his 1988 novel. Ph: Andrew Dunn. Pro Des: Jan Roelfs and Michael Seirton. Ed: Tariq Anwar. M: Anne Dudley. Costumes: Colleen Atwood and Graham Churchyard. (Imagine Entertainment/Xingu Films–Starlight.) Rel: 14 June 1996. 98 mins. Cert 18. UK. 1995.

Guiltrip

A day and night in the life of an Irish married couple, *Guiltrip* plays like a thriller while refusing to resort to the excesses of the genre. Thus, an innocuous shopping trip takes on all the foreboding of an imminent bloodbath, while the worst thing that happens is the slip of a lie. The film's suspense is achieved by the simple trick of focusing on the trivial and mundane and by casting the imposing Andrew Connolly as the husband. Resembling Liam Neeson in build and presence, Connolly (who previously starred in the underrated 1988 Irish film *Joyriders*) makes the most of every threatening gesture, while never lifting a finger. *Guiltrip* deals with the psychological violence of a doomed marriage, our recognition of the domestic details causing our hackles to rise. First-time director Gerard Stembridge fuels the tension with sly cross-cutting across time, building to a climax loaded with horror and irony.

Cast: Andrew Connolly (Liam), Jasmine Russell (Tina), Peter Hanly (Ronnie Mac), Michelle Houlden (Michele), Frankie McCafferty (Frankie O'Malley), Pauline McLynn (Joan), Mikel Murfi (Petey), Fintan Lee (the kid).
   Dir and Screenplay: Gerard Stembridge. Pro: Ed Guiney. Ex Pro: Stephen Bradley and David Collins. Co-Pro: Domenico Procacci and Giuseppe Pedersoli. Line Pro: Noelette Buckley. Ph: Eugene O'Connor. Pro Des: David Wilson. Ed: Mary Finlay. M: Brendan Power. Costumes: Marie Tierney. (Temple Films/Fandango and Smile/MC4 and La Sept Cinema/Euskal Media/The Irish Film Board-Starlight Films.) Rel: 7 June 1996. 90 mins. Cert 15. Ireland. 1995.

Hackers

Some kids swap CDs, others stamps. The kids at Stanton High, New York, trade stories of computer derring-do. Phantom Phreak can phone anywhere in the world for free. Joey can programme cash dispensers to spit out money at predesignated times. Dade Murphy – aka Zero Cool – crashed 1,507 computers on Wall Street at the age of nine. Now the teenage cyberpunks find themselves beaten at their own game by The Plague, a master hacker who's framing them for a multi-million corporate scam ... Visually imaginative, skilfully plotted and edited at the speed of a video game, this slick, entertaining paean to computer nerds everywhere widens the generation gap with pizzazz and energy. Log on. FYI: Angelina Jolie, who plays the androgynous whiz kid Acid Burn, is the daughter of actor Jon Voight.

Cast: Jonny Lee Miller (Dade Murphy/Zero Cool), Angelina Jolie (Kate Libby/Acid Burn), Fisher Stevens (Eugene/The Plague), Jesse Bradford (Joey), Matthew Lillard (Cereal Killer), Laurence Mason (Lord Nikon), Renoly Santiago (Phantom Phreak), Alberta Watson (Lauren Murphy), Lorraine Bracco (Margo), Wendell Pierce (Agent Dick Gill), Penn Jillette (Hal), Bob Sessions (Duke Ellingson), Darren Lee, Peter Y. Kim, Ethan Browne, Michael Gaston, Marc Anthony, Liza Walker, Terry Porter, Sam Douglas, Annemarie Zola, Nancy Ticotin.
   Dir and Ex Pro: Iain Softley. Pro: Michael Peyser and Ralph Winter. Co-Pro: Janet Graham. Screenplay: Rafael Moreu. Ph: Andrzej Sekula. Pro Des: John Beard. Ed: Christopher Blunden and Martin Walsh. M: Simon Boswell; numbers performed by Orbital, Massive Attack, Prodigy, Leftfield and John Lydon, Underworld, Deep Cover, Squeeze, Stereo MC's, etc. Costumes: Roger Burton. (United Artists–UIP.) Rel: 3 May 1996. 105 mins. Cert 12. USA. 1995.

The long arm of les gendarmes: Said Tagh-maoui and Hubert Kounde are 'interviewed' by police in Mathieu Kassovitz's impassioned La Haine *(from Metro Tartan)*

La Haine - Hate

With nary a wedge of brie or glass of burgundy in sight, Mathieu Kasso-vitz's disturbing, frenzied drama lifts the rug to reveal a very different side to the traditional view of Paris. Utilising edgy hand-held camerawork and bleached-out black-and-white photography, Kassovitz concentrates on 24 hours in the lives of three friends from a run-down housing project. Vinz, a working-class Jew, is psyching himself up to kill his first policeman; Hubert, an aspiring boxer, has just lost his gym in a riot; while Said, an Arab, is more interested in girls. Meanwhile, the tension between the police and the locals is heating up to boiling point … Thanks to three remarkable performances from his leading actors and a bravura filmmaking style, Kassovitz keeps us on the edge of our seats while knotting our sympathies. With hate blinding both sides of the social line, who are the villains?

Cast: Vincent Cassel (Vinz), Hubert Kounde (Hubert), Said Taghmaoui (Said), Karim Belkhadra (Samir), Edouard Montoute (Darty), Francois Levantal (Asterix), Solo Dicko, Marc Duret, Helroise Rauth, Rywka Wajsbrot, Tadek Lokcinski.

Dir and Screenplay: Mathieu Kassovitz. Pro: Christophe Rossignon. Line Pro: Gilles Sacuto. Assoc Pro: Adeline Lacailler and Alain Rocca. Ph: Pierre Aim. Ed: Kassovitz and Scott Stevenson. Pro Des: Giuseppe Ponturo. M: numbers performed by Bob Marley, Isaac Hayes, Zapp and Roger, Cut Killer, Cameo, The Gap Band, Ripple, Klay M, Solo, The Beastie Boys, etc. Costumes: Virginie Montel. Sound: Vincent Tulli. (Les Productions Lazennec/Canal Plus/La Sept Cinema–Metro Tartan.) Rel: 17 November 1995. 85 mins. Cert 18. France. 1995.

Haunted

Sussex, England; 1925. Straight forward, very English adaptation of James Herbert's romantic ghost story, the tale of an American professor of

Tales of the Expected: Aidan Quinn dreams of Anna Massey in Lewis Gilbert's Haunted *(from Entertainment)*

The hot zone: Robert De Niro and Val Kilmer take on the streets in Michael Mann's gut-kicking Heat *(from Warner)*

parapsychology (Aidan Quinn) who is lured to a haunted mansion by a freak coincidence. There, he spends more time flirting with the comely lady of the manor (Kate Beckinsale) than sorting out the demons of mad Nanny Tess (Anna Massey). Then, gradually ... With its traditionally quaint period reference points – the large stately home, vintage cars barrelling down narrow country lanes and a cameo from John Gielgud – this feels more like an extended episode of *Tales of the Unexpected* than a feature thriller. Indeed, it's tempting to ponder what somebody like Nicolas Roeg would have made of such fertile source material – particularly with Francis Ford Coppola as executive producer.

Cast: Aidan Quinn (David Ash), Kate Beckinsale (Christina Mariell), Anthony Andrews (Robert Mariell), John Gielgud (Dr Doyle), Anna Massey (Nanny Tess), Alex Lowe (Simon Mariell), Geraldine Somerville (Kate), Linda Bassett (Madame Brontski), Victoria Shalet, Peter England,

Liz Smith, Alice Douglas, Hilary Mason.
Dir: Lewis Gilbert. Pro: Gilbert and Anthony Andrews. Co-Pro: William P. Cartlidge. Ex Pro: Francis Ford Coppola, Fred Fuchs, Jeff Kleeman and Ralph Kamp. Screenplay: Gilbert, Tim Prager and Bob Kellett. Ph: Tony Pierce-Roberts. Ed: Johnny Jympson. Pro Des: John Fenner and Brian Ackland-Snow. M: Debbie Wiseman. Costumes: Jane Robinson and Candy Patterson. (Double 'A' Pictures/American Zoetrope/Lumiere–Entertainment.) Rel: 27 October 1995. 110 mins. Cert 15. UK/USA. 1995.

Heat

A gang of ruthless, highly skilled thieves are cleaning up Los Angeles. Masterminded by the meticulous professional criminal Neil McCauley, their increasingly ambitious operations are dumbfounding the police. Yet LAPD lieutenant Vincent Hanna is as cunning and determined as his unknown quarry – and he knows that sooner or later they have to trip up ... A handsome, gripping crime drama, *Heat* is a masterful example of its genre, although it tries too hard to be all things. The film positively groans under the weight of its colourful characters, but it cannot serve them all, resulting in

confusion. We want to know more about Val Kilmer, but because of the profusion of subplots introducing secondary characters (just so they can be killed off), we are left with a fractured mosaic. More troubling still is the shift of sympathies between Pacino and De Niro. As the cop, Pacino is the one we should be rooting for, but with his deteriorating marriage and self-indulgent pronouncements ('all I am is what I'm going after'), De Niro comes off as the more attractive proposition – particularly as his romantic future seems more assured.

Cast: Al Pacino (Vincent Hanna), Robert De Niro (Neil McCauley), Val Kilmer (Chris Shiherlis), Tom Sizemore (Michael Cheritto), Diane Venora (Justine Hanna), Amy Brenneman (Eady), Ashley Judd (Charlene Shiherlis), Mykelti Williamson (Det. Drucker), Wes Studi (Det. Casals), Ted Levine (Bosko), Jon Voight (Nate), Dennis Haysbert (Breedan), William Fichtner (Van Zant), Natalie Portman (Lauren Hanna), Tom Noonan (Kelso), Kevin Gage (Waingro), Hank Azaria (Marciano), Susan Traylor (Elaine Cheritto), Kim Staunton, Danny Trejo, Henry Rollins, Jerry Trimble, Marty Ferrero, Ricky Harris, Tone Loc, Hazelle Goodman, Jeremy Piven, Xander Berkeley, Rick Avery, Paul Herman, Brian

Libby, Phillip Robinson, Yvonne Zima, Bud Cort.

Dir and Screenplay: Michael Mann. Pro: Mann and Art Linson. Ex Pro: Arnon Milchan and Pieter Jan Brugge. Ph: Dante Spinotti. Pro Des: Neil Spisak. Ed: Dov Hoenig, Pasquale Buba, William Goldenberg and Tom Rolf. M: Elliot Goldenthal; numbers performed by Brian Eno, Terje Rypdal, Moby, William Orbit, James, Lisa Gerrard, Solitaire, Eric Clapton, B.B. King, House of Pain, New World Beat, etc. Costumes: Deborah L. Scott. (Regency Enterprises/Forward Pass–Warner.) Rel: 26 January 1996. 170 mins. Cert 15. USA. 1996.

Heaven's Prisoners

An ex-cop and reformed alcoholic, David Robicheaux has settled for a quiet life supplying boats to fishermen in the Louisiana swampland. With a beautiful wife and comfortable home, David would seem to have everything he could wish for – except, perhaps, a child to share his future. Then abruptly his subconscious wishes are answered when he rescues a little girl from a plane crash. But his new blessing proves to be a nightmare in disguise when some unsavoury characters come looking for her ... Based on the book by James Lee Burke, *Heaven's Prisoners* makes the most of its exotic locations, while director Joanou lays on the atmosphere with a trowel. However, a lumpy script and some dubious acting weakens the brew, resulting in a ponderous, schematic tale punctuated by outbursts of sudden violence and unspeakable dialogue ('I'm one guy – I'm not a crime wave'). Still, Kelly Lynch makes the most of her thankless role as David's wife and George Fenton supplies a fine score.

Cast: Alec Baldwin (David 'Streak' Robicheaux), Mary Stuart Masterson (Robin Gaddis), Kelly Lynch (Annie Robicheaux), Teri Hatcher (Claudette Rocque), Eric Roberts (Bubba Rocque), Vondie Curtis Hall (Minos P. Dautrieve), Samantha Lagpacon (Alafair), Tuck Milligan (Jerry Falgout), Joe Viterelli (Didi Giancano), Badja Djola, Hawthorne James, Carl A. McGee, Don Stark, Gray Frederickson, Paul Guilfoyle, Chuck Zito.

Dir: Phil Joanou. Pro: Andre E. Morgan and Albert S. Ruddy. Ex Pro: Hildy Gottleib. Co-Ex Pro: Gray Frederickson. Screenplay: Harley Peyton and Scott Frank. Ph: Harris Savides. Pro Des: John Stoddart. Ed: William Steinkamp. M: George Fenton; numbers performed by John Lee Hooker, B.B. King, Stevie Ray Vaughan,

etc. Costumes: Aude Bronson-Howard. (New Line/Savoy Pictures/Rank/PVM Entertainment–Rank.) Rel: 28 June 1996. 132 mins. Cert 15. USA. 1996.

Heavy

Fine ensemble acting from its six leading players cannot save *Heavy* from being an oppressive view of loners living out a drab existence. Set in a remote roadside diner in New York state, this first feature from James Mangold, a Sundance prizewinner, does, however, have its admirers. But the central misfit, a fat mother's boy unable to make an independent life for himself (excellently played by Pruitt Taylor Vince), arouses discomfort rather than pity for his situation. For this, Mangold's screenplay is to blame. [*Mansel Stimpson*]

Cast: Shelley Winters (Dolly), Liv Tyler (Callie), Deborah Harry (Delores), Evan Dando (Jeff), Pruitt Taylor Vince (Victor), Joe Grifasi (Leo), David Patrick Kelly, Marian Quinn, Meg Hartig, Zandy Hartig.

Dir and Screenplay: James Mangold. Pro: Richard Miller. Ex Pro: Herbert Beigel. Assoc Pro: Scott Ferguson and Jane Wright. Line Pro: Gretchen McGowan. Ph: Michael Barrow. Pro Des: Michael Shaw. Ed: Meg Reticker. M: Thurston Moore. Costumes: Sara Jane Slotnick. (Available Light–Artificial Eye.) Rel: 29 December 1995. 104 mins. Cert 15. USA. 1995.

Choose your stereotype: Jennifer Connelly and Kristy Swanson in John Singleton's impassioned Higher Learning *(from Columbia)*

Higher Learning

Three new students at the (fictitious) institute of Columbus University find that their identities are becoming radically altered. Indeed, the campus they looked on as a haven of education and as a springboard of opportunity turns out to be a microcosm of the racial, cultural and sexual tensions of the rest of America. The third film from John Singleton – writer-director of *Boyz N the Hood* and *Poetic Justice* – this is the first not based on actual experiences. However, the emotional engineering is all too obvious, with every black, white, Jew and lesbian neatly slotted into his or her place (with the exception of Kristy Swanson who, at least, plays a bisexual). A powerful, well-made polemic, but far from convincing.

Cast: Omar Epps (Malik Williams), Kristy Swanson (Kristen Connor), Michael Rapaport (Remy), Jennifer Connelly (Taryn), Ice Cube (Fudge White), Jason Wiles (Wayne), Tyra Banks (Deja), Cole Hauser (Scott Moss), Laurence Fishburne (Professor Maurice Phipps), Regina King (Monet), Jay Ferguson (Billy), Bradford English, Busta Rhymez, Andrew Bryniarski, Trevor St John, Talbert Morton, Adam Goldberg, J. Trevor Edmond, Bridgette Wilson, Kari Salin, John Walton Smith Jr., Randall Batinkoff, D-Knowledge, Ernie Singleton, Mista Grimm, Colleen Ann Fitzpatrick.

Dir and Screenplay: John Singleton. Pro: Singleton and Paul Hall. Co-Pro: Dwight Alonzo Williams. Ph: Peter Lyons Collister. Ed: Bruce Cannon. Pro Des: Keith Brian Burns. M: Stanley Clarke; numbers performed by Ice Cube, The Brand New Heav-

ies, Mista Grimm, Rage Against the Machine, Tony Toni Toné, OutKast, Dramarama, Zhane, Tori Amos, Eve's Plum, D-Knowledge and Black/Note, Mrs God, Al Green, Aretha Franklin, Curtis Mayfield, Blanket Party, Cotton Mather, Sons of Elvis, The Watts Prophets, Final Cut, Minnie Riperton, etc. Costumes: Carol Oditz. Title Sequence: Elaine and Saul Bass. (New Deal–Columbia.) Rel: 15 September 1995. 128 mins. Cert 15. USA. 1995.

Hold Me, Thrill Me, Kiss Me

Zany comedy in which a good-hearted thief, Eli, is caught red-handed by the daughter of a millionaire he is burgling. In return for her silence and $200,000, he reluctantly agrees to a shotgun wedding in which he ends up shooting the bride. Escaping to a trailer camp, he finds that his criminal problems are nothing compared to the romantic ones he's getting into ... Fortified by some wonderful dialogue ('Deep down I'm a sensitive and vulnerable girl – don't let my dildos, vibrators and handcuffs fool you'), Joel Hershman's first film (made two months after the director left New York University), bursts with promise but is deflated by some dodgy performances. Ex-Bruce Weber model Max Parrish looks the part as the handsome innocent Eli, and ex-porn star Andrea Naschak knows how to strut her stuff, but their acting sucks.

Shotgun wedding: Sean Young demands 'I do' from Max Parrish in Joel Hershman's promising Hold Me, Thrill Me, Kiss Me *(from Art House Productions)*

Cast: Max Parrish (Eli/Bud/Fritz), Adrienne Shelly (Dannie), Andrea Naschak (Sabra), Diane Ladd (Lucille), Sean Young (Twinkle), Timothy Leary (Mr Jones), Bela Lehoczky (Lazslo), Ania Suli (Olga), Vic Trevino (Julio), Joseph Anthony Richards, Allan Warnick, Mary Lanier, Travis Swords, John Auxier, Alain Joel Silver, Gus the dog (himself).

Dir and Screenplay: Joel Hershman. Pro: Travis Swords. Ex Pro: Martin Ira Rubin. Co-Ex Pro: Bela Lehoczky. Ph: Kent Wakeford. Ed: Kathryn Himoff. Pro Des: Dominic Wymark. M: Gerald Gouriet; numbers performed by Mel Carter, Violent Femmes, The Pixies, Fred Schneider, The Jazz Butcher, Elvis Hitler, The Cramps, etc. Costumes: Cathy Cooper. (Mad Dog Pictures–Art House Productions.) Rel: 1 September 1995. 92 mins. Cert 18. USA. 1992.

The Horseman on the Roof – Le Hussard sur le Toit

1832; Provence. In France to warn his fellow exiles of a brutal posse of Austrian assassins, Angelo Pardi, a young Italian colonel, finds himself plunged into the midst of a devastating epidemic of Asian cholera. Chased by paranoid mobs and hunted by trigger-happy dragoons, he meets up with a proud, beautiful noblewoman, Pauline de Theus, and takes it on himself to escort her to safety. However, Pauline has her own agenda, although Angelo's chivalry refuses to let her out of his sight. And so the headstrong duo embark on an escapade of narrow escapes and almost certain infection ... Following the triumph of his fifth film, *Cyrano de Bergerac*, writer-director

Jean-Paul Rappeneau moves up two centuries – to the 1830s – and takes on Jean Giono's epic romantic novel (written between 1946 and '51). Capturing the intoxicating beauty of the Provence countryside – in marked contrast to the grotesque cadavers littering the streets – Rappeneau has produced a visually sumptuous epic. Yet beyond the sword fights and thrilling flights on horseback, the film is an intimate romance of raging, suppressed passion. A magnificent celebration of cinema.

Cast: Juliette Binoche (Pauline de Theus), Olivier Martinez (Angelo Pardi), Pierre Arditi (Mr Peyrolle), Francois Cluzet (the doctor), Jean Yanne (the pedlar), Isabelle Carre, Jean-Marie Winling, Jacques Sereys, Claudio Amendola, Carlo Cecchi, Paul Freeman, Gerard Depardieu, Nathalie Krebs, Christophe Odent, Yolande Moreau, Jean-Claude Dumas, Beatrice Bertrand.

Dir: Jean-Paul Rappeneau. Pro: René Cleitman. Ex Pro: Bernard Bouix. Screenplay: Rappeneau, Nina Companeez and Jean-Claude Carrière. Ph: Thierry Arbogast. Pro Des: Ezio Frigerio. Ed: Noelle Boisson. M: Jean-Claude Petit; Brahms. Costumes: Franca Squarciapino. Sound: Pierre Gamet. Stunts: William Hobbs. (Hachette Première et Cie/France 2 Cinema–Artificial Eye.) Rel: 5 January 1996. 136 mins. Cert 15. France. 1995.

How to Make an American Quilt

Grasse, California. For quilt read marriage, or at least romantic commitment. Here, seven women of varying ages and background meet up to sew together an elaborate love quilt to 'commemorate' young Finn's eventual wedlock. However, Finn, a fickle 26-year-old student, is not so sure she even wants to get married, and after hearing the various romantic escapades of her elders (the stories themselves incorporated into the designs on the quilt), is even less sure that a permanent commitment is what she needs ... Directed by the Australian Jocelyn Moorehouse (*Proof*), scripted by the playwright Jane Anderson and produced by a variety of female executives, *How to Make an American Quilt* is, inescapably, a women's picture. Yet this is not to be taken in a derogatory sense, as the film is a warm, intelligent and low-key celebration of love in all its many guises. None the less, some heavy-handed symbolism and the

Love in the time of cholera: Olivier Martinez cuts a swathe through Provence in Jean-Paul Rappeneau's rousing The Horseman on the Roof *(from Artificial Eye)*

patchwork nature of the film's structure smacks of theatre. Even Janusz Kaminiski's immaculate lighting, Thomas Newman's tender score and a magnificent cast cannot rustle up a cinematic momentum.

Cast: Winona Ryder (Finn), Anne Bancroft (Glady Joe), Ellen Burstyn (Hy), Kate Nelligan (Constance), Alfre Woodard (Marianna), Maya Angelou (Anna), Kate Capshaw (Sally), Loren Dean (Preston), Samantha Mathis (young Sophia), Dermot Mulroney (Sam), Derrick O'Connor (Dean), Jean Simmons (Em), Lois Smith (Sophia), Rip Torn (Arthur), Mykelti Williamson (Winston), Johnathon Schaech (Leon), Maria Celedonio (young Anna), Adam Baldwin, Denis Arndt, Melinda Dillon, Joanna Going, Tim Guinee, Richard Jenkins, Tamala Jones, Esther Rolle, Gail Strickland, Jared Leto, Claire Danes, Alicia Goranson, Holland Taylor.

Dir: Jocelyn Moorhouse. Pro: Sarah Pillsbury and Midge Sanford. Ex Pro: Walter Parkes, Laurie MacDonald and Deborah Jelin Newmyer. Co-Pro: Patricia Whitcher. Screenplay: Jane Anderson,

based on the novel by Whitney Otto. Ph: Janusz Kaminski. Pro Des: Leslie Dilley. Ed: Jill Bilock. M: Thomas Newman. Costumes: Ruth Myers. (Universal/ Amblin Entertainment–UIP.) Rel: 14 June 1996. 116 mins. Cert 15. USA. 1995.

Crimes against nurture: Fairuza Balk and Harvey Keitel in Anthony Drazan's Imaginary Crimes *(from Warner)*

Imaginary Crimes

Unsavoury and awkwardly related fable in which a con man struggles to raise his two daughters in Portland, Oregon. Forever inventing 'revolutionary' gadgets that will make his fortune, Ray Weiler tramples over the dignity and hopes of his family with a trail of broken promises. While it's obvious why Harvey Keitel was attracted

Wake-up call: John Hannah and Annabella Sciorra uncover police corruption in Scott Michell's The Innocent Sleep *(from Starlight)*

to playing this blinkered failure, the actor's edge is repeatedly blunted by tasteful filters and soft, omnipresent music. It's not until the final reel that the film's emotional grip finally exerts itself.

Cast: Harvey Keitel (Ray Weiler), Fairuza Balk (Sonya Weiler), Kelly Lynch (Valery Weiler), Vincent D'Onofrio (Mr Webster), Chris Penn (Jarvis), Seymour Cassel (Ed-

Small wonder: Hal Scardino examines his new friend in Frank Oz's beguiling The Indian in the Cupboard *(from Columbia TriStar)*

die), Amber Benson (Margaret), Elisabeth Moss (Greta Weiler), Diane Baker (Abigale Tate), Richard Venture (Judge Klein), Tori Paul, Melissa Bernstein, Annette O'Toole, Bill Geisslinger, William Shilling, Chad Burton.

Dir: Anthony Drazan. Pro: James G. Robinson. Ex Pro: Gary Barber, Ted Field and Robert W. Cort. Screenplay: Kristine Johnson and Davia Nelson, based on the book by Sheila Ballantyne. Ph: John J. Campbell. Ed: Elizabeth King. Pro Des: Joseph T. Garrity. M: Stephen Endelman; numbers performed by The Skyliners, Bobby Day, Hank Thompson, Julie London ('June In January' and 'In The Middle Of A Kiss'), Jim Gatlin, etc. Costumes: Susan Lyall. (Morgan Creek–Warner.) Rel: 21 July 1995. 105 mins. Cert PG. USA. 1994.

The Indian in the Cupboard

Who knows what simple ingredients, when arbitrarily tossed together, can activate a whole new world? For nine-year-old Omri, it is a second-hand cupboard, a key given to his mother by his great-grandmother and a three-inch plastic Iroquois Indian. Together these inanimate objects cast a magic spell that brings the Indian to life in contemporary Brooklyn. Enchanted by his new miniature friend, Omri is propelled into the role of protector and father and quickly learns the responsibilities of playing god with real beings, however small. Utilising all the technical know-how of Industrial Light & Magic, *The Indian in the Cupboard* never pushes the special effects too far, other than to create a credible universe in which the boy and his proud lilliput-

ian companion can react. Rather, Melissa Mathieson's masterful adaptation of Lynne Reid Bank's successful children's book chooses to explore the wonder of its scenario, while slyly side-stepping the inherent cliches of the 'my little secret' genre. Surprisingly unsentimental (after all, Mathieson *did* script *E.T.*), the film addresses a number of important issues while never losing sight of its entertainment value.

Cast: Hal Scardino (Omri), Litefoot (Little Bear), Lindsay Crouse (Jane), Richard Jenkins (Victor), Rishi Bhat (Patrick), David Keith (Boone), Steve Coogan (Tommy Atkins), Sakina Jaffrey, Vincent Kartheiser, Nestor Serrano, Ryan Olson, Cassandra Brown, Christopher Moritz.

Dir: Frank Oz. Pro: Kathleen Kennedy, Frank Marshall and Jane Startz. Ex Pro: Bernie Williams, Robert Harris and Marty Keltz. Screenplay: Melissa Mathieson. Ph: Russell Carpenter. Pro Des: Leslie McDonald. Ed: Ian Crafford. M: Randy Edelman; numbers performed by Litefoot, Tracey Shenandoah, and Motley Crue. Costumes: Deborah L. Scott. Visual Effects/Animation: Industrial Light & Magic. (Paramount/Columbia/Kennedy/Marshall/Scholastic Prods–Columbia TriStar.) Rel: 22 December 1995. 96 mins. Cert PG. USA. 1995.

The Innocent Sleep

London; today. Following a night on the tiles, a young vagrant dosses down in a deserted warehouse by Tower Bridge and witnesses a gangland murder. Spotted by one of the assailants, he runs to the police – only to find the inspector in charge of the investigation is also the killer... A first-time production in the true sense of the phrase, this serviceable thriller marks the feature debut of the father-and-son producing-directing team of Rod Michell and Scott Michell, as well as of the cinematographer, writer, composer, etc. A polished, character-driven piece inspired by the suspicious circumstances surrounding the 'suicide' of the Vatican banker Roberto Calvi, *The Innocent Sleep* is to be commended for its brave casting-against-type and unusual London locations. However, a melodramatic score and ill-judged cockney villain from Michael Gambon strains credibility.

Cast: Rupert Graves (Alan Terry), Annabella Sciorra (Billie Hayman), Michael Gambon (Matheson), Graham Crowden (George), Franco Nero (Cavani),

John Hannah (James), Oliver Cotton (Lusano), Struan Rodger (Peter Samson), Peter Howells, Chris Jury, Crispin Redman, Stephen Yardley, Tony Bluto, Robert James, Susan Gilmore, Peter Cartwright, Peter Howell.

Dir: Scott Michell. Pro: Scott Michell and Matthew Vaughn. Ex Pro: Rod Michell. Line Pro: Michael Dreyer. Screenplay: Ray Villis. Ph: Alan Dunlop. Pro Des: Eve Mavrakis. Ed: Derek Trigg. M: Mark Ayres; 'Someone To Love' performed by East 17. Costumes: Stephanie Collie. (Timedial–Starlight.) Rel: 26 January 1996. 99 mins. Cert 15. UK. 1995.

Institute Benjamenta or This Dream People Call Human Life

This suspense feature debut by the Brothers Quay draws freely on Robert Walser's novella *Jakob von Gunten* but shows clearly why that work was an influence on Kafka. Jakob joins the institute of the title where servants are trained and is drawn to the proprietor's sister, Lisa, who responds with emotions which could bring her truly to life. Echoes of *Sleeping Beauty* don't prevent this tale taking on meaning as a wider comment on the nature of society in which power comes from control and represssion. More accessible than many of the short films by the Brothers Quay, but still demanding, the film is notable for its brilliantly textured black-and-white photography, its subtle music score and performances from Mark Rylance, Alice Krige and others which are not overwhelmed by their setting. [*Mansel Stimpson*]

Cast: Mark Rylance (Jakob von Gunten), Alice Krige (Lisa Benjamenta), Gottfried John (Johannes Benjamenta), Daniel Smith (Kraus), Joseph Alessi (Pepino), Jonathan Stone, Cesar Sarachu, Peter Lovstrom, Peter Whitfield.

Dir: Brothers Quay. Pro: Keith Griffiths and Janine Marmot. Co-Pro: Karl Baumgartner and Katsue Tomiyama. Screenplay: Alan Passes and Brothers Quay. Ph: Nic Knowland. Pro Des: Jennifer Kernke. Ed and Sound: Larry Sider. M: Lech Jankowski. Costumes: Nikky Gillibrand. (British Screen/Channel Four/Image Forum/Pandora Film–ICA Projects.) Rel: 17 November 1995. 104 mins. No Cert. UK. 1995.

In the Bleak Midwinter

With his career on the skids, actor Joe Harper decides to stage *Hamlet* at a

Putting the ham in Hamlet: John Sessions and Richard Briers as Gertrude and Claudius in Kenneth Branagh's dismal In the Bleak Midwinter *(from Rank)*

disused church where he grew up. With only his meagre savings to finance the production, Joe gathers around him a bunch of six losers to play all 24 roles in Shakespeare's play, leading to a showdown that will either destroy or liberate the assembled company. Wheeling out all the old caricatures of this over-fed genre – the screaming queen, alcoholic failure, bitter veteran, glitzy agent, campy costume designer – writer-director Kenneth Branagh has created a squelchy love note to the worse excesses and insanities of the theatre. Following inexplicable attacks on him in the media for egomania and 'luvviness', Branagh has picked up a red flag and waved it at his critics with this, his most navel-centric and self-indulgent film yet (shot in pretentious black and white, no less). Having said that, the film's dramatic moments do occasionally work, but for the most part this is a simply embarrassing comedy inviting a chorus of disapproval. Branagh, incidentally, is to play Hamlet himself in an imminent big-screen version.

Cast: Richard Briers (Henry Wakefield/Claudius), Hetta Charnley (Molly Harper), Joan Collins (Margaretta D'Arcy), Nick Farrell (Tom Newman/Laertes), Mark

The usual suspect: Femme fatale du jour Linda Fiorentino taunts her sleazy husband Chazz Palminteri in William Friedkin's jaded Jade *(from UIP)*

Brothers in arms: Allen Payne and Bokeem Woodbine flex their differences in Doug McHenry's overly familiar Jason's Lyric *(from Rank)*

Hadfield (Vernon Spatch/Polonius), Gerard Horan (Carnforth Greville Branch/ Horatio/Rosencrantz/ Guildenstern), Celia Imrie (Fadge), Michael Maloney (Joe Harper/ Hamlet), Julia Sawalha (Nina Raymond/Ophelia), John Sessions (Terry Du Bois/Gertrude), Jennifer Saunders (Nancy Crawford), Robert Hines, James D. White, Ann Davies, Brian Petifer, Patrick Doyle.

Dir and Screenplay: Kenneth Branagh. Pro: David Barron. Assoc Pro: Iona Price and Tamar Thomas. Ph: Roger Lanser. Ed: Neil Farrell. Pro Des: Tim Harvey. M: Jimmy Yuill. Costumes: Caroline Harris. (Castle Rock/Midwinter Films–Rank.) Rel: 1 December 1995. 99 mins. Cert 15. UK. 1995.

Intimate With a Stranger

Los Angeles; now. Disillusioned with a future in philosophy, Jack Hawkins switches from the cerebral to the carnal to make his living, setting himself up as a gigolo, catering to a variety of women as emotionally lost as himself. Truly abysmal attempt to insert some intellectual class into an erotic scenario, this would-be *sex, lies and videotape* is emasculated by appalling acting, iffy production values and cod philosophy. Has sex ever been so boring? Not surprisingly, first-time director/co-writer Mel Woods has had no previous film-making experience. [*Ewen Brownrigg*]

Cast: Roderick Mangin Turner (Jack Hawkins), Daphne Nayar (Michelle), Janis Lee (Summer), Amy Tolsky (Carol), El-

lenor Wilkinson (Vicki), Lorelie King (Ellen), Darcy Ferrer (Barbara), Kaethe Cherney, Colleen Passard, Sara Mason, Francesca Wilde.

Dir: Mel Woods. Pro: Roderick Mangin Turner. Line Pro: Deborah Thompson. Screenplay: Woods and Turner. Ph: Nicholas Tebbet. Ed: Brian Smedley-Aston. Pro Des: Graeme Story. M: Ledsam & Pugh. Costumes: Tabitha Doyle. (Independent International Pictures.) Rel: 11 August 1995. 94 mins. Cert 18. UK. 1994.

Jade

San Francisco; the present. Accompanied by the orchestral hysteria of James Horner's score, an eminent millionaire is hacked to death in his stately home. Assistant DA David Corelli discovers that the fingerprints of an old flame, Trina Gavin, are all over the murder weapon. Worse still, she has a motive and no alibi. Luckily, she is married to the celebrated defence attorney Matt Gavin, who is determined to fight her case. Of course, she's innocent – she looks too guilty not to be. Paramount paid $2.5 million for Joe Eszterhas's two-page outline, and that's exactly what the film looks like: an outline. William Friedkin dresses up the action with desperate cinematic flourishes, but no amount of gloss can disguise the cold, calculating nature of this jaded piece of plotting. Characters who didn't speak in sound bites would've been nice.

Cast: David Caruso (David Corelli), Linda Fiorentino (Trina Gavin), Chazz Palminteri (Matt Gavin), Michael Biehn (Bob Hargrove), Richard Crenna (Governor Edwards), Donna Murphy (Karen Heller), Ken King (Petey Vasko), Angie Everhart (Patrice Jacinto), Holt McCallany, David Hunt, Kevin Tighe, Jay Jacobus, Drew Snyder, Darryl Chan, Ron Ulstad, Olimpia Saravia, Victor Wong.

Dir: William Friedkin. Pro: Robert Evans, Craig Baumgarten and Gary Adelson. Ex Pro: William J. McDonald. Screenplay: Joe Eszterhas. Ph: Andrzej Bartkowiak. Ed: Augie Hess. Pro Des: Alex Tavoularis. M: James Horner. Costumes: Marilyn Vance. (Paramount–UIP.) Rel: 3 November 1995. 95 mins. Cert 18. USA. 1995.

Jason's Lyric

Familiar good brother/bad brother tale, in which an honest, upright (and athletic) Joe is plagued by flashbacks of his father's death. Like many characters of literature, Jason Alexander (no relation to the actor-director) must choose between family duty and his new love, the lyrically named Lyric (Jada Pinkett). Lyric seems by far the better option, as whenever she's on screen there's sweet music, sunsets, flowers and butterflies. But when Jason's brother Josh turns up, it's time for blood, guns, profanity and urban decay. Mawkish, profane, hackneyed.

Cast: Allen Payne (Jason Alexander), Jada Pinkett (Lyric Greer), Forest Whitaker ('Maddog' Alexander), Bokeem Woodbine (Joshua Alexander) Suzzanne Douglas (Gloria Alexander), Anthony 'Treach' Criss (Alonzo), Lisa Carson (Marti), Eddie Griffin, Lahmard Tate, Clarence Whitmore, Asheamu Earl Randle.

Dir: Doug McHenry. Pro: McHenry and George Jackson. Co-Pro: Dwight Williams and Bobby Smith Jr. Ex Pro: Suzanne Broderick and Clarence Avant. Screenplay: Smith Jr. Ph: Francis Kenny. Ed: Andrew Mondshein. Pro Des: Simon Dobbin. M: Afrika and Matt Noble. (PolyGram/Propaganda Films–Rank.) Rel: 7 June 1995. 119 mins. Cert 18. USA. 1994.

Jeanne la Pucelle - Joan of Arc

Filmed on a budget that couldn't cover the cost of one battle scene from *Braveheart*, Jacques Rivette's minimalist biography of Joan of Arc fails to grip, inspire or convince. Soldiers and peasants stand around uncomfortably looking like waxworks in a museum, while the comically understaffed battle sequences are cut off with captions declaring, 'and many died that night'. Attempting to show the human face of Joan, Rivette is rewarded with a commanding, sparky performance from the ethereal Sandrine Bonnaire, but the rest of his cast blend into the aged stonework (actually, it's unlikely that the houses and castles looked that old in the 15th century). Ingrid Bergman, Michele Morgan, Jean Seberg and other previous Joans should lose little sleep. Incidentally, this four hour version (shown in two parts, *Les Batailles* and *Les Prisons*) has been cut by almost two hours from the French original.

Cast: Sandrine Bonnaire (Jeanne La Pucelle), Jean-Marie Richier (Durand Laxart), Baptiste Roussillon (Baudricourt), Jean-Luc Petit (Henri Le Royer), Olivier Cruveiller (Jean de Metz), Andre Marcon (Charles, Dauphin of France), Bernard Sobel (Pierre de Versailles), Guy Martinez (Pierre Seguin), Martine Pascal (Yolande d'Aragon), Patrick Le Mauff (Jean, Batard of Orleans), Florence Darel (Jeanne

Following her faith: Sandrine Bonnaire rides into battle in Jacques Rivette's torpid Jeanne la Pucelle *(from Artificial Eye/Mayfair Film)*

d'Orleans), Quentin Ogier (Raymond), Stephane Boucher (La Hire), Francois Chattot (Arthur de Richemont), Jean-Pierre Becker (Jean d'Aulon), Nathalie Richard (Catherine de la Rochelle), Philippe Morier-Genoud (Philippe the Good, Duke of Burgundy), Michel Berto (Guillaume Erard).

Love means never having to say you're positive: Steven Weber and Michael T. Weiss work up a sweat in Christopher Ashley's Jeffrey *(from Film Four Distributors Ltd)*

Dir: Jacques Rivette. Pro: Martine Marignac. Ex Pro: Pierre Grise. Screenplay: Pascal Bonitzer and Christine Laurent. Ph: William Lubtchanskuy. Ed: Nicole Lubtchanskuy. Pro Des: Manu de Chauvigny. M: Jordi Savall. Costumes: Laurent. (La Sept Cinema/France 3 Cinema/Canal Plus–Artificial Eye.) Rel: 1 September 1995. 240 mins. Cert PG. France. 1994.

Jeffrey

New York; today. Fed up with the rigours of safe sex, gay waiter and struggling actor Jeffrey opts for a life of celibacy. But as he strives to channel his energies into more positive directions, he becomes a bystander to the

Giving head: Keanu Reeves loans out his cerebrum in Robert Longo's chaotic Johnny Mnemonic *(from Fox)*

real issues of gay ideology and denies himself the very essence of life. Ten years ago Aids was too new, too terrifying and too apocalyptic to laugh at. But time has a habit of fine-tuning all viewpoints and this flipside to such Aids documents as *The Normal Heart* and *Longtime Companion* – adapted by Paul Rudnick from his own Obie-winning play – addresses a number of

'I knew you'd say that': Sylvester Stallone doles out the wit in Danny Cannon's Judge Dread*ful (from Guild)*

vital questions with the refreshing perspective of humour. Briskly paced by the play's original director and acted by an outstanding cast, *Jeffrey* introduces a welcome element of wit – while never balking from the task of making us think twice.

Cast: Steven Weber (Jeffrey), Patrick Stewart (Sterling), Michael T. Weiss (Steve Howard), Bryan Batt (Darius), Sigourney Weaver (Debra Moorhouse), Irma St Paule (Mother Teresa), Robert Klein (Skip Winkley), Peter Maloney (dad), Debra Monk (mom), Nathan Lane (Father Dan), Olympia Dukakis (Mrs Marcangelo), Gregory Jbara (Angelique), Nicky Paraiso, Patrick Kerr, Peter Bartlett, Christine Baranski, Victor Garber, Camryn Man-

heim, Kathy Najimy, J. Smith Cameron, Ethan Phillips, Nancy Ticotin, Michael Duvert, Alice Drummond.

Dir: Christopher Ashley. Pro: Mark Balsam, Mitchell Maxwell and Victoria Maxwell. Ex Pro: Kevin McCollum. Co-Ex Pro: Dan Markely, Andrea Pines and Mike Skipper. Line Pro: Harry Knapp. Screenplay and Co-Pro: Paul Rudnick. Ph: Jeffrey Tufano. Pro Des: Michael Johnston. Ed: Cara Silverman. M: Stephen Endelman. Choreography: Jerry Mitchell. (Workin' Man Films/The Booking Office–Film Four Distributors Ltd.) Rel: 22 March 1996. 92 mins. Cert 18. USA. 1995.

Johnny Mnemonic

2021; Beijing/The Free City of Newark. A courier of the future jettisons his childhood memories to make cerebral space for top-secret coded information – fed into a computer chip in his brain. Then, during a power struggle between the Yakuza and Chinese Mafia, Johnny Mnemonic is overloaded with crucial data that everybody wants a byte of. Johnny's got a headache – but is there anywhere safe that he can download his software? Based on cyberpunk William Gibson's ingenious short story, *Johnny Mnemonic* is a frantic mess, a collision of ideas and technology that fails to grab a foothold on cohesion. Still, a film that features Keanu Reeves, a rap star, Japanese film director, Swedish karate champion, rock 'n' roll singer, Fassbinder protegeé and a dolphin cannot be dismissed lightly. And Keanu Reeves screaming for room service in a dystopian landscape must go down in history as one of the greatest moments of cod cinema.

Cast: Keanu Reeves (Johnny), Dolph Lundgren (Street Preacher), Takeshi (Takahashi), Ice-T (J-Bone), Dina Meyer (Jane), Henry Rollins (Spider), Barbara Sukowa (Anna K), Denis Akiyama (Shinji), Udo Kier (Ralfi), Tracy Tweed, Falconer Abraham, Don Francks, Diego Chambers, Susan Tsagkaris, Robin Crosby.

Dir: Robert Longo. Pro: Don Carmody. Ex Pro: Robert Lantos, Victoria Hamburg and B.J. Rack. Supervising Pro: Jean Desormeaux. Screenplay: William Gibson. Ph: Francois Protat. Pro Des: Nilo Rodis Jamero. Ed: Ronald Sanders. M: Brad Fidel; numbers performed by KMFDM, Orbital, Helmet, Bono and The Edge, Stabbing Westward, Rollins Band, God Lives Underwater, and Cop Shoot Cop. Costumes: Olga Dimitrov. Visual Consultant: Syd Mead. Japanese Interpreter: Ayana Osada. (Peter Hoffman and Staffan

Game for a laugh: Robin Williams (seen here with Bonnie Hunt) is floored by the special effects in Joe Johnston's frenetic Jumanji *(from Columbia TriStar)*

Ahrenberg/Alliance Communications–Fox.) Rel: 9 February 1996. 96 mins. Cert 15. USA. 1995.

Judge Dredd

In the year 2139 AD crime has become so rampant that an elite corps of law enforcers – the judges – have been bestowed with the power to act as instantaneous judge, jury and executioner. In the giant metropolis of Mega City One (population: 65 million), formerly known as New York, one such lawman has become a legend in his own time: Judge Dredd. Then, as Joe Dredd starts showing signs of megalomania, he is framed on a murder charge – just when the Big Apple needs him the most ... The main competitor of *Batman Forever* in the box-office wars of the summer of '95, this $80m behemoth based on the 2000 AD comic strip at least has the semblance of a story and a recognisable sense of humour. However, it is nowhere near

as funny as *Demolition Man* or as atmospheric as *Blade Runner*, two films it superficially resembles. Nobody can accuse Sylvester Stallone of being a great thespian, but he reaches new depths here with an exaggerated snarl and a walk that suggests painful constipation. Armand Assante as the criminal mastermind is not much better, while such predictable acting choices as Max Von Sydow and Jurgen Prochnow play out their roles along the dotted line. Nigel Phelps's production design is the real star, although Mega City One looks like a huge set with digital enhancement.

Cast: Sylvester Stallone (Judge Joseph Dredd), Armand Assante (Rico), Diane Lane (Judge Hershey), Rob Schneider (Fergie), Joan Chen (Ilsa), Jurgen Prochnow (Judge Griffin), Max Von Sydow (Judge Fargo), Joanna Miles (McGruder), Balthazar Getty (Olmeyer), Maurice Roeves (Miller), Ian Dury, Chris Adamson, Ewen Bremner, Peter Marinker, Angus MacInnes, Louise Delamere, Pat Starr, Mitchell Ryan, James Remar, James Earl Jones (narrator).
    Dir: Danny Cannon. Pro: Charles M. Lippincott and Beau E.L. Marks. Ex Pro: Andrew G. Vajna and Edward R. Pressman.

Assoc Pro: Tony Munafo and Susan Nicoletti. Screenplay: William Wisher and Steven E. de Souza, from a story by Wisher and Michael De Luca. Ph: Adrian Biddle. Ed: Alex Mackie and Harry Keramidas. Pro Des: Nigel Phelps. M: Alan Silvestri; numbers performed by The Cure, The The, Cocteau Twins, White Zombie, and Leftfield. Costumes: Emma Porteous. Visual Effects: Joel Hynek. Dredd armour: Gianni Versace. (Cinergi–Guild.) Rel: 21 July 1995. 96 mins. Cert 15. USA. 1995.

Jumanji

When young Alan Parrish unearths an arcane board game from a building site, he is transported into a terrifying world in which no normal laws apply. Anything, it seems, can happen, and soon the game's characters – giant mosquitoes, malevolent monkeys, a ferocious lion, a herd of rhino and a deadly big game hunter – are rampaging all over the quiet New Hampshire town. The art is to stay alive long enough to work out the rules ... Based on the best-selling children's book by Chris Van Allsburg, this is very much a rollercoaster ride for older children and adults. The special effects are truly exhilarating, but being the creation of

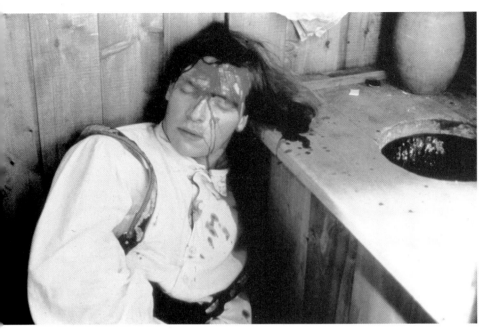

Enigma of the chattering classes: Andre Eiserman, as Kaspar Hauser, becomes a victim of his own celebrity (from Arrow)

a board game they are never too realistic for comfort.

Cast: Robin Williams (Alan Parrish), Bonnie Hunt (Sarah Whittle), Kirsten Dunst (Judy Shepherd), Bradley Pierce (Peter Shepherd), Bebe Neuwirth (Aunt Nora), David Alan Grier (Carl Bentley), Jonathan Hyde (Sam Parrish/Van Pelt), Adam Hann-Byrd (young Alan Parrish), Laura Bell Bundy (young Sarah Whittle), Patricia Clarkson (Carol Parrish), James Handy, Gillian Barber, Brandon Obray, Malcolm Stewart, Annabel Kershaw, Frank Welker.
  Dir: Joe Johnston. Pro: Scott Kroopf and William Teitler. Ex Pro: Ted Field, Robert W. Cort and Larry J. Franco. Screenplay: Jonathan Hensleigh, Greg Taylor and Jim Strain, from a story by Taylor, Strain and Chris Van Allsburg. Ph: Thomas Ackerman. Pro Des: James Bissell. Ed: Robert Dalva. M: James Horner; Rossini, Dvorak; 'Locomotive Breath' performed by Jethro Tull. Costumes: Martha Wynne Snetsinger. Visual Effects: Stephen L. Price and Ken Ralston. Animatronics: Alec Gillis and Tom Woodruff Jr. (TriStar/ Interscope Communications/Teitler Film–Columbia TriStar.) Rel: 16 February 1996. 100 mins. Cert PG. USA. 1995.

The Juror

New York; 1995. An avant-garde sculptress and single mother, Annie Laird is pressurised to single-handedly hang a jury and then acquit the defendant in the trial of a notorious mobster. Threatened with the death of her beloved son, Annie has no choice but to compromise her principles ... Given the melodramatic nature of its subject and its eerie similarities to the 1994 thriller *Trial by Jury* (see *Film Review 1995-6*), *The Juror* is an effective psychological chiller buoyed by two polished performances from its A-list stars. However, it is Ted Tally's accomplished script, Jamie Anderson's wide-screen photography and some wonderful supporting performances (particularly from Anne Heche, James Gandolfini and Frances Foster) that nudges this above the run-of-the-mill. Tally, incidentally, won an Oscar for his screenplay to *The Silence of the Lambs*.

Cast: Demi Moore (Annie Laird), Alec Baldwin (The Teacher), Joseph Gordon-Levitt (Oliver Laird), Anne Heche (Juliet), James Gandolfini (Eddie), Lindsay Crouse (Tallow), Tony Lo Bianco (Louie Boffano), Michael Constantine (Judge Weitzel), Matt Craven (Boone), Michael Rispoli (Joseph Boffano), Matthew Cowles (Rodney), Todd Susman, Julie Halston, Frank Adonis, Polly Adams, Jack Gilpin, Tom Signorelli, Frances Foster, Chuck Zito, Anne Bobby, Fiona Gallagher.
  Dir: Brian Gibson. Pro: Irwin Winkler and Rob Cowan. Ex Pro: Patrick McCormick. Screenplay: Ted Tally, based on the book by George Dawes Green. Ph: Jamie Anderson. Pro Des: Jan Roelfs. Ed: Robert Reitano. M: James Newton Howard; 'The Sidewinder Sleeps Tonite' performed by REM. Costumes: Colleen Atwood. (Columbia Pictures–Columbia TriStar.) Re: 14 June 1996. 118 mins. Cert 18. USA. 1996.

Kaspar Hauser - Verbrechen am Seelenleben eines Menschens

It seems that every country has its national enigma (ours being Jack the Ripper), but few have been as perplexing as the case of Kaspar Hauser, the 16-year-old boy who, in 1828, appeared out of nowhere in the marketplace of Nuremberg. Werner Herzog had his own crack at the story in 1974, artfully casting the authentically curious Bruno S in the title part. This version concentrates on the 'boy born to be king' theory, and makes a compelling and convincing case. In an attempt to sever the line to the throne of Baden, the baby crown prince is swapped with the terminally ill child of a servant woman. Locked away in a cellar, Kaspar is deprived of light, comfort and human contact. Then, 12 years later, he is dumped in Nuremberg unable to walk, talk or comprehend the sudden beauty and cruelty of the world around him. Taken in by a caring professor, Kaspar gradually becomes the toast of Europe, a man-child at the mercy of every temptation and the whim of those out to exploit him... An interesting companion piece to the Australian *Bad Boy Bubby*.

Cast: Andre Eiserman (Kaspar Hauser), Udo Samel (Tutor Daumer), Jeremey Clyde (Lord Stanhope), Katharina Thalbach (Grafin Hochberg), Cecile Paoli (Stefanie von Baden), Anja Schiller (Sophie von Baden), Uew Ochsenknecht (Ludwig von Baden), Dieter Laser (Ludwig I. von Bayern), Tilo Nest (Carl von Baden), Hansa Czypionka, Herann Beyer, Dieter Mann, Peter Lohmeyer, Valerie Vail, Jan Skvar, Jennifer Chamberlain.
  Dir and Screenplay: Peter Sehr. Pro: Andreas Meyer. Ph: Gernot Roll. Ed: Susanne Hartmann. Pro Des: O. Jochen Schmidt and Karel Vacek. M: Nikos Mamangakis. Costumes: Diemut Remy. (Multimedia Munchen–Arrow.) Rel: 17 November 1995. 125 mins. Cert 18. Germany. 1993.

Katia Ismailova - Podmoskovnye Vechera

Married to the nerdish son of Irina Dmitrievna, a top-selling Russian novelist, Katia Ismailova types out the manuscripts of her mother-in-law with resigned good nature. Yet beneath her impenetrable calm lies a well of untapped emotion. When the Dmitri-evnas' handyman, the dashing Sergey, seduces Katia on a fateful, rain-swept night, he inadvertently sets in motion a string of calamitous events ... It's extraordinary how different people perceive the same film. *Katia Ismailova* has been described as both a picture about 'violent passion' and as 'a wearying watch'. As usual, the truth falls somewhere in between. Katia herself, numbed by the mediocrity of typing out the grim prose of her mother-in-law, craves a life of palpable adventure. When she's (reluctantly) seduced by the handyman, she sees an outlet. However, her homicidal actions are not mere crimes of passion, but meditative acts of almost subliminal angst. We are in Russia, after all. Relayed with admirable simplicity, Katia's story unfolds in deliberate, atmospheric strokes, the action never sensationalised nor over-explained. Yet while the surface belies a studied calm, the subtext seethes with turmoil. Aka *Moscow Nights*.

Cast: Ingeborga Dapkounaite (Katia Ismailova), Alice Friendlikh (Irina Dmitrievna), Vladimir Machkov (Sergey), Alexandre Feklistov (Mitia), Youri Kouznetsov (Romanov), Natali Tchoukina (Sonia), Avangard Leontive (editor).

Dir: Valeri Todorovski. Pro: Marc Ruscart and Igor Tolstounov. Ex Pro: Alexandre Gnedenko and Mikhail Zonenechvili. Screenplay: Alla Krinitsina, Francois Guerif and Cecile Vargaftig, based on the novel by Marina Cheptounova and Stanislav Govourkhine. Ph: Serguei Kozlov. Pro Des and Costumes: Alexandre Ossipov. Ed: Helene Gagarine and Alla Strelnikova. M: Leonid Deciatnikov. (Studiia TTL/Les Films–Metro Tartan.) Rel: 2 February 1996. 88 mins. Cert 18. France/Russia. 1994.

Kids

New York; today. Unemployed and unsupervised, 17-year-old Telly is a self-styled 'virgin surgeon' whose hobby is deflowering underage virgins. Although physically unprepossessing, Telly has a knack for turning on an engaging sincerity when it suits him and is managing to spread more than disillusionment among the trail of broken hearts he leaves behind. Utilising a pseudo-documentary style, first-time

director and acclaimed photographer Larry Clark certainly brings an edge of naturalism to his grim story. For once the kids on screen (all non-professionals) look their age (if not younger) and act with startling spontaneity and candour. If nothing else, Clark shows an

Typecast: Ingeborga Dapkounaite takes to her keys in Valeri Todorovski's Katia Ismailova *(from Metro Tartan)*

Mouthing off: Sarah Henderson and Leo Fitzpatrick indulge in adult pleasures in Larry Clark's headline-grabbing Kids *(from Electric)*

Louder than words: Rosana Pastor and Marc Martinez in Ken Loach's highly acclaimed Land and Freedom *(from Artificial Eye)*

extraordinary ability for coaxing credible performances from his young cast who behave as if they're completely unaware of the camera. As it happens, the film is meticulously scripted, brazenly chronicling the malaise of a juvenile subculture with easy access to drugs, alcohol and willing sexual partners. A terrifying, eye-opening call-to-arms for parents everywhere, *Kids* is a prime example of an art form serving to reflect contemporary mores and stimulate debate. FYI: Clark, now 52, once served 19 months in prison for 'assault and battery with a deadly weapon with intent to kill'.

Cast: Leo Fitzpatrick (Telly), Chloe Sevigny (Jennie), Justin Pierce (Casper), Yakira Peguero (Darcy), Rosario Dawson (Ruby), Sarah Henderson, Sajan Bhagat, Billy Valdes, Julia Stube-Glorhus, Harold Hunter, Joe Abrahams, Michele Lockwood.
  Dir: Larry Clark. Pro: Cary Woods. Ex Pro: Gus Van Sant, Patrick Panzarella and Michael Chambers. Co-Pro: Cathy Konrad, Christine Vachon and Lauren Za-

laznick. Ph: Eric Alan Edwards. Pro Des: Kevin Thompson. Ed: Chris Tellefson. M: Louis Barlow; numbers performed by The Beastie Boys, Average White Band, Nine, Sonny Rollins, Brand Nubian, The Crooklyn Dodgers, Sebadoh, John Coltrane, A Tribe Called Quest, E Rule, O.C., etc. Costumes: Kim Druce. (Shining Excalibur/ Independent Pictures/The Guys Upstairs– Electric.) Rel: 17 May 1996. 93 mins. Cert 18. USA. 1995.

Land and Freedom

Fired up by a lecture given by the communist party, an out-of-work Liverpudlian decides to join the fight against fascism in the Spanish Civil War. Yet while the struggle gives David a focus in his life, he is never entirely sure who – or why – he is fighting. Heavily praised at Cannes, Ken Loach's humanist tract on the Spanish Civil War is remarkable for its immediacy, in spite of the odd, ill-judged lapse into slow-motion. The film is also frequently wordy and extended discussions on the war hint at facile exposition. A long-cherished project for Loach and his scriptwriter Jim Allen (*Hidden Agenda*, *Raining Stones*), *Land and Freedom* encapsulates the futility of

the Spanish conflict even though, ultimately, it falls down as human drama. The dramatic centre piece - the first battle – is the film's *coup de theatre*: here there is no comforting orchestra, just the sound of shouting, sobbing men and the whistle of bullets.

Cast: Ian Hart (David), Rosana Pastor (Blanca), Iciar Bollain (Maite), Tom Gilroy (Lawrence), Marc Martinez (Vidal), Frederic Pierrot (Bernard), Angela Clarke (Kitty), Raffaele Cantatore, Paul Laverty, Jurgen Muller, Emili Sampler, Suzanne Maddock, Mandy Walsh, Miguel Cabrillana, Jordi Dauder, Pep Molina.
  Dir: Ken Loach. Pro: Rebecca O'Brien. Ex Pro: Sally Hibbin, Gerardo Herrero and Ulrich Felsberg. Assoc Pro: Marta Esteban. Screenplay: Jim Allen. Ph: Barry Ackroyd. Ed: Jonathan Morris. Pro Des: Martin Johnson. M: George Fenton. Costumes: Ana Alvargonzalez. (British Screen/Television Espanola/Canal Plus/BBC Films/Parallax Pictures/Messidor Films/Road Movies– Artificial Eye.) Rel: 6 October 1995. 109 mins. Cert 15. UK/Spain/Germany. 1995.

Last of the Dogmen

Montana; today. Haunted by the death of his wife in a drowning accident, Lewis Gates has resorted to the bottle, but, 'drunk or sober,' says his

Sharing the wilderness: Tom Berenger and Barbara Hershey find themselves reluctantly drawn to each other in Tab Murphy's Last of the Dogmen *(from Guild). Incidentally, Murphy also co-scripted Disney's* The Hunchback of Notre Dame

father-in-law, Sheriff Deegan, he's 'still the best bounty hunter there is.' Gates prefers to think of himself as a civil servant, but he agrees to hunt down a trio of escaped convicts in the Montana wilderness when he's threatened with disciplinary action for breaching the local 'leash laws'. Then, in the forest – '4,000 square miles of the roughest country ever put on a map' – he and his faithful Australian Cattle Dog discover the aftermath of a bloodbath. And only a Cheyenne arrowhead remains of the massacre ... Boasting a terrific concept and some of the most breathtaking scenery of North America ever captured on film, *Last of the Dogmen* ravishes the eye, stirs the blood and ignites the imagination. Inspired by actual historical documentation, former forestry scholar Tab Murphy wrote this screenplay 15 years ago (before receiving an Oscar nomination for co-scripting *Gorillas in*

the Mist). Filmed in the Canadian Rockies and at the Zempoala National Park south of Mexico City.

Cast: Tom Berenger (Lewis Gates), Barbara Hershey (Professor Lillian Sloan), Kurtwood Smith (Sheriff Deegan), Steve Reevis (Yellow Wolf), Andrew Miller (Briggs), Gregory Scott Cummins (Sears), Mark Boone Jr (Tattoo), Dawn Lavand (Indian girl), Helen Calahasen, Eugene Blackbear, Sidel Standing Elk, Molly Parker, Parley Baer, Anthony Holland, Graham Jarvis, Zip (Zip), Wilford Brimley (narrator).
    Dir: Tab Murphy. Pro: Joel B. Michaels. Ex Pro: Mario Kassar. Assoc Pro: Don Heitzer. Ph: Karl Walter Lindenlaub. Pro Des: Trevor Williams. Ed: Richard Halsey. M: David Arnold. Costumes: Elsa Zamparelli. (Carolco/Savoy–Guild.) Rel: 14 June 1996. 117 mins. Cert PG. USA. 1995.

The Lawnmower Man 2: Beyond Cyberspace

Los Angeles – the future. Jobe Smith, the antichrist of computer nerds, may have had his chips at the end of *The Lawnmower Man*, but thanks to the miracles of virtual reality he is painstakingly reconstructed – and ends up looking like a bald version of Max Headroom's Matt Frewer (which must come as a shock when you used

to look like Jeff Fahey). Unhinged by this cosmetic turnaround, Jobe embarks on his plan to colonise the world's computer networks, enabling him to control the military, global currency and any other perks he can think of. Building on the premise of the first film and expanding it from there, *Beyond Cyberspace* is a perfect example of what a sequel should be: an extension of the original. However, the script itself is so poorly developed that the lapses in logic and credibility reduce this to bargain basement video fodder. Good special effects, though. Budget: $20 million (twice that of the original).

Cast: Patrick Bergen (Benjamin Trace), Matt Frewer (Jobe Smith), Austin O'Brien (Peter Parkette), Ely Pouget (Dr Cori Platt), Camille Cooper (Jennifer), Kevin Conway (Jonathan Walker), Crystal Celeste Grant (Jade), Richard Fancy (Senator Greenspan), Patrick La Brecque, Sean Parhm, Trever O'Brien, Amanda Hillwood, John Benjamin Martin.
    Dir and Screenplay: Farhad Mann, from a story by Mann and Michael Miner, based on *The Lawnmower Man* by Brett Leonard and Gimel Everett. Pro: Edward Simons and Keith Fox. Ex Pro: Steve Lane, Robert Pringle, Peter McRae, Clive Turner and Avram Butch Kaplan. Ph: Ward Russell. Pro Des: Ernest Roth. Ed: Peter Berger and

Message in a bottle: Nicolas Cage in his award-laden role, in Mike Figgis's heavily stylised Leaving Las Vegas *(from Entertainment)*

Joel Goodman. M: Robert Folk. Costumes: Deborah Everton. Digital Visual Effects: Cinesite. (Allied Entertainment/Fuji Eight-First Independent.) Rel: 29 March 1996. 92 mins. Cert 12. USA. 1995.

Leaving Las Vegas

With his career in tatters and his marriage a thing of the past, Hollywood scriptwriter and alcoholic Ben Sanderson decides to drink himself to death in Las Vegas. Resigned to his fate, Ben experiences an unexpected release and it is his carefree disposition that draws Sera, a prostitute, into his life. Accepting each other for who they are, Ben and Sera embark on a romance to the death ... Exploring the complex nature of human attraction, director Mike Figgis has coaxed naked performances out of his two stars, but has directed the film like a stylised slice of film noir. Thus, while we cannot but

admire the filmmaking process, the tortured souls of these pathetic people escape our deeper sympathies. Based on the semi-autobiographical book by John O'Brien, who killed himself two weeks after selling the movie rights. According to O'Brien's father, the novel was his son's suicide note.

Cast: Nicolas Cage (Ben Sanderson), Elisabeth Shue (Sera), Julian Sands (Yuri), Richard Lewis (Peter), Valeria Golino (Terri), Steven Weber, Kim Adams, Emily Procter, Stuart Regen, Holly, Carey Lowell, Anne Lange, Thomas Kopache, Vincent Ward, Lucinda Jenney, Ed Lauter, Mike Figgis, R. Lee Ermey, Mariska Hargitay, Danny Huston, Laurie Metcalf, David Brisbin, Shawnee Smith, Paul Quinn, Julian Lennon, Bob Rafelson, Susan Barnes, Marc Coppola, Xander Berkeley, Lou Rawls.

Dir, Screenplay and M: Mike Figgis, from the novel by John O'Brien; numbers performed by Sting, Michael McDonald, Don Henley, Nicolas Cage, and The Palladinos. Pro: Lila Cazes and Annie Stewart. Ex Pro: Paige Simpson and Stuart Regen. Ph: Declan Quinn. Pro Des: Waldemar Kalinowski. Ed: John Smith. Costumes: Laura Goldsmith and Vivienne Westwood. Drinking coach: Tony Dingman. (Initial–Entertainment.) Rel: 19 January 1996. 112 mins. Cert 18. USA. 1995.

The Life and Extraordinary Adventures of Private Ivan Chonkin

Set shortly before the Second World War in Stalinist Russia, this adaptation of Vladimir Voinovich's acclaimed novel (smuggled out of Russia in 1968, resulting in Voinovich's persecution at the hands of the authorities), *Ivan Chonkin* is a simple delight that gathers comic momentum as it trundles along. Assigned to guard a broken-down plane in the remote community of Red End (formerly Dead End), the doltish Private Ivan Chonkin soon takes advantage of the ample charms of a farm girl and becomes a catalyst in the hamlet's shaky political bureaucracy. But, when push comes to shove, Chonkin turns out to be every bit a hero – even if the army has forgotten him. Taking enormous delight in reflecting the absurdities of the Communist regime in the simple confusion of these rural folk, director Jiri Menzel has created a work of enormous charm and humanism. Deceptively straightforward in its execution, the film exercises a fine satirical bite. Menzel, incidentally, is the acclaimed Czech director of such films as *Closely Observed Trains*,

Royal academy: Liesel Matthews adds more than a hint of blue blood to Miss Minchin's School For Girls in Alfonso Cuaron's magical A Little Princess *(from Warner)*

Problems in the garden of Communism: Alexei Zharkov and Zoya Buryak fight amid the tomato plants in Jiri Menzel's engaging The Life and Extraordinary Adventures of Private Ivan Chonkin *(from Portobello Pictures)*

Capricious Summer and *My Sweet Little Village.*

Cast: Gennadiy Nazarov (Ivan Chonkin), Zoya Buryak (Nyura), Vladimir Ilyin (Golubev), Valeriy Zolotukhin (Kilin), Alexei Zharkov (Gladyshev), Yuriy Dubrovin (Volkov), Sergei Stepanchenko, Sergei Garmash, Zinoviy Gerdt, Marian Labuda, Maria Vinogradova, Tatyana Gerbachevskaya, Vyacheslav Molokov.

Dir: Jiri Menzel. Pro: Eric Abraham. Co-Pro: Katya Krausova. Screenplay: Zdenek Sverek and Vladimir Voinovich. Ph: Jaromir Sofr. Ed: Juri Brozek. Pro Des: Milan Bycek. M: Jiri Sust. Costumes: Irina Ginno. (Portobello Pictures/MK2/Canal Plus/La Sept Cinema/CNC/Fandango/Kable Plus/Studio 89/KF/Trite/Channel Four–Portobello Pictures.) Rel: 27 October 1995. 104 mins. Cert 15. UK/France/Italy/Czech Republic/Russia. 1994.

A Little Princess

1914; New York. Having enjoyed an idyllic life in India, young Sara Crewe is moved to the imposing Miss Minchin's School For Girls in New York when her father is called off to war. Instantly winning friends with her romantic tales of India (and her insistence that all little girls are princesses), Sara finds her fortunes dramatically altered with the news of her father's death... Following the success of *The Secret Garden*, from the 1911 novel by Frances Hodgson Burnett, Warner Brothers quickly greenlighted this adaptation of Burnett's 1905 story. While sharing numerous comparisons to the former film (a ten-year-old girl from India is left to fend for herself at a forbidding foreign establishment,

Focal hero: Ted Danson and James Frain zoom in on the myth of Loch Ness *(from PolyGram)*

forcing her to fall back on her imagination and transforming the lives of those around her in the process), *A Little Princess* glides head and shoulders over its predecessor. In spite of the odd concession to its limited budget (a motionless Atlantic, shaky studio walls), this is a captivating, deeply moving dramatisation of a wonderful story. From the beguiling central performance of Liesel Matthews to the exquisite score (a rare thing in Hollywood), *A Little Princess* conveys just the right balance of fantasy and realism and should entrance generations to come. Previously filmed in 1917 with Mary Pickford and in 1939 with Shirley Temple.

Cast: Eleanor Bron (Miss Minchin), Liam Cunningham (Captain Crewe/Prince Rama), Liesel Matthews (Sara Crewe), Rusty Schwimmer (Amelia Minchin), Arthur Malet (Charles Randolph), Vanessa Lee Chester (Becky), Errol Sitahal (Ram Dass), Heather DeLoach (Ermengarde), Taylor Fry (Lavinia), Alison Moir (Princess

Sita), Time Winters (Frances the Milkman), Kelsey Mulrooney, Lomax Study, Vincent Schiavelli.

Dir: Alfonso Cuaron. Pro: Mark Johnson. Co-Pro: Dalisa Cohen. Ex Pro: Alan C. Blomquist and Amy Ephron. Screenplay: Richard LaGravenese and Elizabeth Chandler. Ph: Emmanuel Lubezki. Pro Des: Bo Welch. Ed: Steven Weisberg. M: Patrick Doyle. Costumes: Judianna Makovsky. (Mark Johnson/Baltimore Pictures–Warner.) Rel: 9 February 1996. 97 mins. Cert U. USA. 1995.

Living in Oblivion

Considering the recent spate of features set in the world of the movie industry (*Ed Wood, In the Soup, Mistress, The Player, The Big Picture*, etc), you'd think the genre was pretty worn out. It is, but Tom DiCillo's mordant comedy spotlights the agony of the filmmaking process with a wry, fresh light. Near the beginning of the film a young woman confronts her mother with an awful truth – as it happens, it's a riveting scene from a low-budget movie within a low-budget movie, but then an intrusive boom destroys the shot. The take is repeated, but this time dissolves out of focus. Take Three is interrupted by rowdy street noise. And

so it goes on, with the two actresses gradually losing patience (and one forgetting her lines) as the scene mislays its spontaneity and veracity. But DiCillo, who directed the criminally underrated *Johnny Suede*, has many more tricks up his sleeve as he unveils the terrifying pressures that arise from producing one decent moment of celluloid. FYI: Made on a budget of $35,000, *Living in Oblivion* was partially financed by members of the cast who 'bought' themselves roles in the movie.

Cast: Steve Buscemi (Nick Reve), Catherine Keener (Nicole Springer), Dermot Mulroney (Wolf), Danielle Von Zernick (Wanda), James LeGros (Chad Palomino), Peter Dinklage (Tito), Hilary Gilford, Michael Griffiths, Matthew Grace, Robert Wightman, Kevin Corrigan, Tom Jarmusch, Francesca Dimauro.

Dir and Screenplay: Tom DiCillo. Pro: Michael Griffiths and Marcus Viscidi. Ex Pro: Hilary Gilford. Co-Ex Pro: Frank Von Zernick and Robert Sertner. Co-Pro: Meredith Zamsky. Assoc Pro: Danielle Von Zerneck, Dermot Mulroney and Jane Gil. Ph: Frank Prinzi. Ed: Camilla Toniolo. Pro Des: Therese Deprez. M: Jim Farmer. Costumes: Ellen Lutter. (Cinergi/JDI Productions/Lemon Sky–Entertainment.)

Rel: 10 November 1995. 90 mins. Cert 15. USA. 1995.

Loch Ness

American zoologist Jonathan Dempsey has made a fool of himself hunting for Bigfoot and the Yeti, then, with his credibility and financial standing in tatters, he is blackmailed into hunting down the Loch Ness monster. Disillusioned and disgusted, Dempsey is determined to disprove the existence of the 'kelpie' as quickly as possible ... Borrowing more from the temperament of *Local Hero* than *Jurassic Park*, *Loch Ness* is a contemplative movie with a monster of a heart. As the cynical American, Ted Danson is at his most easy-going and charismatic and is well matched by eight-year-old newcomer Kirsty Graham as the little psychic who utters the film's most telling line, 'You've got to believe it to see it.' A likeable film – if not a remarkable one.

Cast: Ted Danson (Dr Jonathan Dempsey), Joely Richardson (Laura MacFeteridge), Ian Holm (water bailiff), Harris Yulin (Dr Mercer), James Frain (Adrian Foote), Keith Allen (Gordon Shoals), Nick Brimble (Andy Maclean), Kirsty Graham (Isabel MacFeteridge), Harry Jones, Joseph Greig, John Dair, Deborah Weston, Wolf Kahler, Julian Curry, Roger Sloman, Brian Pettifer, Pamela Kelly, Janette Foggo, John Savident, Richard Vernon.
  Dir: John Henderson. Pro: Tim Bevan, Eric Fellner and Stephen Ujlaki. Co-Pro: Nicky Kentish Barnes and Judith Hunt. Assoc Pro: Debra Hayward. Screenplay: John Fusco. Ph: Clive Tickner. Pro Des: Sophie Becher. Ed: Jon Gregory. M: Trevor Jones. Costumes: Nic Ede. Sound: Mark Auguste. Animatronics: Jim Henson's Creature Shop. (Working Title–PolyGram.) Rel: 9 February 1996. 100 mins. Cert PG. UK. 1994.

A Low Down Dirty Shame

Unashamedly borrowing from blaxploitation films, TV cop shows and buddy-buddy movies, director-scenarist Keenen Ivory Wayans rewrites the standard shoot-'em-up and tailors the lead for himself as black action hero Andre Shame. He's an ex-LA cop who's woefully underemployed until a government agent hires him to find twenty million dollars of drug money. In the midst of this unimaginative plot are two extra-spunky women: heroine Jada Pinkett, Shame's attitude-laden

assistant, and anti-heroine Salli Richardson, the beautiful woman of Shame's past. Despite its predictability, lacklustre acting and direction, this comedic actioner is extremely watchable. For all its faults, it feels more authentic than other formula films and is certainly grittier than *Bad Boys*. High marks go to Pinkett's boisterous performance (as a girl who wants some of the action) and Wayans' generous sprinkling of snappy comebacks. [*Karen Krizanovich*]

Cast: Keenen Ivory Wayans (Andre Shame), Charles S. Dutton (Rothmiller), Jada Pinkett (Peaches), Salli Richardson (Angela Flowers), Andrew Divoff (Ernesto Mendoza), Corwin Hawkins (Wayman), Gary Cervantes, Gregory Sierra, Kim Wayans, Andrew Shaifer, John Capodice.
  Dir and Screenplay: Keenen Ivory Wayans. Pro: Joe Roth and Roger Birnbaum. Ex Pro: Eric L. Gold and Lee R. Mayes. Ph: Matthew F. Leonetti. Ed: John F. Link. Pro Des: Robb Wilson King. M: Marcus Miller; numbers performed by Evelyn Champagne King, Santana, Sidney James, Smooth, Jellybean, Tito Puente, Zhane, Silk, etc. Costumes: Francine Jamison-Tanchuck. (Caravan Pictures/ Hollywood Pictures–Buena Vista.) Rel: 1 September 1995. 100 mins. Cert 18. USA. 1994.

Madagascar Skin

Chris Newby's follow up to *Anchoress* confirms his individual cinema eye, but, with its distant echoes of Beckett

Daughter for the slaughter: Raquel Santamaria stares at the weapon that killed her mother in Juanma Bajo Ulloa's unpredictable La Madre Muerta *(from Metro Tartan)*

and Pinter, the new film has a tiresomely pretentious edge. This tells against the effect of the intelligent performances of John Hannah and Bernard Hill. The former plays a young gay man inhibited by the birthmark on his face (to which the title refers), the latter a crook grateful to the other man for saving his life. The friendship-cum-romance which develops makes for an interesting comment on sexuality, but Newby's screenplay limits its impact both as comedy and drama. [*Mansel Stimpson*]

Cast: Bernard Hill (Flint), John Hannah (Harry), Mark Anthony (Adonis), Mark Petit, Danny Earl, Alex Hooper, Susan Harries.
  Dir and Screenplay: Chris Newby. Pro: Julie Baines. Ex Pro: Ben Gibson. Assoc Pro: Sarah Daniel. Ph: Oliver Curtis. Pro Des: Paul Cross. Ed: Newby and Annabel Ware. M: Mozart; numbers performed by The Peppermint Lounge, Nellie Melba, Sarah Hopkins, etc. Costumes: Annie Symons. (BFI/Channel Four/Dan Films–ICA Projects.) Rel: 26 January 1996. 93 mins. No cert. UK. 1995.

La Madre Muerta

Events of catastrophic significance are frequently set in motion by the most frivolous details. For a thief called Ismael it is a half-eaten bar of chocolate. Making his escape – empty-handed – from a religious repair shop, he notices the chocolate just as he's exiting the premises by window. Climbing back in, Ismael is disturbed by a little girl, the daughter of the woman he shot

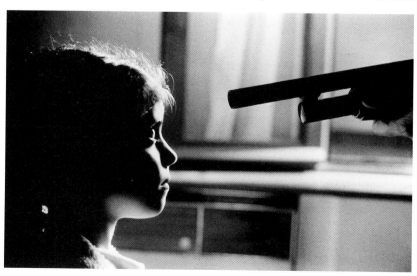

dead a moment earlier. With barely a moment's hesitation, he lifts his shot-gun, steadies it between the girl's eyes and pulls the trigger. Years later he is still haunted by the angelic image of the girl he blew away. Then, shortly before the start of a fresh crime spree, Ismael observes her likeness in the face of a mentally retarded girl crossing the street. It couldn't be his avenging angel, but Ismael will have to kill her just in case ... Shocking, artfully crafted and totally unpredictable, *La Madre Muerta* is one of the most original and disturbing thrillers to emerge from Europe in the 1990s. Loaded with metaphor and blind alleys, the film delivers a number of unforgettable scenes, not least Ismael's first, accident-prone kidnap of the girl and his later attempts to make her laugh.

Cast: Karra Elejalde (Ismael Lopez De Matauko), Ana Alvarez (Leire), Lio (Maite), Silva Marso (Blanca), Marisol Saez (the dead mother), Elena Irureta, Ramon Barea, Gregoria Mangas, Raquel Santa-maria.
  Dir and Pro: Juanma Bajo Ulloa. Ex Pro: Fernando Bauluz. Screenplay: Juanma and Eduardo Bajo Ulloa. Ph: Javier Agirre-sarobe. Pro Des: Satur Idarreta. Ed: Pablo Blanco. M: Bingen Mendizabal. Costumes: Kontxa Agirretxe. (Gasteizko Zinema–Metro Tartan.) Rel: 1 March 1996. 107 mins. Cert 18. Spain. 1993.

Gor, Blarney! Albert Finney and Rufus Sewell in Suri Krishnamma's A Man of No Importance *(Winstone Films)*

The Man in My Life - L'Homme da Ma Vie

Tired of learning new languages for jobs that repeatedly evaporate, Aimee decides to become a kept woman and announces to her foster mother that she'll be married by Christmas. Maurice, the first man on her list of prospective husbands – a smiling misanthropic bookseller – turns out to be heading for the poor house, but instantly falls in love with her. Discarded as unsuitable marital material, Maurice becomes Aimee's best friend and together they try to navigate the hazardous currents of romantic, sexual and material love ... Typically oddball, disarming French romantic comedy – ripe for Hollywood plagiarism – *The Man in My Life* saunters along at its own amiable pace (beautifully scored by Raymond Alessandrini), dispensing a guffaw here and there and a continuous stream of charm. From the director of *Cousin Cousine*.

Cast: Maria De Medeiros (Aimee), Thierry Fortineau (Maurice), Jean-Pierre Bacri (Malcolm), Anne Letourneau (Catherine), Ginette Garcin (Arlette), Ginette Mathieu (Prudence), Alain Doutey, Alix De Konopka, Carmela Valente, Bertrand Lacy.
  Dir and Screenplay: Jean-Charles Tacchella. Pro: Gabriel Boustani. Co-Pro: Justine Heroux. Ph: Dominique Le Rigoleur. Ed: Marie-Aimee Debril. Pro Des: Serge Douy. M: Raymond Alessandrini. Costumes: Sylvie De Segonzac. (Optima/Cineroux Films/Cine Cinq/Prodeve–Gala.) Rel: 25 August 1995. 104 mins. Cert 12. France/Canada. 1993.

A Man of No Importance

Dublin; 1963. Alfie Byrne, a poetry-spouting bus conductor and amateur theatre director, decides to put on a production of Oscar Wilde's *Salome* at the church hall, thus sowing the seeds of his downfall. Seldom has the blarney been laid on so thick, with overly robust performances from Albert Finney and Michael Gambon, nostalgic advertising papering the screen at every opportunity and an irritatingly exuberant score (largely appropriating Cole Porter's 'Let's Do It'). Worse still, it's all terribly predictable, with nudge-nudge wink-wink references to Stephen Ward, Oscar Wilde and 'the love that dare not speak its name'. An interesting antidote to *An Awfully Big Adventure*.

Cast: Albert Finney (Alfie Byrne), Brenda Fricker (Lilly Byrne), Michael Gambon (Carney), Tara Fitzgerald (Adele Rice), Rufus Sewell (Robbie Fay), Joe Pilkington (Ernie Lally), David Kelly (Baldy), Anna Manahan, Brendan Conroy, Pat Killalea, John Killalea, Joan O'Hara, Eileen Reid, Mick Lally, Stuart Dunne, Patrick Malahide, Dylan Tighe, Jimmy Keogh.
  Dir: Suri Krishnamma. Pro: Jonathan Cavendish. Ex Pro: James Mitchell, Guy East, Robert Cooper and Mark Shivas. Screenplay: Barry Devlin. Ph: Ashley Rowe. Ed: David Freeman. Pro Des: Jamie Leonard. M: Julian Nott. Costumes: Phoebe De Gaye. (Majestic/Newcomm/BBC Films/Little Bird Prods–Clarence Films/Winstone Films.) Rel: 21 July 1995. 100 mins. Cert 15. UK. 1994.

Man of the Year

The year's most novel conceit, *Man of the Year* is a mockumentary starring, written and directed by *Playgirl* magazine's Centrefold of the Year. A bona fide filmmaker (his short *Lace Ladies* was nominated for a student Academy Award), Dirk Shafer inadvertently became a celebrity slab of cheesecake following an innocent photo shoot. Committed to *Playgirl* for the duration of 1992, Shafer did the best he could to represent the Ideal Man, dispensing 'expert' advice on radio and TV talk shows on what women want and need from a guy. However, Shafer's biggest hurdle was keeping his homosexuality a secret. Largely made up of dramatic reenactments (but also including genuine documentary footage), the film plays its hand a little broadly, although it is never less than entertaining and

Would you give him one? Writer-director-star Dirk Shafer (seen with Phil Donahue) wins first place in a best buns contest in Man of the Year *(from BFI)*

frequently very funny and revealing (how do you photograph an erection without it looking like an erection?). Claudette Sutherland, as Dirk's long-suffering, straight-laced mother, is a standout. FYI: Shafer's lover, played by Michael Ornstein, not only has a small part in the film himself, but served as costume designer, production designer and location scout.

Cast: Dirk Shafer (himself), Vivian Paxton (herself/Chris), Claudette Sutherland (Tammy Shafer), Michael Ornstein (Mike Mueller), Cal Bartlett (Ken Shafer), Mary Stein (Angela Lucassey), Beth Broderick (Kelly Bound), Cynthia Szigeti (Betty Levy), Bill Brochtrup (Pledge Cartwright), Rhonda Dotson (Lady La Flame), Deidra Shafer (herself), Paul Fow (Rex Chandler), Dennis Bailey, Charles Sloane, Lu Leonard, Thom Collins, Michael Mueller, Fabio, Merri Biechler, Joan Rivers, Phil Donahue.
   Dir and Screenplay: Dirk Shafer. Pro: Matt Keener. Ex Pro: Christian Moeyaert. Co-Pro: Simon Bowler. Ph: Stephen Timberlake. Pro Des and Costumes: Michael

Mueller. Ed: Barry Silver and Ken Soloman. M: Peitor Angell; numbers performed by The Village People, The J. Geils Band, Moonstone, Odds, The Story, etc. (Artisan Productions/The Documentary Foundation–BFI.) Rel: 21 June 1996. 87 mins. Cert 15. USA. 1995.

Martha & Ethel

One of the best films in recent years, this feature-length documentary contrasts the lives, outlooks and personalities of two nannies, Martha, a refugee from Nazi Germany, and Ethel, a black woman from the American South. Each became attached to one particular American family, and their stories are told by various members of these families and by Martha and Ethel themselves. The film triumphs both as a double portrait and an insightful dissection of family life – which proves how vital childhood influences can be. *Martha & Ethel* is touching, revealing, amusing and, finally, uplifting. A joy. [*Mansel Stimpson*]

Dir and Pro: Jyll Johnstone. Co-Pro: Barbara Ettinger. Assoc Pro: Gretchen McGowan and Christina Houlihan. Writers: Ettinger, Houlihan, Johnstone, Alysha Cohen, Frank Ortega and Sharon Woods. Ph:

Joseph Friedman. Ed: Toby Shimin. M: Sarah Franklyn and John Casey; Bach, Chopin; numbers performed by Phil Aaberg, Keith Jarrett, Fats Waller, Cab Calloway, Country Joe and the Fish, Billie Holiday, etc. (Canobie Films–Columbia TriStar.) Rel: 28 July 1995. 77 mins. Cert U. USA. 1993.

Mary Reilly

A wealthy Victorian doctor, Dr Jekyll, invites a mysterious assistant to work at his private laboratory – much to the consternation of Jekyll's housemaid, Mary Reilly, who harbours an unspoken affection for the good doctor ... It's hard to see what attracted screenwriter Christopher Hampton and director Frears to such timeworn material as the Dr Jekyll and Mr Hyde story. It's less hard, maybe, to see what drew John Malkovich and Glenn Close to work with Frears and Hampton again (all four reunited from *Dangerous Liaisons*) – and with such material. Jekyll and Hyde is a devil of a part and Malkovich supplies his customary unpredictable edge to it, creating a mental rather than physical transformation of Jekyll, with teeth bared and tongue going like the clappers. Close, in a

Mary, Mary, Not Too Scary: John Malkovich (right) attempts to inhibit Julia Roberts' awful Irish accent in Stephen Frears' awful Mary Reilly *(from Columbia TriStar)*

jumped-up cameo, lays on a lipsticked sneer and something bordering on a Cockney accent, while Julia Roberts, as Mary Reilly, runs through a catalogue of wide-eyed reaction shots. Unfortunately, Ms Roberts' Irish accent is possibly the worst ever committed to film, reducing this bloated, Hollywood folly into a large rusty nail in the coffin of the actress's career. She was, incidentally, paid $10 million to appear in the film.

Cast: Julia Roberts (Mary Reilly), John Malkovich (Dr Jekyll/Mr Hyde), George Cole (Mr Poole), Michael Gambon (Mary's father), Kathy Staff (Mrs Kent), Glenn Close (Mrs Farraday), Michael Sheen (Bradshaw), Bronagh Gallagher (Annie), Linda Bassett, Henry Goodman, Ciaran Hinds, David Ross, Stephen Boxer.
  Dir: Stephen Frears. Pro: Ned Tanen, Nancy Graham Tanen and Norma Heyman. Ex Pro: Lynn Pleshette. Co-Pro: Iain Smith. Screenplay: Christopher Hampton, based on the novel by Valerie Martin. Ph: Philippe Rousselot. Pro Des: Stuart Craig.

Ed: Lesley Walker. M: George Fenton. Costumes: Consolata Boyle. (TriStar Pictures–Columbia TriStar.) Rel: 3 May 1996. 109 mins. Cert 15. USA. 1996.

Mighty Aphrodite
After the shock of seeing a Woody Allen film open in a Greek amphitheatre, *Mighty Aphrodite* cuts back to the more familiar terrain of Manhattan, marital friction and neurotic insecurity, i.e. Woodyworld. The premise of the film is a good one: a man underhandedly befriending the natural mother of his adopted son. However, the idiotic conceit of framing the story with a jokey Greek chorus belongs in another movie, probably directed by Mel Brooks. Furthermore, much of the film's humour is propelled at the expense of characters less bright than the director (Michael Rapaport: 'Who were the bad guys in *Schindler's List*?'), which is not only smug but cheap. Mira Sorvino, so good in *Barcelona*, resorts to obvious caricature here as the brainless hooker who falls for Woody, echoing the strident performance of Jennifer Tilly in *Bullets Over Broadway*.

Cast: F. Murray Abraham (leader of Greek Chorus), Woody Allen (Lenny), Claire

Bloom (Amanda's mother), Helena Bonham Carter (Amanda), Olympia Dukakis (Jocasta), Michael Rapaport (Kevin), Mira Sorvino (Linda Ash/Judy Cum), David Ogden Stiers (Laius), Jack Warden (Tiresias), Peter Weller (Jerry Bender), Donald Symington (Amanda's father), Dan Moran (Ricky), J. Smith Cameron, Steven Randazzo, Jeffrey Kurland, Jimmy McQuaid, Rosemary Murphy, Jennifer Greenhut, William Addy, Danielle Ferland, Paul Herman, Tony Sirico, Tony Darrow, George De La Pena.
  Dir and Screenplay: Woody Allen. Pro: Robert Greenhut. Ex Pro: Jean Doumanian and J.E. Beaucaire. Co-Ex Pro: Jack Rollins, Charles H. Joffe and Letty Aronson. Co-Pro: Helen Robin. Ph: Carlo DiPalma. Pro Des: Santo Loquasto. Ed: Susan E. Morse. M: Dick Hyman; numbers performed by Erroll Garner, The Dave Brubeck Quartet, Ramsey Lewis, The Count Basie Orchestra, Dick Hyman, The Benny Goodman Orchestra, etc. Costumes: Jeffrey Kurland. (Miramax International/Magnolia Pictures/Sweetland Films–Buena Vista.) Rel: 12 April 1996. 95 mins. Cert 15. USA. 1995.

Mighty Morphin Power Rangers: The Movie
Trapped for 6,000 years in a giant egg, the remarkably powerful and thoroughly evil Ivan Ooze is accidentally

Struggling down a familiar path: Alessandra Martines, Salome Lelouch, Michel Boujenah and Jean-Paul Belmondo in Claude Lelouch's award-winning Les Miserables *(from Warner)*

released by workmen on a building sight in Angel Grove, USA. Imbued with the power to transform his phlegm into a loyal fighting force, Ivan proceeds to take over the world, starting by relieving the Power Rangers of their supernatural powers ... In spite

The teen team: David Yost, Karan Ashley, Jason David Frank, Amy Jo Johnson, Steve Cardenas and Johnny Yong Bosch prepare for action in Bryan Spicer's, er, ebullient Mighty Morphin Power Rangers: The Movie *(from Fox)*

of all expectations, the feature film adaptation of the cult, violence-driven children's TV series is not so terrible. Buoyed by high spirits, some wit and imaginative graphics, the film is a good deal less painful than either *Batman Forever* or *Judge Dredd*. True, a lot of the good humour is unintentional, but the colour-coordinated, racially balanced and sexually harmonious Rangers are so earnest and fun-loving that it's hard to lower a censorious eyebrow.

Cast: Karan Ashley (Aisha/Yellow Ranger), Johnny Yong Bosch (Adam/Black Ranger), Steve Cardenas (Rocky/Red Ranger), Jason David Frank (Tommy/White Ranger), Amy Jo Johnson (Kimberly/Pink Ranger), David Yost (Billy/Blue Ranger), Paul Schrier (Bulk), Jason Narvy (Skull), Paul Freeman

(Ivan Ooze), Gabrielle Fitzpatrick (Dulcea), Nicholas Bell (Zordon), Peta-Maree Rixon (Alpha 5), Mark Ginther (Lord Zedd), Jamie Croft (Fred Kelman), Jean Paul Bell, Kerry Casey, Julia Cortez, Peter Mochrie, Robyn Gol.

Dir: Bryan Spicer. Pro: Haim Saban, Shuki Levy and Suzanne Todd. Screenplay: Arne Olsen, from a story by Olsen and John Kamps. Ph: Paul Murphy. Ed: Wayne Wahrman. Pro Des: Craig Stearns. M: Graeme Revell; numbers performed by Red Hot Chilli Peppers, They Might Be Giants, Dan Hartman, Devo, Shampoo, Van Halen, Snap, Carl Douglas, Power Jet, etc. Costumes: Joseph Porro. (Saban Entertainment/Toei Co.–Fox.) Rel: 21 July 1995. 95 mins. Cert PG. USA. 1995.

Les Miserables –
Les Miserables du Vingtieme Siecle

Typically flamboyant romantic epic from Claude Lelouch, translating, updating and mirroring Victor Hugo's classic 1842 novel of defeat, despair and the extraordinary resilience of mankind. Beginning shortly after the birth of the cinema and spanning most of the twentieth century, Lelouch's self-consciously stylistic film follows the destiny of two men, both called Henri Fortin (and both played by Jean-Paul Belmondo) who, as father and son, discover that fate has a nasty way of repeating itself. Unable to read or write, the second Henri asks a Jewish lawyer to read Hugo's masterpiece to him in return for driving the lawyer and his wife and daughter to safety. As it transpires, Henri shares uncanny similarities with Hugo's protagonist, Jean Valjean, as did Henri's father. Furthermore, what the country went through in the French Revolution, it is now undergoing at the hands of the Nazi occupation. Miserable times indeed ... Through the use of repetition, allegory, coincidence, elliptical detail and sweeping cuts across time, Lelouch paints a passionate and moving tapestry of humanity, forever just one step away from happiness and redemption. A master storyteller himself, Lelouch has managed to bring the preeminent masterwork of French literature alive through a twentieth century perspective, while exploring the very mechanics of storytelling itself. Winner of the Golden Globe award for best foreign language film.

Cast: Jean-Paul Belmondo (Henri Fortin/Jean Valjean), Michel Boujenah (Andre Ziman), Alessandra Martines (Elise Ziman), Salome Lelouch (Salome Ziman), Annie Girardot (Theardiere farmer woman), Philippe Leotard (Theardiere farmer man), Clementine Celarie (Catherine/Fantine), Philippe Khorsand (policeman/Javert), Rufus (Theardiere father and son), Jean Marais (Bishop Myriel), Micheline Presle (Mother Superior), Ticky Holgado, Nicole Croisille, William Leymergie, Darry Cowl, Antoine Dulery, Robert Hossein, Cyrielle Claire, Paul Belmondo, Jacques Bonnot.

Spar excellence: Wesley Snipes sizes up the opposition (Jennifer Lopez) in Joseph Ruben's cheerfully entertaining Money Train *(from Columbia TriStar)*

Dir, Pro, Screenplay and Ph: Claude Lelouch. Ex Pro: Tania Zazulinsky. Pro Des: Jacques Bufnoir. Ed: Helene de Luze. M: Francis Lai, Philippe Servain, Erik Berchot, Michel Legrand and Didier Barbelivien. Costumes: Dominique Borg. (Les Films 13/TFI Films/Canal Plus–Warner.) Rel: 2 February 1996. 174 mins. Cert 12. France. 1995.

Money Train

They're as different as chalk and cheddar, but John and Charlie are foster brothers who are now working together as transit cops in the New York subway. John is diligent, selfless and black; Charlie is carefree, irresponsible and white. The only thing they have in common is a burning hatred for their boss – and an unhealthy interest in the cargo of the money train ... Having hit it off in *White Men Can't Jump*, Wesley Snipes and Woody Harrelson return to knock sparks off each other in the ultimate buddy movie. The chemistry works a treat, with Wesley in particular making the most of his loose cannon. Throw in some terrific stunts, machine gun repartee and a feisty, alluring female distraction (the lovely Jennifer Lopez) and you have an action comedy that delivers. Daft, but entertaining. FYI: While the stash that Wesley and Woody drool over on the money train amounts to $4m, the stars' combined income from the movie was $11m.

Cast: Wesley Snipes (John), Woody Harrelson (Charlie), Jennifer Lopez (Grace Santiago), Robert Blake (Donald Patterson), Chris Cooper (Torch), Scott Sowers (Mr

Brown), Skip Sudduth (Kowalski), Joe Grifasi, Vincent Patrick, Aida Turturro, Alvaleta Guess, John Norman Thomas, Enrico Colantoni, Moss Porter, Bill Nunn.

Dir: Joseph Ruben. Pro: Jon Peters and Neil Canton. Ex Pro: Tracy Barone, Adam Fields and Frederick Pierce. Screenplay: Doug Richardson and David Loughery. Ph: John W. Lindley. Pro Des: Bill Groom. Ed: George Bowers and Bill Pankow. M: Mark Mancina; numbers performed by Shaggy and Ken Boothe, 112, Skee-Lo, Men of Vizion, Gloria Estefan, Terry Ellis, Samuelle, Melissa Etheridge, Enigma, Juster, Luther Vandross, 4.0, The Neville Brothers, etc. Costumes: Ruth E. Carter. (Peters Entertainment–Columbia TriStar.) Rel: 17 May 1996. 110 mins. Cert 18. USA. 1995.

A Month By the Lake

In May, 1937, a middle-aged spinster and bachelor from England meet while holidaying on the shores of Lake Como in Italy. Drawn to each other by dint of their age and nationality, the unlikely couple find their romantic paths diverted by the presence of a young American nanny and a dashing local Adonis ... Adapted from the novella by H.E. Bates, this sunny romance is as happy and carefree as *Feast of July* is grim and funereal. Edward Fox, imaginatively cast as the affable, pipe-smoking English major, overacts atrociously, yet Vanessa Redgrave, who is cast against type, cannot blot out the memory of her more dramatic oeuvre just by smiling incessantly. Sunglasses would be advisable – not for the Italian sunshine, but for the glaring bonhomie.

Cast: Vanessa Redgrave (Miss Bentley), Edward Fox (Major Wilshaw), Uma Thurman (Miss Beaumont), Alida Valli (Mrs Fascioli), Alessandra Gassman (Vittorio Balzari), Carlo Cartier (Mr Bonizzoni), Sonia Maertinelli (Maria), Paola Lombardi, Frances Nacman, Veronica Wells, Ajanta Barilli.

Dir: John Irvin. Pro: Robert Fox. Screenplay: Trevor Bentham. Ph: Pasqualino de Santis. Pro Des: Giovanni Giovagnoni. Ed: Peter Tanner. M: Nicola Piovani. Costumes: Lia Morandini. (Miramax–Buena Vista.) Rel: 21 June 1996. 93 mins. Cert PG. USA. 1995.

Moonlight and Valentino

Four women – a struggling wife, single student, divorcee and widow – find themselves polarised and then drawn together when tragedy strikes. Affect-

Understanding sex: Gwyneth Paltrow and Elizabeth Perkins discuss the finer details of love-making in David Anspaugh's funny, insightful Moonlight and Valentino *(from PolyGram)*

ing a facade of control and togetherness, the women realise that the only path to redemption is for an emotional catharsis. If that sounds heavy, it's not, as *Moonlight and Valentino* works equally well on a number of levels, not least as a comedy about the contemporary female psyche. Witty, moving and extremely well observed, the film is served by some terrific performances, particularly from Elizabeth Perkins and Gwyneth Paltrow as sisters coming to terms with love and death and the whole damned thing. Many moments leave a lasting impression, not least the seemingly insignificant ones, like Perkins trying to leave the perfect message on her answering machine or instructing Paltrow on how to get the best out of sex. Imaginatively adapted by Ellen Simon from her own play.

Cast: Elizabeth Perkins (Rebecca Trager Lott), Gwyneth Paltrow (Lucy Trager), Jon Bon Jovi (house painter), Kathleen Turner (Alberta Russell), Whoopi Goldberg (Sylvie Morrow), Josef Sommer (Thomas Trager), Jeremy Sisto (Steven), Shadia Simmons (Jenny Morrow), Peter Coyote (Paul), Erica Luttrell, Matthew Koller, Kelli Fox, Carlton Watson.

Dir: David Anspaugh. Pro: Alison Owen, Eric Fellner and Tim Bevan. Co-Pro: Mary McLaglen. Assoc Pro: Liza Chasin. Screenplay: Ellen Simon. Ph: Julio Macat. Pro Des: Robb Wilson King. Ed: David Rosenbloom. M: Howard Shore; Rossini; numbers performed by REM, The Temptations, Joan Armatrading, Toni Childs, Lone Justice, etc. Costumes: Denise Cronenberg. (PolyGram/Working Title–PolyGram.) Rel: 28 June 1996. 104 mins. Cert 15. USA. 1995.

Mortal Kombat

Having fought and won nine tournaments against mortal man, the sorcerer Shang Tsung, from the nether kingdom of Outworld, needs only one more victory to take over earth. His sole setback is that he can only use 'mortal combat' to overpower his human competitors, although some psychological sorcery is not out of the question. Which leaves the whining, arrogant movie star Johnny Cage, the ballsy, vengeful Sonya Blade and the grieving, intense Liu Kang to confront their own inner fears before they can take their best shot. Based on the top-selling video game, the film certainly delivers plenty of combat and backs it up with some eye-opening, digitally enhanced effects and Gigeresque production design. It's all way over the top, retarded by banal Saturday matinee humour (and some suspect acting), but the bone-crunching stunts should keep diehards drooling.

Cast: Linden Ashby (Johnny Cage), Cary-Hiroyuki Tagawa (Shang Tsung), Robin Shou (Liu Kang), Bridgette Wilson (Sonya Blade), Talisa Soto (Princess Kitana), Trevor Goddard (Kano), Christopher Lambert (Lord Rayden), Chris Casamassa (Scorpion), Francois Petit, Keith H. Cooke, Hakim Alston, Kenneth Edwards, Lloyd Kino.

Dir: Paul Anderson. Pro: Lawrence Kasanoff. Ex Pro: Bob Engelman and Danny Simon. Assoc Pro: Alison Savitch. Screenplay: Kevin Droney. Ph: John R. Leonetti. Ed: Martin Hunter. Pro Des: Jonathan Carlson. M: George S. Clinton; numbers performed by The Immortals, Mutha's Day Out, Stabbing Westward, Fear Factory, KMFDM, Napalm Death, Traci Lords, Gravity Kills, etc. Costumes:

Ha Nguyen. (Threshold Entertainment/New Line Cinema–First Independent.) Rel: 20 October 1995. 101 mins. Cert 15. USA. 1995.

Moscow Nights
See *Katia Ismailova.*

The Most Desired Man - Der Bewegte Mann
Cologne; 1994. If Axel's libido wasn't enough trouble, his association with a gay admirer lands him in even deeper water with his exasperated pregnant girlfriend. A series of further misunderstandings conspire to alienate Axel and Doro in spite of their basic love for one another. Billed as the most successful German film of all time, this goofy, engaging comedy ploughs old ground with the credibility of a British sitcom. None the less, there are some priceless moments, not least the scene in which three hooligans mistakenly attend a screening of Visconti's *Death in Venice.*

Cast: Til Schweiger (Axel), Katja Riemann (Doro), Joachim Krol (Norbert), Rufus Beck (Walter), Armin Rohde (Metzger), Antonia Lang (Elke Schmidt), Nico Van Der Knaap, Martina Gedeck, Judith Reinartz, Kai Wiesinger, Helmut Buchel, Monty Arnold.
   Dir and Screenplay: Sonke Wortmann, from the comics *The Most Desired Man* and *Pretty Baby* by Ralf Koenig. Pro: Bernd Eichinger. Ex Pro: Martin Moszkowicz, Molly Von Furstenberg, Harry Kugler and Elvira Senft. Ph: Gernot Roll. Pro Des: Monika Bauert. Ed: Ueli Christen. M: Torsten Breuer. Costumes: Katharina Von Martius. (Neue Constantin Film/Olga Film–Gala.) Rel: 26 January 1996. 98 mins. Cert 18. Germany. 1994.

Armed to the teeth: A hunky contender from Outworld flexes his advantage – in Paul Anderson's Mortal Kombat *(from First Independent)*

Laid in Germany: Katja Riemann and Til Schweiger in Sonke Wortmann's The Most Desired Man *(from Gala)*

The Most Terrible Time in My Life - Waga Jinsei Saiaku No Toki
Seemingly established as a Japanese 'art house' director with *Circus Boys*, Kaizo Hayashi now surprises us with a popular thriller. Although it could be read as a comment on the immigrant element in Japanese society, the film is better taken as a surface entertainment featuring Masatoshi Nagase (from *Mystery Train* and *Cold Fever*) as an accident prone private eye, Maiku Hama. The name, so close to Mickey Spillane's pulp hero Mike Hammer, is a hint that his investigations concerning a missing person will echo the *film*

Music makes his day: Richard Dreyfuss lends inspiration to Alicia Witt in Stephen Herek's Mr Holland's Opus *(from PolyGram)*

noir style of the forties. But, with black comedy and violent action incongruously intermingled, the appeal here is to contemporary audiences whose taste is for thrills and giggles combined. [*Mansel Stimpson*]

Cast: Masatoshi Nagase (Maiku Hama), Shiro Sano (Kanno), Kiyotaka Nanbara (Hoshino), Yang Haitin (Yang Hai Tin), Hou De Jian, Akaji Maro, Shinya Tsukamoto, Joe Shishido.
 Dir: Kaizo Hayashi. Pro: Hayashi, Yutaka Goto, Sunshuke Koga and Yu Wei Yen. Ex Pro: Yoshiharu Saga. Screenplay: Hayashi and Daisuke Tengan. Ph: Yuichi Nagata. Art: Takeo Kimura. (For Life Records/Film Detective Office/Shutter Pictures–ICA Projects.) Rel: 15 March 1996. 92 mins. No cert. Japan. 1993.

Mr Holland's Opus
Determined to make his name as a classical composer, Glenn Holland gives up playing piano at weddings and bar mitzvahs to become a music teacher – so that he can write music in his spare time. However, Mr Holland never anticipated the demands that came with a job he considered a stopgap ... A heartfelt tribute to the spirit of teaching, *Mr Holland's Opus* starts out like yet another *To Sir, With Love* clone, then veers into *Forrest Gump* territory, covering thirty years in the life of a singular character, complete with topical news footage and hit songs. Yet despite its unwieldy unevenness and lapses of cinematic fine-tuning (and some temperamental camera moves), the film achieves considerable emotional power. Richard Dreyfuss, looking as credible as a 30-year-old as he does an old man (the actor is actually 48), turns in another remarkable performance in a film spotted with brilliant moments.

Cast: Richard Dreyfuss (Glenn Holland), Glenne Headly (Iris Holland), Jay Thomas (Bill Meister), Olympia Dukakis (Principal Jacobs), William H. Macy (Vice Principal Wolters), Alicia Witt (Gertrude Lang), Terrence Howard (Louis Russ), Jean Louisa Kelly (Rowena Morgan), Alexandra Boyd (Sarah Olmstead), Joseph Anderson (Cole, at 15 years old), Damon Whitaker, Nicholas John Renner, Anthony Natale, Joanna Gleason, Beth Maitland, Benjamin J. Dixon, Kathryn Arnett, Freeman O. Corbin, John Henry Redwood.

 Dir: Stephen Herek. Pro: Ted Field, Michael Nolin and Robert W. Cort. Ex Pro: Patrick Sheane Duncan and Scott Kroopf. Co-Pro: William Teitler and Judith James. Screenplay: Duncan. Ph: Oliver Wood. Pro Des: David Nichols. Ed: Trudy Ship. M: Michael Kamen; numbers performed by Len Barry, The Kingsmen, The Spencer Davis Group, Richard Dreyfuss, Stevie Wonder, John Lennon, Jackson Browne, Jean Louisa Kelly, Ray Charles, Julian Lennon, and Shawn Stockman. Costumes: Aggie Guerard Rodgers. (PolyGram/Interscope Communications/Charlie Mopic-PolyGram.) Rel: 10 May 1996. 143 mins. Cert PG. USA. 1995.

Muppet Treasure Island
Cacophonous, fitfully amusing remake of Robert Louis Stevenson's classic tale of pirates, buried treasure and betrayal should appeal to children and adults alike, within reason. Although Kermit claims that this is his first real action adventure epic, the frog shows no sign of stretching himself as an actor. Miss Piggy, too, is limited to her usual self-indulgent, narcissistic histrionics, leaving only Fozzie Bear, as the simple-minded son of an aristocratic ship builder, to reveal a degree of

And a bottle of rum: The implacable Sam Eagle and a carefree Kermit in Brian Henson's Muppet Treasure Island *(from Buena Vista)*

versatility. However, the human actors – Tim Curry and Billy Connolly, in particular – throw themselves with brio into the spirit of the enterprise, while the elaborate sets are worthy of a better film. The musical numbers aren't bad, either, and the script, mar-

Fighting for justice: Kevin Bacon and Christian Slater take on the Establishment in Marc Rocco's hard-hitting Murder in the First *(from Guild)*

rying Stevenson's gutsy 18th century lingo with a number of contemporary allusions, is top-notch. Funnier than *CutThroat Island*. Previous Muppet movies include *The Muppet Movie, The Great Muppet Caper, The Muppets Take Manhattan* and *The Muppet Christmas Carol*.

Cast: Kermit the Frog (Captain Samuel Smollett), Miss Piggy (Benjamina Gunn), The Great Gonzo (Gonzo), Rizzo the Rat (Rizzo), Tim Curry (Long John Silver), Kevin Bishop (Jim Hawkins), Billy Connolly (Billy Bones), Jennifer Saunders (Mrs Bluveridge), Fozzie Bear (Squire Trelawney), Sam Eagle (Mr Arrow), Wal-dorf, Beaker, Peter Geeves, Harry Jones, Frederick Warder.

Dir: Brian Henson. Pro: Henson and Martin G. Baker. Ex Pro: Frank Oz. Line Pro: Selwyn Roberts. Screenplay: Jerry Juhl, Kirk R. Thatcher and James V. Hart. Ph: John Fenner. Pro Des: Val Strazovec. Ed: Michael Jablow. M: Hans Zimmer. Songs: Barry Mann and Cynthia Weil. Costumes: Polly Smith. Visual Effects: Thomas G. Smith. (Walt Disney Pictures/Jim Henson Productions–Buena Vista.) Rel: 24 May 1996. 102 mins. Cert U. USA. 1996.

Murder in the First

1938-41; San Francisco. For his very first turn in the courtroom, 24-year-old attorney James Stamphill is asked to defend a convict who killed a fellow inmate in front of 200 witnesses. The legal greenhorn is expected to lose the open-and-shut case, but the experience should be good for him. Right. Based on a true story, *Murder in the First* stokes our moral indignation as young Stamphill turns the case round, taking on the prison authorities at Alcatraz and the establishment itself. It appears that Henri Young, incarcerated for stealing $5 from a local post office (so that he could feed his starving sister), was submitted to three years and two months in solitary confinement after attempting to escape. There, in the 'hole', he is deprived of light, clothes, heat, a bed and toilet facilities, and is only allowed 30 minutes a year in the exercise yard. Kevin Bacon, looking disturbingly thin, plays Young with a tortured commitment, while Gary Oldman as the sadistic warden is no less impressive. Only some fancy camera moves occasionally detract from the potency of this gripping, harrowing film.

Cast: Christian Slater (James Stamphill), Kevin Bacon (Henri Young), Gary Oldman (Associate Warden Glenn), Embeth Davidtz (Mary McCasslin), Brad Dourif (Byron Stamphill), William H. Macy (William McNeil), R. Lee Ermey (Judge Clawson), Stephen Tobolowsky (Mr Henkin), Stefan Gierasch (Warden James Humson), Mia Kirshner, Ben Slack, Kyra Sedgwick, Charles Boswell.

Dir: Marc Rocco. Pro: Marc Frydman and Mark Wolper. Ex Pro: Rocco and David L. Wolper. Co-Pro: Deborah Lee. Screenplay: Dan Gordon. Ph: Fred Murphy. Ed: Russell Livingstone. Pro Des: Kirk M. Petruccelli. M: Christopher Young; 'Tuxedo Junction' performed by The Andrews Sisters. Costumes: Sylvia Vega

Vasques. (Canal Plus/Wolper Organisation–Guild.) Rel: 1 December 1995. 122 mins. Cert 15. USA. 1994.

Mute Witness

The surroundings and premise are certainly unusual. Originally set in Chicago, the action has been shifted to Moscow where a small Russian-American crew is filming a low-budget slasher movie. When the mute make-up and special effects girl gets locked in the studio overnight, she witnesses the making of a snuff film and soon becomes embroiled in a plot involving a crime syndicate, the police and the KGB. Technically a very accomplished effort for first-time British director Anthony Waller (particularly considering the number of obstacles he faced), *Mute Witness* doesn't entirely work. The twists are not as surprising as they should be (by being overstated) and many of the cinematic effects are clearly borrowed from other films, from *The Stunt Man* and *The Shining* via *The Spiral Staircase*. Even the abrupt cut from a death blow to a knife sawing through a slab of beef is lifted straight from Bram Stoker's *Dracula*. Still, there is much to admire, not least the nocturnal Moscow locations and the engaging central performance from Russian actress Marina Sudina.

Cast: Marina Sudina (Billie Hughes), Fay Ripley (Karen Hughes), Evan Richards (Andy Clarke), Oleg Jankowskij (Larsen), Igor Volkov (Arkadi), Sergej Karlenkov (Lyosha), Alec Guinness (The Reaper), Alexander Buriev, Alexander Piatov, Nikolai Pastuhov, Stephen Bouser, Nikolai Chindjaikin, Olga Tolstetskaya, Uri Sherstiniov.

Dir and Screenplay: Anthony Waller. Pro: Waller, Alexander Buchman and Norbert Soentgen. Ex Pro: Richard Claus. Co-Pro: Grigory Riazhsky and Alexander Atanesjan. Ph: Egon Werdin. Pro Des: Matthias Kammermeier. Ed: Peter Adam. M: Wilbert Hirsch. Costumes: Svetlana Luzanova. (Cobblestone Pictures–Columbia TriStar.) Rel: 19 January 1996. 96 mins. Cert 18. UK/Germany/ Russia. 1995.

My Family - Mi Familia

East Los Angeles; the 1920s-1980s. Having walked all the way to Los Angeles from Mexico, young Jose Sanchez is determined to establish deep roots there and build a life for

Bathtime for Billie: Marina Sudina hears no evil in Anthony Waller's accomplished Mute Witness *(from Columbia TriStar)*

All in the family: Jennifer Lopez struggles with the currents of fate in Gregory Nava's marvellous My Family *(from Entertainment)*

'Sickness makes you stronger': Sami Frey as the petulant poet in Gerard Mordillat's My Life and Times With Antonin Artaud *(from Metro Tartan)*

himself and future generations. And so, by the sweat of his brow and with the help of God and his dignity, Jose does just that – and watches in bemusement, horror and love as his family grows, sways and rocks with the brutal currents of time. An affectionate, passionate, sweeping, unflinching and gloriously photographed portrait of Hispanic life in America, *My Family* achieves the impossible by bringing the world of the Sanchez clan so vividly to life – in a little over two hours. Portraying the lives of so many characters over a period of seventy years, writer-director Gregory Nava (*El Norte*, *A Time of Destiny*) has proved again what an accomplished storyteller he is. Indeed, this is a film of enormous resonance that knows the difference between false sentimentality and real heart.

Cast: Jimmy Smits (Jimmy Sanchez), Esai Morales (Chucho Sanchez), Eduardo Lopez Rojas (Jose Sanchez), Elpidia Carrillo (Isabel Magana), Jenny Gago (Maria Sanchez), Edward James Olmos (Paco Sanchez, narrator), Jacob Vargas (young Jose Sanchez), Leon Singer (El Californio), Jennifer Lopez (young Maria), Constance Marie (Toni Sanchez), Maria Canals (young Irene Sanchez), Michael De-

Lorenzo (Butch Mejia), Lupe Ontiveros (Irene Sanchez), Enrique Castillo (Memo 'Bill'), Paul Robert Langdon (Carlitos), Mary Steenburgen, Scott Bakula, Alicia Del Lago, Benito Martinez, Greg Albert, Jonathan Hernandez, Jeanette Jurado, Seidy Lopez, Brian Lally, Ernie Lively, Peter Mark Vasquez, Ruben Sierra, Angelina Estrada, Dedee Pfeiffer, Bibi Besch, Bruce Gray.

Dir: Gregory Nava. Pro: Anna Thomas. Ex Pro: Francis Ford Coppola, Tom Luddy, Guy East, Lindsay Law and Sergio Molina. Screenplay: Nava and Thomas. Ph: Edward Lachman. River Ph: Carroll Ballard. Ed: Nancy Richardson. Pro Des: Barry Robinson. M: Mark McKenzie; Pepe Avila; numbers performed by Los Folkloristas, Jeanette Jurado, Mariachis Los Camperos, All 4-One, Mana, Los Lobos, James and Bobby Purify, Juan Luis Guerra y 4:40, Banda Machos, etc. Costumes: Tracy Tynan. (American Zoetrope/New Line Cinema/Newcomm/Majestic Films/American Playhouse–Entertainment.) Rel: 6 October 1995. 126 mins. Cert 15. USA. 1994.

My Life and Times With Antonin Artaud - En Compagnie d'Antonin Artaud

Paris; 1946-48. A poet, actor and theatrical impresario little known outside his native France, Antonin Artaud (1896-1948) exercised some influence on twentieth century theatre. Ahead of his time, Artaud was fiercely interested in acupuncture, astrology, tarot and Yoga, experimented with drugs and

obscure religions, revolted against conventional literature and founded the seminal Theatre of Cruelty. Notwithstanding, this does not make him an ideal subject for cinematic scrutiny. Mordillat's profile, shot in black and white and filmed in contemporary Paris (with little regard for period accuracy), follows the last two years of Artaud's life as seen through the eyes of devotee and fellow poet Jacques Prevel (on whose memoir this is based). As played with some command by Sami Frey, Artaud is a singularly unpleasant man ravaged by drugs and dying of cancer, whose unconventional remarks ('every time a child is born drains blood from my heart' and 'sickness makes you stronger') leads more to involuntary chuckles than philosophical insight. Enough to put you off poetry for life.

Cast: Sami Frey (Antonin Artaud), Marc Barbe (Jacques Prevel), Julie Jezequel (Jany), Valerie Jeannet (Rolande), Clotilde de Bayser (Marthe), Charlotte Valandrey (Colette), Anne Barbe.

Dir: Gerard Mordillat. Pro: Denis Freyd. Screenplay: Mordillat and Jerome Prieur. Ph: Francois Cantonne. Pro Des: Jean-Pierre Clech. Ed: Sophie Rouffio. M: Jean-

A little night musing: Elina Lowensohn (above) seduces Galaxy Craze in Michael Almereyda's intriguing Nadja *(from ICA Projects)*

Claude Petit. Costumes: Caroline de Vivaise. (Archipel 33/Laura Productions/La Sept/France 2–Metro Tartan.) Rel: 31 May 1996. 90 mins. No cert. France. 1993.

Nadja

Although the novelty of Brooklyn vampirism has been bled dry by such movies as *Def by Temptation, Innocent Blood* and *Vampire in Brooklyn*, reinventing the genre in the image of Hal Hartley is a welcome one. It's hard to imagine a more perfect actress for the role of the mysterious, deadly Nadja than Elina Lowensohn (*Amateur, Simple Men*), the biggest star to come out of Romania since Edward G. Robinson. Rambling on poetically, she speaks of 'the pain of fleeting joy', complains about European restaurants, yet admits, 'I'm not really much good for anything.' However, she can walk through walls, dispatch psychic faxes and turn on a mean nose bleed. At its best, *Nadja* is a wry, irreverent and spacey parody of horror films, fortified by a number of deadpan performances and much throwaway humour. Unfortunately, the film's supposed trump card – the 'breakthrough' use of pixelvision on 35mm – reduces the key scenes (the death of Dracula, the seduction of Lucy, etc) into distorted shadow-play. Still, any picture featuring a tarantula called Babar that eats potato salad and has a learning disability can't be totally ignored.

Cast: Suzy Amis (Cassandra), Galaxy Craze (Lucy), Martin Donovan (Jim), Peter Fonda (Dr Van Helsing), Karl Geary (Reinfield), Jared Harris (Edgar Drarkoola), Elina Lowensohn (Nadja), David Lynch (morgue receptionist), Jack Lotz, Isabel Gillies.
   Dir and Screenplay: Michael Almereyda. Pro: Mary Sweeney and Amy Hobby. Ex Pro: David Lynch. Ph: Jim Denault. Pro Des: Kurt Ossenfort. Ed: David Leonard. M: Simon Fisher Turner; numbers performed by Portishead, Space Hog, The Verve. Costumes: Prudence Moriarty. Sound: Stuart Levy. (David Lynch/Kino Link–ICA Projects.) Rel: 5 April 1996. 90 mins. Cert 15. USA. 1994.

Nelly and Mr Arnaud

Paris; today. Trapped in a sterile marriage and six months behind on the rent, Nelly is struggling to stay sane. Then, out of the blue, she meets Mr Arnaud, a polite, shrewd and elderly

Not on his nelly: Michel Serrault observes the sleeping form of Emmanuelle Beart in Claude Sautet's meticulous Nelly and Mr Arnaud *(from Guild)*

gentleman who seems willing to put her life to rights ... Having last displayed the mastery of his medium with the award-winning *Un Coeur en Hiver*, the 72-year-old Claude Sautet again shows what a fine dramatist he is with this impeccably crafted, beautifully acted and superlatively realised film (with not a nuance misplaced). Yet while his characters inhabit entirely credible lives, the canvas on which they interact is dramatically wanting. And without a strong narrative to engage us, we can hardly be expected to savour the ride.

Cast: Emmanuelle Beart (Nelly), Michel Serrault (Mr Arnaud), Jean-Hugues Anglade (Vincent), Claire Nadeau (Jacqueline), Francoise Brion (Lucie), Michele Laroque (Isabelle), Michel Lonsdale (Dollabella), Charles Berling (Jerome), Jean-Pierre Lorit, Michel Albertini, Coraly Zahonero, Judith Vittet.
   Dir: Claude Sautet. Pro: Alain Sarde. Ex Pro: Antoine Gannage. Screenplay: Sautet, Jacques Fieschi and Yves Ulmann. Ph: Jean-Francois Robin. Pro Des: Carlos Conti. Ed: Jacqueline Thiedot. M: Philippe Sarde. Costumes: Corinne Jorry. (Les Films Alain Sarde/TFI Films/Cecchi Gori Group Tiger Cinematografica/Canal Plus–Guild.) Rel: 12 April 1996. 106 mins. Cert PG. France. 1995.

The Neon Bible

In the Deep South a 16-year-old boy reflects on his life in a small God-fearing town. Burdened by poverty, his mother and father suffered an unhappy marriage, but there was always Aunt Mae, a flamboyant woman who lived precariously in her own past ... If the camera is moved slowly enough and the odd popular song plonked on the soundtrack, a certain amount of atmosphere can be evoked. Indeed, Terence Davies's deadly slow adaptation of John Kennedy Toole's novel is excessively strong on nuance and production design – but little else. There are good performances from Gena Rowlands and Diana Scarwid, to be sure, but the film's lingering views of doorways and other inanimate tableaux will test the patience of most filmgoers. The most boring film since *The Long Day Closes* in 1992.

Cast: Gena Rowlands (Aunt Mae), Diana Scarwid (Sarah), Denis Leary (Frank), Jacob Tierney (David, aged 15), Leo Burmester (Bobbie Lee Taylor), Tom Turbiville (Clyde), Drake Bell (David, aged 10), Dana Dick (Jo Lynne), Frances Conroy, Peter McRobbie, Joan Glover, Bob Hannah, Virgil Graham Hopkins.
   Dir and Screenplay: Terence Davies. Pro: Elizabeth Karlsen and Olivia Stewart. Ex Pro: Nik Powell and Stephen Woolley. Ph: Mick Coulter. Ed: Charles Rees. Pro Des: Christopher Hobbs. M: various. Costumes: Monica Howe. (Channel Four Films/Scala/Miramax–Artificial Eye.) Rel: 13 October 1995. 92 mins. Cert 15. UK. 1995.

About-interface: Sandra Bullock gets lost on the Infopike in Irwin Winkler's riveting The Net *(from Columbia TriStar)*

The Net

Angela Bennett is a freelance analyst who isolates viruses and irons out bugs in adolescent computer games. Then, one day, she hacks into a bizarre prototype of a new Internet programme. Her inadvertent discovery results in her immediate deletion from society: her passport, driving licence, credit cards and even her identity are wiped off the collective computers of America. In their place, Angela is mysteriously installed with a new name and an instant criminal record. All she's got left is her life; for now... From the opening shot of the camera sweeping through the skylight of Angela Bennet's attic, *The Net* trawls the viewer into its complex web. Warning of both the personal and global dangers of living life through the Internet, Irwin Winkler's breakneck, unbearably suspenseful thriller logs on to a number of our most primal neuroses. Sandra Bullock, as the vulnerable, adorable computer nerd denied access to her own life, provides another heroine to root for, while the Orwellian high-tec villainy rings frighteningly true.

Cast: Sandra Bullock (Angela Bennett), Jeremy Northam (Jack Devlin), Dennis Miller (Dr Alan Champion), Diane Baker (Mrs Bennett), Wendy Gazelle (imposter), Ken Howard (Bergstrom), Ray McKinnon (Dale Hessman), Robert Gossett (Ben Phillips), Daniel Schorr, Margo Winkler, Gene Kirkwood, Charles Winkler, Rick Snyder, Gerald Berns, Adam Winkler, David Winkler, Rich Bracco, Andrew Amador.

Dir: Irwin Winkler. Pro: Winkler and Rob Cowan. Screenplay: John Brancato and Michael Ferris. Ph: Jack N. Green. Ed: Richard Halsey. Pro Des: Dennis Washington. M: Mark Isham; 'A Whiter Shade Of Pale' sung by Annie Lennox. Costumes: Linda Bass. 2nd Unit Director and Stunt Coordinator: Buddy Van Horn. (Columbia.) Rel: 6 October 1995. 114 mins. Cert 12. USA. 1995.

Nightwatch

Something is rotten in the state of Denmark. A psykopat is on the loose and 'his' frequent attacks on prostitutes are beginning to intrude on the carefree lives of Martin, Kalinka, Jens and Lotte. Martin in particular feels the shadow of the killer when, to support his law studies, he takes a job on the nightwatch at the local morgue ... An ingeniously plotted, slickly crafted and morally dubious thriller, *Nightwatch* is not recommended to those who take scalping, necrophilia and mutilation too seriously. All rather unsettling – and brilliantly done.

Cast: Nikolaj Waldau (Martin Bork), Sofie Graaboel (Kalinka Martens), Kim Bodnia (Jens Arnkiel), Lotte Andersen (Lotte), Ulf Pilgaard (Inspector Peter Wormer), Rikke Louise Andersson (Joyce), Stig Hoffmeyer (Rolf), Gyrd Lofquist (old nightwatchman).

Dir and Screenplay: Ole Bornedal. Pro: Michael Obel. Ex Pro: Jesper Boas Smith. Ph: Dan Laustsen. Ed: Camilla Skousen. Pro Des: Soeren Krag Soerensen. M: Joachim Holbek; numbers performed by Sort Sol, The Sandmen, etc. Costumes: Margrethe Rasmussen. (Thura Film/DR TV Fikton/Danske Filminstitut–Metro Tartan.) Rel: 13 October 1995. 104 mins. Cert 18. Denmark. 1994.

Nine Months

When Samuel Faulkner, a carefree and happy psychotherapist, discovers that his long-term girlfriend is pregnant, he sees his idyllic lifestyle go out the

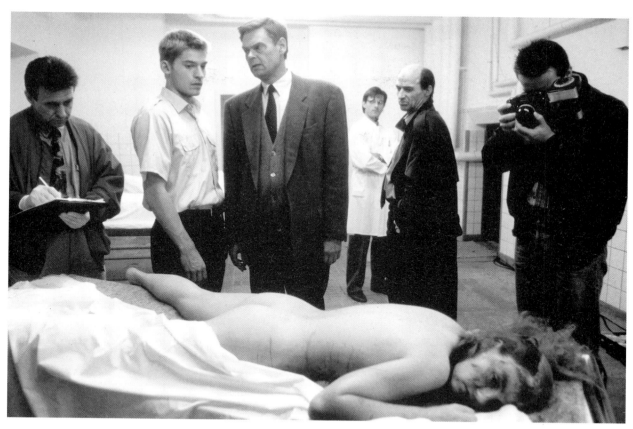

Morgue the merrier: Nikolaj Waldau and Ulf Pilgaard survey some grisly evidence in Ole Bornedal's chilling, darkly humorous Nightwatch *(from Metro Tartan)*

English agony: Julianne Moore and Hugh Grant look forward to an obstetric future in Chris Columbus's frantic Nine Months *(from Fox)*

window. Tormented by a pushy couple ('breeders') and their obnoxious children and further unnerved by an inept Russian obstetrician, Samuel must face up to his worst fears. With Hugh Grant's personification of the embarrassed Englishman, Jeff Goldblum's hip and cynical asides and Robin Williams's linguistic acrobatics

– not to mention director Chris Columbus's aptitude for high farce – *Nine Months* offers a smorgasbord of comedy styles, most of which hit home runs. Inject a dose of wholesome values and a high cute factor, and you have commercial engineering elevated to an art form. Of course, similar territory was explored with greater skill and credibility in the British *Jack & Sarah*, but, heh, this is Hollywood. FYI: The actor Christopher Lambert executive produces.

Cast: Hugh Grant (Samuel Faulkner), Julianne Moore (Rebecca Taylor), Tom Arnold (Marty Dwyer), Joan Cusack (Gail Dwyer), Jeff Goldblum (Sean Fletcher), Robin Williams (Dr Kosevich), Mia Cottet (Lily), Joey Simmrin, Ashley Johnson, Alexa Vega, Charles A. Martinet, Brendan Columbus, Eleanor Columbus, Anna Barnathan, Zelda Williams, Betsy Monroe, Irene Columbus, Violet Columbus, Britanny Radcliffe, Porscha Radcliffe, Kristin Davis, Emily Yancy, Paul Simon.

Dir and Screenplay: Chris Columbus, from the film *Neuf Mois* by Patrick Braoude. Pro: Columbus, Anne Francois, Mark Radcliffe and Michael Barnathan. Ex Pro: Joan Bradshaw and Christopher Lambert. Ph: Donald McAlpine. Ed: Raja Gosnell. Pro Des: Angelo P. Graham. M: Hans Zimmer;

Here lies ... : Anthony Hopkins in his Oscar-nominated turn as Richard Milhous Nixon (from Entertainment)

Morrison, Marvin Gaye, The Ronettes, Tyrone Davis, and The Rolling Stones. Costumes: Jay Hurley. (1492–Fox.) Rel: 20 October 1995. 103 mins. Cert 12. USA. 1995.

Nixon

A man driven to succeed and be loved becomes the most powerful figure in the world – and then blows it ... It's hard to imagine how such a shifty, arrogant, uncharismatic and haunted character ever made it into the White House, let alone succeed in capturing a second term. Yet writer-director-producer Oliver Stone insists on concealing the cunning and charisma that Richard Milhous Nixon exercised to worm his way into the presidency, boost his popularity, open up Russia and China to the West and end the Vietnam war. It's also hard to get over the fact that Nixon is played by Anthony Hopkins, a classical Welsh actor with rounded features. These grievances aside, Stone's marathon biography of the shamed 37th president is a bloated, fragmentary and pretentious affair designed to tax even the most resilient bottom. Of course, there are moments of brilliance and a sterling cast and accomplished crew pull out all the stops in this highly personal, brave and misjudged attempt to blend 'historical fact, interpretation and conjecture'.

Cast: Anthony Hopkins (Richard Milhous Nixon), Joan Allen (Pat Nixon), Powers Boothe (Alexander Haig), Ed Harris (E. Howard Hunt), Edward Herrmann (Nelson Rockefeller), Bob Hoskins (J. Edgar Hoover), E.G. Marshall (John Mitchell), David Paymer (Ronald Ziegler), David Hyde Pierce (John Dean), Paul Sorvino (Henry Kissinger), Mary Steenburgen (Hannah Nixon), J.T. Walsh (John Ehrlichman), James Woods (H.R. Haldeman), Brian Bedford (Clyde Tolson), Kevin Dunn (Chuck Colson), Fyvush Finkel (Murray Chotiner), Annabeth Gish (Julie Nixon), Tony Goldwyn (Harold Nixon), Larry Hagman (Jack Jones), Madeline Kahn (Martha Mitchell), Robert Beltran (Frank Sturgis), Corey Carrier (Richard Nixon at 12), John Diehl (G. Gordon Liddy), David Barry Gray (Richard Nixon at 19), Joshua Preston (Arthur Nixon), Michael Chiklis, Joanna Going, Dan Hedaya, Tony Lo Bianco, Tony Plana, George Plimpton, Saul Rubinek, John Cunningham, John C. McGinley, Lenny Vullo, Enrique Castillo, Drew Snyder, Sean Stone, Julie Condra Douglas, Howard Platt, Bridgitte Wilson, Pamela Dickerson, O'Neal Compton, John Bedford Lloyd, Mikey Stone, Robert Marshall, James Karen, Richard Fancy, Ric Young, Jon Tenney, Julie Araskog, Donna Dixon, John Stockwell, Boris Sichkin (Leonid Brezhnev), Fima Noveck (Andre Gromyko), Marilyn Rockafellow.

Dir: Oliver Stone. Pro: Stone, Clayton Townsend and Andrew G. Vajna. Co-Pro: Eric Hamburg and Dan Halsted. Assoc Pro: Richard Rutowski. Screenplay: Stone, Stephen J. Rivele and Christopher Wilkinson. Ph: Robert Richardson. Pro Des: Victor Kempster. Ed: Hank Corwin and Brian Berdan. M: John Williams; Schubert, Chopin, Vivaldi; numbers performed by Sarah Vaughan, Peggy Lee, etc. Costumes: Richard Hornung. (Illusion Entertainment Group/Cinergi–Entertainment.) Rel: 15 March 1996. 192 mins. Cert 15. USA. 1995.

Now and Then

Shelby, Indiana; 1970/1995. Fulfilling a pact to meet twenty years after the summer they all turned twelve, four childhood friends reminisce on the good old days. Days when they experienced the first flushes of puberty and discovered the importance of friendship. Now, although divided by their adult differences (one is a successful writer, one a Hollywood movie star – you know, the usual stuff girls turn into) the quartet promise to strengthen their ties ... Produced by Demi Moore from a semi-autobiographical screenplay by I. Marlene King, this distaff *Stand by Me* is so syrupy you expect it to stick in the projector gate. Unevenly lit and punctuated by a raft of well-worn songs, the film resembles a greatest hits album set to the constant image of four 12-year-old girls cycling down a sun-lit country lane. Nevertheless, the quartet of young actresses are uniformly wonderful, prompting the paternal fear that they'll all lose their talent and end up like Demi Moore, Melanie Griffith & co. Still, it's fun to imagine the on-set barbecues with the girls' other halves: Bruce Willis, Antonio Banderas and Tom Hanks (Mrs Rita Wilson). Previously known as *The Gaslight Addition*.

Cast: Christina Ricci (young Roberta Martin), Thora Birch (young Teeny Tercell), Gaby Hoffmann (young Samantha Albertson), Ashleigh Aston Moore (young Chrissy DeWitt), Melanie Griffith (Tina Tercell), Demi Moore (Samantha Albertson), Rosie O'Donnell (Roberta Martin), Rita Wilson (Christina DeWitt), Janeane Garofalo (Wiladene), Hank Azaria (Bud Kent), Bonnie Hunt (Mrs DeWitt), Cloris Leachman (Grandma Albertson), Devon Sawa (Scott Wormer), Lolita Davidovich (Mrs Albertson), Walter Sparrow (Crazy Pete), Brendan Fraser (Vietnam vet), Willa Glen, Travis Robertson, Justin Humphrey, Bradley Coryell, Beverly Shelton, T.S. Morgan.

Dir: Lesli Linka Glatter. Pro: Suzanne Todd and Demi Moore. Ex Pro: Jennifer Todd. Co-Pro: Eric McLeod. Screenplay: I. Marlene King. Ph: Ueli Steiger. Pro Des: Gershon Ginsburg and Anne Kuljian. Ed: Jacqueline Cambas. M: Cliff Eidelman; numbers performed by Stevie Wonder, Sophie B. Hawkins, The Jackson 5, The Allmann Brothers, The Staple Singers, The Supremes and The Temptations, The Monkees, The Hollies, Freda Payne, Nancy Sinatra, Badfinger, Tony Orlando and Dawn, Vanity Fare, Free, The Archies, Susanna Hoffs, etc. Costumes: Deena Appel. (Moving Pictures–First Independent.) Rel: 7 June 1996. 102 mins. Cert PG. USA. 1995.

Othello

Venice; 1570. The reason that the works of Shakespeare have endured for so long is because of the exquisite poetry of their language. Take that away and you have overly complex and melodramatic plays that have little to say to contemporary audiences. The dialogue's the thing, with its resonance, canny insights and elaborate play on words. A fine example of this is when Othello meditates on the irony of extinguishing the candle before he ex-

Put out the text: Irene Jacob and Laurence Fishburne flout convention in Oliver Parker's impotent Othello *(from Rank)*

tinguishes the light of his life: Desdemona. It is the most famous, moving and poetically powerful passage in the play, and to cut it out is rather like deleting 'To be or not to be' from *Hamlet*. First-time director Oliver Parker has attempted to give Othello 'a more cinematic drive' by jettisoning half the dialogue, but in so doing he has squeezed the blood out of the meat. In recompense Parker could have produced a cinematically visual feast (as Branagh did with *Henry V* and *Much Ado About Nothing*), but even falls down on that level. As Othello, Laurence Fishburne is suitably dashing and charismatic, although one wonders why he has the title role, as Branagh, playing Iago, monopolises the screen, abducting the audience by directly addressing the camera.

Cast: Laurence Fishburne (Othello), Irene Jacob (Desdemona), Kenneth Branagh (Iago), Nathaniel Parker (Cassio), Michael Maloney (Roderigo), Anna Patrick (Emilia), Nicholas Farrell (Montano), Indra Ove (Bianca), Michael Sheen (Lodovico), Gabriele Ferzetti (The Duke of Venice), Pierre Vaneck (Brabantio), Andre Oumansky, Philip Locke, John Savident.

Dir and Screenplay: Oliver Parker. Pro: Luc Roeg and David Barron. Ex Pro: Jonathan Olsberg. Ph: David Johnson. Pro Des: Tim Harvey. Ed: Tony Lawson. M: Charlie Mole. Costumes: Caroline Harris. (Castle Rock/Dakota Films/Imminent Films–Rank.) Rel: 16 February 1996. 123 mins. Cert 12. UK. 1995.

Panther

1967; Oakland, California. After years of persecution by police in the San Francisco suburb of Oakland, a group of young black residents establish a vigilante movement to uphold law and order and protect their own. Insisting that their fight is against racism and not whites, The Black Panther Party for Self-Defense find their cause twisted by the FBI and the media, tainting them as Communist terrorists. Based on Melvin Van Peebles' novel, this is a fictionalised account of the movement, focusing on a young Panther used as a patsy by police to fabricate incriminating evidence against his brothers. Utilising extreme close-ups, mock documentary footage and a free-wheeling camera style, director Mario Van Peebles (Melvin's mixed-origin son) ensures that the interest is engaged, even when the plotting becomes confused. However, by portraying every white cop as a Nazi,

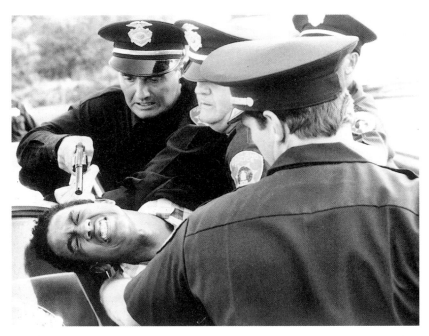

A pig of a day: Wesley Jonathan comes under the strong arm of the law in Mario Van Peebles' Panther *(from PolyGram)*

the film loses some dramatic credibility, further augmented by largely ignoring the internal tensions and criminal transgressions of the party. Thus what could have been a disturbing, provocative, historical document ends up as an entertaining slice of MTV propaganda.

Cast: Kadeem Hardison (Judge), Bokeem Woodbine (Tyrone), Joe Don Baker (Brimmer), Courtney B. Vance (Bobby Seale), Marcus Chong (Huey Newton), Tyrin Turner (Cy), James Russo (Rodgers), Nefertiti (Alma), M. Emmet Walsh (Dorsett), Anthony Griffith (Eldridge Cleaver), Bobby Brown (Rose), Jenifer Lewis (Rita), Michael Wincott (Tynan), Richard Dysart (J. Edgar Hoover), Lahmard Tate (Gene McKinney), Jay Koch (Governor Reagan), Angela Bassett (Betty Shabazz), Mario Van Peebles (Stokley Carmichael), Chris Rock, Roger Guenveur Smith, Wesley Jonathan, Dick Gregory, Kool Moe Dee, Melvin Van Peebles, Tony Toni Toné, Yolanda Whitaker, James LeGros, Joseph Culp, Robert Culp, Chris Tucker, Manny Perry.

Dir: Mario Van Peebles. Pro: Preston L. Holmes, Mario Van Peebles and Melvin Van Peebles. Ex Pro: Eric Fellner and Tim Bevan. Screenplay: Melvin Van Peebles. Ph: Edward Pei. Ed: Earl Watson. Pro Des: Richard Hoover. M: Stanley Clarke; numbers performed by JOE, Blackstreet, Funkadelic, Bobby Brown, Aaron Hall, Female, Tony Toni Toné, etc. Costumes: Paul

Simmons. (Working Title/Tribeca Productions/MVP Films–PolyGram.) Rel: 10 November 1995. 124 mins. Cert 15. USA. 1995.

The Passion of Darkly Noon

Driven out of the religious community that has housed him all his life, the biblically-named Darkly Noon is an innocent trapped in an easy-going, secular world. Nursed back to health by a backwoods beauty called Callie, Darkly is invited to stay but cannot reconcile himself to the evil he sees around him: free love, exposed flesh and cigarettes. While Callie feels nothing but pity for the handsome stranger, the latter sees his new life through a glass, darkly ... Portraying the everyday in a surreal light, English director Philip Ridley (*The Reflecting Skin*) reveals the confusion Darkly faces within himself while simultaneously unnerving the viewer. Furthermore, by investing the film with a palpable sexuality, Ridley has produced a psychological thriller that pricks the carnal while stirring the intellect. Top marks, too, to the fine camerawork of John de Borman and the distinctive, telling music of Nick Bicat. FYI: Although set in Southern redneck country, *Darkly Noon* was actually filmed in Germany.

Cast: Brendan Fraser (Darkly Noon), Ashley Judd (Callie), Viggo Mortensen (Clay), Loren Dean (Jude), Grace Zabriskie

(Roxy), Lou Myers (Quincy), Kate Harper, Mel Cobbs, Josse De Pauw, Maximilian Paul.

Dir and Screenplay: Philip Ridley. Pro: Dominic Anciano, Frank Henschke and Alain Keytsman. Ex Pro: Jim Beach and Ray Burdis. Co-Ex Pro: Shelly Bancroft. Ph: John de Borman. Pro Des: Hubert Pouille. Ed: Leslie Healey. M: Nick Bicat; 'Who Will Love Me Now?' performed by P.J. Harvey, 'Look What You've Done (To My Skin)' by Gavin Friday. Costumes: Gabi Binder and Anne Verhoeven. Sound: Nigel Galt. (Fugitive Features/Die Hauskunst/Keytsman–Entertainment.) Rel: 28 June 1996. 101 mins. Cert 18. UK/Germany/Belgium. 1995.

The Pebble and the Penguin

In the lore of the far south a pebble presented to a penguin of the fairer sex is a proposition of undying love. However, the better the pebble the greater the opportunity for a match made in heaven. But for poor love-struck Hubie a lack of courage prevents him from popping the pebble between the patient wings of the winsome Marina. Then, no sooner does he pluck up his nerve, he is cast out to sea by the dastardly Drake ... Inspired by a National Geographic documentary (the setting, if not the narrative), *The Pebble and the Penguin* holds so much promise but is let down by crude characterisations, mediocre production values and a weak story. There are a few good scenes – the opening credit sequence performed on a sea of sheet music and an enthralling attack by killer whales – but there is little charm or wit.

Voices: Martin Short (Hubie), James Belushi (Rocko), Tim Curry (Drake), Annie Golden (Marina), Shani Wallis (narrator), Scott Bullock, Louise Vallance, Angeline Ball, B.J. Ward, Hamilton Camp, Will Ryan, Stanley Jones.

Dir: Don Bluth. Pro: Russell Boland. Ex Pro: James Butterworth. Screenplay: Rachel Koretsky and Steve Whitestone. Pro Des: David Goetz. Ed: Thomas V. Moss. M: Mark Watters; supervisor: Barry Manilow; songs: Manilow (music) and Bruce Sussman (lyrics). (Don Bluth Ireland–Warner.) Rel: 16 February 1996. 74 mins. Cert U. USA. 1995.

Persuasion

Persuaded to break off her engagement to the handsome naval officer Frederick Wentworth because of his limited funds, Anne Elliot, the second daughter of the haughty Sir Walter Elliot, is plunged into despair. Then the

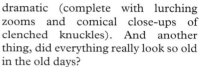

A good hair day: Pocahontas and her pet raccoon Meeko enjoy the spectacular Virginia scenery in Disney's triumphant Pocahontas

Elliots find themselves on equally shaky financial ground and are forced to rent out the ancestral home and move to more modest quarters in Bath. Meanwhile, Wentworth is making his fortune overseas … Anybody with a passing acquaintance with the works of

Social butterflies: Victoria Hamilton, Emma Roberts and Sophie Thompson in Roger Michell's dry translation of Jane Austen's Persuasion *(from BBC/Winstone)*

Jane Austen (and that has to be half the country by now), will not be surprised by the turn of events in this adaptation of the author's 1815 novel. Once again we have the financial dilemma of the upper classes, an unspoken love of the century and a dashing, but dastardly seducer. Originally made for television (and screened twice by the BBC), *Persuasion* did well on theatrical release in the US, prompting a belated engagement in British cinemas. Yet next to the Beeb's *Pride and Prejudice* and Emma Thompson's *Sense and Sensibility*, this Austen is lifeless and predictable, not to say downright melodramatic (complete with lurching zooms and comical close-ups of clenched knuckles). And another thing, did everything really look so old in the old days?

Cast: Amanda Root (Anne Elliot), Ciaran Hinds (Captain Frederick Wentworth), Susan Fleetwood (Lady Russell), Corin Redgrave (Sir Walter Elliot), Fiona Shaw (Mrs Croft), John Woodvine (Admiral Croft), Phoebe Nicholls (Elizabeth Elliot), Samuel West (Mr Elliot), Sophie Thompson (Mary Musgrove), Judy Cornwell (Mrs Musgrove), Simon Russell Beale (Charles Musgrove), Felicity Dean (Mrs Clay), Roger Hammond (Mr Musgrove), Emma Roberts (Louisa Musgrove), Victoria Hamilton (Henrietta Musgrove), Richard McCabe (Captain Benwick), Helen Schlesinger (Mrs Smith), Jane Wood (Nurse Rooke), Robert Glenister, David Collings, Darlene Johnson, Cinnamon Faye.

Dir: Roger Michell. Pro: Fiona Finlay. Ex Pro: George Faber and Rebecca Eaton. Screenplay: Nick Dear. Ph: John Daly. Pro Des: William Dudley. Ed: Kate Evans. M: Jeremy Sams. Costumes: Alexander Byrne. (BBC Films/WGBH/Mobil Masterpiece Theatre/Millesime Prods–BBC/Winstone.) Rel: 19 January 1996. 106 mins. Cert U. UK. 1995.

Pocahontas

Besides a mischievous triumvirate of raccoon, hummingbird and pug (none of whom speak), Disney's 33rd animated feature takes a giant step away from the cosy fantasy world of the

Stamp of approval: Massimo Troisi and Philippe Noiret admire the charms of Maria Grazia Cucinotta in Michael Radford's exquisite Il Postino *(from Buena Vista)*

anthropomorphic and leaps on to the politically correct bandwagon of revisionist history. Clearly aiming for an older audience, *Pocahontas* recreates the legend of the Algonquin princess who falls for the English explorer John Smith, thus thwarting the almost certain massacre of her people. While taking the usual liberty with the facts, the film is a visually stunning, persuasive and moving celebration of the dignity and wisdom of the American Native (in spite of claims by some minority groups that they have, yet again, been misinterpreted). Be that as it may, this is the most convincing case yet for handing America back to its rightful owners. Standouts: the production numbers 'Listen With Your Heart', 'Colors Of The Wind' and 'Savages', and the character of Grandmother Willow, a wily, wise old tree with a sense of humour.

Voices: Irene Bedard (Pocahontas), Mel Gibson (John Smith), David Ogden Stiers (Governor Ratcliffe/Wiggins), Russell Means (Powhatan), Billy Connolly (Ben), Linda Hunt (Grandmother Willow), Christian Bale (Thomas), John Kassir (Meeko), Danny Mann (Percy), Joe Baker (Lon), Frank Welker (Flit), Michelle St John (Nakoma), James Apaumut Fall (Kocoum), Gordon Tootoosis (Kekata).

Dir: Mike Gabriel and Eric Goldberg. Pro: John Pentecost. Assoc Pro: Baker Bloodworth. Screenplay: Carl Binder, Susannah Grant and Philip Lazebnik. Ed: H. Lee Petersen. Art: Michael Giaimo. M: Alan Menken; songs: Menken (music), Stephen Schwartz (lyrics); 'Colors Of The Wind' sung by Vanessa Williams. (Walt Disney–Buena Vista.) Rel: 6 October 1995. 81 mins. Cert U. USA.

Il Postino - The Postman

Tired of the life of a fisherman, Mario Ruoppolo takes the job of a postman on a remote, tranquil island off the coast of Naples. Actually, few letters pass between the hands of the fishing community, until the arrival of the renowned, exiled Chilean poet Pablo Neruda, whose fan mail and business correspondence necessitates an extra employee at the local post office. Fascinated by the new celebrity, Mario establishes a liaison of sorts with the poet, garnering the power of metaphor and simile from him. Armed with these new figures of speech, Mario advances on the local barmaid ... Unfolding from the opening credits with a bewitching, poetic simplicity, *Il Postino* paints a seductive scenario that dares not be disturbed by anything as intrusive as a plot. Yet, as these straightforward, endearing folk follow their uncomplicated routines, so the film glides into a narrative amble that never disturbs the calm and charm of its idyllic waters. Philippe Noiret, as ever, is a wonder to behold as the amiable bard, but it is Massimo Troisi's gentle, ingenuous portrayal of the postman that transcends acting. FYI: Troisi, who co-scripted the film and brought the novel to the attention of director Radford, died the day after completion of principal photography, aged 41.

Cast: Philippe Noiret (Pablo Neruda), Massimo Troisi (Mario), Maria Grazia Cucinotta (Beatrice), Linda Moretti (Rosa), Renato Scarpa (telegraph operator), Anna Bonaiuto (Matilde), Mariano Rigillo (Di Cosimo), Sergio Solli, Carlo di Maio, Nando Neri.

Dir: Michael Radford. Pro: Mario Cecchi Gori, Vittorio Cecchi Gori and Gaetano

The rage of innocence: Richard Gere pitches his case for Edward Norton in Gregory Hoblit's engrossing Primal Fear *(from UIP)*

Daniele. Ex Pro: Albert Passone. Screenplay: Radford, Anna Pavignano, Furio Scarpelli, Giacomo Scarpelli and Massimo Troisi, from the novel *Burning Patience* by Antonio Skarmeta, itself based on a true incident. Ph: Franco Di Giacomo. Ed: Roberto Perpignani. Pro Des: Lorenzo Baraldi. M: Luis Enrique Bacalov. Costumes: Gianni Gissi. (Tiger Cinematographica/Pentafilm Esterno/Mediterraneo/Blue Dahlia/Canal Plus–Buena Vista.) Rel: 20 October 1995. 108 mins. Cert PG. Italy/France. 1994.

Primal Fear

Hotshot Chicago attorney Martin Vail likes to see his face on the six o'clock news and relishes the money that goes with the territory. However, when a 19-year-old altar boy is arrested for hacking an archbishop to death, Vail sets his ambition to one side to fight for the boy's rights. But can Vail relinquish his career moves even in a case that is beginning to work on his emotions? In spite of the politically correct clichés (the black female judge, the Oriental anchorwoman, an unsympathetic character's addiction to cigarettes), the film is so efficiently directed by Gregory Hoblit (executive producer and director of *L.A. Law*) that you forgive it everything. Richard Gere is on particularly good form, transforming a headline-chasing careerist into a sympathetic character even though he refuses to spell out his moral agenda. However, it is Edward Norton (in his first film role) who, as the stammering bumpkin convicted of a brutal murder, bestows the film with its true calibre.

Cast: Richard Gere (Martin Vail), Laura Linney (Janet Venable), John Mahoney (John Shaughnessy), Alfre Woodard (Judge Miriam Shoat), Frances McDormand (Dr Molly Arrington), Edward Norton (Aaron Stampler), Terry O'Quinn (Bud Yancy), Andre Braugher (Tommy Goodman), Maura Tierney (Naomi Chance), Steven Bauer (Joey Pinero), Joe Spano (Captain Abel Stenner), Stanley Anderson (Archbishop Rushman), Jon Seda (Alex), Reg Rogers (Jack Connerman), Tony Plana, Kenneth Tigar, Brian Reddy, Wendy Cutler, Linda Yu, Clarence Williams Jr.

Dir: Gregory Hoblit. Pro: Gary Lucchesi. Ex Pro: Howard W. Koch Jr. Screenplay: Steve Shagan and Ann Biderman, based on the novel by William Diehl. Ph: Michael Chapman. Pro Des: Jeannine Oppewall. Ed: David Rosenbloom. M: James Newton Howard; Mozart. Costumes: Betsy Cox. (Paramount/Rysher Entertainment–UIP.) Rel: 24 May 1996. 130 mins. Cert 18. USA. 1996.

The Quick and the Dead

John Herod rules the dead-end town of Redemption, Arizona, with a fist of Smith & Wesson. Setting up a gunfighting contest, he challenges anybody to end his rein with a draw. But nobody is as quick as John Herod – although a young preacher, Herod's own son and a female stranger are gonna try ... From the opening strum of a guitar to the close-up of horses' hooves and a silhouette in the sun, the clichés of the western are promptly established. Yet while boldly yanking the funny bone, this testosterone-heavy, leather-coated odyssey never signals the laughs in advance in the tradition of *Blazing Saddles*. Somehow the comedy and the western have been uneasy allies and this is the closest they're likely to come in entertaining harmony. A blatant spoof of the stylistic horse

Making the sparks fly: Wu Gang and Ning Jing play with fire in He Ping's nuanced Red Firecracker, Green Firecracker *(from Electric)*

operas of Sergio Leone, *The Quick and the Dead* has enough dramatic ballast to keep its boots on.

Cast: Sharon Stone (Ellen), Gene Hackman (John Herod), Russell Crowe (Cort), Leonardo DiCaprio (Kid), Tobin Bell, Roberts Blossom, Kevin Conway, Keith David, Lance Henriksen, Pat Hingle, Gary Sinise, Mark Boone Junior, Olivia Burnette, Fay Masterson, Raynor Scheine, Woody Strode, Jerry Swindall, Scott Spiegel, Jonothon Gill, Sven-Ole Thorsen, Lennie Loftin, Bruce Campbell, Michael Stone, Oliver Dear.
    Dir: Sam Raimi. Pro: Joshua Donen, Allen Shapiro and Patrick Markey. Ex Pro: Toby Jaffe and Robert Tapert. Co-Pro: Chuck Binder and Sharon Stone. Screenplay: Simon Moore. Ph: Dante Spinotti. Ed: Pietro Scalia. Pro Des: Patrizia Von Brandenstein. M: Alan Silvestri. Costumes: Judianna Makovsky. (Japan Satellite Broadcasting/IndieProd–TriStar.) Rel: 22 September 1995. 107 mins. Cert 15. USA. 1995.

Red Firecracker, Green Firecracker - Paoda Shuang Deng

Niu Bao, a proud itinerant painter, arrives in a remote village in Northern China at the turn of the century. Here

firework manufacture is the order of the day, with the constant whiz and bang of firecrackers rending the air. Hired to paint 76 doors at the Cai palace, Bao is drawn to the Cai 'Master', a strict, aloof figure indoctrinated by tradition. The 'Master' is in fact Chun Zhi, a very beautiful 19-year-old woman whose life has been dedicated to the lucrative production of firecrackers. While in command of her own business empire, Zhi is green to the ways of love until her dormant cravings are sparked by the brash, incendiary overtures of Bao – leading, inevitably, to fireworks of a different nature. Yet another masterly example of the power of intimation and subtext, beautifully conveyed by Yang Lun's unobtrusive camerawork and a performance of restrained passion and dignity from Ning Jing as Zhi.

Cast: Ning Jing (Chun Zhi, The 'Master'), Wu Gang (Niu Bao, the painter), Zhao Xiaorui (Mr Mann), Gai Yang (Mr Zhao), Xu Zhengyun (Mr Xu, the one-armed master), Zhao Liang, Ju Xingmao, Li Yushen.
    Dir: He Ping. Pro: Chen Chunkeung and Yung Naiming. Ex Pro: Naiming. Screenplay: Da Ying, based on the novel by Feng Jicai. Ph: Yang Lun. Ed: Yuan Hong. Art: Qian Yunxiu. M: Zhao Jiping. Costumes: Chen Changmin. (Yung & Associate/Xi'an Film Studio/ Beijing Salon Films–Electric.) Rel: 8 September 1995. 111 mins. Cert 15. Hong Kong/China. 1993.

Rendez-vous in Paris - Les Rendez-vous de Paris

The haunting refrain 'there are sometimes misunderstandings and often surprises' links three short stories in this engaging if modest low-budget offering. The film charts the course of a young woman who suspects her boyfriend of infidelity; a married woman and her ardent suitor exploring the possibilities of a future together; and a young artist whose obligation to escort a Swedish girl around town is overwhelmed by a chance encounter with another girl. But the real subject of this gentle and humorous film is Paris itself – its changing moods and contrasting locations benignly determining the destiny of those within. [*Nigel Mulock*]

Cast: *The Seven O'Clock Rendez-vous*: Clara Bellar (Esther), Antoine Basler (Horace), Judith Chancel (Aricie), Mathias Megard (the flirt). *The Benches of Paris*: Aurore Rauscher (the woman), Serge Renko (the man). *Mother and Child*: Michael Kraft (the painter), Benedicte Loyen (the young woman), Veronika Johansson (the Swedish woman).
    Dir: Eric Rohmer. Pro: Francois Etchegaray. Ph: Diane Baratier. Ed: Mary Stephen. M: Sebastien Erms. (Compagnie Eric Rohmer/Canal Plus–Artificial Eye.) Rel: 9 February 1996. 98 mins. Cert PG. France. 1995.

Restoration

England; 1663-6. A medical student in disease-plagued London, Robert Merivel is bestowed with a rare gift for healing the sick – although his interest in anatomy is torn between the medical and the carnal. When Robert is invited to the court of Charles II to help save the life of the king's pet spaniel, his hedonistic instincts get the better of him. Conferred with a knighthood and country estate (not to mention a lavish wardrobe), he promptly forgets his true vocation. But the Restoration, a period of extraordinary transition, holds many surprises in store for Robert ... Philosophically rich and visually beguiling, *Restoration* abounds with many pleasures. Sam Neill makes a splendid Merry Monarch, while Eugenio Zanetti's opulent production design and James Acheson's costumes are out of this world. But the film's leaden pacing and Robert Downey Jr's uncharismatic turn in the central role let the side down. Worse, James Newton Howard's incessant, droning score robs the film of any emotional light and shade.

Cast: Robert Downey Jr (Robert Merivel), Sam Neill (King Charles II), David Thewlis (Dr John Pearce), Polly Walker (Celia Clemence), Meg Ryan (Katherine), Ian McKellen (Will Gates), Hugh Grant (Finn), Ian McDiarmid (Ambrose), Benjamin Whitrow (Merivel's father), Mary Macleod, Sandy McDade, Rosalind Bennett, Willie Ross, David Gant, Bryan Pringle, Roy Evans, Roger Ashton-Griffiths, David Ryall, Jenny Runacre.

Dir: Michael Hoffman. Pro: Cary Brokaw, Andy Paterson and Sarah Ryan Black. Ex Pro: Kip Hagopian. Co-Pro: Bob Weinstein, Harvey Weinstein and Donna Gigliotta. Screenplay: Rupert Walters, based on the novel by Rose Tremain. Ph: Oliver Stapleton. Pro Des: Eugenio Zanetti. Ed: Garh Craven. M: James Newton Howard; Henry Purcell. Costumes: James Acheson. (Segue Prods/Avenue Pictures/Oxford Film Company–Buena Vista.) Rel: 8 March 1996. 118 mins. Cert 15. USA. 1995.

Richard III

While Oliver Parker stripped down the text of *Othello* to make it more cinematic on its own terms, Ian McKellen and Richard Loncraine have decimated *Richard III* for their own. Thus, the conniving, hunchbacked royal imposter has been mutated into an Oswald Mosley-like gangster, and 15th-century Britain into 1930s Fascist England. And it works. Although based on McKellen's own triumphant performance of the play, nothing theatrical remains. Scatter-gun pacing, inspired visuals, an all-star cast and plenty of violence hoists the text on to a new and vastly entertaining plane. Thus, rather than confiding in the camera with his stilted 'now is the winter of our discontent' monologue, McKellen turns it into grand oratory by addressing a stately congregation. Likewise, the 'A horse! A horse! My kingdom for a horse!' speech makes perfect sense when Richard's fleeing jeep gets stuck in the mud. McKellen himself, eloquent, demonic and self-mocking, transforms Richard from a theatrical rogue into a seductive vision of the devil himself. Inspired cinema – and a welcome re-evaluation of the Bard.

Cast: Ian McKellen (Richard III), Annette Bening (Queen Elizabeth), Kristin Scott

Ian McKellen, determined to prove a villain, in his greatest screen role as Richard III *(from Guild)*

Thomas (Lady Anne), Jim Broadbent (Buckingham), Robert Downey Jr (Earl Rivers), Maggie Smith (Duchess of York), Nigel Hawthorne (Clarence), Jim Carter (Lord Hastings), Dominic West (Henry Richmond), John Wood (Kind Edward IV), Bill Paterson (Richard Ratcliffe), Adrian Dunbar (Corp. James Tyrell), Tim McInnery (Sir William Catesby), Kate Steavenson-Payne (Princess Elizabeth), Edward Hardwicke (Lord Stanley), Roger Hammond (Archbishop of Canterbury), Donald Sumpter, Matthew Groom, Marc Williamson, Michael Elphick.

Dir: Richard Loncraine. Pro: Lisa Katesalas Pare and Stephen Bayly. Ex Pro: Ellen Dinerman Little, Ian McKellen, Joe Simon and Maria Apodiacos. Screenplay: McKellen and Loncraine, based on the stage adaptation by Richard Eyre. Ph: Peter Biziou. Pro Des: Tony Burrough. Ed: Paul Green. M: Trevor Jones. Costumes: Shuna Harwood. (Mayfair Entertainment International/British Screen/United Artists/First Look Pictures–Guild.) Rel: 26 April 1996. 103 mins. Cert 15. UK. 1995.

The Rock

Stanley Goodspeed is an expert in chemical warfare who drives a beige Volvo. John Mason is a sixty-year-old man who has spent the last thirty years

Granite testosterone: Executive producer and sometime actor Sean Connery gets to grips with the hardware in Michael Bay's dynamic The Rock *(from Buena Vista)*

(Jade Angelou), Vanessa Marcil (Carla Pestalozzi, Stanley's girlfriend), Jim Maniaci, Greg Collins, Gregory Sporleder, Brendan Kelly, David Bowe, Howard Platt, Marshall Teague, Danny Nucci, Willie Garson, Anthony Clark (the barber), Sam Whipple, Tom Towles.

Dir: Michael Bay. Pro: Don Simpson and Jerry Bruckheimer. Ex Pro: William Stuart, Sean Connery and Louis A. Stroller. Screenplay: David Weisberg, Douglas S. Cook and Mark Rosner. Ph: John Schwartzman. Pro Des: Michael White. Ed: Richard Francis-Bruce. M: Nick Glennie-Smith and Hans Zimmer; numbers performed by Scott McKenzie, Elton John, and Buddy Holly and The Crickets. Costumes: Bobbie Read. (Hollywood Pictures–Buena Vista.) Rel: 21 June 1996. 129 mins. Cert 15. USA. 1996.

Rough Magic

1950; Los Angeles/Mexico. When magician's assistant Myra Shumway (Fonda) sees her boss shot dead by her incredibly wealthy fiancé, she flees to Mexico. There, she meets up with a seedy but charismatic drifter (Crowe), unaware that he is an agent hired by her ex. But romance would appear to have its own agenda, as would the genuine sorcery of a local shaman... While attempting to capture the spirit of those tough, screwball romantic escapades of yesteryear, *Rough Magic* falls down by feeding Bridget Fonda and Russell Crowe duff lines and inane situations. The film works best as a magic surrealist comedy, with the ever-dependable Jack Russell terrier Barkley (*This Boy's Life*, *Clean Slate*) again stealing every scene he's in. FYI: Director-writer Clare Peploe is the wife of Bernardo Bertolucci.

Cast: Bridget Fonda (Myra Shumway), Russell Crowe (Alex Ross), Jim Broadbent (Doc Ansell), D.W. Moffet (Cliff Wyatt), Paul Rodriguez (Diego), Euva Anderson (Tojola/Diego's wife), Kenneth Mars (Ivan the Terrific), Andy Romano (Clayton), Richard Schiff (Marvin Wiggins), Michael Ensign, Chris Otto.

Dir: Clare Peploe. Pro: Laurie Parker and Declan Baldwin. Ex Pro: Yves Attal, Andrew Karsch and Jonathan Taplin. Screenplay: Peploe, Robert Mundy and William Brookfield, from the novel *Miss Shumway Waves a Wand* by James Hadley Chase. Ph: John J. Campbell. Pro Des: Waldemar Kalinowski. Ed: Suzanne Fenn. M: Richard Hartley. Costumes: Richard Hornung. (UGC Images/Recorded Picture Company–Fox.) Rel: 17 May 1996. 105 mins. Cert 12. France/UK. 1995.

inside a cell. They're an unlikely match, but they are both educated men and share a love of the classics. They are also the last-ditch hope of the Pentagon to break into Alcatraz, the former fortress that's just been taken over by an elite army of terrorists ... A thinking man's action movie, if there is such a thing, *The Rock* diminishes the familiarity of its premise (terrorists, hostages, bomb, ransom) with the infusion of an A-list cast. Directed by

Michael Bay (*Bad Boys*) with the dementia of an emergency room surgeon, the film deploys MTV cutting to keep the adrenaline flowing. Ultimately, however, *The Rock* is more exhausting than suspenseful, although the stunts and techno-babble are top of the range.

Cast: Sean Connery (John Patrick Mason), Nicolas Cage (Stanley Goodspeed), Ed Harris (General Francis X. Hummel), Michael Biehn (Charles Anderson), William Forsythe (Eddie Paxton), David Morse (Major Tom Baxter), John C. McGinley (Marine Captain Hendrix), Bokeem Woodbine (Sergeant Crisp), Tony Todd (Captain Darrow), John Spencer (FBI Director Womack), Claire Forlani

Rudy

Inexplicably belated release of this captivating story of a small-town boy from Illinois who struggles to realise his dreams against impossible odds. Predestined to end up working at the local industrial plant, Rudy fights for a place at the University of Notre Dame in order to join the legendary Fighting Irish football team – in spite of his small stature and academic under-performance. While laying on the romanticism, the film sidesteps pure corn thanks to intelligent writing and a driving spirit that gives this well-packaged tonic genuine pedigree. Charles S. Dutton and Jason Miller in supporting turns are particularly effective. Based on a true story. [*Charles Bacon*]

Cast: Sean Astin (Daniel E. 'Rudy' Ruettiger), Ned Beatty (Daniel Ruettiger Snr), Charles S. Dutton (Fortune), Jason Miller (Ara Parseghian), Lili Taylor (Sherry), Robert Prosky (Father Cavanaugh), Greta Lind (Mary), Jon Favreau (D-Bob), Chelcie Ross, Ron Dean, Scott Benjaminson, Christopher Reed, Mary Ann Thebus, Robert J. Steinmiller Jr.

Dir: David Anspaugh. Pro: Robert N. Fried and Cary Woods. Ex Pro: Lee R. Mayes. Co-Pro and Screenplay: Angelo Pizzo. Ph: Oliver Wood. Ed: David Rosenbloom. Pro Des: Robb Wilson King. M: Jerry Goldsmith; numbers performed by Johnny Cash, Patsy Cline, Creedence Clearwater Revival, etc. Costumes: Jane Anderson. (TriStar–Columbia TriStar.) Rel: 14 July 1995. 113 mins. Cert PG. USA. 1993.

All the right moves: Christopher Reed and Sean Astin drink to ambition in David Anspaugh's Rudy *(from Columbia TriStar)*

The Run of the Country

County Cavan, Ireland; today. When his mother dies of a heart attack, eighteen-year-old Danny is forced to face the future and his tyrannical father on his own. While resembling a number of recent Irish offerings (*Circle of Friends* and *The Playboys* in particular), Peter Yates's *The Run of the Country* has enough gutsy flavour of its own to mark it out as a passionate original. Based on the novel by Shane Connaughton (*My Left Foot*), the film gathers steam in its final passages to resemble the poetic power of *Ryan's Daughter*. Photography, music and editing are all top-notch, while Anthony Brophy as the coarse, good-natured 'Coco' Prunty is a marvel.

Cast: Albert Finney (Father), Matt Keeslar (Danny), Victoria Smurfit (Annagh), Anthony Brophy (Prunty), David Kelly (Father Gaynor), Dearbhla Molloy (Mother), Carole Nimmons (Mrs Prunty), Dawn Bradfield (Daphne), Joan Sheehy (Widdy McGinn), Vinnie McCabe, P.J. Brady, Declan Mulholland, Maureen Dow, Eileen Ward, Thomas Lappin, Antoine Byrne, Mary Reilly.

Country matters: Matt Keeslar and Victoria Smurfit in Peter Yates's absorbing The Run of the Country *(from Rank)*

Dir: Peter Yates. Pro: Yates and Ruth Boswell. Ex Pro: Nigel Wooll. Screenplay and Assoc Pro: Shane Connaughton. Ph: Mike Southon. Pro Des: Mark Geraghty. Ed: Paul Hodgson. M: Cynthia Millar; numbers performed by Titanic Cinq, The Saw Doctors, and Patsy Cline. Costumes: Rosemary Burrows. Second Unit Director: Toby Yates. Focus Puller: Simon Finney. (Castle Rock Entertainment/Channel Four/One Two Nine Rank.) Rel: 12 January 1996. 108 mins. Cert 15. Ireland. 1995.

Sabrina

Once upon a time on the north shore of Long Island lived one of America's richest families, the Larabees. And

Lifestyle of the rich and fabulous: Julia Ormond and Harrison Ford in Sydney Pollack's impossibly romantic Sabrina *(from UIP)*

there Sabrina, the bespectacled daughter of the chauffeur, spied on the two handsome heirs of the Larabee fortune: the stiff, buttoned-up and dependable Linus, and his dashing, debonair and self-centred younger brother, David. Sabrina Fairchild had been smitten with David for as long as she could remember, but who would ever look twice at a poor servant girl? Fairy tale romances are few and far between, and gold-plated, eight-cylinder ones as sophisticated and bewitching as this are as good as extinct. Updated from Billy Wilder's sparkling 1954 comedy of the same name (which starred Humphrey Bogart, Audrey Hepburn and William Holden), *Sabrina* strays little from the original save for passing concessions to mobile phones, laptop computers and Concorde. The joy of Sydney Pollack's polished remake is that the humour is never overstated, nor the strings of the deception plucked too hard. While Julia Ormond lacks the ethereal magic

of Audrey Hepburn, she makes a spunky, credible heroine, and is supported by a sterling cast (spearheaded by Nancy Marchand, John Wood and Richard Crenna).

Cast: Harrison Ford (Linus Larrabee), Julia Ormond (Sabrina Fairchild), Gregg Kinnear (David Larrabee), Nancy Marchand (Maude Larrabee), John Wood (Fairchild), Lauren Holly (Elizabeth Tyson), Angie Dickinson (Ingrid Tyson), Richard Crenna (Patrick Tyson), Dana Ivey (Mack), Elizabeth Franz (Joanna), Fanny Ardant (Irene), Patrick Bruel (Louis), Miriam Colon (Rosa), Valerie Lemercier, Becky Ann Baker, Paul Giamatti, Margo Martindale, J. Smith Cameron, Michael Dees, Carmen Chaplin.
Dir: Sydney Pollack. Pro: Pollack and Scott Rudin. Ex Pro: Ronald Schwary and Lindsay Doran. Screenplay: Barbara Benedek and David Rayfield, based on the screenplay by Billy Wilder, Samuel Taylor and Ernest Lehman, itself based on the play by Taylor. Ph: Giuseppe Rotunno. Pro Des: Brian Morris. Ed: Frederic Steinkamp. M: John Williams; songs by Williams (music) and Alan Bergman and Marilyn Bergman (lyrics); numbers performed by Michael Dees, Massive Attack, Tino Rossi, etc, 'Moonlight' sung by Sting. Costumes: Ann Roth. (Paramount/Constellation Films/

Mirage/Scott Rudin/Sandollar–UIP.) Rel: 26 January 1996. 127 mins. Cert PG. USA. 1995.

Safe

Isolated in physical comfort and a passionless marriage, 'homemaker' Carol White is insulated from the virulence of the outside world. By all intents and purposes living in one of the last 'safe' zones on earth, Carol gradually deteriorates in her sterile cocoon, succumbing to depression, vomiting and coughing fits ... It's hard to determine whether writer-director Todd Haynes is warning us of the ills of our society or mocking the New Age sensibilities depicted in his film. Either way, his pessimistic satire is masterly engineered (Carol's sense of detachment constantly reinforced by the oppressive architecture of her home) and is fortified by a selfless, unforgettable performance from Julianne Moore as the victim of her own apathy. Suitably disturbing. Haynes, incidentally, is obsessed by illness, his first film, *Superstar: The Karen Carpenter Story*, chronicling the fatal anorexia of the eponymous singer, and his previous work, *Poison*, exploring both mental and physical disorders.

Cast: Julianne Moore (Carol White), Peter Friedman (Peter Dunning), Xander Berkeley (Greg White), Susan Norman (Linda), Kate McGregor Stewart (Claire), James LeGros (Chris), Martha Velez-Johnson (Fulvia), Jessica Harper (Joyce), Mary Carver, Steven Gilborn, April Grace, Peter Crombie, Ronnie Farer, Jodie Markell, Lorna Scott, Wendy Haynes.
Dir and Screenplay: Todd Haynes. Pro: Christine Vachon and Lauren Zalaznick. Ex Pro: James Schamus, Lindsay Law and Ted Hope. Ph: Alex Nepomniaschy. Pro Des: David Bomba. Ed: James Lyons. M: Ed Tomney; numbers performed by Madonna, Brian Eno, Billy Ocean, Belinda Carlisle, Kenny Loggins, George Benson, etc. Costumes: Nancy Steiner. (American Playhouse/Chemical Films/Good Machine/Kardana Prods/Channel Four Films/Arnold Semler–Metro Tartan.) Rel: 26 April 1996. 118 mins. Cert 15. USA. 1995.

Safe Passage

New Jersey; today. Torn apart by the passage of time and irreconcilable differences, the Singer family – Mag, Patrick and their seven sons – finds itself drawn together when Percival Singer goes missing in a terrorist bomb

The usual suspects: Tim Allen (second from left) is the real thing in John Pasquin's The Santa Clause *(from Buena Vista)*

attack in the Sinai. Susan Sarandon, as the mother of mothers, has never been better (and that's saying something), mining a quarry of conflicting emotions that all ring true. Sam Shepard, too, as her estranged, easy-going husband, is on excellent form, bringing credibility to his own convictions.

With an extraordinarily complex film to orchestrate, stage director Ackerman knows exactly where to place his camera, allowing his story's innate drama to speak for itself as it plucks at a number of exposed nerves and heart strings.

Family dies: Susan Sarandon and Sam Shepard discover that home is where the heart is in Robert Allan Ackerman's engrossing Safe Passage *(from Entertainment)*

Cast: Susan Sarandon (Mag Singer), Sam Shepard (Patrick Singer), Robert Sean Leonard (Alfred Singer), Nick Stahl (Simon Singer), Jason London (Gideon Singer), Marcia Gay Harden (Cynthia), Matt Keeslar (Percival Singer), Philip Bosco (Mort), Philip Arthur Ross (Merle Singer), Steven Robert Ross (Darren Singer), Sean Astin (Izzy Singer), Priscilla Reeves, Jesse Lee, Jeffrey DeMunn, Rutanya Alda.

Dir: Robert Allan Ackerman. Pro: Gale Anne Hurd. Ex Pro: David Gale, Betsy Beers and Ruth Vitale. Line Pro: Diana Pokorny. Screenplay: Deena Goldstone, based on the novel by Ellyn Bache. Ph: Ralf Bode. Ed: Rick Shaine. Pro Des: Dan Bishop. M: Mark Isham; Wagner, Modest Mussorgsky ('Pictures At An Exhibition'); numbers performed by Carly Simon ('Touched By The Sun'), Kool Moe Dee, Raffi, Marshall Crenshaw, 10,000 Maniacs, The Cranberries, etc. Costumes: Renee Ehrlich Kalfus. (Pacific Western-Entertainment.) Rel: 25 August 1995. 98 mins. Cert 15. USA. 1994.

The Santa Clause

Following a somewhat strained Christmas Eve with his eight-year-old son, divorced father and toy executive Scott Calvin accidentally causes the death of Santa Claus. Then, after donning Santa's suit in order to placate his

Crimson tide: Gary Oldman (centre) makes peace with the Algonquin people in Roland Joffé's powerful look at early American history, The Scarlet Letter (from Entertainment)

son, Calvin develops a worrying weight problem and an accelerated growth of white beard ... Unashamedly reworking the spirit of *A Christmas Carol* (dressed up with some impressive prosthetic make-up), Disney's *The Santa Clause* is a fitfully amusing fantasy aimed squarely at that lump in the throat. Yet while much of the concept works a treat, a good deal of credibility is lost in thoughtless slapstick. However, for every drop of treacle, there are some nice adult asides, not least a bizarre allusion to Armand Assante. A wonderfully eclectic soundtrack includes ZZ Top and The Chipmunks' 'Santa Claus Is Comin' To Town'.

Cast: Tim Allen (Scott Calvin), Judge Reinhold (Neal), Wendy Crewson (Laura), David Krumholtz (Bernard - head elf), Peter Boyle (Mr Whittle), Eric Lloyd (Charlie Calvin), Paige Tamada (Elf - Judy), Larry Brandenburg, Mary Gross, Judith Scott,

Jayne Eastwood, Joyce Guy, John Pasquin. Dir: John Pasquin. Pro: Brian Reilly, Jeffrey Silver and Robert Newmyer. Ex Pro: Richard Baker, Rick Messina and James Miller. Screenplay: Leo Benvenuti and Steve Rudnick. Ph: Walt Lloyd. Ed: Larry Bock. Pro Des: Carol Spier. M: Michael Convertino; numbers performed by The Drifters, ZZ Top, The Chipmunks, Johnny Hawksworth, Brenda Russell and Howard Hewett, Loreena McKennitt, etc. Costumes: Carole Ramsey. Elf wrangler: Christy Garland. (Walt Disney Pictures–Buena Vista.) Rel: 1 December 1995. 98 mins. Cert U. USA. 1994.

The Scarlet Letter

Massachusetts; mid-17th century. Arriving in Boston from England to help forge an exciting, free New World, Hester Prynne discovers nothing but hypocrisy and prejudice – a paranoia fuelled by the fear of the surrounding wilderness and native Algonquin people. But by refusing to compromise her own integrity, beliefs and code of Christianity, Hester suffers a terrible fate for one night of passion ... Damned by the critics as the turkey of the year, this 'free' interpretation of

Nathaniel Hawthorne's verbose 1850 novel has much to offer. Skilfully photographed by Alex Thomson, handsomely designed by Roy Walker and sensitively scripted by Douglas Day Stewart, the film is yet another impassioned, eloquent and heartfelt cry against the injustices of history from the director of *The Killing Fields*, *The Mission* and *City of Joy*. And, far from being a vanity vehicle for the temperamental Demi Moore (whose strongest ally remains the camera lens), *The Scarlet Letter* features a volcanic turn from Gary Oldman as the spiritually tortured adulterer, a compassionate reading from Joan Plowright as the plain-speaking widow Harriet Hibbons (only sketchily shaded in the book) and an extraordinary portrait of restrained evil from Robert Duvall. A powerful, accomplished recreation of early American history that deserves re-appraisal.

Cast: Demi Moore (Hester Prynne), Gary Oldman (Arthur Dimmesdale), Robert Duvall (Roger Prynne/Roger Chillingworth), Lisa Jolliff-Andoh (Mituba), Edward Hardwicke (John Bellingham), Robert Prosky (Horace Stonehall), Roy Dotrice (Thomas Cheever), Joan Plowright (Harriet

Hibbons), Tim Woodward (Brewster Stonehall), Eric Schweig (Metacomet), Jodhi May (voice of Pearl), Malcolm Storry, Jim Bearden, Larissa Lapchinski, Amy Wright, George Aguilar, Joan Gregson, Dana Ivey, Diane Salinger, Kennetch Charlette.

Dir: Roland Joffé. Pro: Joffé and Andrew G. Vajna. Ex Pro: Dodi Fayed and Tova Laiter. Co-Pro: Robert Colesberry. Screenplay: Douglas Day Stewart. Ph: Alex Thomson. Ed: Thom Noble. Pro Des: Roy Walker. M: John Barry. Costumes: Gabriella Pescucci. Demi Moore's Body Make-Up Artist: Jeanie Fielder. (Hollywood Pictures/Lightmotive/Allied Stars/Cinergi/Moving Pictures–Entertainment.) Rel: 17 November 1995. 135 mins. Cert 15. USA. 1995.

Screamers

2078; outer space. Designed to hunt down and shred enemy intruders on the planet Sirius 6B, screamers are the ultimate weapon of the future: subterranean, self-replicating machines made of circular saws. But during a lengthy civil war the 'machines' have taken on a life of their own. Utilising the methane gas from rotting bodies as fuel, the screamers have upgraded themselves into intelligent life forms that can adopt any shape they like ... Based on the short story *Second Variety* by Philip K. Dick, *Screamers* thankfully refrains from subscribing to the MTV school of filmmaking, instead developing a more thoughtful, laid-back style. Peter Weller, as the opera-loving commander abandoned by his superiors, lends some intellectual gravity and irony to the exercise, keeping the hightec excesses in their place ('Morse code used to be better than this virtual reality shit'). There are also plenty of nice little touches, while the matte shots and creature effects are top of the range.

Cast: Peter Weller (Joseph A. Hendrickson), Roy Dupuis (Becker), Jennifer Rubin (Jessica), Andy Lauer (Ace Jefferson), Charles Powell (Ross), Michael Caloz (David), Bruce Boa (Secretary Green), Ron White, Liliana Komorowska, Jason Cavalier.

Dir: Christian Duguay. Pro: Tom Berry and Franco Battista. Ex Pro: Charles W. Fries. Supervising Pro: Antony I. Ginnane. Co-Ex Pro: Josee Bernard and Masao Takiyama. Assoc Pro: Stefan Wodoslawsky. Screenplay: Dan O'Bannon and Miguel Tejada-Flores. Ph: Rodney Gibbons. Pro Des: Perri Gorrara. Ed: Yves Langlois. M:

And another cup of tea: Brenda Blethyn (right), in the performance that won her the best actress award at Cannes, makes a surprising discovery in Mike Leigh's blissful Secrets & Lies *(from Film Four). Marianne Jean-Baptiste looks on*

Normand Corbeil. Costumes: Trixi Rittenhouse. Digital Effects: Richard Ostiguy. Visual Effects: Ernest Farino. (Triumph Films/Fuji Eight/Fries Film/Allegro Films–Columbia TriStar.) Rel: 28 June 1996. 108 mins. Cert 18. US/Canada/Japan. 1995.

Secrets and Lies

Hortense is an intelligent, attractive and cultured young black woman who holds down a good job as an optometrist. Adopted from birth, she decides to seek out her biological mother following the funeral of her adoptive mother of 26 years. To her surprise, Hortense discovers that her real mother is Cynthia, who is white. Cynthia, who has become virtually isolated from the rest of mankind, lives alone with her abusive, chain-smoking 20-year-old daughter, Roxanne, a road sweeper. Cynthia herself puts the slits into the sides of cardboard boxes and lives a life of absolute misery. And she has no idea of the whereabouts, gender or race of her first child ... The com-

pelling thing about the work of Mike Leigh is that the writer-director has an uncanny knack for pinpointing the banal in people's lives, whatever their class or creed. Here, he introduces his traditional roster of caricatures, but gives them a stronger than usual narrative on which to work. Brenda Blethyn, who builds on the performance she created for Leigh's *Grown Ups*, is a tower of selfless wretchedness, whose frequent loss of control veers uneasily between mirth and despair. Similarly, we, the audience, don't know whether to laugh or shudder. But then Cynthia observes, 'You've got to laugh, ain't you, sweetheart? Else you'd cry.'

Cast: Timothy Spall (Maurice), Brenda Blethyn (Cynthia), Phyllis Logan (Monica), Marianne Jean-Baptiste (Hortense), Claire Rushbrook (Roxanne), Elizabeth Berrington (Jane), Michele Austin (Dionne), Lee Ross (Paul), Lesley Manville (social worker), Ron Cook (Stuart), Emma Amos, Brian Bovell, Trevor Laird, Clare Perkins, June Mitchell, Hannah Davis, Terence Harvey, Lucy Sheen, Peter Wight, Gary McDonald, Alison Steadman, Liz Smith, Sheila Kelley, Philip Davis, Ruth Sheen.

Dir and Screenplay: Mike Leigh. Pro: Simon Channing-Williams. Pro Ex: Phillip Kenny. Ph: Dick Pope. Pro Des: Alison Chitty. Ed: Jon Gregory. M: Andrew Dickson. Costumes: Maria Price. (CiBy 2000/Thin Man Films/Channel Four–Film Four.) Rel: 24 May 1996. 141 mins. Cert 15. UK/France. 1995.

A bonnet tonic: Kate Winslet and Emma Thompson ruminate on the multitudinous ramifications of love in Ang Lee's heavenly Sense and Sensibility *(from Columbia TriStar)*

Sense and Sensibility

The late 1700s; England. Two sisters find their fortunes dramatically compromised when their late father's estate is left to his son by his first marriage. Only love, it seems, can salvage the women's wellbeing, but then love is a precarious animal ... Generally considered to be Jane Austen's weakest novel, *Sense and Sensibility* has been given a sensitive and voluptuous treatment here, scripted by Emma Thompson over a period of five years. Visually glorious, frequently very funny and impeccably acted (with stand-out turns from Hugh Laurie, Elizabeth Spriggs and Harriet Walter), the film's narrative weaknesses reflect the novel's, dipping perilously in the final quarter. However, some resolute wit and outstanding production values save the day. FYI: So determined was director Ang Lee to avoid sentimentality, that when two swans swam into shot during a romantic clinch the scene had to be filmed again.

Cast: Emma Thompson (Elinor Dashwood), Alan Rickman (Colonel Brandon), Kate Winslet (Marianne Dashwood), Hugh Grant (Edward Ferrars), James Fleet (John Dashwood), Tom Wilkinson (Mr Dashwood), Harriet Walter (Fanny Dashwood), Gemma Jones (Mrs Dashwood), Emile Francois (Margaret Dashwood), Elizabeth Spriggs (Mrs Jennings), Robert Hardy (Sir John Middleton), Greg Wise (John Willoughby), Imelda Staunton (Charlotte Palmer), Imogen Stubbs (Lucy Steele), Hugh Laurie (Mr Palmer), Richard Lumsden (Robert Ferrars), Ian Brimble, Isabelle Amyes, Oliver Ford Davies.

Dir: Ang Lee. Pro: Lindsay Doran. Ex Pro: Sydney Pollack. Co-Pro: James Schamus and Laurie Borg. Screenplay: Emma Thompson. Ph: Michael Coulter. Pro Des: Luciana Arrighi. Ed: Tim Squyres. M: Patrick Doyle. Costumes: Jenny Beavan and John Bright. Food Stylist: Debbie Brodie. (Columbia Pictures/Mirage Prods–Columbia TriStar.) Rel: 23 February 1996. 136 mins. Cert U. UK. 1995.

La Separation

From the moment Anne jerks her hand away from Pierre's at the cinema, their relationship starts to unravel like a picked pullover. The parents of a 15-month-old boy, Pierre and Anne share an apartment in Paris, but the little irritations are building into grievances. He no longer pays her the attention she should, she is hardly ever at home ... Although the minutiae of the emotional cracks ring resoundingly true, there is a surprising lack of personal background here. While passing reference is made to some book Pierre is finishing, the professional life of Anne is totally ignored. Nevertheless, the dialogue and Auteuil and Huppert's remarkably detailed performances make this a most absorbing drama.

Cast: Isabelle Huppert (Anne), Daniel Auteuil (Pierre), Jerome Deschamps (Victor), Karin Viard (Claire), Laurence Lerel (Laurence), Louis Vincent (Loulou), Nina Morato (Marie).

Dir: Christian Vincent. Pro: Claude Berri. Ex Pro: Pierre Grunstein. Screenplay: Vincent and Dan Franck, from the novel by Franck. Ph: Denis Lenoir. Ed: Francois Ceppi. Set Des: Christian Vallerin. M: Johann Sebastian Bach's 'Goldberg Variations' interpreted by Glenn Gould. Costumes: Sylvie Gautrelet. (Renn Productions/France 2/DA Films/CMV/Canal Plus–Guild.) Rel: 1 September 1995. 88 mins. Cert PG. France. 1994.

Deadly signs: Morgan Freeman sifts through the human wreckage in David Fincher's accomplished Seven *(from Entertainment)*

Seven

A faceless, methodical and scholarly psychopath is loose in a faceless North American city. In a tribute to Chaucer and Dante, the killer engineers the deaths of his victims to suit their sins. Thus, an obscenely overweight man is gutted in the name of gluttony; an extortionate defence attorney is killed for his greed, and so on. It takes Lt. Det. William Somerset little time to predict that five more murders will complete the Seven Deadly Sins. But Somerset's adversary leaves no clues: no fingerprints, no witnesses, no motive ... Following the vacuous ostentation of David Fincher's *Alien 3*, the raw power and human complexity of Fincher's stunning thriller comes as a huge surprise. While brandishing his distinctive style like a badge, Fincher showers fragments of narrative across a blanket of sheer atmosphere. This is eminently watchable cinema which, with unique flair and vivid nuance, electrifies a timeworn genre – the black cop and his white partner on the trail of a serial killer.

Cast: Brad Pitt (Det. David Mills), Morgan Freeman (Lt. Det. William Somerset), Gwyneth Paltrow (Tracy), John C. McGinley (California), R. Lee Ermey (police captain), Kevin Spacey (John Doe), Richard Roundtree (Talbot), Richard Portnow (Dr Beardsley), Julie Araskog, Mark Boone Junior, Daniel Zacapa, John Cassini, Peter Crombie, Reg. E. Cathey, Charline Su,

Too close for comfort: Isabelle Huppert and Daniel Auteuil inhabit separate worlds in Christian Vincent's absorbing La Separation *(from Guild)*

Pamela Tyson, Emily Wagner, Martin Serene, Richard Schiff, Richmond Arquette.

Dir: David Fincher. Pro: Arnold Kopelson and Phyllis Carlyle. Ex Pro: Gianni Nunnari, Dan Kolsrud and Anne Kopelson. Co-Ex Pro: Lynn Harris and Richard Saperstein. Co-Pro: Stephen Brown, Nana Greenwald and Sanford Panitch. Ph: Darius Khondji. Pro Des: Arthur Max. Ed: Richard Francis-Bruce. M: Howard Shore. Costumes: Michael Kaplan. (New Line–Entertainment.) Rel: 5 January 1996. 127 mins. Cert 18. USA. 1995.

Sgt. Bilko

In the tradition of *Dragnet* and *The Flintstones*, Universal Pictures unearths this chestnut from the golden age of television. Sgt. Ernest G. Bilko

Welcome to Shanghai: Gong Li in Zhang Yimou's vacuous Shanghai Triad *(from Electric)*

is officially in charge of the 'motor pool' at the US army's Fort Baxter, but he is more concerned with setting up scams and gambling operations than national security. Then an old foe, Major Thorn, turns up to expose Bilko's unethical practices – by fair means or foul ... Bravely leaping into the shoes of Phil Silvers, Steve Martin makes an engaging old clod, even though his treatment of his long-suffering girlfriend (Glenne Headly) borders on the inhumane. There are a few moments of comic invention (and a great sight gag involving a horse), but the odd good joke cannot alleviate the mediocrity. Alan Silvestri supplies the moronic score. N.B. The filmmakers gratefully acknowledge the total lack of cooperation from the US army.

Cast: Steve Martin (Sgt. Ernest G. Bilko), Dan Aykroyd (Colonel Hall), Phil Hartman (Major Thorn), Glenne Headly (Rita Rob-

Soldier of fortunes: Steve Martin tramples over the memory of Phil Silvers in Jonathan Lynn's Sgt. Bilko *(from UIP)*

bins), Daryl Mitchell (Wally Holbrook), Eric Edwards (Duane Doberman), John Marshall Jones (Sgt. Henshaw), Pamela Segall (Sgt. Raquel Barbella), Max Casella, Dan Ferro, Brian Leckner, Austin Pendleton, Chris Rock, Catherine Silvers (daughter of Phil), Debra Jo Rupp, Richard Herd, Dale Dye, Rance Howard, Travis Tritt (himself).

Dir: Jonathan Lynn. Pro: Brian Grazer. Co-Pro: Mary McLaglen. Screenplay: Andy Breckman, based on characters from CBS TV's The Phil Silvers Show created by Nat Hiken. Ph: Peter Sova. Pro Des: Lawrence G. Paull. Ed: Tony Lombardo. M: Alan Silvestri; numbers performed by The Steve Miller Band, ZZ Top, Chuck Berry, Stevie Ray Vaughan, David Lee Roth, Mick Jagger, Elvis Presley, Glenn Frey, Travis Tritt, Charlie Rich, Emmylou Harris, Steve Winwood, etc. Costumes: Susan Becker. (Universal/Imagine Entertainment–UIP.) Rel: 29 March 1996. 95 mins. Cert PG. USA. 1996.

Shanghai Triad

Tang Shuisheng is a 14-year-old country boy employed to serve Xiao Jinbao, a nightclub singer in 1930s Shanghai. The latter is also the mistress of the local Godfather – The Boss – who lavishes unimaginable riches, if little attention, on her. Consequently, Jinbao has become entirely spoilt, has taken a lover and treats her servants with cruel contempt. Through Shuisheng's eyes, we witness the absolute corruption – and inevitable tragedy – of wealth and power. Masterfully composed, visually exhilarating and aurally dynamic, *Shanghai Triad* is a model of film as art. However, by choosing not to include any sympathetic central characters (even Shuisheng comes off as a surly wimp), director Zhang (whose seventh feature this is) has created a work of sensual wonder that fails to solicit the emotions. Incidentally, production of the film was temporarily halted when Zhang's last picture, *To Live*, was shown at Cannes without the approval of the Chinese authorities.

Cast: Gong Li (Xiao Jinbao aka 'Bijou'), Li Baotian (Tang, The Boss), Li Xuejian (Uncle Liu Shu), Shun Chun (Song), Wang Xiao Xiao (Tang Shuisheng), Jiang Baoying (Cuihua, the widow), Yang Qianquan (Ajiao), Fu Biao, Chen Shu, Liu Jiang.
  Dir: Zhang Yimou. Pro: Jean Louis Piel, Yves Marmion and Wu Yigong. Ex Pro: Wang Wei and Zhu Yongde. Screenplay: Bi Feiyu, from the novel *Gang Law* by Li Xiao. Ph: Lu Yue. Ed: Tu Yue. Pro Des: Cao Jiu Ping. M: Zhang Guangtian; numbers performed by Gong Li. Costumes: Tong Hua Miao. (Shanghai Film Studios/Alpha Films/UGC Images/La Sept Cinema–Electric.) Rel: 17 November 1995. 108 mins. Cert 15. China/France. 1995.

The Shooter

Czech-born US Marshal Dolph Lundgren has his hands full when he agrees to extradite a French assassin-cum-lesbian out of Prague. But is she really the killer of the Cuban ambassador to the UN? Does Dolph know what he's doing? Do we care? Dolph looks vaguely more sane than in the moronic Johnny Mnemonic, but Dutch actress Maruschka Detmers pilfers any acting honours going. The rest – direction, script, photography, reason – is decidedly sub-par. Filmed in Toronto and the Czech Republic. [*Ewen Brownrigg*]

Cast: Dolph Lundgren (Michael Dane), Maruschka Detmers (Simone Rosset), Assumpta Serna (Marta), Gavan O'Herlihy (Dick Powell), John Ashton (Alex Reed), Simon Andreu (Alberto Torena), Pablo Scola, Petr Drozda, Alexandra Kotcheff, Thomas Kotcheff.
  Dir: Ted Kotcheff. Pro: Paul Pompian and Silvio Muraglia. Ex Pro: Craig Baumgarten, Daniel Jakub Sladek and Gary Adelson. Assoc Pro: Jan Bilek. Screenplay: Yves Andre Martin, Meg Thayer and Billy Ray.

Flash dancers: Gina Gershon and Elizabeth Berkley strut their stuff in Paul Verhoeven's reviled Showgirls *(from Guild)*

Ph: Fernando Arguelles. Pro Des: Brian Eatwell. Ed: Ralph Brunjes. M: Stefano Mainetti. Costumes: Winkie McPherson. Second Assistant Director: Joshua Kotcheff. (Newmarket Capital Group/Canal Plus/Conquistador Entertainment/Arco Films/Etamp-Netto/Ricochet Prods/ Rominvest/Transatlantique Films–PolyGram.) Rel: 15 December 1995. 104 mins. Cert 18. UK/USA/Spain/Czech Republic. 1994.

Showgirls

Arriving in Las Vegas to make her fortune as a dancer, a mysterious, uptight beauty attempts to strip her way to the top ... Setting aside all the hype, the inflated salaries and the scathing reviews, *Showgirls* is still an X-rated musical. And that must count for something, right? Wrong. *Showgirls* is no more a musical than *Flashdance* was – which, incidentally, was also scripted by Joe Eszterhas. Here, Eszterhas was paid $3.2 million for his adult reworking of *All About Eve*, and although he delivers plenty of snappy one liners, he has made his heroine so unpleasant that it's hard to get an emotional foothold. Worse, newcomer Elizabeth Berkley is so bad in the central role that the film disintegrates around her. Which leaves the erotic production numbers. Well, with more buttocks and breasts on show than in any other Hollywood film before it, *Showgirls* delivers in spades – in that department. The bodies are beautiful and the choreography invigorating, so it's not a total waste of time.

Cast: Elizabeth Berkley (Nomi Malone), Kyle MacLachlan (Zack Carey), Gina Gershon (Cristal Connors), Glenn Plummer (James Smith), Robert Davi (Al Torres), Alan Rachins (Tony Moss), Gina Ravera (Molly Abrams), Lin Tucci (Henrietta Bazoom), Greg Travis (Phil Newkirk), William Shockley (Andrew Carver), Michelle Johnston (Gay Carpenter), Rena Riffel (Penny), Ungela Brockman (Annie), Al Ruscio, Patrick Bristow, Dewey Weber, Melinda Songer, Melissa Williams, Jack McGee, Jim Ishida, Bobbie Phillips, Dante McCarthy, Caroline Key Johnson, Lisa Boyle, Julie Pop, Paul Bates, Michael Cooke.
  Dir: Paul Verhoeven. Pro: Alan Marshall and Charles Evans. Ex Pro: Mario Kassar. Co-Pro: Ben Myron. Screenplay: Joe Eszterhas. Ph: Jost Vacano. Pro Des: Allan Cameron. Ed: Mark Goldblatt and Mark Helfrich. M: David A. Stewart; numbers performed by Dwight Yoakam, Swell, My Life With The Thrill Kill Kult, David Bowie, The Artist Formerly Known As Prince, Rena Riffel, Freaks of Desire, Elastica, Sisters of Mercy, Killing Joke, U2, George Strait, Siouxsie and The Banshees, etc. Costumes: Ellen Mirojnick. Choreography: Marguerite Pomerhn-Derricks. (MGM/UA/Chargeurs–Guild.) Rel: 12 January 1996. 131 mins. Cert 18. USA. 1995.

Steve Martin discovers the perfect cravat (on Gabriel Byrne) in Gillies Mackinnon's A Simple Twist of Fate *(from Buena Vista)*

A Simple Twist of Fate

When a fun-loving expectant father discovers that his wife's child is not his, he retreats into a life of miserly solitude. Only years later, when a little girl wanders into his house, is the man transformed into his former self. But for how long can he resist the darker forces of fate? An unlikely vehicle for Steve Martin, *A Simple Twist of Fate* was adapted by the actor himself from George Eliot's *Silas Marner*, a labour of love which took him four years to write on a portable word processor. Repressing his more maniacal tendencies, Martin makes a most moving Silas, his innate skill for working with children underlining the irony of his own childlessness. After a clumsy, somewhat schematic start, the film settles into a gentle, leisurely tale of some heart until finally turning into an underwhelming court room drama. Still, Gabriel Byrne's mercurial accent is fun.

Cast: Steve Martin (Michael McCann), Gabriel Byrne (John Newland), Catherine O'Hara (April Simon), Stephen Baldwin (Tanny Newland), Laura Linney (Nancy Newland nee Lammeter), Alana Austin (Mathilda McCann, aged 10), Ed Grady (Judge Marcus), Amelia Campbell (Marsha Swanson), Alyssa Austin, Byron Jennings, Michael des Barres, Tim Ware, David Dwyer, Kellen Crosby, Carolyn McCormick, Terry Loughlin, Eric Brooks, Shauna Leigh Austin, Michelle Benjamin-Cooper, Boyce Holleman, Judson Vaughn, Janell McLeod, Kathrin Nicholson, Mary Nell Santacroce.

Dir: Gillies Mackinnon. Pro: Ric Kidney. Ex Pro and Screenplay: Steve Martin. Ph: Andrew Dunn. Ed: Humphrey Dixon. Pro Des: Andy Harris. M: Cliff Eidelman. Costumes: Hope Hanafin. (Touchstone–Buena Vista.) Rel: 22 September 1995. 107 mins. Cert PG. USA. 1994.

Prologue to murder: Jodhi May dreams of a better future in Nancy Meckler's masterly Sister My Sister *(from Arrow)*

Sister My Sister

Le Mans, France; 1932-33. In the ordered household of Madame Danzard everything has its place. Every item and duty is fixed in its wheel of function. And Madame Danzard, a wealthy widow with a frumpy grown-up daughter, is blessed in her choice of domestic help: two discreet, hard-working maidservants, sisters, who work for the price of one. But in this sterile, regimented universe, suffocated desires and the simplest grievances are magnified out of all proportion ... Stepping eloquently into the bloodstains of *Heavenly Creatures*, *Fun* and *Butterfly Kiss*, this atmospheric, impeccably acted drama is based on a real-life double murder (previously dramatised by Jean Genet in *The Maids*). And like *Heavenly Creatures*, Wendy Kesselman's adaptation of her play *My Sister in This House* convincingly examines the cause of such terrible violence. A sublime case of less delivering more. Theatre director Nancy Meckler (wife of David Aukin, head of drama at Channel Four) makes her feature film debut with controlled assurance.

Cast: Julie Walters (Madame Danzard), Joely Richardson (Christine), Jodhi May (Lea), Sophie Thursfield (Isabelle Danzard), Amelda Brown, Lucita Pope, Kate Gartside.
Dir: Nancy Meckler. Pro: Norma Heyman. Assoc Pro: Joyce Herlihy. Screenplay: Wendy Kesselman. Ph: Ashley Rowe. Ed: David Stiven. Pro Des: Caroline Amies. M: Stephen Warbeck; 'Sleep My Little Sister, Sleep,' performed by Joely Richardson. Costumes: Lindy Hemming. (Film Four International/British Screen/NFH–Arrow.) Rel: 1 December 1995. 89 mins. Cert 15. UK. 1994.

Small Faces

Set in the tenement wasteland of Glasgow in 1968, *Small Faces* chronicles the lives of the brothers Maclean. The eldest, Bobby, is dyslexic and troubled by nightmares; Alan, the most easygoing, aspires to becoming an artist and exhibits enormous promise; and Lex, 13, the youngest, dreams of becoming a member of the local gang. It is through Lex's eyes that we view this little-seen side of Glasgow in the late

Tobacco Road: William Hurt and Harvey Keitel share the blue stuff in Wayne Wang's delicious Smoke *(from Artificial Eye)*

sixties, a harsh world of drinking, brawling and loss. What's a boy to do? Securing faultless performances from his cast of young unknowns and trotting out the events of his narrative in an unhurried, naturalistic way, director Gillies MacKinnon (*The Playboys, A Simple Twist of Fate*) has forged a potent, compelling drama that is funny,' touching and horrifying. Intelligently scripted by MacKinnon and his own brother, Billy.

Cast: Clare Higgins (Lorna Maclean), Iain Robertson (Lex Maclean), Joseph McFadden (Alan Maclean), J.S. Duffy (Bobby Maclean), Laura Fraser (Joanne MacGowan), Garry Sweeney (Charlie Sloan), Kevin McKidd (Malky Johnson), Mark McConnochie (Gorbals), David Walker (Fabio), Ian McElhinney (Uncle Andrew), Steven Singleton, Paul Doonan, Debbie Welch, Monica Brady, Elizabeth McGregor.
Dir: Gillies MacKinnon. Pro: Billy MacKinnon and Steve Clark-Hall. Ex Pro: Mark Shivas and Andrea Calderwood. Screenplay: Gillies MacKinnon and Billy MacKinnon. Ph: John De Borman. Pro Des: Zoe Macleod. Ed: Scott Thomas. M: John Keane; numbers performed by Iain Robertson, Clare Higgins, Ian McElhinney, The Spencer Davies Group, Zager and Evans, Georgie Fame, Cream, etc. Costumes: Kate Carin. (BBC Films/BBC Scotland/The Glasgow Film Fund/Skyline–Guild.) Rel: 5 April 1996. 108 mins. Cert 18. UK. 1995.

The Swingeing Sixties: Iain Robertson contemplates the future in Gillies MacKinnon's Small Faces *(from Guild)*

Smoke

Brooklyn; 1990. Via a fascinating anecdote, Brooklyn novelist Paul Benjamin relates how Sir Walter Raleigh measured the weight of smoke. First, he weighed a cigar; then, after it had been smoked, he weighed the butt and ash. Answer: the subtracted sum equals the weight of the smoke. A number of characters passing through The Brooklyn Cigar Company store (on the corner of 3rd Street and Seventh Avenue) weigh in with a good deal of colourful anecdotage, smoke screens of bullshit, lies and distorted truths – lit up with the convivial glow of cheroot and cigarette smoke. This is a most genial marriage of good company and conversation, illuminated by a first-rate cast, with atmospheric direction from Wayne Wang and sly camerawork from Adam Holender (*Midnight Cowboy, Fresh*). Light up, sit back and inhale. Inspired by Paul Auster's short fiction *Auggie Wren's*

Cole), Jared Harris (Jimmy Rose), Victor Argo (Vinnie), Mary Ward (April Lee), Mel Gorham (Violet Jalapeno), Jose Zuniga, Stephen Gevedon, Daniel Auster, Deirdre O'Connell, Michelle Hurst, Erica Gimpel, Malik Yoba, Clarice Taylor.

Dir: Wayne Wang. Pro: Greg Johnson, Peter Newman, Hisami Kuriowa and Kenzo Horikoshi. Ex Pro: Bob Weinstein, Harvey Weinstein and Satoru Iseki. Screenplay: Paul Auster. Ph: Adam Holender. Pro Des: Kalina Ivanov. Ed: Maysie Hoy. M: Rachel Portman; numbers performed by Jerry Garcia Band, Group Home, Louis Prima, Tom Waits, Sophia George, Screaming Jay Hawkins, etc. Costumes: Claudia Brown. William Hurt's Dialect Coach: Lileen Mansell. (Miramax/NDF/ Euro Space/Peter Newman/Internal–Artificial Eye.) Rel: 19 April 1996. 108 mins. Cert 15. USA. 1995.

Pillow talk: Dennis Quaid and Julia Roberts face up to some sticky dilemmas in Lasse Hallstrom's Something To Talk About *(from Warner)*

Mother of intervention: Alberta Watson reaches out for her retiring son, Jeremy Davies, in David O. Russell's provocative Spanking the Monkey *(from Metro Tartan)*

Christmas Story, originally published in *The New York Times*.

Cast: William Hurt (Paul Benjamin), Harvey Keitel (Auggie Wren), Stockard Channing (Ruby McNutt), Harold Perrineau Jr (Thomas Jefferson 'Rashid' Cole), Giancarlo Esposito (Tommy), Ashley Judd (Felicity McNutt), Forest Whitaker (Cyrus

Something To Talk About

Grace King Bichon has a picture-perfect life. The eldest daughter of a wealthy Southern family, she has a beautiful, spunky daughter, an affluent, dashing husband and two rewarding jobs. Then, one day, her world falls apart – and Grace sees her life for the sham that it is. Is it too late for compromise? From an original screenplay by Callie Khouri (*Thelma & Louise*), directed by Lasse Hallstrom (*My Life as a Dog*, *What's Eating Gilbert Grape?*), photographed by the legendary Sven Nykvist and executive-produced by Goldie Hawn, *Something To Talk About* promises great things. Indeed, there are some marvellous scenes, good performances (particularly from Dennis Quaid and Kyra Sedgwick) and telling lines. Ultimately, however, the film takes on too many subplots and changes in tone to create a credible, compelling whole, with only the dramatic moments occasionally hitting home. Previously known as *Grace Under Pressure*.

Cast: Julia Roberts (Grace King Bichon), Robert Duvall (Wyly King), Dennis Quaid (Eddie Bichon), Gena Rowlands (Georgia King), Kyra Sedgwick (Emma Rae King), Brett Cullen (Jamie Johnson), Haley Aull (Caroline), Muse Watson (Hank Corrigan), Anne Shropshire (Aunt Rae), Terence P. Currier (Dr Frank Lewis), David Huddleston (Jack 'Maddog' Pierce), Ginnie Randall, Rebecca Koon, Rhoda Griffis, Lisa Roberts, Shannon Eubanks.

Dir: Lasse Hallstrom. Pro: Anthea Sylbert and Paula Weinstein. Ex Pro: Goldie Hawn. Co-Pro: William Beasley.

Here, let me give you a back rub: Whip Hubley in decidedly hot water in Roger Donaldson's loopy Species *(from UIP)*

Screenplay: Callie Khouri. Ph: Sven Nykvist. Pro Des: Mel Bourne. Ed: Mia Goldman. M: Hans Zimmer and Graham Preskett; numbers performed by Bonnie Raitt, Wayne Fontana and The Mindbenders, Vince Gill and Little Feat, Therese Willis, etc. Costumes: Aggie Guerard Rodgers. Choreography: Toni Basil. (Spring Creek–Warner.) Rel: 5 January 1996. 106 mins. Cert 15. USA. 1995.

Spanking the Monkey

Connecticut; today. Raymond Aibelli is a frustrated 23-year-old stranded at home looking after his invalid mother. Unable to find adequate privacy or to consummate a relationship with a local girl, Ray is hormonally charged and frustrated. His mother, laid up in bed for weeks, is in the same boat. When the latter receives an irate phone call from the father of Ray's girlfriend – who has accused Ray of manhandling her – Susan Aibelli feels duty-bound to demonstrate the rules of seduction to her callow son. Fuelled by an extensive quantity of vodka, both Ray and his mother succumb to the unspeakable ... Taking a taboo subject and making it credible, *Spanking the Monkey* is a remarkable achievement for a first-time director. Whether the film succeeds as black comedy, however, is in question. It certainly touches on areas previously unexplored in the cinema, such as the difficulty of masturbating when your pet is watching. Mesmerising.

Cast: Jeremy Davies (Raymond Aibelli), Alberta Watson (Susan Aibelli), Carla Gallo (Toni Peck), Benjamin Hendrickson (Tom Aibelli), Judette Jones (Aunt Helen), Elizabeth Newitt, Matthew Puckett, Zak Orth, Josh Weinstein, Judah Domke, Neil Connie Wallace, Lleana Stratton, Richard Husson.
    Dir and Screenplay: David O. Russell. Pro: Dean Silvers. Ex Pro: Russell, Stanley F. Buchthal and Janet Grillo. Assoc Pro: Cheryl Miller Houser. Ph: Michael Mayers. Ed: Pamela Martin. Pro Des: Susan Block. M: David Carbonara; numbers performed by Morphine. Costumes: Carolyn Greco. Dog trainer: David Russell. (Buckeye Communications/Swelter Films–Metro Tartan.) Rel: 11 August 1995. 98 mins. Cert 18. USA. 1994.

Species

With actors of the calibre of Ben Kingsley, Michael Madsen, Alfred Molina and Forest Whitaker one would have hoped for something more than a cheesy monster movie. Yet the most interesting thing about *Species* is what happens before the movie even starts. Receiving a response to earth's galactic package of terrestrial data and human DNA, a covert government body injects alien DNA into a human ovum. The result is a baby girl who grows at a supernatural rate, entering puberty in a matter of weeks. Fearing that he has overstepped the mark, government scientist Ben Kingsley decides to terminate the experiment, only to see his inscrutable prize break out of the confines of his security base. Predictable mayhem ensues. Guilty of some ludicrous dialogue ('something bad happened here,' Whitaker notes, peering into a room filled with goo and a dead body), *Species* is basically *Alien* on earth with a number of other movies glued on (*The Hidden*, *Split Second*, etc). Michael Crichton it ain't.

Cast: Ben Kingsley (Xavier Fitch), Michael Madsen (Press Lennox), Alfred Molina (Arden), Forest Whitaker (Dan Smithson), Marg Helgenberger (Dr Laura Baker), Natasha Henstridge (Sil), Michelle Williams (young Sil), Whip Hubley, Jordan Lund, Don Fischer, Jayne Luke, Herta Ware, Gary Bullock, Caroline Barclay, Matthew Ashford, Anthony Guidera, Richard Fancy, Marliese K. Schneider, Frank Welker (voice of alien Sil).
    Dir: Roger Donaldson. Pro: Frank Mancuso Jr. and Dennis Feldman. Ex Pro: David Streit. Screenplay: Feldman. Ph: Andrzej Bartkowiak. Ed: Conrad Buff. Pro Des: John Muto. M: Christopher Young; numbers performed by Daryl D. Bonneau, Crystal Method, Joyce Sims, Enchanted, etc. Costumes: Joe I. Tompkins. Visual Effects: Richard Edlund. Creature Effects: Steve Johnson. 'Sil' Design: H.R. Giger. (MGM–UIP.) Rel: 13 October 1995. 108 mins. Cert 18. USA. 1995.

Spy Hard

As usual, Leslie Nielsen overacts wildly as clumsy Agent WD-40, battling the armless General Rancor (whose turn it is to dominate the world). The Bond spoofing ranges from silhouetted swimming girls to Marcia Gay Harden's Moneypenny-like turn as Miss Cheevers, whose sexy double entendres make things hard for our hero. The mickey's also taken out of *In the Line of Fire*, *True Lies*, *Butch Cassidy*, *Speed* (with Ray Charles as the bus driver!), *Home Alone*, *Sister Act*, *E.T.* and *Pulp Fiction*. Supremely silly – but fun for fans of the genre (although there's no O.J. Simpson). [*Simon Rose*]

Cast: Leslie Nielsen (Dick Steele, Agent WD-40), Nicollette Sheridan (Veronqiue Ukrinsky, Agent 3.14), Charles Durning (The Director), Marcia Gay Harden (Miss Cheevus), Barry Bostwick (Norman Coleman), John Ales (Kabul), Andy Griffith (General Rancor), Elya Baskin, Mason Gamble, Carlos Lauchu, Stephanie Romanov, Curtis Armstrong, Michael Berryman, Julie Brown, Eddie Deezen, Clyde Kusatsu, Katherine Moffat, Shari Shattuck, Dr Joyce Brothers, Ray Charles, Roger Clinton, Robert Culp, Fabio, Robert Guillaume, Hulk Hogan, Pat Morita, Alexandra Paul, Mr T.
   Dir: Rick Friedberg. Pro: Friedberg, Doug Draizin and Jeffrey Konvitz. Ex Pro: Robert L. Rosen and Leslie Nielsen. Screenplay: Rick Friedberg, Dick Chudnow, Jason Friedberg and Aaron Seltzer. Ph: John R. Leonetti. Pro Des: William Creber. Ed: Eric Sears. M: Bill Conti; numbers performed by 'Weird Al' Yankovich, B.J. Thomas, and Chuck Berry. Costumes: Tom Bronson. (Hollywood Pictures–Buena Vista.) Rel: 24 May 1996. 81 mins. Cert PG. USA. 1996.

Stolen Hearts

In an attempt to patch up things with his girlfriend, petty thief Frank O'Brien executes the theft of a Matisse two days ahead of schedule. This way, he reasons, he and the missus can share a romantic weekend on a secluded island in New England as they await the arrival of the buyer ... If Denis Leary (who co-scripted) had allowed his character an iota of charm or intelligence, then this film might've had a fighting chance. As it is, Leary attempts to mate a romantic comedy with a moronic cartoon in which the villains are portrayed as low-life goons and where the 'hero' spends half the time falling over. Only Yaphet Kotto, as a fiercely unsentimental cop, occasionally brings a smile to the face. US title: *Two If By Sea*. FYI: Leary and Sandra Bullock previously worked together on *Demolition Man*.

Cast: Denis Leary (Frank Michael O'Brien), Sandra Bullock (Roz), Stephen Dillane (Evan Marsh), Yaphet Kotto (O'Malley), Jonathan Tucker (Todd), Wayne Robson (Beano), John Friesen (Sheriff Herbert Horn), Mike Starr, Michael Badalucco, Lenny Clarke, Jonny Fido, Don Gavin, Shaun R. Clark, Markus Parilo, Angela Moore.
   Dir: Bill Bennett. Pro: James G. Robinson. Ex Pro: Gary Barber and Bill Todman Jr. Co-Pro: Michael MacDonald. Screenplay: Denis Leary and Mike Armstrong, from a story by Leary, Armstrong and Ann Lembeck. Ph: Andrew Lesnie. Pro Des: David Chapman. Ed: Bruce Green. M: Nick Glennie-Smith and Paddy Maloney of The Chieftains; numbers performed by Shane MacGowan and The Popes with Sinead O'Connor, The Pointer Sisters, Belinda Carlisle, Shelby Lynne, Alannah Myles, etc. Costumes: Olga Dimitrov. Product Placement: Miranda Beeson. (Morgan Creek–Warner.) Rel: 5 April 1996. 96 mins. Cert 15. USA. 1996.

Stonewall

New York; 1969. On the night following the funeral of Judy Garland in late June, 1969, police raided the transvestite bar Stonewall Inn in Greenwich Village, prompting the historical riot that was to initiate the Gay Rights Movement. In order to bring Martin Duberman's social documentary *Stonewall* to life, this touching, eye-opening film focuses on the lives of a handful of fictitious gay characters, bringing a little-known but momentous event in the history of homosexual persecution into sharp relief. Featuring a cast of talented unknowns, *Stonewall* takes a fresh look at the whole gay hierarchy, from closet homosexuals and conservative activists to the more outlandish drag queens. Punctuated by a number of musical interludes in which a trio of queens mime to fashionable numbers (see music credits), the film entertains as it enlightens. Nigel Finch, who previously directed the acclaimed BBC film *The Lost Language of Cranes*, died from Aids during post-production.

Cast: Guillermo Diaz (LaMiranda), Frederick Weller (Matty Dean), Brendan Corbalis (Ethan), Duane Boutte (Bustonia), Bruce MacVittie (Skinny Vinnie), Peter Ratray (Burt), Dwight Ewell (Helen Wheels), Matthew Faber (Mizz Moxie), Michael McElroy (Princess Ernestine), Luis Guzman, Joey Bedio, Isaiah Washington, Chuck Pfeifer, Jose Zuniga, Aida Turturro.
   Dir: Nigel Finch. Pro: Christine Vachon. BBC Pro: Ruth Caleb. Ex Pro: George Faber and Anthony Wall. Screenplay: Rikki Beadle Blair. Ph: Chris Seager. Pro Des:

Pigskin parade: A cop hassles drag queen Duane Boutte in Nigel Finch's eye-opening Stonewall *(from Metro Tartan)*

Therese DePrez. M: Michael Kamen; numbers performed by Brian Eno, The Shangri-Las, The Ad-Libs, Shirelles, The Soul Brothers, Patti LaBelle and The Bluebelles, Judy Garland, Bessie Banks, Bare Naked Ladies, etc. Costumes: Michael Clancy. (BBC–Metro Tartan.) Rel: 10 May 1996. 98 mins. Cert 15. UK. 1995.

Strange Days

Los Angeles; December 30, 1999. On the eve of the new millennium it's business as usual for Lenny Nero. An ex-cop, Lenny is now into selling 'playback clips' on the black market. A virtual reality device developed by the FBI to replace the old surveillance wire, a clip records anything the wearer undergoes for thirty minutes, including the sights, sounds, smells, tastes and even the feel of the experience. The software is now a booming business, with human 'recorders' willing to risk ever greater adrenaline rushes – from sexual encounters to petty crime. However, Lenny refuses to deal in 'blackjacks' or 'death clips', but when a snuff clip is anonymously slipped into his possession, the bootlegger finds himself embroiled in a plot that could detonate LA. While Lenny's good friend Lornette makes the crucial point that we must live life for the moment and not rely on prepackaged dreams, the film's message is diluted in a visual MTV overkill that defeats the moral of its argument. Worse, we, the viewer, are forced into the role of voyeur, allowing us the vicarious thrill of a snuff filmmaker. It could get addictive – and on video one can fast forward over the message.

Cast: Ralph Fiennes (Lenny Nero), Angela Bassett (Lornette 'Mace' Mason), Juliette Lewis (Faith Justin), Tom Sizemore (Max Peltier), Michael Wincott (Philo Gant), Vincent D'Onofrio (Burton Steckler), Glenn Plummer (Jeriko One), Brigitte Bako (Iris), Richard Edson (Tick), William Fichtner (Dwayne Engelman), Josef Sommer (Palmer Strickland), Joe Urla, Nicky Katt, Michael Jace, Louise LeCavalier, David Carrera, Jim Ishida, Todd Graff, Brandon Hammond, James Acheson.
Dir: Kathryn Bigelow. Pro: James Cameron and Steven-Charles Jaffe. Ex Pro: Rae Sanchini and Lawrence Kasanoff. Screenplay: Cameron and Jay Cocks. Ph: Matthew F. Leonetti. Pro Des: Lilly Kilvert. Ed: Howard Smith. M: Graeme Revell; numbers performed by Prong and Ray Manzarek, Quo, Marilyn Mason, H. Beno, Deep Forest, Bob Marley, Tricky, Glenn

Read my clips: Juliette Lewis provokes in Kathryn Bigelow's Strange Days *(from UIP)*

Plummer, Satchel, Season to Risk, Kate Gibson, P.J. Harvey, Lords of Acid, Bokie Loc, Diatribe, Juliette Lewis, Testament, Skunk Anansie, Peter Gabriel, etc. Costumes: Ellen Mirojnick. Sound: Gary Rydstrom. (Lightstorm Entertainment/ Universal–UIP.) Rel: 1 March 1996. 139 mins. Cert 18. USA. 1995.

Sudden Death.

Pittsburgh; today. Following an accident in which a little girl is killed, French-Canadian fireman Darren McCord has lost his will for heroism. However, his little daughter, Emily, still idolises him, although his son, Tyler, shows nothing but contempt. Then, when an army of terrorists take the Vice-President of the United States hostage at a championship ice-hockey match, McCord appears to be the only man able to stop them ... *Sudden Death*, or rather *Die Hard On Ice*, pushes all the right buttons with vigour and skill, eliciting gasps, stunned silence and, where appropriate, smiles. Jean-Claude Van Damme still has a thing or two to learn about charisma, but his sincerity and high kicks take up a lot of slack, while Powers Boothe makes the villain suitably odious (after killing a number of people he asks, politely, if he can smoke). The clumsy opening aside, I was glued to my seat throughout.

Cast: Jean-Claude Van Damme (Darren Thomas McCord), Powers Boothe (Joshua Foss), Raymond J. Barry (Vice President), Whittni Wright (Emily McCord), Ross Malinger (Tyler McCord), Dorian Harewood (Hallmark), Kate McNeil (Kathi), Audra

Infested waters: Kevin Spacey (with Michelle Forbes) puts on his best glower in George Huang's compulsive Swimming With Sharks *(from Starlight Films)*

Lindley (Mrs Ferrara), Paul Mochnick (Andre Ferrara), Michael Gaston, Brian Delate, Karen Baldwin, William Cameron, Luc Robitaille.

Dir and Ph: Peter Hyams. Pro: Moshe Diamant and Howard Baldwin. Ex Pro: Ash R. Shah, Sundip R. Shah, Anders P. Jensen and Sunil R. Shah. Line Pro: Deborah Lee. Assoc Pro: Karen Baldwin. Screenplay: Gene Quintano, based on a story by Karen Baldwin. Pro Des: Philip Harrison. Ed: Steven Kemper. M: John Debney; 'Rock and Roll Part II' performed by Gary Glitter. Costumes: Dan Lester. (Universal Pictures/ Signature/Baldwin Cohen/Imperial Entertainment–UIP.) Rel: 26 April 1996. 110 mins. Cert 18. USA. 1995.

Suite 16

Suite 16, Hotel West End, Nice; 1995. Most unpleasant, sordid little fable in which a wealthy cripple and a penniless hustler serve each other's perverted ends. While the former has more money than he can spend, his condition prohibits him from enjoying solid foods, alcohol or sex. Conversely, the hustler has no money with which to satisfy his voracious appetites. So, in exchange for a slice of the good life, the young man allows his benefactor to spy on his sexual exploits. Dredging the seedier excesses of the abuse of power, voyeurism and greed, *Suite 16* is a claustrophobic wallow in dire need of a good laugh.

Cast: Pete Postlethwaite (Glover), Antonie Kamerling (Chris), Geraldine Pailhas (Helen), Tom Jansen (Paul), Bart Slegers (Rudy), Suzanne Colin, Viviane de Muynck, Dirk Roofthooft, Vic Deruddere.

Dir: Dominique Deruddere. Pro: Paul Breuls. Co-Pro: Frank Bak. Screenplay: Charles Higson and Lise Mayer. Ph: Jean-Francois Robin. Ed: Kant Pan. Pro Des: Niek Kortekaas. M: Walter Hus. Costumes: Loret Meus. (Corsan Prods/Theorema Prods–Feature Film Co.) Rel: 18 August 1995. 106 mins. Cert 18. UK/Belgium. 1994.

The Swan Princess

Predetermined to marry from childhood, Prince Derek and Princess Odette show contempt for each other until – too late – Odette is turned into a daytime swan by the evil sorcerer Rothbart. But is Derek up to the task of saving her? On a scale of *Thumbelina* to *The Lion King*, this falls somewhere in between. Based on the ballet *Swan Lake*, the film's story does exercise a grip and the animated backdrops are inspirational (especially the water effects). However, the human drawings are of morning TV standard (i.e. crude) and many of the animal comic foils miss their mark (in particular Steven Wright's witless turtle and a puffin sporting a wide range of British accents).

Voices: Jack Palance (Rothbart), Howard McGillin (Prince Derek), Michelle Nicastro (Princess Odette), Liz Callaway (singing voice of Princess Odette), John Cleese (Jean-Bob), Steven Wright (Speed), Steve Vinovich (Puffin), Mark Harelik (Lord

Rogers), James Arrington (Chamberlain), David Gaines (singing voice of Chamberlain), Joel McKinnon Miller (Bromley), Dakin Matthews (King William), Sandy Duncan (Queen Uberta).

Dir: Richard Rich. Pro: Rich and Jared F. Brown. Ex Pro: Brown and Seldon Young. Co-Ex Pro: Matt Mazer. Co-Pro: Terry L. Noss and Thomas J. Tobin. Screenplay: Brian Nissen, from a story by Rich and Nissen. M: Lex de Azevedo; songs by de Zevedo and David Zippel; 'Far Longer Than Forever' performed by Regina Belle and Jeffrey Osborne. Character Design: Steven E. Gordon. Art: Mike Hodgson and James Coleman. (Nest Entertainment/Rich Animation Studios–Fox.) Rel: 15 December 1995. 89 mins. Cert U. USA. 1994.

Swimming With Sharks

A young film school graduate is engaged as the new assistant of Buddy Ackerman, a senior executive of a Hollywood film studio. Ruthless, selfish and remarkably cruel, Ackerman takes satanic delight in humiliating his young charge. But the worm can only take so much punishment before he turns ... Although *Swimming With Sharks* is yet another picture about the cutthroat world of moviemaking in Hollywood, it could be set in any business milieu. The strength of the film lies in the conflict between the master and his servant and the depths to which the underling will suffer for his ambition. George Huang's deliciously cruel screenplay (Buddy: 'You're happy – I hate that!') and the restrained power of Kevin Spacey's performance make this compulsive entertainment. Previously known as *The Buddy Factor*.

Cast: Kevin Spacey (Buddy Ackerman), Frank Whaley (Guy), Michelle Forbes (Dawn Lockard), Benicio Del Toro (Rex), T.E. Russell (Foster Kane), Roy Dotrice (Cyrus Miles), Matthew Flynt, Patrick Fischler, Jerry Levine.

Dir and Screenplay: George Huang. Pro: Steve Alexander and Joanne Moore. Co-Pro: Kevin Spacey and Buzz Hays. Ex Pro: Jay Cohen and Stephen Israel. Line Pro: Louis Nader. Assoc Pro: Kevin Reidy. Ph: Steven Finestone. Pro Des: Veronika Merlin and Cecil Gentry. Ed: Ed Marx. M: Tom Heil; numbers performed by Vibes Alive, Gigolo Aunts, The Vibrettes, Love Spit Love, Sarah McLachlan, etc. Costumes: Kristen Everberg. (Cineville/Neofight Film/ Mama'z Boy Entertainment–Starlight Films.) Rel: 5 April 1996. 93 mins. Cert 15. USA. 1994.

Things To Do in Denver When You're Dead

Smooth operator Jimmy The Saint has put his criminal past behind him and is now running a video business in which the soon-to-be-deceased record messages ('afterlife advice') for their bereaved. Then Jimmy's former boss, The Man With the Plan, invites him to pull off one last 'action' – to scare off the boyfriend of Meg, the latter being the love interest of The Man's disturbed son. Recruiting his old partners-in-crime, Jimmy sets out for one profitable night of scaremongering ... Stealing into extremely familiar territory with his first full-length feature film, director Gary Fleder guides his gritty, quirky material with a sure hand, eliciting a roster of colourful performances from a powerhouse cast. But it is Scott Rosenberg's inventive screenplay, with its twisted clichés and distinctive dialogue, that stamps the film with a fresh, arresting identity.

Cast: Andy Garcia (Jimmy the Saint), Christopher Walken (The Man With the Plan), Christopher Lloyd (Pieces), William Forsythe (Franchise), Bill Nunn (Easy Wind), Treat Williams (Critical Bill Dooley), Jack Warden (Joe Heff), Steve Buscemi (Mister Shhh), Fairuza Balk (Lucinda), Gabrielle Anwar (Dagney), Michael Nicolosi (Bernard), Josh Charles (Bruce), Sarah Trigger (Meg), Cheree Jaeb, Phil Boardman, Bill Coess, Archie Smith, Willie Garson, Selina Mathews, David Stratton, Marshall Bell, Glenn Plummer, Don Cheadle, Tiny Lister Jr., Bill Erwin.

Dir: Gary Fleder. Pro: Cary Woods. Co-Pro: Cathy Konrad. Ex Pro: Bob Weinstein, Harvey Weinstein and Marie Cantin. Screenplay: Scott Rosenberg. Ph: Elliot Davis. Pro Des: Nelson Coates. Ed: Richard Marks. M: Michael Convertino; numbers performed by Blues Traveller, The Neville Brothers, Morphine. Costumes: Abigail Murray; Giorgio Armani. (Miramax/Woods Entertainment–Buena Vista.) Rel: 3 May 1996. 115 mins. Cert 18. USA. 1995.

A Thin Line Between Love and Hate

'If God had meant all women to be happy,' notes playboy Darnell Wright, 'he would have made all men like me.' Indeed, Darnell has a knack for seducing the ladies, with his street patter, sharp threads and industrious tongue. Then, when he is rebuffed by a glacial beauty way out of his league, he embarks on a romantic assault course.

But his courtship is a little too effective ... Conceived, co-written, executive produced, directed by and starring Martin Lawrence, *A Thin Line...* really has only one person to blame for its unmitigated failure. For a comedy-thriller, the film is surprisingly light on thrills and laughs, while Lawrence plays each scene like a third-rate stand-up routine, slowing the narrative to a sluggish amble. FYI: Described by producer McHenry as 'the male side to the *Waiting to Exhale* coin,' the film also stars the singer Bobby Brown, husband of Whitney Houston.

Cast: Martin Lawrence (Darnell Wright), Lynn Whitfield (Brandi Web), Regina King (Mia), Bobby Brown (Tee), Della Reese (Ma Wright), Malinda Williams (Erica), Daryl 'Chill' Mitchell (Earl), Roger E. Mosley (Smitty), Miguel A. Nunez Jr (Reggie), Simba Khali, Tangie Ambrose, Wendy Robinson, Stacii Jae Johnson, Faizon Love, Tiny Lister.

Dir and Ex Pro: Martin Lawrence. Pro: Douglas McHenry nd George Jackson. Co-Pro: William C. Carraro, Suzanne Broderick and David Raynr. Screenplay: Lawrence, Bentley Kyle Evans, Kenny Buford and Kim Bass. Ph: Francis Kenny. Pro Des: Simon Dobbin. Ed: John Carter. M: Roger Troutman; numbers performed by H-town, Dark Complexion, Smooth, Dru Down, etc. Costumes: Eduardo Castro. (New Line Cinema/Savoy Pictures/You Go Boy!–Entertainment.) Rel: 28 June 1996. 108 mins. Cert 18. USA. 1996.

Three Wishes

1955; California. Running down a hobo in the street, widow and mother-of-two Jeanne Holman feels obliged to put the man up until his broken leg

Wish upon a stud: Patrick Swayze (with canine co-star Rosa) out to change lives in Martha Coolidge's life-affirming Three Wishes *(from Entertainment)*

Blood runs thicker ... Julia Devin and Daryl Hannah join in the manipulation in Wesley Strick's excessive The Tie That Binds *(from PolyGram)*

heals. The neighbours do not approve, but the stranger is not all he appears to be ... Not a sequel to *Aladdin*, but a romantic fantasy set in middle American suburbia where one man, whose decision 'to be himself', transforms a household in need of a miracle or two, or three. Patrick Swayze, Hollywood's most constantly miscast actor, seems a tad too clean-cut for the enigmatic hobo, but his eyes speak volumes, backing up such significant aphorisms as, 'everything contains its opposite' and 'if you don't have much, you don't need much'. Displaying the sentimental acuity of *It's a Wonderful Life*, this engaging fable promises more than can fight its way out of the clinging molasses. Can this really be from the director of *Rambling Rose*?

Cast: Patrick Swayze (Jack McCloud), Mary Elizabeth Mastrantonio (Jeanne Holman), Joseph Mazzello (Tom Holman), Seth Mumy (Gunny Holman), David Marshall Grant (Phil), Jay O. Sanders (Coach Schramka), Michael O'Keefe (adult Tom Holman), Diane Venora (Joyce), Moira Harris (Katherine Holman), Rosa (Betty Jane), John Diehl, David Zahorsky, Brian Flannery, Brock Pierce, David Jacob Carey, David Hart, Scott Patterson, Michael Laskin, Simone Study, Neil McDonough, Bill Mumy, Colleen Camp, D.B. Sweeney.

Dir: Martha Coolidge. Pro: Gary Lucchesi, Clifford Green and Ellen Green. Ex Pro: Larry Y. Albucher and Keith Samples. Ph: Johnny E. Jensen. Ed: Stephen Cohen. Pro Des: John Vallone. M: Cynthia Millar; numbers performed by The Lovin' Spoonful, The Penguins, Doris Day, The Flamingos, Bill Haley & The Comets, Nat King Cole, etc. Costumes: Shelley Komarov. Sound: Leslie Shatz. (Rysher Entertainment–Entertainment.) Rel: 15 December 1995. 115 mins. Cert PG. USA. 1995.

The Tie That Binds

Russell Clifton is a successful architect, Dana Clifton a successful commercial photographer. Young, well-off and desperately in love, Russell and Dana would appear to have everything – everything except the child that would give their lives meaning. Then, when they adopt the angelic, six-year-old Janie, their lot would seem to be complete. But because of the law prohibiting adopters knowing the identity of their child's biological parents, Russell and Dana have no idea what they have taken on. Then, as old ghosts start to surface, Janie starts behaving very oddly indeed ... Relentlessly playing on our worst fears, *The Tie That Binds* slips from psychological drama into Grand Guignol thriller, which is no surprise when you consider that three of the producers colluded on *The Hand That Rocks the Cradle*. However, first-time director Wesley Strick, whose screenwriting credits include *Arachnophobia*, *Cape Fear*, *Final Analysis* and *Wolf*, has picked up some very bad habits from the worst excesses of those who directed his scripts. Just when Janie seems to promise some intriguing psychological insight, she's turned into a blip in a violent video game.

Cast: Daryl Hannah (Leann Netherwood), Keith Carradine (John Netherwood), Moira Kelly (Dana Clifton), Vincent Spano (Russell Clifton), Julia Devin (Janie), Ray Reinhardt (Sam Bennett), Barbara Tarbuck (Jean Bennett), Ned Vaughn (Officer David Carrey), Jenny Gago (Maggie Hass), Cynda Williams (Lisa-Marie Chandler), Bruce A. Young (Gil Chandler), Kerrie Cullen, Carmen Argenziano, Dana Gladston, Andrea Sandahl.

Dir: Wesley Strick. Pro: David Madden, Patrick Markey, John Morrissey and Susan Zachary. Ex Pro: Ted Field, Jon Brown and Robert W. Cort. Screenplay: Michael Auerbach. Ph: Bobby Bukowski. Ed: Michael N. Knue. Pro Des: Marcia-Hinds Johnson. M: Graeme Revell; numbers performed by The Commotion, Willie Nelson and Leon Russell, Asleep At the Wheel, Billie Holiday, etc. Costumes: Betsy Heimann. (Interscope Communications/PolyGram–PolyGram.) Rel: 15 December 1995. 102 mins. Cert 18. USA. 1995.

To Die For

Director Joel Schumacher (*Batman Forever*) has called her 'obsessive-compulsive', but Nicole Kidman is the first to admit that she's ambitious. In *To*

Die For she plays a manipulative young woman who will do anything to get a slice of the spotlight, a part, so Ms Kidman told director Gus Van Sant, that she 'was destined to play'. Suzanne Stone, modelled on real-life megalomaniac Pamela Smart, declares, 'You're not anybody unless you're on television.' And, sure enough, Suzanne Stone would just kill to get on TV ... Yet another botched job from America's most overrated independent filmmaker, *To Die For* is a satire on crime, the media and blonde ambition – like this is new or something. Kidman, bless her, eats the screen up with a spoon, but it is Joaquim Phoenix (formerly Leaf Phoenix), as the inarticulate, tortured tool of Suzanne's machinations, who gives a performance to die for. Label it *Serial Mom* without the laughs.

Cast: Nicole Kidman (Suzanne Stone), Joaquim Phoenix (Jimmy), Matt Dillon (Larry Maretto), Casey Affleck (Russell), Illeana Douglas (Janice Maretto), Alison Folland (Lydia Mertz), Dan Hedaya (Joe Maretto), Wayne Knight (Ed Grant), Kurtwood Smith (Earl Stone), Holland Taylor, Susan Traylor, Maria Tucci, Tim Hopper, Michael Rispoli, Buck Henry, Gerry Quigley, Nicholas Pasco, David Cronenberg, George Segal.
Dir: Gus Van Sant. Pro: Laura Ziskin. Ex Pro: Jonathan Taplin and Joseph M. Caracciolo. Screenplay: Buck Henry, from the novel by Joyce Maynard. Ph: Eric Alan Edwards. Ed: Curtiss Clayton. Pro Des: Missy Stewart. M: Danny Elfman; numbers performed by Billy Preston, Nailbomb, Strawpeople, Lynyrd Skynyrd, Eric Carmen, Donovan, etc. Costumes: Beatrix Aruna Pasztor. (Columbia Pictures–Rank.) Rel: 27 October 1995. 107 mins. Cert 15. USA. 1995.

Tommy Boy
Affable, exuberant comedy from the *Saturday Night Live* stable, produced by Lorne Michaels and featuring the big, warm, cuddly Chris Farley in his starring debut. Also on hand is David Spade, another SNL alumni, who is a perfect foil for the cosy excesses of his frequent co-star. Here Farley dominates the action as Tommy Callahan, the moronic son of an auto parts manufacturer, who is forced to pull his socks up when his father's death pitches him into the centre of a business crisis. While the film is guilty of recycling old jokes, it does deliver a few novel gags, not least an uncredited

Blonde ambition: Nicole Kidman straddles the opposition (husband Matt Dillon) in Gus Van Sant's To Die For *(from Rank)*

Rob Lowe cast as Bo Derek's son, a deer breaking out of Spade's car, some scary hair from Dan Aykroyd and the now traditional dig at The Carpenters. It could've been a lot worse.

Cast: Chris Farley (Tommy Callahan), David Spade (Richard Hayden), Bo Derek (Beverly), Brian Dennehy (Big Tom Callahan), Dan Aykroyd (Zalinsky), Julie Warner (Michelle), Sean McCann (Rittenhauer), Rob Lowe (Paul), Zach Grenier, James Blendick, Philip Williams, David 'Skippy' Malloy, Roy Lewis, William Dunlop, David

Belles with balls: John Leguizamo, Wesley Snipes and Patrick Swayze strut their stuff in To Wong Foo, Thanks For Everything! Julie Newmar *(from UIP)*

Hemblen, Addison Bell, Colin Fox, Lorri Bagley, Lynn Cunningham, Michael Ewing, Lindsay Leese, Sandi Stahlbrand.
Dir: Peter Segal. Pro: Lorne Michaels. Co-Pro: Barnaby Thompson. Ex Pro: Robert K. Weiss. Assoc Pro: Michael Ewing. Screenplay: Bonnie Turner, Terry Turner and Fred Wolf. Ph: Victor J. Kemper. Ed: William Kerr. Pro Des: Stephen J. Lineweaver. M: David Newman; numbers performed by Paul Westerberg, Primal Scream, Chris Farley and Brian Dennehy, Patsy Cline, The Carpenters, Brenda Lee, Buckwheat Zydeco, Timbuk 3, Dexys Midnight Runners, REM, Soul Coughing, Smoking Popes, Phunk Junkeez, etc. Costumes: Patti Unger. (Paramount–UIP.) Rel: 17 November 1995. 97 mins. Cert PG. USA. 1995.

To Wong Foo, Thanks for Everything! Julie Newmar
Teetering in the footsteps of *The Adventures of Priscilla Queen of the Desert*,

The magic toy shop: Woody holds court in John Lasseter's breakthrough Toy Story *(from Buena Vista)*

the equally cumbersomely titled *Wong Foo* covers very similar territory with much less pizzazz, wit or glorious scenery. Two drag queens, who tie for the crown in a New York beauty pageant, take pity on a whimpering Latino also-ran and decide to swap their prize plane tickets to Hollywood for a Cadillac drive cross country. On the way they meet inevitable hostility, while leaving behind them broader, happier minds and a strong whiff of Coco Chanel. While preaching the need for tolerance, *To Wong Foo* manages to insult practically every minority, not least the inevitable 'redneck' community of Middle America which, as Hollywood would have it, is terminally naive, prejudiced and ignorant. Filmed in New York and Nebraska.

Cast: Wesley Snipes (Noxeema Jackson), Patrick Swayze (Vida Boheme), John Leguizamo (Chi Chi Rodriguez), Stockard Channing (Carol Ann), Blythe Danner (Beatrice), Arliss Howard (Virgil), Jason London (Bobby Ray), Chris Penn (Sheriff Dollard), Melinda Dillon (Merna), Beth Grant (Loretta), Alice Drummond (Clara), Jennifer Milmore (Bobby Lee), Julie Newmar (herself), Robin Williams (John Jacob Schmidt), Marceline Hugot, Jamie Harrold, Mike Hodge, Michael Vartan, RuPaul, Joel Story, Naomi Campbell, Quentin Crisp.

Dir: Beeban Kidron. Pro: G. Mac Brown. Ex Pro: Bruce Cohen. Screenplay: Douglas Carter Beane. Ph: Steve Mason. Ed: Andrew Mondshein. Pro Des: Wynn Thomas. M: Rachel Portman; numbers performed by Salt-N-Pepa, Tom Jones, Crystal Waters, Barbra Streisand, Chaka Khan, The Commodores, Labelle, Eartha Kitt, Johnny Mathis, Charlie Rich, B.J. Thomas, Cyndi Lauper, etc. Costumes: Marlene Stewart. Choreography: Kenny Ortega. Best Baby: Noah Kidron Style. (Universal/Amblin–UIP.) Rel: 10 November 1995. 107 mins. Cert 12. USA. 1995.

Toy Story

As we all know, toys have a life of their own and when left to their own devices inhabit a wondrous world of fun and enchantment. As long as they fulfil their one purpose in life – to bring happiness to their young owner – toys can get up to any old mischief they like. And all is hunky dory in six-year-old Andy's crowded bedroom until the arrival of Buzz Lightyear, a spaceman action figure who doesn't realise he's a plaything ... The first totally computer-animated feature film, *Toy Story* takes a terrific concept and infuses it with wit, narrative panache and extraordinary visual invention. From the exceptionally fine vocal interpretations (Tom Hanks alone deserves an Oscar), to the crackerjack editing, superlative score and outstanding sound, *Toy Story* stimulates the same sense of wonder as *2001* and *Star Wars* did when they first appeared. In fact, the animation is so magical that one almost forgets it's just a cartoon. Even those who normally avoid cartoons should get a buzz out of this.

Voices: Tom Hanks (Woody), Tim Allen (Buzz Lightyear), Don Rickles (Mr Potato Head), Jim Varney (Slinky Dog), Wallace Shawn (Rex), John Ratzenberger (Hamm), Annie Potts (Bo Peep), John Morris (Andy), Erik Von Detten (Sid), Laurie Metcalf (Mrs Davis), R. Lee Ermey, Sarah Freeman, Penn Jillette.

Dir: John Lasseter. Pro: Ralph Guggenheim and Bonnie Arnold. Ex Pro: Edwin Catmull and Steven Jobs. Screenplay: Joss Whedon, Andrew Stanton, Joel Cohen and

Anoraks unite: Ewen Bremner and Ewan McGregor share the low-life in Danny Boyle's kaleidoscopic Trainspotting *(from PolyGram)*

Alec Sokolow, from a story by Lasseter, Stanton, Pete Docter and Joe Ranft. Art Director: Ralph Eggleston. Ed: Robert Gordon and Lee Unkrich. M: Randy Newman; songs written and performed by Newman. Sound: Gary Rydstrom. Supervising Animator: Pete Docter. Supervising Technical Director: William Reeves. (Pixar/Walt Disney Pictures–Buena Vista.) Rel: 22 March 1996. 81 mins. Cert PG. USA. 1995.

Trainspotting

Leith, Edinburgh; today. One naturally approaches the second film from the creators of *Shallow Grave* with some caution. *Shallow Grave* was such a fresh, vivid and savagely entertaining film that no other British work of 1995 could equal it in originality or impact. Whatever followed would inevitably disappoint. However, this critic was not expecting an in-your-face comedy extolling the virtues of heroin, nor a film with the visual panache and daring of a Scottish *Clockwork Orange*. It's got it all here: drugs, violence, drugs,

diarrhoea, drugs, underage sex, drugs, infant mortality, drugs, the dementia of cold turkey and the clinical detail of needles penetrating veins. 'We're not stupid, you know,' proclaims Mark Renton, the eloquent mouthpiece for Scottish junkie youth. 'Imagine your best orgasm and magnify it a thousand times. And you still can't describe the high.' Nor, in mere words, can you express the horror that follows. A fantastic script, inspired direction and a score boasting the cutting edge of contemporary British music proves a heady cocktail by any standards.

Cast: Ewan McGregor (Mark Renton), Ewen Bremner (Spud), Jonny Lee Miller (Sick Boy), Kevin McKidd (Tommy), Robert Carlyle (Begbie), Kelly Macdonald (Diane), James Cosmo (Mr Renton), Eileen Nicholas (Mrs Renton), Susan Vidler (Allison), Pauline Lynch (Lizzy), Shirley Henderson (Gail), Peter Mullan, Stuart McQuarrie, Irvine Welsh, Dale Winton, Keith Allen, Kevin Allen, Annie Louise Ross, Billy Riddoch, Fiona Bell, Vincent Friel, Finlay Welsh.

   Dir: Danny Boyle. Pro: Andrew Macdonald. Screenplay: John Hodge, based on the novel by Irvine Welsh. Ph: Brian Tufano. Pro Des: Rachael Fleming. Ed:

Masahiro Hirakubo. M: Bizet, J.S. Bach; numbers performed by Iggy Pop, Brian Eno, Primal Scream, Heaven 17, Sleeper, New Order, Blur, Lou Reed, Underworld, Ice MC, Pulp, Bedrock featuring Kyo, Elastica, Ewen Bremner, Leftfield, etc. Costumes: Lesley Stewart. (Channel Four/Figment Film/Noel Gay–PolyGram.) Rel: 23 February 1996. 93 mins. Cert 18. UK. 1995.

Twelve Monkeys

Drawing on a number of his cherished themes – madness, dreams, re-birth, the homeless, unorthodox men, an Orwellian future – Terry Gilliam creates an epic sci-fi love story that both touches the heart and challenges the mind. Opening with the bold statement that 'five billion people will die from a deadly virus in 1997,' the film leaps into an elegant, operatic medley of *Brazil*, *The Fisher King*, *The Terminator* and *Outbreak*. A prisoner from the next century has been accidentally dropped into 1990 to collect evidence leading to a viral epidemic that is to relegate the future to history. Of course, nobody believes him and so he is locked up in an asylum where, significantly, he meets both his romantic and

Making history of the future: Bruce Willis models the latest in designer macs in Terry Gilliam's brilliant Twelve Monkeys *(from PolyGram)*

predestined catalysts. Yet the past becomes so seductive to the time traveller that when he returns to the future he believes he is hallucinating. While narratively complex, *Twelve Monkeys* is so well constructed that each piece of the mosaic falls perfectly into place at its allotted time, revealing another spiral to this fascinating, gripping and rousing story. Visually provocative, intellectually tantalising and darkly humorous, *Twelve Monkeys* will blow your mind.

Cast: Bruce Willis (James Cole), Madeleine Stowe (Kathryn Railly), Brad Pitt (Jeffrey Goines), Christopher Plummer (Dr Leland Goines), Jon Seda (Jose), Frank Gorshin (Dr Fletcher), David Morse (Dr Peters), Joseph Melito, Michael Chance, H. Michael Walls, Bob Adrian, Simon Jones, Carol Florence, Bill Raymond, Joey Perillo, Fred Strother, Rick Warner, Anthony 'Chip' Brienza, Charles Techman, Harry O'Toole, Christopher Meloni, Paul Meshejian, Kevin Thigpen, Annie Golden, Lisa Talerico.
Dir: Terry Gilliam. Pro: Charles Roven. Ex Pro: Robert Cavallo, Gary Levinsohn and Robert Kosberg. Co-Pro: Lloyd Phillips. Screenplay: David Peoples and Janet Peoples, inspired by the Chris Marker short *La Jetée* (1962). Ph: Roger Pratt. Pro Des: Jeffrey Beecroft. Ed: Mick Audsley. M: Paul Buckmaster; numbers performed by B.J. Cole, Louis Armstrong, Fats Domino, Link Wray and the Wraymen, The Chantays, Tom Waits, etc. Costumes: Julie Weiss. (Universal Pictures/Atlas Entertainment/Classico–PolyGram.) Rel: 19 April 1996. 129 mins. Cert 15. USA. 1995.

Two Deaths

December 22, 1989; Bucharest. For Daniel Pavenic, an eminent Romanian surgeon, the slow death of his soul began when he first touched the ankle of Ana Puscasu. That moment also heralded a kind of death for Ana, whose voluptuous beauty consumed the tall stranger, forever uniting their lives. Pavenic reveals his bizarre pact with Ana, now his housekeeper and mistress, to three old school friends who meet for a sumptuous banquet to mark their 19th reunion. Outside, on the streets of Bucharest, the 15-year-old Socialist regime of President Ceausescu is crumbling, with random killing staining the conscience of Romania … Blending Pinter with Dennis Potter spiced with traditional Nicolas Roeg, *Two Deaths* is a chilling piece of cinematic theatre. As the conversation drifts from convivial small talk to shocking revelation, Roeg cuts to the carnage on the streets to heighten the atmosphere of unease. A close-up of a fish being gutted, the scene of a tragic abortion, a young man shot in the head, all reinforce the sense of imminent death (both psychological and literal) in typical Roeg style. Filmed on location in Bucharest and Kingston-on-Thames, Surrey.

Cast: Michael Gambon (Daniel Pavenic), Sonia Braga (Ana Puscasu), Patrick Malahide (George Bucsan), Ion Caramitru (Carl Dalakis), Nickolas Grace (Marius Vernescu), John Shrapnel (Cinca), Sevilla Delofski (Ilena), Lisa Orgolini (young Ana), Niall Refoy (young Pavenic), Ravil Isyanov, Matthew Terdre, Amanda Royle, Karl Tessler, Andrew Tiernan, Rade Serbedzija, Laura Davenport.
Dir: Nicolas Roeg. Pro: Carolyn Montagu and Luc Roeg. Ex Pro: Allan Scott, Jonathan Olsberg and Mark Shivas. Screenplay: Scott, from the novel *The Two Deaths of Senora Puccini* by Stephen Dobyns. Ph: Witold Stok. Pro Des: Don Taylor. Ed: Tony Lawson. M: Hans Zimmer. Costumes: Elizabeth Waller. (BBC Films/British Screen–Metro Tartan.) Rel: 14 June 1996. 96 mins. Cert 18. UK. 1994.

Two If by Sea
See *Stolen Hearts*.

Ulysses' Gaze – To Vlemma Tou Odyssea – Regard d'Ulysse

Returning to the provincial town of Ptolemais after 35 years, Greek filmmaker 'A' embarks on a quest to find three reels of undeveloped Balkan film from 1905. His search – leading him through the bleak landscapes of

Greece, Albania, Macedonia, Bulgaria, Romania, Serbia and Bosnia – develops into an odyssey of self-revelation, enlightenment and catharsis as 'A' rediscovers his forgotten country. Theo Angelopoulos, the director of such works as *The Travelling Players* (1975) and *Landscape in the Mist* (1988), has been described by film historian David Thomson as one of the three greatest filmmakers still working (alongside Rivette and Godard). This, his tenth film, is by turns self-indulgent, morose, obtuse, bloated and ponderous. Then, halfway through, a masterpiece begins to take shape as the story gels and a note of optimism is sounded. Indeed, it is the last third which proves the most memorable, with the spectre of beautiful, ancient buildings ravaged by war and with an orchestra – comprised of Croatian, Serbian and Muslim musicians – playing sweet music in thick fog. Two hours would've done nicely.

Cast: Harvey Keitel ('A'), Erland Josephson (Film Library curator), Maia Morgenstern (Ulysses' 'wives'), Thanassis Vengos (taxi driver), Yorgos Michalakopoulos (journalist friend), Dora Volanaki (old woman).

Dir: Theo Angelopoulos. Pro: Giorgio Silvagni and Eric Heumann. Ex Pro: Phoebe Economopoulos and Marc Soustras. Screenplay: Angelopoulos, Silvagni, Tonino Guerra and Petros Markaris. Ph: Yorgos Arvantis. Pro Des: Giorgos Patsas and Miodrac Mile Nicolic. Ed: Yannis Tsitsopoulos. M: Eleni Karaindrou; violin solo: Kim Kashkashian. Costumes: Yorgos Ziakas. (Centre Du Cinema Grec/ Mega Channel/Paradis Film/La Generale d'Images/La Sept Cinema/Canal Plus/RAI/ Channel Four, etc–Artificial Eye/Mayfair.) Rel: 16 February 1996. 177 mins. Cert PG. Greece/France/Italy. 1995.

Underground

Belgrade; 1941/43/44/61/91. Returning to his love of parable, magic realism and knockabout farce, Yugoslav director Emir Kusturica (*Time of the Gypsies, Arizona Dream*) paints an epic canvas of his country's history from 1941 to 1991. Dividing his film into three acts, Kusturica explores the tragedy of a country brutalised by war, from the Nazi bombing of Belgrade, the Occupation, the bombing by the Allies, the tyranny of Tito and the savage conflict of the 1990s. During all this two best friends, Marko and Blacky, capitalise on their country's suffering through arms dealing, gold

Surreal Sarajevo: Srdan Todorovic and Milena Pavlovic in Emir Kusturica's extraordinary Underground *(from Artificial Eye)*

trafficking and other immoral profiteering, exploiting both Yugoslavia and themselves. Yet behind this rich tapestry of betrayal and misery is a warm, funny and ferocious comedy in which man's instinct for revelry repeatedly surfaces with a vengeance. Droll, harrowing and action-packed, *Underground* is a little too much at times, but always grips the attention. Coincidentally, the film shares many parallels with Claude Lelouche's equally ambitious *Les Miserables*, but replaces the latter's self-indulgent style and romanticism with raw energy and good humour.

Cast: Miki Manojlovic (Marko), Lazar Ristovski (Petar 'Blacky' Popara), Mirjana Jokovic (Natalija), Slavko Stimac (Ivan),

Ernst Stotzner (Franz), Srdan Todorovic (Jovan), Mirjana Karanovic (Vera), Milena Pavlovic (Jelena), Bata Stojkovic, Bora Todorovic, Dragan Nikolic.

Dir: Emir Kusturica. Ex Pro: Pierre Spengler. Screenplay: Kusturica and Dusan Kovacevic. Ph: Vilko Filac. Pro Des: Miljen Kljakovic 'Kreka'. Ed: Branka Ceperac. M: Goran Bregovic. Costumes: Nebojsa Lipanovic. (CiBy 2000/Pandora Film/Novo Film–Artificial Eye.) Rel: 8 March 1996. 167 mins. Cert 15. France/Germany/Hungary. 1995.

The Underneath

Mesmerising chamber drama from Steven Soderbergh, more in keeping with his first film, *sex, lies and videotape*,

Out of the past: Peter Gallagher makes moves on his ex-girlfriend Alison Elliott in Steven Soderbergh's mesmerising The Underneath *(from UIP), a remake of Robert Siodmak's 1949 film* Criss Cross

'If she doesn't move, I'm sure I could hit her from here': Afifi Alaquie trains her sights on Katherine Heigl in Geoff Murphy's faster-than-British Rail Under Siege 2 *(from Warner)*

than his later period pieces, *Kafka* and *King of the Hill*. Again, Peter Gallagher plays the slimy charmer 'skating through life on his looks and luck' who returns to Austin, Texas, ostensibly to attend his mother's wedding. He is, in fact, more interested in resurrecting his relationship with Rachel, whom he had left in the lurch along with the rest of his life. But, to quote his erstwhile girlfriend, 'there's something very powerful about being absent – but you shouldn't have come back.' Cross-cutting across time, Soderbergh slyly drops the shards of his narrative into place, provoking both a curiosity and sense of unease in the viewer. Particularly remarkable is Gallagher who, in an essentially unsympathetic role, elicits our compassion. And full marks to Cliff Martinez' subliminal score which never intrudes on the drama.

Cast: Peter Gallagher (Michael Chambers), Alison Elliott (Rachel), William Fichtner (Tommy Dundee), Adam Trese (David Chambers), Joe Don Baker (Clay Hinkle), Paul Dooley (Ed Dutton), Elisabeth Shue (Susan), Anjanette Comer (Mrs Chambers), Shelley Duvall (nurse), Joe Chrest, Dennis Hill, Harry Goaz, Mark Feltch, Vincent Gaskins, Richard Linklater, Helen Cates, John Martin, Steve Shearer.

Dir: Steven Soderbergh. Pro: John Hardy. Ex Pro: Joshua Donen, William Reid and Lionel Wigram. Screenplay: Sam Lowry and Daniel Fuchs. Ph: Elliot Davis. Pro Des: Howard Cummings. Ed: Stan Salfas. M: Cliff Martinez. Costumes: Kristen Anacker. (Universal/Populist Pictures–UIP.) Rel: 19 January 1996. 99 mins. Cert 15. USA. 1995.

Under Siege 2

When a secret government body activates a satellite with unparalleled optical and destructive powers, Travis Dane, the sacked designer, commandeers the device for his own nefarious ends. Hijacking the mile-long Grand Continental train for his mobile command centre, Dane and a small army of mercenaries embark on a mission to nuke Washington DC. Their only problem: that cook from *Under Siege* is on board ... While Steven Seagal strides through the film with his customary indifference (looking uncannily like a bored Jim Belushi), he is buoyed by a terrific supporting cast, with Everett McGill's monolithic sadist (who uses mace as a breath freshener) winning top honours by a whisker. Add to this seat-wetting stunts, helter skelter pacing and spectacular views of the Rockies and you have Escapism with a capital E. This is what action cinema is all about. Sadistic, but fun.

Cast: Steven Seagal (Casey Ryback), Eric Bogosian (Travis Dane), Everett McGill (Penn), Katherine Heigl (Sarah Ryback), Morris Chestnut (Bobby Zachs), Andy Romano (Admiral Bates), Brenda Bakke (Gilder), David Gianopoulos (David Trilling), Nick Mancuso (Breaker), Kurtwood Smith (General Cooper), Peter Greene, Patrick Kilpatrick, Scott Sowers, Afifi Alaquie, Sandra Taylor, Jonathan Banks, Royce D. Applegate, Dale Dye, Silan Smith, Rick Wiles, D.C. Douglas, Thom Adcox Hernandez.

Dir: Geoff Murphy. Pro: Steven Seagal, Steve Perry and Arnon Milchan. Ex Pro: Gary Goldstein, Jeffrey Neuman and Martin Wiley. Co-Pro: Julius R. Nasso. Screenplay: Richard Hatem and Matt Reeves, based on characters created by J.F Lawton. Ph: Robbie Greenberg. Ed: Michael Tronick. Pro Des: Albert Brenner. M: Basil

Poledouris; 'After the Train Has Gone' co-written, co-produced and co-sung by Seagal. Costumes: Richard Bruno. Visual Effects Supervisor: Richard Yuricich. (Regency Enterprises–Warner). Rel: 27 October 1995. 99 mins. Cert 18. USA. 1995.

Unstrung Heroes

Los Angeles; 1962. Steven Lidz is 12 years old and is somewhat embarrassed by his father, an outspoken inventor of bizarre gadgets who spends most of his time locked away in his workshop. When Steven's beloved mother takes to her bed from a mysterious illness, the boy's isolation is too much to bear – so he runs away to stay with his two uncles. There he discovers a bizarre new world in which paranoia and fantasy run hand in hand. As it happens, this is just what Steven needs to nourish his childhood identity. Skilfully adapted by Richard LaGravanese (*The Fisher King*, *The Bridges of Madison County*) from Franz Lidz's distinctive novel, *Unstrung Heroes* is a work of brave originality. Perfectly pitched by director Diane Keaton (making her theatrical film debut), the film is a bewitching, resonant work. Its sepia-toned photography and detailed screenplay perfectly capturing the otherworldliness of Steven's universe.

Cast: Andie MacDowell (Selma Lidz), John Turturro (Sid Lidz), Michael Richards (Danny Lidz), Maury Chaykin (Arthur Lidz), Nathan Watt (Steven/Franz Lidz), Kendra Krull (Sandy Lidz), Celia Weston (Amelia), Jack McGee (Lindquist), Sean P. Donahue (Ralph Crispi), Joey Andrews, Candice Azzara, Anne DeSalvo, Lillian Adams, Lou Cutell, Rabbi Harold M. Schulweis, Wayne Duvall.
  Dir: Diane Keaton. Pro: Susan Arnold, Donna Roth and Bill Badalato. Screenplay: Richard LaGravanese. Ph: Phedon Papamichael. Ed: Lisa Churgin. Pro Des: Garreth Stover. M: Thomas Newman; 'You Are My Sunshine' performed by Ray Charles. Costumes: Jill Ohanneson. (Hollywood Pictures–Buena Vista.) Rel: 8 December 1995. 95 mins. Cert PG. USA. 1995.

Unzipped

As New York fashion designer Isaac Mizrahi prepares for his autumn '94 exhibition, fashion photographer Douglas Keeve records in intimate detail his inspirations, despairs and euphoria. A perfect subject for any documentary, Mizrahi waxes enthusiastic about Mary Tyler Moore, ouija boards, Paris and old movies, the last named seeming to inspire most of his sartorial ideas (in particular *Nanook of the North* and *Call of the Wild*). A fly-on-the-wall documentary, *Unzipped* offers fascinating insights into the fashion industry and presents an honest portrait of an extraordinary man who has come to terms with himself. The various camera-friendly celebrities and glowering supermodels add icing to the cake (Cindy Crawford to intrusive camera: 'Hello? My pores are not that small!'). As quirky and entertaining a film as its subject.

Cast: Isaac Mizrahi, Sandra Bernhard, Naomi Campbell, Cindy Crawford, Linda Evangelista, Eartha Kitt, Mark Morris, Kate Moss, Polly Mellen, Candy Pratts, Helena Christensen, Niki Taylor, Cristy Turlington, Ellen Barkin, Richard Gere, Madonna, Liza Minnelli, Roseanne.
  Dir: Douglas Keeve. Pro: Michael Alden. Ex Pro: David Pecker and Nina Santisi. Co-Pro: Paul DeBenedictis and Keith Estabrook. Co-Ex Pro: Dori Berinstein. Assoc Pro: Diana Schmidt. Ph: Ellen Kuras. Ed: Paula Heredia. M: Debussy, Beethoven; numbers performed by Sandra Bernhard, Eartha Kitt, Bobby Darin, Boy George, Isaac Mizrahi, etc. Costumes: Mizrahi. (Hachette Filipacchi/Elle Magazine–Buena

In search of childhood: Nathan Watt and Andie MacDowell in Diane Keaton's haunting, touching Unstrung Heroes *(from Buena Vista)*

Vista.) Rel: 19 April 1996. 73 mins. Cert 15. USA. 1995.

Up Close and Personal

Like Nicole Kidman in *To Die For*, Sally Atwater will do anything to appear on television. Yet when she gets her chance to present the weather on local TV in Miami, she throws up beforehand and freezes during her inaugural performance. However, the station's producer sees through Sally's nerves and decides to nurture her callow talent. But the world of TV news is a tough business. Can Sally hack it? And can she overcome her initial hostility to her mentor? What do you think? It's a sad day indeed when Robert Redford, who's made such canny films about the media as *The Candidate*, *All the President's Men* and *Quiz Show*, should resort to such cinematic bubble gum. Cast as a hard-nosed TV newsman, Redford behaves more like a vaguely weathered matinee idol, while Michelle Pfeiffer reinvents her performance from *Dangerous Minds* (with additional mannerisms). With its gushing score and feeble attempts at comedy, the film resembles a Mills & Boon version of *Broadcast News*. Furthermore, there's something deeply disquieting about watching two such familiar icons exchanging bodily fluids.

Cast: Robert Redford (Warren Justice), Michelle Pfeiffer (Sally 'Tally' Atwater),

Gunning for the truth: Pete Postlethwaite lends an ear to Stephen Baldwin and Gabriel Byrne in Bryan Singer's masterful The Usual Suspects *(from PolyGram)*

Stockard Channing (Marcia McGrath), Joe Mantegna (Bucky Terranova), Kate Nelligan (Joanna Kennelly), Glenn Plummer (Ned Jackson), James Rebhorn (John Merino), Scott Bryce (Rob Sullivan), Raymond Cruz, Dede Pfeiffer, Miguel Sandoval, Noble Willingham, James Karen, Brian Markinson, Heidi Swedberg, Marc Macaulay, Elizabeth Ruscio, Fabian, Dennis Dun.

Dir: Jon Avnet. Pro: Avnet, David Nicksay and Jordan Kerner. Ex Pro: Ed Hookstratten and John Foreman. Co-Pro: Lisa Lindstrom and Martin Huberty. Screenplay: Joan Didion and John Gregory Dunne; suggested by the book *Golden Girl* by Alanna Nash. Ph: Karl Walter Lindenlaub. Pro Des: Jeremy Conway. Ed: Debra Neil-Fisher. M: Thomas Newman; Mozart; numbers performed by Tito Puente, Sheryl Crow, etc; 'Because You Loved Me' sung by Celine Dion. Costumes: Albert Wolsky. (Touchstone Pictures/Cinergi–Entertainment.) Rel: 7 June 1996. 126 mins. Cert 15. USA. 1996.

The Usual Suspects

'The greatest trick the devil ever pulled was convincing the world he didn't exist,' warns Roger 'Verbal' Kint (quoting Baudelaire). A pathetic, crippled crook, Verbal is granted immunity in exchange for his testimony concerning a horrific drug massacre, of which he is the sole intact survivor. Bullied by a tough customs agent, Verbal reluctantly reveals that six weeks earlier he and four other 'usual suspects' were thrown into a cell on trumped-up charges and so plotted their revenge. However, while later puncturing the New York police department's defences they stirred up a different hornet's nest. Inadvertently, they had crossed a Turkish crime lord – nicknamed 'The Devil' – whose speciality of torturing and killing his enemy's parents and children had become legendary. And no amount of police custody is going to save anybody ... An elaborate and ingenious crime caper, *The Usual Suspects* piles on the tension while retaining a macabre sense of humour. Superbly made, too.

Cast: Stephen Baldwin (Michael McManus), Gabriel Byrne (Dean Keaton), Chazz Palminteri (David Kujan), Kevin Pollak (Todd Hockney), Pete Postlethwaite (Kobayashi), Kevin Spacey (Roger 'Verbal' Kint), Benico Del Toro (Fred Fenster), Suzy Amis (Edie Finneran), Giancarlo Esposito (Jack Baer), Dan Hedaya (Jeffrey Rabin), Peter Greene (Redfoot), Paul Bartel, Carl Bressler, Phillip Simon, Jack Shearer, Christine Estabrook, Clark Gregg, Morgan Hunter, Louis Lombardi, Vito D'Ambrosio.

Dir: Bryan Singer. Pro: Singer and Michael McDonnell. Co-Pro: Kenneth Kokin. Ex Pro: Robert Jones, Hans Brockman, Francois Duplat and Art Horan. Screenplay: Christopher McQuarrie. Ph: Newton Thomas Sigel. Ed and M: John Ottman. Pro Des: Howard Cummings. Costumes: Louise Mingenbach. (Spellings Films/Blue Parrot/Bad Hat Harry/Rosco Film–PolyGram.) Rel: 25 August 1995. 106 mins. Cert 18. USA. 1995.

Vampire in Brooklyn

Having overlooked fellow vampires Tom Cruise and Brad Pitt in San Francisco, self-proclaimed 'connoisseur of death' Maximilian journeys to Brooklyn to ensnare, bed and bleed the perfect mate – the last of his kind ... Designed as a vehicle for Wes Craven to break into comedy and for Eddie Murphy to try a splash of horror, *Vampire in Brooklyn* fails to raise a hair or chuckle. An over-directed extravaganza of fog, gore and explosions, the film cribs gags from other movies and then wastes them. Kadeem Hardison, who plays Maximilian's slowly deteriorating sidekick, was better in the low-budget *Def By Temptation* five years ago, about a vampire in Brooklyn.

Cast: Eddie Murphy (Maximilian/Preacher Pauley/Guido), Angela Bassett (Rita Veder), Allen Payne (Warren Justice),

Kadeem Hardison (Julius Jones), Zakes Mokae (Dr Zeko), John Witherspoon (Silas Green), Joanna Cassidy (Dewey), Simbi Khali (Nikki), Messiri Freeman, Nick Corri, Mitch Pileggi, Jerry Hall, Wendy Robie.

Dir: Wes Craven. Pro: Eddie Murphy and Mark Lipsky. Ex Pro: Marianne Maddalena and Stuart M. Besser. Co-Pro: Ray Murphy Jr. Screenplay: Charles Murphy, Michael Lucker and Chris Parker, from a story by Eddie Murphy, Vernon Lynch Jr and Charles Murphy. Ph: Mark Irwin. Ed: Patrick Lussier. M: J. Peter Robinson; numbers performed by Salt 'n' Pepa, Hammer, Hugh Masakela, UB40, etc. Costumes: Ha Nguyen. (Paramount–UIP.) Rel: 7 June 1996. 102 mins. Cert15. USA. 1995.

Waiting to Exhale

Phoenix, Arizona; today. Four affluent Afro-American women are looking for love and happiness – but they aren't finding it with the men they know. In fact, every man who crosses their threshold turns out to be a two-timing bastard (and hopeless in bed). Forest Whitaker's soapy dramatic comedy resembles more the women's pictures of the Fifties than the recent cinema of Spike Lee and John Singleton. With nary a white face in view, racism barely raises its ugly head, although interracial romance is given a pugnacious frown. These feisty women, cloistered in their upper-middle-class ivory towers, seem only affected by the trials and tribulations of the dating arena. The syrup glistens in every scene, complete with rosy sunsets, Whitney Houston numbers and frequent close-ups of hands intertwined. In fact, this is the closest thing you'll find to a celluloid version of a Whitney Houston album.

Cast: Whitney Houston (Savannah Jackson), Angela Bassett (Bernadine Harris), Loretta Devine (Gloria Johnson), Lela Rochon (Robin Stokes), Gregory Hines (Marvin), Dennis Haysbert (Kenneth), Mykelti Williamson (Troy), Michael Beach (John Snr), Leon (Russell), Wendell Pierce (Michael), Donald Adeosun Faison (Tarik Johnson), Giancarlo Esposito (David Johnson), Wesley Snipes (James Wheeler), Jeffrey D. Sams, Jazz Raycole, Brandon Hammond, Kenya Moore, Lamont Johnson, Theo, Starletta DuPois, Luis Sharpe.

Dir: Forest Whitaker. Pro: Ezra Swerdlow and Deborah Schindler. Ex Pro and Screenplay: Terry McMillan and Ronald Bass, based on McMillan's novel. Ph: Toyomichi Kurita. Pro Des: David Gropman. Ed: Richard Chew. M: Kenneth 'Babyface' Edmonds; numbers performed by Whitney

So Emotional: Angela Bassett waits for her man (an uncredited Wesley Snipes) in Forest Whitaker's soapy Waiting to Exhale *(from Fox)*

Houston, Chante Moore, SWV, CeCe Winans, For Real, Brandy, Toni Braxton, Sonja Marie, Faith Evans, Patti LaBelle, Aretha Franklin, Mary J. Blige, TLC, Chaka Khan, De De O'Neal, Shanna, The Whispers, Prince, Oreolando Mallary, Minnie Riperton, Roberta Flack, etc. Costumes: Judy L. Ruskin. (Fox.) Rel: 26 January 1996. 123 mins. Cert 15. USA. 1995.

A Walk in the Clouds

Returning to San Francisco at the end of the Second World War, Paul Sutton discovers that his wife had never bothered to read his countless letters.

'This is what I call a chinwag': Anthony Quinn and Keanu Reeves catch up on the grape in Alfonso Arau's intoxicating A Walk in the Clouds *(from Fox)*

Who'll Stop The War? *Kevin Costner gives Elijah Wood some home-grown advice in Jon Avnet's sadly neglected drama (from UIP)*

Mortified, he takes off for the country-side to re-evaluate his life when he encounters a young pregnant woman, Victoria, who is terrified of facing her tyrannical father – a Mexican vineyard owner. In an act of spontaneous chivalry, Paul offers to stand in as her husband – at least, until the dust settles ... Visually exquisite and intoxicated with old-fashioned story-telling values, *A Walk in the Clouds* just doesn't work in English. While Alfonso Arau's last

film, the critically acclaimed *Like Water for Chocolate*, cast an exotic magic in its native Spanish tongue, Arau's Hollywood debut strains credibility and encourages giggles. Nevertheless, the film boasts many wonderful moments, not least the grape harvest and any scene Anthony Quinn is allowed to stride off with. If this had been made forty years ago, it would probably be a classic by now. But, sadly, times have changed ... Based on the Italian film *Four Steps in the Clouds*.

Cast: Keanu Reeves (Paul Sutton), Aitana Sanchez-Gijon (Victoria Aragon), Anthony Quinn (Don Pedro Aragon), Giancarlo Gi-

annini (Alberto Aragon), Angelica Aragon (Marie Jose Aragon), Evangelina Elizondo (Guadelupe Aragon), Freddy Rodriguez (Pedro Aragon, Jr.), Debra Messing (Betty Sutton), Febronio Covarrubias, Roberto Huerta, Juan Jimenez, Don Amendolia, John Dennis Johnston, Joseph Lindsey, Mark Matheisen, Ivory Ocean.

Dir: Alfonso Arau. Pro: Gil Netter, David Zucker and Jerry Zucker. Ex Pro: James D. Brubaker. Co-Pro: Bill Johnson. Screenplay: Robert Mark Kamen, Mark Miller and Harvey Weitzman, from the screenplay *Quattro Passi Fra le Nuvole*, by Piero Tellini, Cesare Zavattini, Vittorio de Benedetti and Massimo Tellini. Ph: Emmanuel Lubezki. Ed: Don Zimmerman. Pro Des: David Gropman. M: Maurice Jarre. Costumes: Judy L. Ruskin. (Fox.) Rel: 17 November 1995. 103 mins. Cert PG. USA. 1995.

The War

Juliette, Mississippi; 1970. Haunted by nightmares after his ordeal in Vietnam, Stephen Simmons has lost the family's home and is unable to hold down a job. Meanwhile, his son and daughter are being threatened by a neighbouring brood of white trash and Simmons tries hard to instil some pacifist doctrine into his kids before tragedy strikes again. A bold, heartfelt attempt to blend *Stand By Me* with *Platoon*, Jon Avnet's *The War* starts very unpromisingly indeed, awkwardly wedging a Creedence Clearwater Revival track in between snippets of treacly music over the opening credits. Period pop songs continue to pop up at annoying intervals throughout, punctuating the honey-scented photography of dreamy Southern landscapes. Yet once one gets over the rites-of-passage clichés, *The War* turns out to be a moving and gripping drama with plenty to say. A couple of nerve-jangling sequences near the end are particularly well filmed, while 13-year-old actress Lexi Randall gives the piece a real spark.

Cast: Elijah Wood (Stu Simmons), Kevin Costner (Stephen Simmons), Mare Winningham (Lois Simmons), Lexi Randall (Lidia Simmons), LaToya Chisholm (Elvadine), Donald Sellers (Arliss), Raynor Scheine (Mr Lipnicki), Christine Baranski (Miss Strapford), Bruce A. Young (Moe), Leon Sills, Will West, Brennan Gallagher, Adam Henderson, Charlette Julius, Jennifer Tyler, Lucas Black, Justin Lucas, Nick Searcy, Gary Basaraba, Tim Ware.

Dir: Jon Avnet. Pro: Avnet and Jordan Kerner. Co-Pro: Martin Huberty and Lisa

Mad Max at sea: Kevin Costner proves that the battle of the sexes can only get worse in the future, in Waterworld *(from UIP). Jeanne Triplehorn gets the cold stare*

Lindstrom. Ex Pro: Eric Eisner and Todd Baker. Co Ex-Pro and Screenplay: Kathy McWorter. Ph: Geoffrey Simpson. Pro Des: Kristi Zea. Ed: Debra Neil. M: Thomas Newman; numbers performed by Creedence Clearwater Revival, The Lovin' Spoonful, Tony Joe White, The Supremes, Mother Earth, Aretha Franklin, Janis Joplin, Eddie Cochran, Ritchie Havens, Norman Greenbaum, The Rolling Stones, Cat Stevens, The Band, etc. Costumes: Molly Maginnis. (Universal/Island World–UIP.) Rel: 12 January 1996. 125 mins. Cert 12. USA. 1994.

Waterworld

In centuries to come, when global warming has melted the polar ice caps, the world has become submerged by water. What remains of the population now cling to floating cities of scrap metal or drift in makeshift boats. One man, The Mariner, has learned to survive by his own wits and, endowed with gills behind his ears, can swim underwater. In return for aiding his escape from a hostile atoll, he takes a young woman and girl aboard his state-of-the-art trimaran, only to find himself pursued by a flotilla of ruthless killers... Regardless of the fact that, at a budget variously reported to be between $175m and $200m, *Waterworld* is the most expensive movie ever made, it fails on a number of basic points. There is no driving story, no feeling of empathy for the characters, no edge-of-your-seat suspense, no wit in the one-liners, no sense of awe or wonder and a flabbergasting lapse of logic in the final reel. Yet the few scenes which promise any dramatic fireworks (a shark attack, The Mariner's escape from a sea monster and the film's sole hint at sexual intimacy) are skipped over to the point of negligence. Not so much a turkey as a damp squid.

Cast: Kevin Costner (The Mariner), Dennis Hopper (The Deacon), Jeanne Tripplehorn (Helen), Tina Majorino (Enola), Michael Jeter (Gregor), R.D. Call (Enforcer), Gerard Murphy (Nord), Chaim Jeraffi, Ric Aviles, Leonardo Cimino, Zakes Mokae, Lanny Flaherty, Sab Shimono, Robert Joy, John Toley-Bey, Kim Coates.

Dir: Kevin Reynolds. Pro: Charles Gordon, John Davis and Kevin Costner. Ex Pro: Jeffrey Mueller, Andrew Licht and Ilona Herzberg. Screenplay: Peter Rader and David Twohy. Ph: Dean Semler. Ed: Peter Boyle. Pro Des: Dennis Gassner. M: James Newton Howard; Mark Isham. Costumes: John Bloomfield. (Universal/Gordon Company/Davis Entertainment–UIP.) Rel: 11 August 1995. 135 mins. Cert 12. USA. 1995.

When Night is Falling

Camille Baker is a teacher of mythology at a Protestant school in Toronto. Tempted with promotion should she marry her boyfriend and fellow professor, she cannot take the prospect of becoming co-chaplain of the New College of Faith seriously. Then, when her beloved dog dies, she is thrown onto the mercy of her emotions. Just then, a beautiful, mysterious woman from the local avant-garde circus starts making advances ... What is it with the Canucks? Every Canadian film that reaches Britain is either promiscuous, wilfully idiosyncratic or just plain pretentious. *When Night is Falling* is all three, a self-consciously poetic ode to female sexuality that clumsily juggles

Ee, by gum, what it is to be English, lads: Sean Bean celebrates with a pint o' bitter in Maria Giese's misconceived When Saturday Comes *(from Guild)*

magic realism with social statement. While aiming for a kind of heightened naturalism, director Patricia Rozema (*I've Heard the Mermaids Singing, White Room*) has created theatrical stasis.

Girl talk: Rachael Crawford and Pascale Bussieres indulge in a touch of French-Canadian in Patricia Rozema's When Night is Falling *(from Metro Tartan)*

Cast: Pascale Bussieres (Camille Baker), Rachael Crawford (Petra Soft), Henry Czerny (Martin Bergen), David Fox (Rev. DeBoer), Don McKellar (Timothy), Tracy Wright, Clare Coulter, Ruffian (Bob the dog).

Dir and Screenplay: Patricia Rozema. Pro: Barbara Tranter. Ph: Douglas Koch. Ed: Susan Shipton. Pro Des: John Dondertman. M: Lesley Barber. Costumes: Linda Muir. (Crucial Pictures/Telefilm Canada/Ontario Film Development Corp–Metro Tartan.) Rel: 10 November 1995. 93 mins. Cert 18. Canada. 1994.

When Saturday Comes

Contrary to the crowing of John Major's government, not a lot has changed in Northern England since

Lindsay Anderson directed his ground-breaking *This Sporting Life* in 1963. *When Saturday Comes,* inspired by a true story, shows how one man, suffocated by poverty and a bitter, defeated father, attempts to break out of the dead-end existence that Sheffield offers him: i.e. work in the local pits or brewery, boozy evenings at the pub and the odd, perilous flutter at the bookies. Jimmy Muir has a talent for football and a chance to make a decent life with the beautiful, level-headed Annie Doherty, but can he overcome the congenital inhibition that holds him back? In spite of the film's strong characters and a gripping scenario, many of the scenes and much of the dialogue fails to ring true. This is not entirely surprising as producer James Daly commissioned his American wife to write and direct, who shows only a superficial grasp of her subject. It is Sean Bean, himself Sheffield born and bred, whose charismatic portrayal of the hero ultimately wins over our sympathies in spite of the contrivances of the plot. Previously known as *A Pint O'Bitter.*

Cast: Sean Bean (Jimmy Muir), Emily Lloyd (Annie Doherty), Pete Postlethwaite (Ken Jackson), John McEnery (Joe Muir), Craig Kelly (Russell Graham Muir), Ann Bell (Sarah Muir), Mary Muir (Melanie Hill), Chris Walker (Mac), Steve Huison (Jack), Douglas McFerran (Norman), John Higgins, Tim Gallagher, Peter Gunn, Nick Waring, Tony Currie, David Leland, Sharon Jackson, Bill Stewart, Andrew Shepherd, Dave Hill, Philippa Howell, Rebecca Nichols, Freddie Fletcher.

Dir and Screenplay: Maria Giese. Pro: James Daly, Christopher Lambert and Meir Teper. Ex Pro: David Matalon and Peter Koral. Line Pro: Peter McAleese. Ph: Gerry Fisher. Pro Des: Hugo Luczyc-Wyhowski. Ed: George Akers. M: Anne Dudley; numbers performed by such Sheffield musicians as Joe Elliott, Paul Carrack, Glen Gregory, Martin Fry, Dean Ward, etc. Costumes: Kate Carin. (Capitol Films/A Pint O'Bitter–Guild.) Rel: 1 March 1996. 98 mins. Cert 15. UK. 1995.

While You Were Sleeping

Chicago; 1995. Lucy Moderatz works as a humble teller for the Chicago Transit Authority and admires her prince charming from afar. He's Peter Callaghan, who's tall, dark, handsome and, yes, rich. Then, one day, he's pushed onto the track by muggers and

Lucy saves him from the wheels of an oncoming train. Visiting her comatose Romeo in hospital, Lucy is mistaken for his fiancee by his family and is welcomed into the Callaghan home over Christmas. Yet as she falls in love with the Callaghan tribe, she becomes increasingly disillusioned with their scion. Enter Peter's brother Jack, who is not so convinced that Lucy is who she says she is ... Sweet, sentimental, predictable and contrived, *While You Were Sleeping* lacks romantic chemistry but is so damned likeable that it's hard not to root for it. And there are some lovely touches (like the newspaper boy falling off his bike), although Randy Edelman's pushy music is a curse. FYI: Jon Turteltaub previously directed the Disney hit *Cool Runnings*.

Cast: Sandra Bullock (Lucy Moderatz), Bill Pullman (Jack Callaghan), Peter Gallagher (Peter Callaghan), Peter Boyle (Ox Callaghan), Glynis Johns (Elsie), Jack Warden (Saul Tuttle), Micole Mercurio (Midge Callaghan), Jason Bernard (Jerry Wallace), Michael Rispoli (Joe Jr.), Ally Walker (Ashley Bacon), Monica Keena (Mary Callaghan), Ruth Rudnick, Marcia Wright, Dick Cusack, Peter Siragusa, Margaret Travolta.

Dir: Jon Turteltaub. Pro: Joe Roth and Roger Birnbaum. Co-Pro: Charles J.D. Schlissel and Susan Stremple. Ex Pro: Arthur Sarkissian and Steve Barron. Screenplay: Daniel G. Sullivan and Frederic Lebow. Ph: Phedon Papamichael. Ed: Bruce Green. Pro Des: Garreth Stover. M: Randy Edelman; numbers performed by Natalie Cole, Koko Taylor, The Glenn Miller Orchestra, Ella Fitzgerald, Dusty Springfield and Daryl Hall, etc. Costumes: Betsy Cox. (Hollywood Pictures/Caravan Pictures–Buena Vista.) Rel: 1 September 1995. 104 mins. Cert PG. USA. 1995.

The White Balloon

Tehran; today. Seven-year-old Razieh has just one hour, 28 minutes and 30 seconds to buy a goldfish for the New Year celebrations. But, for a seven-year-old, purchasing a goldfish is no easy task, and a myriad of setbacks conspire to block her path to perfect happiness. Perpetually on the edge of tears, Aida Mohammadkhani gives a performance of extraordinary concentration as she stares timorously at the unheeding adults around her, gradually building her resolve as one seeming tragedy follows another. Jafar Panahi, whose first feature this is, art-

fully draws us into the world of his young protagonist, in which a momentarily mislaid fish bowl can precipitate a sense of panic in the viewer. With any luck, this delightful, moving and even suspenseful film should, in the fullness of time, find itself perched proudly

Right on track: Sandra Bullock gets on top of her dreamboat Peter Gallagher in Jon Turteltaub's winning sleeper While You Were Sleeping *(from Buena Vista)*

Giant pleasures in small packages: Aida Mohammadkhani in Jafar Panahi's wonderful The White Balloon *(from Electric)*

Toxic humour: Hugh O'Connor, Roger Lloyd Pack and Charlotte Coleman fail to see the joke in Benjamin Ross's sublime The Young Poisoner's Handbook *(from Electric)*

alongside such children's classics as *Kes* and *The Red Balloon*. Winner of the Camera d'Or and the International Critics' Prize at Cannes '95.

Cast: Aida Mohammadkhani (Razieh), Moshen Kalifi (Ali), Fereshteh Sadr Orfani (mother), Mohammad Shahani (soldier), Anna Bourkowska (old woman), Mohammad Bahktiari (tailor), Aliasghar Samadi (balloon seller).

Dir, Ed and Pro Des: Jafar Panahi. Pro: Kurosh Mazkouri. Screenplay: Abbas Kiarostami, from an idea by Panahi and Parviz Shahbazi. Ph: Farzad Jowdat. (CMI/Institute of Culture-Art/Farabi Cinema/Ferdos Film–Electric.) Rel: 29 December 1995. 84 mins. Cert U. Iran. 1995.

White Squall

1960; the ocean. Based on a true story, *White Squall* chronicles how the captain of the Albatross, a 92-foot brigantine, transforms the lives of 13 students of the Ocean Academy on a voyage that takes them from Bermuda to the Galapagos Islands. Along the way, temperaments clash and friendships

are formed before inevitable tragedy strikes ... Taking some time to establish the identities of the boys and to wriggle out of the clichés of the rites-of-passage genre, *White Squall* settles into a commanding and powerful drama that addresses the importance of community and self-discipline. If that makes it sound like a page torn out of a Baden-Powell sermon, then remember that Ridley Scott previously directed the likes of *Alien*, *Blade Runner* and *Black Rain*. Some scenes are so real (and brilliantly photographed) that they reduce the legs to jelly. Jeff Bridges – as the unflinching skipper with the best interests of his crew at heart – gives another sterling performance while artfully concealing the mechanics of his acting.

Cast: Jeff Bridges (Christopher Sheldon, aka The Skipper), Caroline Goodall (Dr Alice Sheldon), John Savage (McCrea), Scott Wolf (Chuck Gieg), Balthazar Getty (Tod Johnston), Eric Michael Cole (Dean Preston), David Lascher (Robert March), Jason Marsden (Shay Jennings), Julio Oscar Mechoso (Girard Pasqual), Ryan Philippe (Gil Martin), Ethan Embry (formerly Ethan Randall) (Tracy Lapchick), Jeremy Sisto (Frank Beaumont), David Selby (Francis Beaumont), Zeljko Ivanek, Jordan Clarke, Lizbeth Mackay, Jill Larson, James Medina, James Rebhorn, Nicole Ann Samuel, Jordan Scott.

Dir and Ex Pro: Ridley Scott. Pro: Mimi Polk Gitlin and Rocky Lang. Co-Pro: Nigel Wooll and Todd Robinson. Screenplay: Robinson. Ph: Hugh Johnson. Pro Des: Peter J. Hampton and Leslie Tomkins. Ed: Gerry Hambling. M: Jeff Rona and Hans Zimmer; numbers performed by Sting, Fats Domino, Eddie Cochran, Chubby Checker, etc. Costumes: Judianna Makovsky. (Hollywood Pictures/Largo Entertainment/Scott Free–First Independent.) Rel: 10 May 1996. 129 mins. Cert 12. USA. 1996.

The Young Poisoner's Handbook

1961-70; London. Graham Young, serial killer, is not a crazed lunatic. He is an intelligent young man spellbound by the slow-burning effects of his intricate poisoning. With boyish, voyeuristic awe he watches as his stepmother throws up and pulls her hair out. For Graham, this is science exercising all its kinetic wonders. And he is master of the fate of all those around him. Spotlighting a fascinating page from the annuls of true murder, *The Young Poisoner's Handbook* is a painstakingly crafted black comedy that, with a wicked, light touch, sidesteps the Victorian claustrophobia of such heavy-handed films as *The Krays* and *Let Him Have It*. With his misshapen face and projecting ears, Hugh O'Conor (*My Left Foot*, *The Three Musketeers*) makes a perfect blank canvas for the tortured machinations of Graham's mind. From first-time director Benjamin Ross.

Cast: Hugh O'Connor (Graham Young), Antony Sher (Dr Zeigler), Ruth Sheen (Molly Young), Roger Lloyd Pack (Fred Young), Charlotte Coleman (Winnie), Paul Stacey (Dennis), Charlie Creed-Miles (Berridge), Malcolm Sinclair (Dr Triefus), Samantha Edmonds (Sue), Norman Caro, Robert Demeger, Jack Deam, Peter Pacey, Joost Siedhoff, Vilma Hollingbery, Frank Mills, Cate Fowler, Hazel Douglas, Arthur Cox, John Thomson, Jean Warren, Simon Kunz, Frank Coda, Tim Potter, Roger Frost, David Savile.

Dir: Benjamin Ross. Pro: Sam Taylor. Ex Pro: Caroline Hewitt, Eric Stonestrom, Cameron McCracken and Matthew Wilson. Co-Pro: Rainer Kolmel. Screenplay: Ross and Jeff Rawle. Ph: Hubert Taczanowski. Ed: Anne Sopel. Pro Des: Maria Djurkovic. M: Robert Lane and Frank Strobel. Costumes: Stewart Meacham. Poisons: Antimony, Thallium. (Mass Productions/Kinowelt/Haut et Court/British Screen–Electric.) Rel: 15 September 1995. 105 mins. Cert 15. UK. 1994.

Video Releases

Compiled by Charles Bacon

(from July 1995 through to June 1996)

❏ denotes films released theatrically in the US
✳ denotes films of special merit
Additional reviews by James Cameron-Wilson

The Amazing Panda Adventure ❏
Disappointing family adventure that fails to make the most of its political opportunities as an American boy (Ryan Slater, younger bro' of Christian) teams up with his conservationist father to rescue a panda cub from poachers. Rick Baker supplies the special effects, while Sichuan province supplies a somewhat more authentic touch of nature.

Also with Stephen Lang, Yi Ding. Dir: Christopher Cain. U. February 1996 (MGM/UA).

Ariel the Ballerina
Continuing the adventures of the plucky heroine from *The Little Mermaid* (before she got her land legs), this collection of submarine yarns should engage children and even divert some adults. The perfect antidote to the carnage of most Saturday morning television and a lot more watchable than Disney's companion videos featuring Winnie the Pooh. See also *Saltwater Sisters*.

With Ariel, Sebastian, Flounder, etc. U. August 1995 (Walt Disney).

Around the World With Timon & Pumbaa
The wily meerkat and the flatulent wart hog from *The Lion King* are back in their own custom-made video, a series of loose sketches stitched together

The wart hog and meerkat take a break in Disney's dire video original, Around the World With Timon & Pumbaa *(from Disney)*

as a kind of *The Worst of Timon & Pumbaa*. Pumbaa, having been struck by a bolt of lightning, loses his memory and so Timon regales him with tales of their past adventures. Thus, the irritating duo pop up all over the place (Saskatchewan, the Yukon, Brazil, Zaire, etc) like a sub Tom and Jerry act. Personally, I could have done without the farting and vomiting, but the 'Stand By Me' music video is a hoot. My five year old laughed like a drain. [JC-W]

Voices: Nathan Lane, Ernie Sabella, Jim Cummings. Dirs: Tony Craig, Roberts Gannaway, Rob LaDuca, Steve Moore and Jeff DeGrandis. U. May 1996 (Walt Disney).

The Avenging Angel

While Tom Berenger may have left the mainstream behind him, he's still turning out decent little movies that deserve more attention. Here he plays the trigger-happy bodyguard of Mormon leader Brigham Young (Charlton Heston), uncovering a conspiracy to oust his boss just as he's been cast out by his own people. A gripping, handsome video release that captures the flavour of 1880s Mormon life with surprising proficiency. Berenger, incidentally, also co-produces.

Also with James Coburn. Dir: Craig R. Baxley. 12. April 1996 (20.20).

Bad Company ❏

Inexplicably mediocre thriller which ties itself up in knots with double twists. Laurence Fishburne is the ex-CIA agent who gets in over his head when he joins a private organisation with a corrupt agenda. Nice sex, though. Previously known as *The Toolshed* (a much better title).

Also with Ellen Barkin, Frank Langella, Michael Beach, Gia Carides, David Ogden Stiers, Spalding Gray, James Hong, Michael Murphy. Dir: Damian Harris. 15. May 1996 (Touchstone).

Bank Robber ❏

Ponderous tale of a robber who hides out at the Heartbreak Hotel while the law and various low-lifes try to track him down. Slow, quirky, dull.

With Patrick Dempsey, Lisa Bonet, Olivia d'Abo, Forest Whitaker, Judge Reinhold, Michael Jeter. Dir: Nick Mead. 18. August 1995 (Entertainment in Video).

Bitter Vengeance ❏

Routine thriller greased up with some neat camera work and plot twists, in which a bored security guard robs a bank with his sultry mistress and then frames the break-in (and his own murder) on his trusting wife. Pure bunk, but well executed.

With Virginia Madsen, Bruce Greenwood, Kristen Hocking, Eddie Velez, Tim Russ. Dir: Stuart Cooper. Screenplay: Pablo Fenjves. 15. July 1995 (CIC).

Blankman ❏

Although this has been bestowed with a 12 certificate, *Blankman* is a juvenile take on the Superman phenomenon, in which a frustrated inventor adopts the mantle of crimebuster in a lawless society. Got up in bullet proof underwear and his grandmother's housecoat, Damon Wayans strikes a blow for nerds everywhere. Adults beware.

With David Alan Grier, Robin Givens, Lynne Thigpen, Jon Polito, Jason Alexander. Dir: Mike Binder. Screenplay: Wayans and J.F. Lawton. M: Miles Goodman. 12. August 1995 (Columbia TriStar).

Buffalo Girls

Lifeless, disappointing TV adaptation of Larry McMurtry's whimsical reinvention of the Old West, in which Anjelica Huston as Calamity Jane relives her eccentric past on behalf of her new-born baby. Too silly.

Also with Melanie Griffith, Gabriel Byrne, Peter Coyote (as Buffalo Bill), Tracey Walter, Floyd Red Crow Westerman, Jack Palance, Charlayne Woodard, John Diehl, Liev Schreiber, Rusell Means (Chief Sitting Bull), Reba McEntire (Annie Oakley), Sam Elliott (Wild Bill Hickok). Dir: Rod Hardy. M: Lee Holdridge. PG. March 1996 (Guild).

Bushwacked ❏

One of the year's worst films in which a moronic delivery man is framed for murder and ends up impersonating a scout master on a nature trek. Daniel Stern, who is prone to overstatement, mugs his socks off in an attempt to buoy this embarrassing fiasco. Unbelievable.

Also with Jon Polito, Brad Sullivan, Ann Dowd, Anthony Heald. Dir: Greg Beeman. M: Bill Conti. PG. April 1996 (Fox Guild).

China Moon ❏ ✳

Long-delayed film noir thriller tiptoeing menacingly in the footprints of *Double Indemnity*, *The Postman Always Rings Twice*, *Body Heat*, et al. Here Ed Harris plays a cop with designs on an unhappily married Madeleine Stowe, who's had enough of her cruel husband's strange American accent (courtesy of Charles Dance). Superb acting, atmospheric locations (Florida) and some neat twists add to the distinction.

With Benicio Del Toro, Pruitt Taylor Vince. Dir: John Bailey. 18. August 1995 (Columbia).

The Cowboy Way ❏

Moronic action-comedy in which two rodeo cowpokes from New Mexico find themselves in New York City. An inversion of *City Slickers* with a buddy-buddy twist on *Crocodile Dundee*, this commercially driven vehicle for Woody Harrelson and Kiefer Sutherland is too brainless for words. As the straight guy, Sutherland lends some weight as a contemplative Marlboro Man, but Harrelson's tobacco-chewin', yahoo hick is an irritating, offensive jerk. [JC-W]

Also with Dylan McDermott, Ernie Hudson, Cara Buono, Marg Helgenberger, Tomas Milian. Dir: Gregg Champion. 12. October 1995 (CIC).

Cynthia Payne's House of Cyn

A witty and irreverent look at the life and scandals of the notorious madam, this video's greatest triumph is the co-operation of the woman herself. Taking us on a guided tour through her life of suburban misconduct, Cynthia Payne shares her most private photo album of perversions, narrates her own home movies (including a scene in which she takes a mud bath) and tells how she arranged a blow-job for her father. It is the woman's matter-of-factness that is so winning, endowing the world of unnatural sex with all the raciness of a church fete. And, of course, the stories themselves are priceless, not least the one about the bank manager who begged to be tied naked to a bed and had the contents of a hoover emptied over him. 'What a crazy world we live in,' the woman sighs. [JC-W]

Also with Roy Holder, Colin Spaull, David Nicholas Wilkinson and a few naked women. Dir: Richard Kurti. M: J.S.Bach, Spank Corporation. 18. November 1995 (Guerilla Films).

Dancing With Danger
Efficient, racy rip-off of *Basic Instinct*, in which a down-on-his-luck private detective becomes involved with a taxi dancer with a few skeletons in her corset.

With Cheryl Ladd, Ed Marinaro, Miguel Sandoval. Dir: Stuart Cooper. 15. July 1995 (CIC).

Dead Air
Gripping, atmospheric murder mystery in which a top-notch cast bring credibility to a far-out story about a DJ and a mysterious listener with a murderous bent.

With Gregory Hines, Debra Farentino, Beau Starr, Gloria Reuben, Laura Harrington, Veronica Cartwright. Dir: Fred Walton. 12. July 1995 (CIC).

Deadfall ❏
Incredibly muddled film noir thriller in which a conman goes to bits when he accidentally kills his father. Recycled gunk.

With Michael Biehn, Sarah Trigger, Nicolas Cage, James Coburn, Peter Fonda, Charlie Sheen, Talia Shire, Renee Estevez. Dir: Christopher Coppola. 18. April 1996 (Hi-Fliers).

Death Machine
2003; CHAANK Weapons Corporation, Los Angeles. Fast, ruthless and indestructible, the Warbeast is a terrifying cross between *The Alien*, *Robo-Cop 2*, *The Terminator* and a JCB. When Scott Ridley, chairman of CHAANK, threatens the livelihood of the resident techno-nerd, the latter, Jack Dante, unleashes his pet creation ... While mining very familiar territory, *Death Machine* is a gripping, hip and visually arresting $60m sci-fi epic shot for $2m. First-time writer-director Stephen Norrington certainly has a wonderful eye and ear for this sort of thing, and is aided by an admirable performance from his leading lady, newcomer Ely Pouget (tall, angular, masculine: perfect sci-fi fodder). Some of the humour is a little obvious and the acting OTT, but let's not quibble on this budget. [JC-W]

With Brad Dourif, William Hootkins. 18. July 1995 (Entertainment in Video).

Deconstructing Sarah ✳
Extremely well acted, swiftly plotted and unexpected thriller in which the best friend of a missing advertising executive retraces the latter's steps. Soon, the friend (Sheila Kelley) is discovering a side to the businesswoman that she didn't know existed, as her search leads her into the seedier reaches of an alternative nightlife and singles' bars.

Also with Rachel Ticotin, A. Martinez, David Andrews, Jenifer Lewis, Dwier Brown. Dir: Craig R. Baxley. 15. January 1996 (CIC).

The Desperate Trail
Linda Fiorentino scores again in this picturesque, operatic homage to Sergio Leone, the circuitous tale of a wildcat taken to task by a monolithic lawman (Sam Elliott). While P.J. Pesce's directorial flourishes fail to disguise the jaded plot, Fiorentino is always worth watching, as is the spectacular scenery and some thrilling gunplay.

With Craig Sheffer, Frank Whaley. M: Stephen Endelman. 15. July 1995 (Columbia TriStar).

Ernest Goes to School ❏
Yet another spectacularly unfunny vehicle for Jim Varney in which the ex-hamburger spokesman plays the custodian of a high school who's temporarily elevated to the level of genius thanks to a sub-atomic experiment.

With Linda Kash. Dir: Coke Sams. PG. December 1995 (First Independent).

Flight of the Dove
Comely undercover agent Theresa Russell seduces explosives specialist Scott Glenn to help her combat some ruthless assassins. A crisp, well-acted chase thriller that grasps the attention until formula takes over.

With Lane Smith, Joe Pantoliano. Dir: Steve Railsback. 18. November 1995 (Hi-Fliers).

Fluke ❏
An unusual adaptation of James Herbert's novel, which is more *Dead Again* than *Look Who's Talking*. Matthew Modine plays the victim of a fatal car crash who is instantly reincarnated into a dog and seeks to worm his way back into his family's affections.

Combining thrills, suspense, humour, moralising and eventually a generous helping of the cutes, the film defies categorisation. It is, however, stylishly directed by the Italian Carlo Carlei, who previously helmed *Flight of the Innocent*.

Also with Nancy Travis, Eric Stoltz, Max Pomeranc, Ron Perlman, Jon Polito, Bill Cobbs and the voice of Samuel L. Jackson. PG. February 1996 (Warner).

The Glass Shield
Well-meaning but ponderous look at racism inside a sheriff's department in LA. Based on true events by the director of *To Sleep With Anger*.

With Michael Boatman, Lori Petty, Richard Anderson, Ice Cube, Bernie Casey, Elliott Gould, Michael Ironside, Don Harvey, M. Emmet Walsh, Victoria Dillard. Dir: Charles Burnett. 18. January 1996 (Buena Vista).

God's Army
See *The Prophecy*.

The Good Son ❏
When his mother dies, 12-year-old Mark Evans moves in with his cousin Henry, whose idea of play borders on the psychotic. Macaulay Culkin, in his first attempt to escape typecasting as the angel-faced, loveable kid (with ingenuity to spare), here takes on the role of an angel-faced, hateful kid (with ingenuity to spare). Yet in spite of the distinction of an Ian McEwan script (his first original work for Hollywood), *The Good Son* is ultimately just another contrived entry in the fill-in-the-dotted-line-from-hell genre. The film is, however, well acted by all, never boring and boasts some well-executed scenes (Macaulay staging a pile-up on the highway, a thrilling ice skating sequence, etc), but lacks the essential ingredients of credibility and suspense. FYI: Due to be released in January of 1994, the film was withdrawn from theatrical distribution in Britain following the James Bulger episode. [JC-W]

Also with: Elijah Wood, Wendy Crewson, David Morse, Quinn Culkin. Dir: Joseph Ruben. 18. October 1995 (Fox Guild).

Halloween: The Curse of Michael Myers ❏
Jaded return of the fiend in the hockey mask who now seems propelled by some ancient satanic formula. Formula is the order of the day in this sixth

outing in the series that began in 1978, with Donald Pleasence (in his last screen performance) reprising his role as the anxious psychiatrist Dr Loomis.

Also with Mitch Ryan, Marianne Hagan, Paul Rudd. Dir: Joe Chappelle. M: Alan Howarth. 18. January 1996 (Buena Vista).

Handgun ✳
Acutely written, sharply performed low-budget caper in which a gaggle of offbeat low-life characters go in search of half a million stolen dollars stashed in a secret hideaway. First-time writer-director Whitney Ransick shows enormous potential with his material (echoing every genre pic from *Reservoir Dogs* to *Things to Do in Denver When You're Dead*), and gives it a nice dead-pan spin. Treat Williams is particularly effective as a hotheaded crook.

Also with Seymour Cassel, Paul Schulze, Frank Vincent, Luis Guzman. 18. January 1996 (Fox Guild).

Hideaway ❏
Pedestrian if polished adaptation of Dean R. Koontz's literary shocker in which an antique dealer is brought back to life with a Satanist trapped in his soul. Huh? Actually, it's all rather predictable for anybody with a modicum of horror film exposure, although Jeff Goldblum has a knack for enhancing the most execrable material. Christine Lahti's good, too, as his concerned wife.

Also with Alicia Silverstone, Jeremy Sisto, Alfred Molina, Rae Dawn Chong, Kenneth Welsh. Dir: Brett Leonard. M: Trevor Jones. 18. June 1996 (Columbia TriStar).

Houseguest ❏
Frantic vehicle for the talents (?) of Sinbad, in which the chunky stand-up comic plays a debtor posing as an eminent oral surgeon in order to evade the clutches of two bumbling loan sharks. A very basic comedy, this, whose limited success owes more to Sinbad's affable personality than Randall Miller's desperate MTV direction.

Also with Phil Hartman, Jeffrey Jones, Kim Greist, Stan Shaw, Mason Adams. M: John Debney. PG. June 1996 (Buena Vista).

Indictment: The McMartin Trial ✳
Hard-hitting, unapologetic HBO drama chronicling the notorious child abuse case in which seven staff members of a private school were tried for 'rape, animal torture, Satanism and emotional terrorism'. James Woods as the tough defence lawyer is on particularly good form. Includes genuine transcripts used as evidence in the 1983-90 trial. You will believe.

Also with Mercedes Ruehl, Sada Thompson, Shirley Knight, Henry Thomas, Mark Blum, Alison Elliott, Chelsea Field, Richard Bradford, Lolita Davidovich. Dir: Mick Jackson. Ex Pro: Oliver Stone. 15. February 1996 (20.20).

The Infiltrator ✳
Gripping, horrifying and extremely persuasive true-life docudrama in which a third-rate Jewish hack finds himself drawn into the neo-Nazi movement in contemporary Berlin. Deftly side-stepping the inherent cliches of the espionage genre, the film delivers a provocative punch to the conscience.

With Oliver Platt, Arliss Howard, Tony Haygarth, Michael Byrne, Julian Glover, Alex Kingston, Peter Riegert, Alan King. Dir: John Mackenzie. Screenplay: Guy Andrews, based on the book *In Hitler's Shadow* by Yaron Svoray and Nick Taylor. 18. March 1996 (Odyssey).

In Pursuit of Honor ✳
Powerful, astutely scripted drama in which five cavalry officers refuse to comply with the command of General Douglas MacArthur to destroy 400 horses in a step towards modernisation. A real slice of little-known history (set in 1934), *In Pursuit of Honor* is handsomely mounted by the prolific director Ken Olin, better known to his public as Michael Steadman in TV's *thirtysomething*.

With Don Johnson, Craig Sheffer, Gabrielle Anwar, Bob Gunton, Rod Steiger, James B. Sikking, John Dennis Johnston, Robert Coleby. 15. December 1995 (Columbia TriStar).

The Invaders
Based on the 1967-68 TV series, this ambitious update works on a number of levels, promising more to come. Basically it's a Them vs Us scenario, with the invading aliens needing carbon monoxide to survive and resorting to snorting car fumes, chain-smoking and declaring war on environmental militants. A lively pace and a good turn from Elizabeth Pena as an investigative doctor help to fetter the attention.

Also with Scott Bakula, Richard Thomas, Terence Knox, Richard Belzer, Jon Polito, Roy Thinnes (who played David Vincent in the original series), Jon Cypher. Dir: Paul Shapiro. 15. June 1996 (PolyGram).

Iron Will ❏
Routine and predictable Disney pot-boiler about a 17-year-old farm boy who enters a perilous 522-mile dog sled race from Winnipeg to St Paul in Minnesota. Still, the contest itself is rousing and the period (1917) well captured, while Kevin Spacey as an unscrupulous reporter adds some weight.

With Mackenzie Astin, August Schellenberg, David Ogden Stiers, Brian Cox, John Terry. Dir: Charles Haid. U. July 1995 (Buena Vista).

James Herriot's Yorkshire
An intriguing cross between home movie, picturesque travelogue and arty pilgrimage through little-seen corners of England, this is an affectionate, lovingly photographed chronicle of Yorkshire, inspired by James Herriot's book. Christopher Timothy, who played Herriot in the BBC's *All Creatures Great and Small*, guides us over hill and stream and through photogenic hamlet, mixing personal anecdote with historical titbit. A refreshing tonic for those who cannot picture this scepter'd isle beyond its over-populated shopping malls. Rod Bowkett provides the evocative score. [JC-W]

With James Herriot, David Nicholas Wilkinson, Ruth Hudson. Dir: Joy Perino. Cert E (for Exemption). July 1995 (Guerilla Films).

James A. Michener's Texas
See *Texas*.

Judicial Consent
Bonnie Bedelia, who was once *Presumed Innocent*, finds herself at the receiving end of a murder frame-up in this predictable courtroom thriller in which she plays a conscientious lawyer in a dead-end marriage. Bedelia is good, but the plot is strictly mechanical.

With Will Patton, Dabney Coleman, Billy Wirth, Lisa Blount. Dir and Screenplay: William Bindley. 15. July 1995 (Fox/Guild).

Kingfish ✳

Entertaining, liberal TV biography that gamely examines the man behind the public figure of Huey P. Long, the Southern senator and champion of the poor. Incidentally, Broderick Crawford won an Oscar playing a loose variation of Long in Robert Rossen's classic 1949 film, *All the King's Men*. US title: *Kingfish: A Story of Huey P. Long*.

With John Goodman, Matt Craven, Anne Heche, Ann Dowd, Bob Gunton (as FD Roosevelt), Bill Cobbs, Hoyt Axton, Richard Bradford. Dir: Thomas Schlamme. Pro: John Goodman. M: Patrick Williams. 12. October 1995 (20.20).

Lassie ❏

In dog years, the courageous collie is now 371, but with her shining coat and sprightly manner she still looks a fraction of her age. Here, she aids the Turner family settle into their new rural home as they combat rival sheep farmers. From the masterful photography to the canny screenplay, this update of the perennial classic should charm a new generation.

With Thomas Guiry, Helen Slater, Jon Tenney, Frederic Forrest, Richard Farnsworth. Dir: Daniel Petrie. U. August 1995 (CIC).

The Last Great Warrior ❏ ✳

Above-average Disney fare which ventures into *Pocahontas* territory with a theoretical study of what might have happened when the 17th-century Indian brave Squanto was kidnapped and taken to Plymouth, England. An eloquent, thoughtful and beautifully observed piece that deserved more than a direct-to-video burial. US title: *Squanto: A Warrior's Tale*.

With Adam Beach, Mandy Patinkin, Michael Gambon, Nathaniel Parker, Eric Schweig, Donal Donnelly, Alex Norton, Irene Bedard. Dir: Xavier Koller. PG. August 1995 (Walt Disney).

The Lies Boys Tell ✳

Another well-drawn look at old age and family values from Ernest Thompson, creator of *On Golden Pond*. Here Kirk Douglas plays a rascally old man who persuades his middle-aged, ex-hippy son (Craig T. Nelson) to drive him cross-country to his birthplace in California – where he can die in peace. Acting, directing and dialogue are all of the highest order. US title: *Take Me Home Again*.

With Bess Armstrong, Eileen Brennan, Bonnie Bartlett, Ernest Thompson. Dir: Tom McLoughlin. 15. August 1995 (Odyssey).

Live Nude Girls ❏

Don't expect anything approaching *Showgirls* in this talky, modest affair in which a gaggle of women let their hair down during an extended talk-in. Thankfully an extremely talented cast keep things afloat in an entertaining bauble which feels like a good play transposed to the screen.

With Dana Delany, Kim Cattrall, Cynthia Stevenson, Laila Robins, Olivia d'Abo, Tim Choate. Dir and Screenplay: Julianna Lavin. 18. February 1996 (PolyGram).

Losing Isaiah ❏ ✳

Chicago; 1995. After a history of crime, crack and prostitution, Khaila Richards (Halle Berry) is given a chance to get her life back on track. She's even learning to read. But there's one emotional stumbling block: the baby boy she abandoned in a dumpster four years ago. Meanwhile, in the comfortable suburbs on the other side of town, Isaiah is now a happy, much-loved four year old. Finding out that her baby is alive, Khaila starts proceedings to get Isaiah back to his 'rightful' mother. Taking the familiar formula of a TV Movie-of-the-Week, *Losing Isaiah* adds a potent spin by making the baby black and its caring mother an affluent white woman. Thus we have the diametric tug of ghetto vs. suburbs, love vs. need, black vs. white and Kramer vs. Kramer – and every argument for and against is well audited. While some of the characterisation is on the sketchy side, the performances, direction and camerawork – and Mark Isham's trumpet solos – all pull together in an offensive on our judgment calls and tear ducts. [JC-W]

Also with Jessica Lange, David Strathairn, Cuba Gooding Jr, Samuel L. Jackson, Regina Taylor, Marc John Jeffries (Isaiah), Joie Lee, Mike Nussbaum. Dir: Stephen Gyllenhaal. Screenplay: Naomi Foner. 15. June 1996 (CIC).

Love Affair ❏

Considering the hype that surrounded this big-budget re-make of *Love Affair* (1939) and its famous successor *An Affair to Remember* (1957), it's a tad surprising to find it ending up on video without a theatrical release in Britain.

Still, no amount of lush production values can make up for the film's lack of passion or credibility. This is romance of the designer variety, making it hard to care for its materially advantaged characters – although Katharine Hepburn is still wonderful in her brief appearance as Warren Beatty's aunt.

Also with Annette Bening, Garry Shandling, Chloe Webb, Pierce Brosnan, Kate Capshaw, Paul Mazursky, Brenda Vaccaro, Glenn Shadix, Barry Miller, Harold Ramis, Ray Charles. Dir: Glenn Gordon Caron. Pro: Beatty. Screenplay: Beatty and Robert Towne. M: Ennio Morricone. 12. September 1995 (Warner).

Love and a .45 ❏

Very familiar, but entertaining romantic thriller in which a beautiful young couple head for the border with a stash of stolen booty, pursued by the usual quota of low-lifes (and, of course, the cops). Bloody, sexy, funny, derivative.

With Gil Bellows, Renee Zellweger, Rory Cochrane, Jeffrey Combs, Jace Alexander, Ann Wedgeworth, Peter Fonda. Dir: C.M. Talkington. 18. February 1996 (Hi-Fliers).

Love Can Build a Bridge

Competent biopic of the mother-and-daughter Country music act The Judds, chronicling Naomi's teenage years and marriage and then her meteoric ascent to stardom with daughter Wynonna in tow. Some wit, good looking locations and performances keep things buoyant, but it's the music that makes this so watchable.

With Kathleen York (Naomi), Viveka Davis (Wynonna), Bruce Greenwood, Melinda Dillon, Megan Ward (as Ashley), Nick Searcy, Chris Mulkey, Dolly Parton, Paul Bartel, Ashley Judd (narrator). Dir: Bobby Roth. 15. November 1995 (Odyssey).

Mad Love ❏

While gazing at the stars one night, high school student and amateur astrologer Matt Leland (Chris O'Donnell) spots Casey on her jet ski. Of course, it's love at first starlight and soon Matt and Casey are giggling and romping to the Seattle grunge scene. But Casey, who makes up her own rules about life as she goes along, is not all she appears to be... Can puppy love (and a few designer moves) make up for a passion that's one lens short of a telescope? While Drew Barrymore, as Casey, gives a performance of selfless generosity, the camera deals her a dud

On the road again: Drew Barrymore and Chris O'Donnell – and all the songs – in Antonia Bird's Mad Love *(Buena Vista)*

hand, magnifying the spots and spittle of her naked delivery. Furthermore, the actress's natural beauty is constantly upstaged by the tourist-beckoning shots of the Pacific Northwest scenery. Not so much a movie as an idea stretched over a number of MTV opportunities. [JC-W]

Also with Joan Allen, Matthew Lillard, Jude Ciccolella, T.J. Lowther, Kevin Dunn. Dir: Antonia Bird. Screenplay: Paula Milne. 15. June 1996 (Buena Vista).

Mind Ripper
See *Wes Craven Presents: Mind Ripper*.

Mixed Nuts ❑
Disastrous attempt to find humour in the chaotic lives of the staff of a suicide helpline in Venice, California. Then, come Christmas Eve, all hell breaks loose and the film loses its mind. Can this really be from the writer-director of *Sleepless in Seattle*? Based on the 1982 French farce *Le Pere Noel est Une Ordure*.

With Steve Martin, Madeline Kahn, Rita Wilson, Robert Klein, Anthony LaPaglia, Juliette Lewis, Rob Reiner, Adam Sandler, Garry Shandling, Steven Wright. Dir: Nora Ephron. Screenplay: Nora and Delia Ephron. 12. December 1995 (20.20).

My Antonia ✳
Superbly nuanced film version of Willa Cather's 1918 autobiographical novel, focusing on the friendship between a Nebraska farm boy and an immigrant Russian girl. The rural splendour of 1890s Nebraska has been particularly well caught by cinematographer Robert Primes.

With Jason Robards, Eva Marie Saint, Neil Patrick Harris, Elina Lowensohn, Jan Triska. Dir: Joseph Sargent. M: David Shire. PG. December 1995 (CIC).

Naomi & Wynonna: Love Can Build a Bridge
See *Love Can Build a Bridge*.

The New Age ❑
Obscure, very strange 'satire' about a Yuppie LA couple who lose their grip on reality in the materialistic nineties. Forced to find salvation in opposite directions, the pair indulge in strange parties, S & M, a stab at suicide and New Age spirituality. No doubt writer-director Michael Tolkin (*The Player*, *The Rapture*) knew exactly where he was digging, but on screen his vision is self-indulgent and supercilious.

With Peter Weller, Judy Davis, Patrick Bauchau, Corbin Bernsen, Samuel L. Jackson, Adam West. Ex Pro: Oliver Stone. 15. March 1996 (Warner).

New Jersey Drive ❑
Tough, hard-hitting but emotionally underwhelming tale of two teenagers drawn into the world of car-jacking in Newark, New Jersey, and of the dramatic consequences. From the director of *Laws of Gravity*.

With Sharron Corley, Gabriel Casseus, Donald Adeosun Faison. Dir: Nick Gomez. Ex Pro: Spike Lee. 18. December 1995 (CIC).

The Next Karate Kid ❑
Fourth bout in the *Karate Kid* series, with the feisty, abrasive Hilary Swank (replacing Ralph Macchio) as a rebellious girl who needs a bit of martial art to channel and deflect her anger. The reliable Noriyuki 'Pat' Morita is back for more pithy sayings, although the action has been toned down a bit. Incredibly stale.

Also with Michael Ironside, Constance Towers, Chris Conrad. Dir: Christopher Cain. M: Bill Conti. PG. October 1995 (Columbia TriStar).

Night Train to Venice
The film that but for a miracle was never meant to see the light of day. The miracle here is Hugh Grant, a 1993 version, playing a haughty journalist who falls for Tahnee Welch on the Orient Express while the train is besieged by skinheads. Malcolm McDowell looks on with his customary sneer, defying any distributor to release this preposterous, garbled rubbish. Made in Germany.

Dir: Carlo U. Quinterio. 15. July 1995 (Columbia TriStar).

Op Centre
Disappointing TV adaptation of Tom Clancy and Steve Pieczenik's bestseller in which a wooden Mark Hamlin stars as Paul Hood, the businessman-turned-hero with marital and Cold War problems. While the action scenes work well, they are undermined by naff dialogue and banal characterisations. US title: *Tom Clancy's Op Center*.

With Lindsay Frost, Carl Weathers, Kim Cattrall, John Savage, Bo Hopkins, Rod Steiger, Wilford Brimley, Ken Howard. Dir: Lewis Teague. Ex Pro: Clancy and Pieczenik. 15. July 1995 (Hi-Fliers).

Parallel Lives
Slapdash, haphazard affair following the various escapades surrounding a fraternity-sorority reunion. The largely improvised script makes little

sense of the assorted relationships, resulting in the cinematic equivalent of a curry with the spice extracted. Too silly. Incidentally, this is a sequel to the much better *Chantilly Lace*, which was championed by Robert Redford.

With James Belushi, James Brolin, LeVar Burton, Lindsay Crouse, Jill Eikenberry, Ben Gazzara, Jack Klugman, Liza Minnelli, Dudley Moore, Gena Rowlands, Ally Sheedy, Helen Slater, Mira Sorvino, Paul Sorvino, Robert Wagner, Patricia Wettig, JoBeth Williams, Treat Williams. Dir: Linda Yellen. 15. May 1996 (Odyssey).

Pie in the Sky ❏

Shamelessly sentimental and only occasionally amusing romantic comedy in which a nerdy traffic fan (or carspotter) struggles to woo his dreamboat. Some decent performances and a novel hero help to spice up an otherwise predictable scenario from the director of *Career Opportunities*.

With Josh Charles, Anne Heche, Peter Riegert, Christine Ebersole, Wil Wheaton, Christine Lahti, John Goodman, Bob Balaban. Dir and Screenplay: Bryan Gordon. M: Michael Convertino. 15. April 1996 (Entertainment in Video).

Pontiac Moon ❏

Mundane road movie in which Ted Danson plays an eccentric intellectual who drives his son 1,776 miles to Spires of the Moon National Park to commemorate the Apollo 11 moon landing. The film was a tragedy at the US box-office, but at least Danson got to meet his future wife, co-star Mary Steenburgen.

Also with Ryan Todd, Eric Schweig, Cathy Moriarty, Max Gail, Lisa Jane Persky. Dir: Peter Medak. Ex Pro: Danson. M: Randy Edelman. 12. June 1996 (CIC).

Prince of Jutland

Pre-dating Kenneth Branagh's *In the Bleak Midwinter* and *Hamlet*, this loving recreation of the trials of the Melancholy Dane – from the director of *Babette's Feast* – makes for sparse entertainment. While an able cast give of their best and the period detail is to be commended, the proceedings are scuttled by a minuscule budget that cannot overcome the technically threadbare look.

With Gabriel Byrne, Helen Mirren, Christian Bale, Brian Cox, Steven Waddington, Kate Beckinsale, Freddie Jones, Brian

Glover. Dir: Gabriel Axel. 15. November 1995 (First Class Films).

The Prophecy ❏

Audacious spy thriller in which a cop investigates an escalating showdown between an army of bad angels and good angels. Christopher Walken stars as the far-from-angelic Gabriel who attempts to wipe out mankind in a fit of jealousy. The concept – scripted by first-time director Gregory Widen – is so off the wall that it can't help but grip the imagination, in spite of the occasional narrative inconsistency. US title: *God's Army*.

Also with Elias Koteas, Eric Stoltz, Virginia Madsen, Amanda Plummer, Viggo Mortensen. 18. January 1996 (Buena Vista).

The Puppet Masters ❏

Long-delayed film version of Robert A. Heinlein's 1951 novel, in which extraterrestrial beings turn humans into zombies. Poor special effects and cheap thrills rob the story of its inherent suspense, adding to the feel of a film that should've been made 40 years ago.

With Donald Sutherland, Eric Thal, Julie Warner, Keith David, Will Patton, Yaphet Kotto. Dir: Stuart Orme. 18. September 1995 (Hollywood Pictures).

A Pyromaniac's Love Story ❏

A delightfully eccentric romantic comedy in which a kaleidoscope of offbeat characters own up to burning down an inner-city bakery in order to heat up their romantic options. This could've been a hot ticket had Disney not marketed it as a generic burlesque.

With William Baldwin, John Leguizamo, Sadie Frost, Erika Eleniak, Michael Lerner, Joan Plowright, Armin Mueller-Stahl, Mike Starr, Richard Crenna. Dir: Joshua Brand. M: Rachel Portman. PG. March 1996 (Buena Vista).

Radioland Murders ❏

Spectacularly inept, frenzied farce (billed as a 'romantic-mystery-comedy') about a writer suspected of murder on the opening night of a new radio network. Set in 1939 in Chicago and based on a story by George Lucas. Radio fanatics should be advised to check out *Aunt Julia and the Scriptwriter* or *Radio Days* instead.

With Brian Benben, Mary Stuart Masterson, Ned Beatty, George Burns, Michael McKean, Stephen Tobolowsky, Christopher Lloyd, Larry Miller, Corbin Bernsen, Bobcat Goldthwaite, Peter MacNicol. Dir: Mel Smith. 12. July 1995 (CIC).

Reckless Kelly ❏

Yahoo Serious, the writer, director and star of the Australian box-office success *Young Einstein*, takes on more than he can handle with this hit-and-miss farce. Here he directs, produces, scripts, edits, designs the music and visuals and stars as the descendant of Ned Kelly, an outlaw who flees to America to make a quick million. Plenty of neat ideas and a loveable animal cast keep things afloat – just.

With Melora Hardin, Alexei Sayle, Hugo Weaving, Kathleen Freeman, Martin Ferrero. PG. August 1995 (Warner).

Saltwater Sisters

For more commentary of this delightful video for younger viewers, see *Ariel the Ballerina*.

With Ariel, Sebastian, Flounder, etc. U. August 1995 (Walt Disney).

The Scout ❏

Very familiar tale of a luckless baseball talent scout who discovers a dream player in Mexico. No surprises, then, that the would-be star pitcher has a stadium-full of problems, and it's up to the paternal scout to sort the wheat from the clichés. In spite of the dependable presence of Albert Brooks in the title role, *The Scout* fails to engender much humour, interest or even much baseball. No home runs here. Based on an article in the *New Yorker*.

With Brendan Fraser, Dianne Wiest, Lane Smith, Anne Twomey, Michael Rapaport. Dir: Michael Ritchie. 12. July 1995 (Fox Guild).

Seaview Knights

When a painting falls on a young man's head, his concussion leads him to believe he is King Arthur. Were it not for a suitcase containing $1 million, nobody would go along with his barmy misconception – but where has the mythological hero hidden his Holy Grail? At times almost reaching its comedic potential, *Seaview Knights* spins out of control when it dissolves into farce, robbing this original, quirky comedy of its focus and edge. [JC-W]

With James Bolam, Clive Darby, Sarah Alexander, Hildegard Neil, Anita Dobson. Dir: Richard Kurti. 15. June 1996 (Guerilla Films).

Separate Lives ❏
Plodding, overtly familiar 'erotic thriller' in which ex-cop James Belushi becomes involved with a beautiful schizophrenic who believes she may be a killer in her alternative psychological skin.

With James Belushi, Linda Hamilton, Vera Miles, Drew Snyder. Dir: David Madden. 18. August 1995 (Hi-Fliers).

Sizzle Beach ❏
At last! Kevin Costner's first film! Actually, this poor cousin to *Baywatch* (made in 1974) should be labelled Fizzle Beach. US title: *Sizzle Beach, USA*.

Also with Terry Congie, Leslie Brander. Dir: Richard Brander. 18. June 1996 (Troma).

Speechless ❏
Effervescent romantic comedy starring Michael Keaton and Geena Davis as political speechwriters who fall in love before realising they're parked on opposite political posts. Snappy dialogue and engaging performances grease over the film's lighter patches, while the story itself is a fascinating reflection of the real-life duel between US campaigners James Carville and Mary Matalin.

Also with Christopher Reeve, Bonnie Bedelia, Ernie Hudson, Charles Martin Smith, Gailard Sartain, Ray Baker, Mitchell Ryan. Dir: Ron Underwood. Pro: Renny Harlin and Geena Davis. 12. September 1995 (MGM/UA).

Squanto: A Warrior's Tale
See *The Last Great Warrior*.

A Streetcar Named Desire
The third screen version of Tennessee Williams' 1947 drama stars Jessica Lange in her Golden Globe-winning turn as Blanche DuBois – an interesting revelation in light of the critical stoning she received for the same performance on Broadway. As it happens, Lange is the best thing is this uncensored version of the play, which falls down on the miscasting of Alec Baldwin, John Goodman and Diane Lane as, respectively, Stanley Kowalski, Mitch and Stella.

Also with Frederick Coffin, Matt Keeslar, Jerry Harden. Dir: Glenn Jordan. M: David Mansfield. 12. June 1996 (Fox Guild).

Stuart Saves His Family ❏
Weak big-screen vehicle for the self-help authority Stuart Smalley created by Al Franken on *Saturday Night Live*. Here, Smalley loses his cable franchise Daily Affirmation, and so switches his ministrations to his loony, dysfunctional family. Tragically, the film jettisons potential laughs in favour of homespun philosophy.

Also with Laura San Giacomo, Vincent D'Onofrio, Shirley Knight, Harris Yulin, Julia Sweeney. Dir: Harold Ramis. 12. January 1996 (CIC).

Take Me Home Again
See *The Lies Boys Tell*.

Ted and Venus ❏
Marking the directorial debut of Bud Cort, former oddball star of the early seventies (*Brewster McCloud*, *Harold and Maude*), this self-consciously eccentric black comedy misfires on all cylinders. Cort himself plays the hippie poet who pursues his dream woman, a community service worker, forcing her to take desperate measures to discourage his advances. Unpleasant, pointless and unfocused. Released in the US in 1991.

With James Brolin, Kim Adams, Carol Kane, Brian Thompson, Woody Harrelson, Dr Timothy Leary, Martin Mull, Vincent Schiavelli, Rhea Perlman, Gena Rowlands. 18. January 1996 (20.20).

Texas
Cod, unexpectedly engrossing historical saga based on James A. Michener's exhaustive page-turning tome, in which the Yanks, back in 1821, compete against the Mexicans for the Lone Star state. US title: *James A. Michener's Texas*.

With Rick Schroder, Benjamin Bratt, Chelsea Field, Patrick Duffy, Stacy Keach, John Schneider, Anthony Michael Hall, David Keith, Maria Conchita Alonso, Randy Travis, Charlton Heston (as narrator). Dir: Richard Lang. M: Lee Holdridge. 15. May 1996 (PolyGram).

3 Ninjas Kick Back ❏
Spirited if basic sequel to *3 Ninja Kids*, in which the sparring siblings accompany their grandfather to Japan to present a ceremonial dagger to a new

Ninja champion. Trouble follows, as does an acquaintance with a local ninja princess who shows the boys a new side to Japan. But will Rocky, Colt and Tum Tum make it back to LA in time to make their baseball game? The *Karate Kid Part II* meets *The Bad News Bears* with diminishing results.

With Victor Wong, Max Elliott Slade, Sean Fox, Evan Bonifant, Caroline Junko King, Sab Shimono, Joey Travolta. Dir: Charles T. Kanganis. U. July 1995 (20.20).

Tom Clancy's Op Center
See *Op Centre*.

Tyson ✳
Skilfully told, tightly wrought and well-acted biography of the disgraced world heavyweight champion. Newcomer Michael Jai White is particularly effective in the title role, taking on the mantle of the mean man with convincing bravado.

Also with George C. Scott (as trainer Gus D'Amato), Paul Winfield (excellent as Don King), Malcolm-Jamal Warner, Tony Lo Bianco, James B. Sikking, Georg Stanford Brown, Joe Santos, Charles Napier, Tico Wells. Dir: Uli Edel. M: Stewart Copeland. 18. September 1995 (Warner).

UFO: The Untold Stories
A self-consciously dramatic documentary from the files of Carlton Television, *UFO* is promoted as 'the best programme ever made about UFOs'. Uneven in style and focus, the film offers no new startling insights into the subject of visitations or airborne teacups, but goes over old case histories such as Roswell and the Suffolk military base sighting. What it does do is reaffirm the welter of valid documentation on the phenomenon and highlight the unwillingness of military bodies to shed light on the mystery. Thus, it is not the suspect video footage of celestial blobs that intrigues so much as the refusal of governments to enter into the debate. [JC-W]

Dir: Lawrence Moore. Cert E (for Exemption). June 1996 (Odyssey).

Village of the Damned ❏
Only a mildly diverting remake of the British sub-classic of 1960, in which ten women of the coastal town of Midwich give birth to alien albino children. Adapted from John Wyndham's novel *The Midwich Cuckoos*.

With Christopher Reeve, Kirstie Alley, Linda Kozlowski, Michael Pare, Meredith Salenger, Mark Hamill. Dir and M: John Carpenter. 15. February 1996 (CIC).

Wes Craven Presents: Mind Ripper

The result of a genetic engineering experiment, a hideous creature escapes its nest and starts sticking its tentacle where it doesn't belong. Plagiaristic but slickly crafted mayhem.

With Lance Henriksen, Claire Stansfield, John Diehl, Natasha Wagner. Dir: Joe Gayton. 18. August 1995 (Medusa).

White Fang 2: The Myth of the White Wolf

Stodgy sequel to the mild 1991 success, in which the canine wolf and his new owner find love and mysticism in their quest to aid a struggling tribal community.

With Scott Bairstow, Charmaine Craig, Alfred Molina, Geoffrey Lewis, Victoria Racimo, Ethan Hawke. Dir: Ken Olin. U. July 1995 (Buena Vista).

Winnie the Pooh: Helping Others

Four new tales from Disney featuring the cuddly creations of A.A. Milne, namely *Owl's Well That Ends Well*, *A Very, Very Large Animal*, *Caws and Effects* and *To Dream the Impossible Scheme*. While getting increasingly banal, the shorts at least impart worthwhile messages to the very young. Christopher Robin, though, would burn down the nursery (besides, there are no gophers in Ashdown Forest). [JC-W]

With Pooh, Piglet, Rabbit, Gopher, etc. U. August 1995 (Walt Disney).

Winnie the Pooh: Sharing and Caring

More of the same, with the voice of Pooh (courtesy of Jim Cummings) grating on the nerves more than ever. Enough is enough.

U. August 1995 (Walt Disney).

With Honors ❏ ✳

After spending nine months composing his thesis, Monty, a Harvard student, sees the hard disk of his computer self-destruct. On his way to photocopy the single printed manuscript of his work, he slips in the snow and drops his

Joe Pesci and Brendan Fraser meditate on life and higher learning in Alek Keshishian's engaging With Honors *(from Warner)*

future through the grating of a boiler room. Under the pavement, a hard-bitten vagrant sees the thesis as his meal ticket to a better life and – page by page, day by day – sells the work back to the panic-driven Monty: one page for a night's kip, two pages for a bath, and so on. But in his rough, salty way, the hobo is giving Monty far more than his manuscript back ... A literate, witty and intelligent script, crisp direc-

tion and a first-rate cast transform what could have been a sentimental cop-out into one of the most unexpectedly satisfying and moving pictures of the year. While Joe Pesci is a little grating as the smug, know-all bum (Dustin Hoffman would have been perfect), he ultimately pulls off a difficult role. [JC-W]

With Brendan Fraser, Moira Kelly, Patrick Dempsey, Josh Hamilton, Gore Vidal. Dir: Alek Keshishian. Screenplay: William Mastrosimone. Ph: Sven Nykvist. PG. August 1995 (Warner).

Other Video Releases:

The Adventures of Black Feather. Pius Savage. PG. December 1995 (Fox Guild).

The Adventures of Captain Zoom in Outer Space. Daniel Riordan, Ron Perlman, Michelle Nichols. PG. April 1996 (CIC).

The Adventures of the Golden Bear. Mr T, Cheech Marin. U. September 1995 (Fox Guild).

Android Affair. Griffin Dunne, Harley Jane Kozak. 12. December 1995 (CIC).

Angel of Desire. Joan Severance, Anthony John Denison. Dir: Donna Deitch. 18. May 1996 (Hi-Fliers).

As Good as Dead. Judge Reinhold, Traci Lords. PG. October 1995 (CIC).

The Babysitter. Alicia Silverstone, Jeremy London, J.T. Walsh, Lois Chiles, George Segal. Dir: Guy Ferland. 18. June 1996 (First Independent).

The Babysitters. Peter Paul, David Paul, George Lazenby, Jared Martin. Dir: John Paragon. PG. July 1995 (Medusa).

Before the Night. Ally Sheedy, A. Martinez, Frederic Forrest. 18. October 1995 (Hi-Fliers).

Best of the Best 3: No Turning Back. Phillip Rhee, Christopher McDonald, Gina Gershon. Dir: Phillip Rhee. 15. May 1996 (Entertainment in Video).

Between Love and Honour. Maria Pitillo, Grant Show, Robert Loggia. 12. September 1995 (Odyssey).

Big Hearts & Broken Dreams – The Dottie West Story. Michele Lee, William Russ, Larry Gatlin, Kenny Rogers. Ex Pro: Michele Lee. 12. July 1995 (Odyssey).

The Birds II – Land's End. Brad Johnson, Chelsea Field, Tippi Hedren. Dir: Alan Smithee. 15. January 1996 (CIC).

Blood Run. Anna Thomson, David Bradley, Ashley Laurence. 18. April 1996 (Fox Guild).

Body Shot. Robert Patrick, Michelle Johnson, Jonathan Banks. 18. August 1995 (Fox Guild).

Born to be Wild. Will Horneef, Peter Boyle, Helen Shaver. PG. February 1996 (Warner).

The Break. Martin Sheen, Rae Dawn Chong, Valerie Perrine. 12. June 1996 (Medusa).

A Brilliant Disguise. Lysette Anthony, Anthony John Denison, Corbin Bernsen. 18. December 1995 (Hi-Fliers).

Broken Bars. Wings Hauser. 18. March 1996 (Guild).

Caught in the Crossfire. Dennis Franz, Daniel Roebuck. Dir: Chuck Bowman. PG. February 1996 (Hi-Fliers).

Chameleon. Anthony LaPaglia, Kevin Pollak, Wayne Knight. Dir: Michael Pavone. 15. May 1996 (20.20).

Choices of the Heart: The Margaret Sanger Story. Dana Delany, Henry Czerny, Kenneth Welsh, Rod Steiger. Narrated by Jason Priestly. Dir: Paul Shapiro. 15. December 1995 (Odyssey).

A Christmas Romance. Olivia Newton-John, Gregory Harrison. Dir: Sheldon Larry. U. November 1995 (Odyssey).

Circumstances Unknown. Judd Nelson, Isabel Glasser, William R. Moses. 15. November 1995 (CIC).

The Colony. John Ritter, Hal Linden. PG. April 1996 (CIC).

The Companion. Kathryn Harrold, Bruce Greenwood, Brion James. Dir: Gary Fleder. 15. January 1996 (CIC).

Convict Cowboy. Jon Voight, Kyle Chandler, Ben Gazzara, Marcia Gay Harden. January 1996 (MGM/UA).

Courting Justice. Art Hindle, Patty Duke, Linda Dano. Dir: Eric Till. 15. January 1996 (Odyssey).

Crash. Michael Biehn, Leilani Sarelle, Matt Craven, Ed Lauter, Miguel Sandoval. 18. April 1996 (Medusa).

Crazy Hong Kong. Carina Lau. PG. May 1996 (Fox Guild).

Crime Story. Jackie Chan. 18. July 1995 (20.20).

Crosscut. Costas Mandylor, Megan Gallagher. 18. May 1996 (First Independent).

Cyberjack. Michael Dudikoff, Brion James. 18. April 1996 (Columbia TriStar).

Cyber Tracker 2. Don 'The Dragon' Wilson. 18. November 1995 (20.20).

Cyborg Cop 3. Bryan Gennesse. 18. April 1996 (Fox Guild).

Dancing in the Dark. Victoria Principal, Robert Vaughn. 15. December 1995 (Odyssey).

A Dangerous Affair. Connie Sellecca, Gregory Harrison. 15. September 1995 (Odyssey).

Dangerous Indiscretion. C. Thomas Howell, Malcolm McDowell, Joan Severance. 18. February 1996 (Hi-Fliers).

Danielle Steel's Family Album. Jaclyn Smith, Michael Ontkean. PG. December 1995 (20.20).

Danielle Steel's Vanished. George Hamilton. PG. August 1995 (Columbia TriStar).

Darkman II: The Return of Durant. Arnold Vosloo. 18. October 1995 (CIC).

Dead Cold. Chris Mulkey, Peter Dobson, Lysette Anthony. 18. April 1996 (First Independent).

Deadly Nightmare. Lindsay Wagner, Piper Laurie. 15. September 1995 (Fox Guild).

Death of a Cheerleader. Kellie Martin, Tori Spelling, Terry O'Quinn, Valerie Harper. 15. July 1995 (Odyssey).

Deceived by Trust. Stephanie Kramer, Michael Gross. 12. January 1996 (Hi-Fliers).

Decoy. Peter Weller, Robert Patrick, Charlotte Lewis. Dir: Victor Rambaldi. 18. January 1996 (Medusa).

Delta of Venus. Costas Mandylor. 18. January 1996 (First Independent).

Dominion. Brad Johnson, Brion James, Tim Thomerson. 15. June 1996 (20.20).

Dream a Little Dream 2. Corey Haim, Corey Feldman, Robyn Lively. 12. July 1995 (First Independent).

Dream Man. Patsy Kensit, Bruce Greenwood, Andrew McCarthy. Dir: Rene Bonniere. 18. June 1996 (First Independent).

Electra. Shannon Tweed. 18. June 1996 (Entertainment in Video).

Entangled. Judd Nelson, Pierce Brosnan. 18. December 1995 (First Independent).

Enter the Shootfighter. Michael Worth, Matthias Hues, Marshall Teague. 18. December 1995 (Columbia TriStar).

Erotique. Kamala Lopez-Dawson, Priscilla Barnes, Marianne Sagebrecht, Tanita Tikaram. Dir: Lizzie Borden, Monika Treut, Clara Law. 18. March 1996 (Hi-Fliers).

Excessive Force II: Force on Force. Stacie Randall, Jay Patterson. 18. November 1995 (First Independent).

Expect No Mercy. Billy Blanks, Jalal Merhi. 18. August 1995 (20.20).

The Expert. Jeff Speakman, James Brolin, Jim Varney. 18. October 1995 (20.20).

A Family Divided. Faye Dunaway, Stephen Collins. Dir: Philip Rosenberg. 15. March 1996 (Odyssey).

Fight for Justice. Marilu Henner, Doug Savant. 15. January 1996 (Odyssey).

First Degree. Rob Lowe, Leslie Hope. Dir: Jeff Woolnough. 18. April 1996 (Hi-Fliers).

First Light. Michael Pare. 18. January 1996 (Fox Guild).

Flashback. Chuck Norris. 15. May 1996 (Warner).

Flashfire. Billy Zane, Louis Gossett Jr. 18. January 1996 (20.20).

Fleshtone. Martin Kemp, Lise Cutter, Tim Thomerson. 18. December 1995 (Hi-Fliers).

Flight of the Dove. Scott Glenn, Theresa Russell, Lane Smith. Dir: Steve Railsback. 18. January 1996 (Hi-Fliers).

Flinch. Judd Nelson, Gina Gershon, Nick Mancuso. 15. September 1995 (Hi-Fliers).

For Better or Worse. Previously known as *Stranger Things.* With Jason Alexander, Joe Mantegna, Lolita Davidovich, James Woods. 12. June 1996 (Columbia TriStar).

Formula for Death. Nicolette Sheridan, William Devane, Stephen Caffrey, Barry Corbin, William Atherton. Dir: Armand Mastroianni. 15. November 1995 (Odyssey).

Frank and Jesse. Rob Lowe, Bill Paxton, William Atherton, Alexis Arquette. 15. June 1996 (Hi-Fliers).

Fudge-a-Mania. Darren McGavin, Florence Henderson. U. November 1995 (CIC).

Grid Runners. Don 'The Dragon' Wilson, Stella Stevens. Dir: Andrew Stevens. 18. December 1995 (Entertainment in Video).

The Halloween Tree. Voices: Leonard Nimoy, Annie Baker. Animation. U. October 1995 (First Independent).
Hatchet Man. Lance Henriksen, Eric Roberts. 18. May 1996 (Columbia TriStar).
Heatseeker. Keith Cooke, Tom Mathews. 18. November 1995 (Hi-Fliers).
Here Come the Munsters. Edward Herrmann, Robert Morse, Veronica Hamel. PG. June 1996 (CIC).
Her Hidden Truth. Kellie Martin, Reed Diamond. 15. February 1996 (Odyssey).
Heroic Trio. Maggie Cheung. 18. November 1995 (Made in Hong Kong).
Horses and Champions. Quincy David. PG. December 1995 (Guild).
Hostile Intentions. Tia Carrere. 18. March 1996 (Medusa).
Hourglass. C. Thomas Howell, Ed Begley Jr, Timothy Bottoms. Dir and Screenplay: C. Thomas Howell. May 1996 (20.20).
A House in the Hills. Helen Slater, Michael Madsen. 18. October 1995 (Warner).

If Someone Had Known. Kellie Martin, Kevin Dobson, Linda Kelsey. 15. November 1995 (Odyssey).
Illicit Dreams. Andrew Stevens, Shannon Tweed, Joe Cortese. 18. April 1996 (Fox Guild).
The Inside Man. Dennis Hopper, Hardy Kruger. Dir: Tom Klegg. 15. February 1996 (Arrow).
In the Line of Duty: Hunt For Justice. Dan Lauria, Nicholas Turturro, Adam Arkin. 12. May 1996 (Odyssey).
In the Shadow of Evil. Treat Williams, Timothy Busfield, Margaret Colin. 15. October 1995 (Fox Guild).
Iron Eagle IV. Louis Gossett Jr, Sean McCann. PG. June 1996 (Fox Guild).
It Came From Outer Space 2. Brian Kerwin, Elizabeth Pena. PG. May 1996 (CIC).

Jack Reed: One of our Own. Brian Dennehy, Charles S. Dutton, Susan Ruttan, Kevin Dunn, C.C.H Pounder. Dir and Screenplay: Brian Dennehy. M: Lee Holdridge. US title: *Jack Reed: A Killer Amongst Us.* 15. April 1996 (Odyssey).
Jungle Law. Jeff Wincott. 18. February 1996 (Entertainment in Video).

Kansas. Patricia Wettig. PG. February 1996 (Odyssey).
Keys. Marg Helgenberger, Ralph Waite. 15. January 1996 (Odyssey).
A Kiss Goodnight. Al Corley, Lawrence Tierney. 18. March 1996 (Hi-Fliers).
Knight Rider 2010. PG. February 1996 (CIC).

The Langoliers. Patricia Wettig, Dean Stockwell, David Morse, Bronson Pinchot. 15. December 1995 (PolyGram).
Lap Dancers. Elizabeth Wagner. 18. March 1996 (Marquee).
Last Gasp. Robert Patrick, Joanna Pacula, Mimi Craven. 18. August 1995 (Medusa).
Last Man Standing. Jeff Wincott. 18. May 1996 (20.20).
Leapin' Leprechauns! John Bluthal, Sylvester McCoy, James Ellis. U. April 1996 (CIC).
Lion Strike. Don 'The Dragon' Wilson. 18. February 1996 (Columbia Tri-Star).
Lunar Cop. Michael Paré, Billy Drago. 18. April 1996 (Fox Guild).

Madonna: Innocence Lost. Terumi Matthews, Jeff Yagher, Dean Stockwell. 15. July 1995 (FoxVideo).
Malicious. Molly Ringwald. 18. April 1996 (Medusa).
The Man in the Attic. Anne Archer, Len Cariou, Neil Patrick Harris. 15. August 1995 (Fox Guild).
The Man Next Door. Michael Ontkean, Pamela Reed, Annette O'Toole. Dir: Lamont Johnson. 15. March 1996 (Odyssey).
Married People Single Sex 2. Kathy Shower. 18. August 1995 (Fox Guild).
Mask of Death. Lorenzo Lamas, Rae Dawn Chong, Billy Dee Williams. Dir: David Mitchell. 18. May 1996 (Entertainment in Video).
The Matriarch. Stella Stevens, Shannon Whirry. 18. October 1995 (Hi-Fliers).
Midwest Obsession. Courtney Thorne-Smith, Kyle Secor. 15. June 1996 (Odyssey).
Mirage. Sean Young, Edward James Olmos. 18. February 1996 (20.20).

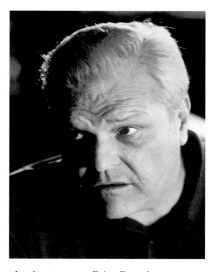

Another true story: Brian Dennehy returns to his role as the tough Chicago cop in Jack Reed: One of our Own *(from Odyssey), which the actor also wrote and directed*

A Mother's Prayer. Linda Hamilton, Bruce Dern, Kate Nelligan. 15. February 1996 (CIC).
Murdered Innocence. Jason Miller. 18. March 1996 (20.20).
Murder Or Memory? Leigh Taylor-Young, Michael Brandon. 15. August 1995 (Hi-Fliers).

National Lampoon's Senior Trip. Matt Frewer, Lawrence Dane, Tommy Chong. Dir: Kelly Makin. 15. February 1996 (First Independent).
Nemesis 2: Nebula. Sue Price. 15. September 1995 (Columbia TriStar).
Night Eyes – The Possession. Shannon Tweed, Ted Prior, Sandahl Bergman, Chad McQueen. 18. July 1995 (New Age).
Night Hunter. Don 'The Dragon' Wilson, Nicholas Guest. 18. April 1996 (Entertainment in Video).
Night of the Demons 2: Angela's Revenge. Bobby Jacoby. Dir: Brian Trenchard-Smith. 18. December 1995 (Fox Guild).
Night of the Scarecrow. Elizabeth Barondes, Dan Blocker. 18. February 1996 (PolyGram).
No Contest. Andrew Dice Clay, Robert Davi, Shannon Tweed. 18. September 1995 (Columbia Tri-Star).
No One Could Protect Her. Joanna Kerns, Dan Lauria, Anthony John Denison. 18. May 1996 (Odyssey).

One Good Turn. James Remar, Suzy

*Mariel Hemingway and Michael York in
September, Colin Bucksey's adaptation of
the Rosamunde Pilcher novel (from Odyssey)*

Amis, Lenny Von Dohlen, John Savage. 18. May 1996 (Medusa).
One Tough Bastard. Brian Bosworth, Bruce Payne, Hammer. Dir: Kurt Wimmer. 18. March 1996 (Guild).
The Other Mother. Frances Fisher. PG. August 1995 (Hi-Fliers).
Out of Annie's Past. Dennis Farina, Catherine Mary Stewart. 15. August 1995 (CIC).

Patriots. Linda Amendola. 18. November 1995 (Fox Guild).
Phantasm III. Angus Scrimm. 18. November 1995 (Fox Guild).
Prehysteria 3. Fred Willard. U. April 1996 (CIC).

Rent-a-Kid. Leslie Nielsen, Christopher Lloyd. U. November 1995 (Columbia TriStar).
Replikator. Michael St Gerard, Brigitte Bako, Ned Beatty. 18. August 1995 (Hi-Fliers).
Road to Vengeance. Chuck Norris, Noble Willingham. September 1995 (Warner).
Robin Cook's Mortal Fear. Joanna Kerns, Gregory Harrison, Robert Englund. 15. August 1995 (Odyssey).

Saints and Sinners. Damian Chapa,

Jennifer Rubin, William Atherton. Dir: Paul Mones. 18. May 1996 (Hi-Fliers).
Scanner Cop 2: Volkin's Revenge. 18. July 1995 (First Independent).
The Secretary. Mel Harris, Sheila Kelly, Barry Bostwick, James Russo. 15. August 1995 (First Independent).
Secret Games 3. Woody Brown. 18. September 1995 (20.20).
September. Jacqueline Bisset, Edward Fox, Michael York, Jenny Agutter, Mariel Hemingway. Dir: Colin Bucksey. PG. March 1996 (Odyssey).
Serial Killer. Tobin Bell, Kim Delaney. 18. January 1996 (First Independent).
The Set-Up. Billy Zane, Mia Sara, James Russo, James Coburn. 15. January 1996 (MGM/UA).
Sexual Outlaws. Mitch Gaylord. 18. January 1996 (20.20).
Sharon's Secret. Mel Harris, Alex McArthur. 15. May 1996 (CIC).
She Fought Alone. Tiffani-Amber Thiessen. 15. February 1996 (Odyssey).
Sherlock: Undercover Dog. Benjamin Eroen. PG. July 1995 (Entertainment in Video).
She Stood Alone: The Tailhook Scandal. Gail O'Grady, Bess Armstrong, Hal Holbrook, Rip Torn, Robert Urich. Dir: Larry Shaw. 15. December 1995 (Odyssey).
Shrunken Heads. Aeryk Egan, Meg Foster, Julius W. Harris. 18. August 1995 (Entertainment in Video).
The Sister-in-Law. Shanna Reed, Kate Vernon, Craig Wasson, Kevin McCarthy. 15. May 1996 (CIC).
Sketch Artist II. Jeff Fahey, Courtney Cox. January 1996 (MGM/UA).
Sleep Baby Sleep. Tracey Gold, Kyle Chandler, Joanna Cassidy. PG. May 1996 (Odyssey).
Sleep Stalker. Jay Underwood. 18. March 1996 (20.20).
Someone Else's Child. Lisa Hartman Black, Bruce Davison, Louise Fletcher. PG. July 1995 (Odyssey).
Someone to Die For. Corbin Bernsen, Ally Walker. 18. June 1996 (Medusa).
Space Rangers: 3rd War of Grakka. Jeff Kaake, Cary-Hiroyuki Tagawa. PG. August 1995 (Fox Guild).
The Stranger. Kathy Long, Andrew Divoff. 18. January 1996 (20.20).
Stranger Things. See *For Better or Worse*.

Tall Dark and Deadly. Jack Scalia, Kim Delaney. 15. December 1995 (CIC).
Temptation. Jeff Fahey, David Keith, Alison Doody. 18. February 1996 (PolyGram).
Terminal Force. Brigitte Nielsen, Richard Moll, Craig Fairbrass, Sam Raimi. 15. January 1996 (Columbia TriStar).
They Call Me Macho Woman. Paul Henri. 18. June 1996 (Troma).
3 Ninjas Knuckle Up. Victor Wong, Max Elliott Slade, Sean Fox, Sab Shimono. PG. August 1995 (Columbia TriStar).
A Time to Heal. Nicollette Sheridan, Gary Cole. PG. June 1996 (Odyssey).
To the Limit. Anna Nicole Smith, Joey Travolta. 18. March 1996 (20.20).
Trail of Tears. Katey Segal, Pam Dawber. 15. January 1996 (Odyssey).
Trapped. Paul Winfield. 18. August 1995 (New Age).
Trapped and Deceived. Jennie Garth, Jill Eikenberry, Helen Shaver. 15. July 1995 (Odyssey).
Trial by Fire. Keith Carradine, Gail O'Grady. Dir: Alan Metzger. 15. March 1996 (Odyssey).

Undercover. Anthena Massey, Meg Foster. 18. November 1995 (Hi-Fliers).
Unforgivable. John Ritter, Harley Jane Kozak. 15. June 1996 (Odyssey).
The Unspoken Truth. Lea Thompson, Patricia Kalember, Robert Englund, James Marshall. Dir: Peter Werner. 15. December 1995 (Odyssey).

The Viking Sagas. Ralph Moeller, Sven-Ole Thorson. 15. January 1996 (Entertainment in Video).

When the Bullet Hits the Bone. Jeff Wincott. 18. May 1996 (Entertainment in Video).
When the Dark Man Calls. Joan Van Ark, Geoffrey Lewis. 15. March 1996 (CIC).
White Tiger. Cary-Hiroyuki Tagawa, Matt Craven. 18. April 1996 (Fox Guild).
Witchboard: The Possession. David Nerman. 18. May 1996 (Hi-Fliers).

Xtro 3 – Watch the Skies. Sal Landi, Andrew Divoff, Robert Culp. 18. January 1996 (Columbia TriStar).

Movie Quotations of the Year

'She threatened me, I patronised her. We didn't have anything to eat – I felt we had a good connection.'

Michael Douglas on his first meeting with Annette Bening, in *The American President*

'Men like to be insulted. It makes them feel loved.'

Gail Strickland in *The American President*

'You know that Easter vacation trip? There might be a slight change in destination. Maybe say the moon.'

Tom Hanks to his wife (Kathleen Quinlan) in *Apollo 13*

'Houston, we have a problem.'

Tom Hanks, as Captain James A. Lovell, understating the problem in *Apollo 13*

'That'll do, pig.'

James Cromwell heaping praise on his prize-winning porker in *Babe*

'Time sure flies when you're young and jerking off.'

Leonardo DiCaprio in *The Basketball Diaries*

...mie, overhearing *sotto voce* insult from ...is mother: 'I heard that.' Mother: 'You ...ould hear a zit burst in Australia, you ...ould.'

Glen Berry and Linda Henry in *Beautiful*

'Every now and then I think everybody is entitled to too much perfection.'

Christian Slater in *Bed of Roses*

'I wish I could give you a part of myself. But that's not something I have in my possession right now.'

Mary Stuart Masterson to Christian Slater in *Bed of Roses*

'In some cultures women are said to be worth their weight in hens. And a man's wealth is measured by the size of his cock.'

Robin Williams in *The Birdcage*

'The trouble with being a journalist for too long is that you stop giving yourself permission to invent.'

Clint Eastwood on the creative perils of his trade, in *The Bridges of Madison County*

'This much certainty comes but once in a lifetime.'

Clint Eastwood, revealing his true feelings to Meryl Streep in *The Bridges of Madison County*

Christian Slater, to a reprehensible John Travolta: 'Are you out of your mind?' Travolta: 'Yeah. Ain't it cool?'

From *Broken Arrow*

'If I push this button, the South-West will be a quiet neighbourhood for about 10,000 years.'

John Travolta toying with Armageddon, in *Broken Arrow*

'He who hesitates masturbates.'

Jim Carrey advising Matthew Broderick to 'go for it' in *The Cable Guy*

'Don't you understand, Steven? Somebody has to kill the babysitter.'

Jim Carrey to Matthew Broderick at the end of *The Cable Guy*

'Running a casino is like robbing a bank with no cops around. For guys like me, Las Vegas washes away your sins. It's like a mortality car wash. It does for me what Lourdes does for hunchbacks and cripples.'

Robert De Niro in *Casino*

'The public is always ahead of us in what they're ready for.'

Shirley MacLaine on the reticence of Hollywood to explore new ideas, in *The Celluloid Closet*

Eclipsing the quips: Jim Carrey in The Cable Guy.

'A man's stature is determined by his enemies, not by his friends.'

New York mayor Al Pacino, in *City Hall*

'Tis a far, far better thing like when you do stuff for other people.'

Alicia Silverstone learning altruism in *Clueless*

Cher: 'Dionne, would you call me selfish?' Dionne: 'No. Not to your face.'

Alicia Silverstone and Stacey Dash in *Clueless*

'Searching for a boy in high school is as hopeless as looking for meaning in a Pauly Shore movie.'

Alicia Silverstone in *Clueless*

'These guys are like viruses. There's always a new mutation.'

Sigourney Weaver on the serial killer in *Copycat*

'Do you know, Helen, that more books have been written about Jack the Ripper than Abraham Lincoln?'

William McNamara to Sigourney Weaver in *Copycat*

'There's trouble in Russia.'

Gene Hackman understating the obvious in *Crimson Tide*

Gene Hackman, exhaling a blanket of cigar smoke: 'I don't trust air I can't see.'

From *Crimson Tide*

'A true enemy cannot be destroyed. In the nuclear world the true enemy is war itself.'

Denzel Washington in *Crimson Tide*

'We're here to preserve democracy – not to practise it.'

A gung-ho Gene Hackman in *Crimson Tide*

'Death is . . . you know, it's not for everyone.'

Tim Daly attempting to cheer up a grieving friend in *Denise Calls Up*

'Bless me, Father, for I have just killed quite a few men.'

El Mariachi (Antonio Banderas) in the confessional in *Desperado*

El Mariachi to Carolina: 'Did I thank you?' Carolina: 'No, you didn't.' El Mariachi: 'I will.'

Antonio Banderas and Salma Hayek in *Desperado*

'An artist doesn't create beauty – he simply removes what prevents us from seeing it.'

Gerard Depardieu in *Elisa*

'If you drop your gun now, I promise not to kill you.'

An apparently defenceless Arnold Schwarzenegger, held at gunpoint by James Caan in *Eraser*

'What *is* semtex, officer?'

Highly trained (but surprisingly ignorant) lawyer Cindy Crawford to William Baldwin, in *Fair Game*

'The only control anybody has is which hand they use to wipe their ass.'

Mickey Rourke, dabbling in a bit of philosophy in *Fall Time*

'A man who fears nothing, loves nothing. And if you love nothing, what joy is there in your life?'

Sean Connery as King Arthur in *First Knight*

'There once was a man who loved you too much to change you.'

Lancelot (Richard Gere) announcing his honourable intentions to Queen Guinevere (Julia Ormond) in *First Knight*

'Their marriage had one overriding problem. One was a man and one was a woman.'

A cynical Julie Kavner on the wedlock of Billy Crystal and Debra Winger in *Forget Paris*

'There are two types of comedians. There's a funny bones comedian and a non-funny bones comedian. They're both funny. One is funny; the other tells funny. Tommy, it's time you knew – and this kills me the most – but you're neither. You're not funny.'

Jokemeister Jerry Lewis to his son, aspiring comic Oliver Platt, in *Funny Bones*

'If I want sarcasm I'll talk to my children.'

Judi Dench as M, head of MI6, reprimanding Michael Kitchen in *Goldeneye*

'Unlike the American government, we prefer not to get our bad news from CNN.'

Judi Dench in *Goldeneye*

M to James Bond: 'I think you are a sexist, misogynistic dinosaur.'

Judi Dench in *Goldeneye*

Q, while exhibiting his latest gadgets: 'Need I remind you, 007, you have a licence to kill – not to break traffic laws.'

Desmond Llewelyn reprimanding Pierce Brosnan in *Goldeneye*

'There is no right or wrong. There is only fun and boring.'

Fisher Stevens in *Hackers*

'Deep down I'm a sensitive and vulnerable girl. Don't let my dildos, vibrators and handcuffs fool you.'

Ex-porn star Andrea Naschak in *Hold Me, Thrill Me, Kiss Me*

'How can you give up sex when there are children in Europe who can't get a date?'

Old woman in church in *Jeffrey*

'Think of Aids as the guest that won't leave. But remember, it's still our party.'

Bryan Batt, a gay victim of the disease, in *Jeffrey*

'I want room service! I want the club sandwich! I want the cold Mexican beer! I want a $10,000-a-night hooker!'

Keanu Reeves screaming his head off in the middle of nowhere in *Johnny Mnemonic*

'I knew you'd say that.'

Catchphrase of Sylvester Stallone's ever-mocking *Judge Dredd*

'Homosexuality is the disease, Aids is the cure.'

Straight-talking priest Charles Durning in *The Last Supper*

A grieving Julia Roberts: 'My mother died.' John Malkovich (as a malevolent Mr Hyde): 'Oh, well, she's not the only one.'

From *Mary Reilly*

Woody Allen, to his young son: 'I'm the boss, Mommy's only the decision maker.'

From *Mighty Aphrodite*

'Achilles only had his heel, I've got an Achilles body.'

Woody Allen in *Mighty Aphrodite*

Mira Sorvino, on Woody Allen's offer of an evening together: 'I can't stay in, I've got six dates.' Woody: 'Six dates? A slow night for you, right?'

From *Mighty Aphrodite*

'I will use anything – from Bach to rock and roll – if I think it will help to teach a student to love music.'

Richard Dreyfuss, on his teaching tactics, in *Mr Holland's Opus*

William Petersen, as he is about to be dealt some underhand justice: 'You can't do this. This is America.' Nick Nolte: 'This isn't America, Jack. This is L.A.'

From *Mulholland Falls*

'I eat so I don't think about food all the time.'

Chazz Palminteri, defending his constant gormandising in *Mulholland Falls*

'I want to be over this. I want to move on. I'm going to give up smoking. Learn a new language.'

Galaxy Craze, following her traumatic liaison with a Transylvanian vampire, in *Nadja*

'Nothing sells like sincerity.'

Sales manager John Cunningham in *Nixon*

'I'll put on the old Nixon charm.'

Anthony Hopkins as Richard Milhous Nixon

Larry Hagman: 'Dick, your country needs you.' Anthony Hopkins: 'Unfortunately, the country isn't available right now.'

From *Nixon*

'The world will see only what I show them.'

Anthony Hopkins as *Nixon*

John Travolta, to Kyra Sedgwick: 'Will you love me for the rest of my life?' Kyra Sedgwick: 'No. I will love you for the rest of *my* life.'

From *Phenomenon*

'Everything is on its way to somewhere.'

A profound John Travolta in *Phenomenon*

'What I love most about rivers is, You can't step in the same river twice; The water's always changing, always flowing.'

Irene Bedard, on the soundtrack of *Pocahontas*

'But still I cannot see, If the savage one is me, How can there be so much that you don't know?'

Irene Bedard, on the soundtrack of *Pocahontas*

'When your mother says she loves you, get a second opinion.'

Hotshot attorney Richard Gere in *Primal Fear*

'If you want justice, go to a whorehouse. If you want to be fucked, go to court.'

Hotshot attorney Richard Gere in *Primal Fear*

'Why gamble with money when you can gamble with people's lives?'

Hotshot attorney Richard Gere in *Primal Fear*

'I suggest you start representing your client and stop representing yourself.'

Judge Alfre Woodard to hotshot attorney Richard Gere, in *Primal Fear*

'It's easier to beat a child than raise it. Love is hard work.'

Morgan Freeman in *Seven*

'We see a deadly sin on every street corner and we tolerate it. Because it's normal.'

Serial killer Kevin Spacey in *Seven*

John Travolta as the phenomenal George Malley in Disney's feel-good Phenomenon

'All I ever wanted was an honest week's pay for an honest day's work.'

Steve Martin as *Sgt Bilko*

'She looks better than a ten-inch dick.'

Lin Tucci bestowing her greatest compliment on Elizabeth Berkley in *Showgirls*

'You've gotta gamble if you're gonna win.'

Dewey Weber in *Showgirls*

'I would just like to know if anybody else in here has slept with my husband?'

Cuckolded wife Julia Roberts to a large female assembly in *Something to Talk About*

'Avoid women directors. They ovulate!'

Movie tycoon Kevin Spacey dispensing advice in *Swimming With Sharks*

'Give it a name.'

Catchphrase of Andy Garcia, William Forsythe and Christopher Lloyd in *Things To Do in Denver When You're Dead*

A few words from the celebrations on *Independence Day*:

US president Bill Pullman, summing up the international situation: 'We're being exterminated!'

US president Bill Pullman to invading alien, speaking on behalf of the human population: 'What is it you want us to do?' Alien: 'Die.'

'Nuke 'em.'
US president Bill Pullman, delivering orders to combat the alien visitors

James Rebhorn, protesting against Judd Hirsch's impromptu prayer service: 'I'm not Jewish.' Hirsch: 'Nobody's perfect.'

'Elvis has left the building.'
Ace fighter pilot Will Smith as he and Jeff Goldblum narrowly escape the alien mother ship

'Didn't I promise you fireworks?'
Ace fighter pilot Will Smith to his son as the alien intruders meet their come-uppance

Will Smith and Jeff Goldblum exchange wisecracks in Independence Day

Say that again (continued from last year):

'I don't even think I could get on to Oprah with that one, these days.'
Mary Stuart Masterson, after explaining her life story to Christian Slater, in *Bed of Roses*

'Look, lover boy, we're not on Oprah.'
Edward Burns in *The Brothers McMullen*

'When I catch your monster I'm gonna put it on Oprah Winfrey!'
'Beastie' hunter Ted Danson in *Loch Ness*

'Was there a thing on Oprah?'
Denis Leary rejecting his girlfriend's own idea in *Stolen Hearts*

'Don't we hear this on Sally and Oprah every day?'
Lena Rochon in *Waiting to Exhale*

Definition of a drag queen: 'A gay man with way too much fashion sense for one gender.'
Wesley Snipes in *To Wong Foo, Thanks for Everything! Julie Newmar*

Woody (to Buzz Lightyear): 'You – are – a – toy!' Buzz Lightyear: 'You are a sad, strange little man.'
Tom Hanks and Tim Allen, on the soundtrack of *Toy Story*

'To infinity and beyond!'
Buzz Lightyear's catchphrase in *Toy Story*

'I chose not to choose life. Reasons? Who needs reasons when you've got heroin?'
Ewan McGregor in *Trainspotting*

'People get trapped in their own history. Unless someone shows them a way out.'
Michael Richards in *Unstrung Heroes*

'The greatest trick the devil ever pulled was convincing the world he didn't exist.'
Kevin Spacey in *The Usual Suspects*

'Ouch.'
Mitch Pileggi – after having his heart ripped out of his rib cage by Eddie Murphy – in *Vampire in Brooklyn*

'I can't tell you never to fight. But if you want to know what I think ... I think the only thing that truly keeps people safe and happy is love. And in the absence of love, there's nothing in this world worth fightin' for.'
Kevin Costner in *The War*

'For goodness sake, somebody shoot something.'
Dennis Hopper - as the villainous Deacon – barking orders in *Waterworld*

And some of the year's most memorable tag lines (those blurbs dreamed up by marketing people to put on movie posters):

'... makes *Waterworld* look like the most expensive film ever made ...'
From *A Fistful of Fingers*

'Five criminals. One line up. No coincidence.'
From *The Usual Suspects*

'Love is an adventure when one of you is sure ... and the other is positive.'
From *Jeffrey*

'The Future Is History.'
From *Twelve Monkeys*

'Don't Call Me Babe.'
From *Barb Wire*

Quotes, off-screen (that is, famous lines not scripted):

'We stay at home and talk a lot. Laugh a lot. Jump on the bed. Bark at each other.'

Patricia Arquette on her unique relationship with her new husband Nicolas Cage

'Cor, this is living, ain't it?'

Brenda Blethyn, accepting her award for best actress at the 1996 Cannes film festival

'I was always shocked when I went to the doctor's office and they did my X-ray and didn't find that I had eight more ribs than I should have or that my blood was the colour green.'

Nicolas Cage, regular guy

'One thing I hope I'll never be is drunk with my own power. And anybody who says I am will never work in this town again.'

Jim Carrey

'My idea of a good evening is two beers in front of the fireplace. I drink them. Squeeze the cans. It makes you feel kind of macho. You toss 'em in the wastepaper basket, you belch three times and go to bed.'

Clint Eastwood, macho legend

'If Sylvester Stallone makes $20 million to star in a picture and a director gets $6 to $8 million, I don't think there's anything wrong with the screenwriter getting $2 to $4 million for a script.'

Joe Eszterhas, whose credits include *Hearts of Fire*, *Showgirls* and *Jade*

'Doing sex scenes with people you like is interesting. But doing them with people you don't like can be even more so, because if you don't like somebody, you torture them. It's really fun. You pull their hair, and they think it's a sexual thing when you're really trying to hurt them.'

Linda Fiorentino, who sexed it up with David Caruso in *Jade*

'It swings, man. And the cats will get it.'

Laurence Fishburne on the appeal of *Othello*

'I don't get offered anything but good guys, otherwise it wouldn't be politically correct. Yet villains are much more fun to play. There are directors who want to cast me as the bad guy, then the producer will say, "No, no, no, you can't do that, it's Morgan Freeman." So, yeah, I'm typecast.'

Morgan Freeman

'Think of a film as a product, something created and brought to market, not too dissimilar from breast implants. If something goes wrong with the product, and injury ensues, then its makers are held responsible.'

Bestselling novelist and lawyer John Grisham on the accountability filmmakers face when their pictures incite violence

'If anybody gives me another box of chocolates, I'll gag.'

Tom Hanks

'I enjoy an exploration of sex. I enjoy an exploration of violence. That's why I go to see movies. That's why I go to see plays. Because usually you find out a lot about who people are.'

Holly Hunter

Macho man Clint Eastwood (as he looked in The Bridges of Madison County)

'It was stipulated in the *Showgirls* contract that they could digitally put a penis on the lead man for a hard-on. Had I done it, I'd have supplied my own hard-on thank you very much.'

Actor Dylan McDermott (*In the Line of Fire*, *Miracle on 34th Street*)

'Hollywood is mad. But it has given me everything.'

Michelle Pfeiffer

'In the future, [Kevin] Costner should only appear in pictures he directs himself. That way he can always be working with his favourite actor and his favourite director.'

Kevin Reynolds, the director unceremoniously removed from the troubled production of *Waterworld*

'I found myself wondering, maybe I'm not such a bad boy after all. And that rather annoyed me.'

Nicolas Roeg, on receiving his CBE

'I think there are a lot of women, probably more than men, who are capable of loving both men and women. It's just flesh, and if you're relatively well balanced, you can get your mind around anything.'

Patricia Rozema, director of *I've Heard the Mermaids Singing* and *When Night is Falling*

'The only thing I believe in now is the wisdom of uncertainty. And the only religion I have is a kind of reverence for the luminous, majestic messiness of it all. That, to me, is sacred.'

Patricia Rozema

'I find it very difficult to say what I think. If you are inarticulate you can become a painter or a musician or an actor. And the laziest of these is an actor.'

Kristin Scott Thomas

'I'm 36, I'm watching my butt slide down my legs and everything else is two inches lower. I want to extend my range. Sexpots age fast in Hollywood.'

Sharon Stone, now 38

'Laughter is a celebration of our failings. That's what clowns are for. And that's what I am.'

Emma Thompson

Faces of the
Year

Pamela Anderson Lee

Hardly a promising *face*, Pamela Anderson Lee nevertheless triggered a media event when she donned high heels and pout to straddle her first made-to-measure star vehicle, *Barb Wire*. Forgetting that the film was rubbish (and that the sexual warhead revealed her thespian shortcomings), *Barb Wire* turned up the amperage on the world's most gloated-on property.

While frequently cited as Pambo's film debut, *Barb Wire* was actually the Canadian beauty's third film, following unremarkable appearances in the unremarkable *Snapdragon* (an erotic thriller co-starring Steven Bauer and Chelsea Field) and *Raw Justice* (aka *Good Cop, Bad Cop*).

To be honest, the girl with the tarantula eyelashes and silicone addenda will probably be tomorrow's Bo Derek, but such is her global celebrity she had to be included here for the record.

FACT FILE:

Born: Vancouver Island, British Columbia; 1 June 1967
TV: *Home Improvements* (1991-93); *Baywatch* (the world's most ogled programme, starring Pambo as lifeguard C.J. Parker) (1992-)
Ex-fiancé: Actor Scott Baio (*Bugsy Malone*, TV's *Happy Days*)
Husband: Tattooed musician Tommy Lee, drummer of Motley Crue
Love of her life: Her new-born son, Brandon Thomas
Vital statistic: A 36D cup
Claim to fame: A record six appearances on the cover of *Playboy*

Penetrating quote: 'Sex makes you get real.'

Ben Chaplin

It was not a bad year for unknown British talent in American films. The Bristol-born Jeremy Northam landed the male lead opposite Sandra Bullock in *The Net*. The London-born Stephen Dillane also shared the screen with Ms Bullock in *Stolen Hearts*. But it was Ben Chaplin – as the shy romantic photographer torn between Janeane Garofalo and Uma Thurman in *The Truth About Cats and Dogs* – who really raised the temperature of American cinemagoers.

Indeed, Chaplin displays an uncanny knack for concealing the artifice of his acting, a gift as rare as humility in Bel Air. In *Feast of July*, the partially successful adaptation of the novel by H.E. Bates, he towered over his co-stars in a performance of tortured honesty. Resembling a tongue-tied Antonio Banderas, Chaplin was a gift to the film. But it was *Cats and Dogs*, which triumphed at the US box-office for three weeks, that cemented the actor's tabloid awareness.

Described as a new Hugh Grant, the 26 year old scoffed, 'I've worked with Hugh and he's a lot more clever, more eloquent and more educated than I am.'

FACT FILE:

Born: Windsor, Berkshire; 1970
TV: *Between the Lines*; *The Borrowers*;

Silicone to celluloid: Pamela Anderson Lee in Barb Wire

Minder; *Tuesday*; *A Few Short Journeys of the Heart*; *Game On!*

Films: *Bye Bye Baby* (TV); *The Remains of the Day* (as Charley, first footman)

Guilty secret: He was kicked out of the Guildhall School of Music & Drama before the end of his second year

Finest hour?: Nominated for an Olivier Award for his performance in the West End production of *The Glass Menagerie*

Penetrating quote: On his punishing schedule: 'I just compare it to drama school. Beside that, work is fun and childish. The approach in drama school is not unlike torture. They take you apart but they haven't got the instructions to put you back together again.'

What they say: 'I like him so much it sounds like I'm lying. Ben was like a gift from the studio, better than a fruit basket' – *Cats and Dogs* co-star Janeane Garofalo

The future: He has landed the male lead (Morris) in the big-budget drama *Washington Square*, an adaptation of Henry James's *The Heiress*, directed by Agnieszka Holland. Jennifer Jason Leigh, Albert Finney and Maggie Smith also star

George Clooney

Few stars have rocketed out of the small screen with such speed and force as George Clooney. One minute he was an unknown in an ensemble cast on yet another medical TV series. The next he was being paid a giddy ten million dollars to play the Caped Crusader. That is one giant leap.

Yet Clooney had that indefinable something that set him apart from his blood-splattered colleagues. Strong jawed, velvet voiced and authoritative, he looked more at home on a movie set than in an emergency room.

The nephew of the singers Rosemary and Betty Clooney, GC struggled in B-movie and TV sitcom hell before landing the role of Doug Ross in *ER*. The show's success seemed to do little for

Ben Chaplin: disarmingly earnest

The man most likely to succeed: George Clooney in From Dusk Till Dawn

his co-stars (Anthony Edwards, Sherry Stringfield, Julianna Margulies, Noah Wyle, Eriq La Salle), but it got him noticed all right.

He was cast in the lead of *From Dusk Till Dawn* (a role originally earmarked for Robert Blake), and the movie opened at the top of the box-office charts, grabbing a substantial $10.2 million in its first weekend on release in the US. He was then plunged into the epicentre of a bidding war. He was supposed to play superhero Britt Reid in the big screen version of *The Green Hornet*, but was persuaded by Steven Spielberg (whose Amblin Entertainment produces *ER*) to star in the post-Cold War drama *The Peacemaker* instead – for $3 million.

Then, when Val Kilmer mixed up his cape with his halo to star in *The Saint*, Clooney was brought in to replace him in *Batman and Robin*. Kilmer had got $2 million for *Batman Forever*, but Clooney was pocketing $10m as part of a three-picture deal engineered by Warner Brothers. By the time the ink had dried, the actor was looking at $26 and $28 million from Warner and the

lead in *The Peacemaker*, the flagship movie from DreamWorks (the multimedia company set up by Spielberg, ex-Disney chairman Jeffrey Katzenberg and music mogul David Geffen).

Oh yeah, and he even had time to slip into *One Fine Day*, a romantic comedy with Michelle Pfeiffer.

FACT FILE:

Born: Kentucky; 1962
TV: *Roseanne* (as Roseanne's colleague, Booker); *The Facts of Life* (as handyman George Burnett); *Sunset Beat* (as undercover cop and amateur guitarist Chic Chesbro); *Baby Talk*; *Sisters*; *ER* (as Doug Ross)
The forgettable movie: *Red Surf* (with Dedee Pfeiffer)
Ex-wife: Actress Talia Balsam
Ex-girlfriends: Actress Kelly Preston (now Mrs John Travolta), Cindy Crawford, actress Kimberly Russell
Love of his life: Max, a half-blind, 150-pound pot-bellied pig
Vital statistic: One pierced ear
Claim to fame: A complete stranger asked him to be best man at his wedding
Guilty secret: In 1988 he starred in the risible *Return of the Killer Tomatoes!*

Second guilty secret: He lost the role of JD in *Thelma & Louise* to Brad Pitt
Third guilty secret: He turned down *Reservoir Dogs*
Penetrating quote: 'I'm trying to focus away from being Joe Television'

Chris Farley

Yet another graduate from the comedy stable of TV's *Saturday Night Live*, Chris Farley leapfrogged over his colleagues to rack up a $6 million payday for *Beverly Hills Ninja*. Big, bouncy and good natured, Farley honed his comedy routine at the Second City Theater in Chicago, where he was spotted by *SNL* producer Lorne Michaels.

'He was extremely funny,' notes Michaels, 'but I wasn't sure he was disciplined enough for *Saturday Night Live*. I felt very strongly though that he'd eventually do great on the show, and he has.' Farley joined the revue in the 1990-91 season and made his reputation as the tragically insecure talk show host on *The Chris Farley Show* segment, as well as for his impersonations of Meatloaf, Mama Cass and Tom Arnold.

He also bonded well with co-star David Spade, the Stan Laurel to his Oliver Hardy. Spade observes, 'We're two really different people. Chris is a big, loud, obnoxious guy, and I'm a whole lot quieter and more low-key. The contrast is pretty funny.'

Farley adds: 'It helps too that I love David's sense of humour more than

The big man: Chris Farley

anyone's. David and I spend so much time together that people say we're beginning to look alike.'

Spade and Farley capitalised on their comic chemistry in the SNL spin-off *Coneheads*, but really came into their own in the hit *Tommy Boy*, in which the mismatched duo were supported by Bo Derek, Brian Dennehy, Dan Aykroyd and Rob Lowe. Since then Farley has gone on to star in Penelope Spheeris's *Black Sheep*, with David Spade, Jim Abrahams' *Stanley's Cup*, with Denis Leary, Denis Dugan's *Beverly Hills Ninja*, with Nicolette Sheridan, and Christopher Guest's *Edwards and Hunt*, with Matthew Perry.

FACT FILE:

Love of his life: David Spade
Vital statistics: Don't mention his weight
Claim to fame: That $6m payday
Penetrating quote: 'Tommy Boy is the kind of guy who puts his hand in the cookie jar, gets caught and tries to desperately wriggle his way out. He'd really rather screw around with his buddies than face responsibility. Tommy is truly a lot like me'

Greg Kinnear

With his boyish good looks and halogen smile, Greg Kinnear could've been the next Mel Gibson had *Sabrina* been the hit that Paramount Pictures said it was going to be. As it is, the talk show host exuded enough eight-cylinder charm to guarantee top-billing in his next picture, Garry Marshall's big-budget comedy *Dear God* (in which he plays a conman working for the post office, forced to answer letters addressed to the Almighty).

With virtually no acting experience to his name (he had a bit part in the 1990 TV movie *Murder in Mississippi*), Kinnear was picked to play the love interest of Julia Ormond in *Sabrina*, Sydney Pollack's $50 million remake of the 1954 classic, with Harrison Ford cast as Kinnear's big brother. Tom Cruise had turned the role down and Pollack was getting anxious. 'I'd spoken to a lot of well-known people, and they either didn't want to do it or couldn't,' the director relates. 'I saw him [Kinnear] on *Talk Soup*, and I was so desperate at that point. I thought he was smart and had a lot of charm.'

Kinnear takes up the story: 'I went in to talk to Sydney without a clue. I didn't know the original movie or have much idea what it was. All I knew was that it was Sydney Pollack, and I was a fan. I thought he wanted to be on my TV show.'

Sabrina may not have been a huge hit, but it grossed a respectable $53.5m in the US and Kinnear won the lion's share of the positive reviews. With the director of *Pretty Woman* guiding his next celluloid outing, Kinnear has time yet to prove his box-office smarts.

FACT FILE:

Born: Logansport, Indiana; 1964. He then grew up in Lebanon and Greece
TV: *Life Goes On* (ABC); *College Mad House* (host); the chat shows *Talk Soup* (E! Network) and *Later With Greg Kinnear* (NBC)
Future: The starring role in a drama called *A Smile Like Yours*, with Lauren Holly, Joan Cusack and Jay Thomas in support
Love of his life: An English lass (unnamed)
Vital statistic: Kinetic eyebrows
Penetrating quote: 'If Hollywood ever offers me another opportunity, it will probably be *Porky's 5*'

Ewan McGregor

If *Trainspotting* is *A Clockwork Orange* for the nineties, then Ewan McGregor is shaping up to be a handy successor to

Through a glass darkly: Ewan McGregor as smack addict Mark Renton in Trainspotting

The urbane, prepossessing Greg Kinnear in Sabrina

Malcolm McDowell. McGregor has the same cocky demeanour, the wiry physique and a knack for skating along the cutting edge of British cinema – much as McDowell did in the early seventies (before the latter turned grey and ended up typecast as sci-fi Nazis).

The son of a pair of teachers, McGregor decided he wanted to tread the boards by the age of nine, inspired by the life of his uncle, the Scottish actor Denis Lawson (*Local Hero*). Following experience at the Perth Repertory Theatre, McGregor enrolled at the Guildhall School of Music and Drama in London, but cut short his course in 1992 to appear in Dennis Potter's *Lipstick on Your Collar* on TV.

Since then he won a supporting role in *Being Human*, directed by fellow Scot Bill Forsyth, and moved up through the ranks until landing the role of the wise-cracking cub reporter Alex in *Shallow Grave*, directed by Danny Boyle. The film was a hit, but nothing compared to the next McGregor-Boyle collaboration, *Trainspotting*, which cast the actor as the eloquent smack addict Mark Renton. Since then he has starred

Hot babe: Alicia Silverstone as she simmered in Clueless

in Peter Greenaway's *Pillow Book* and headed off to Hollywood to appear opposite Nick Nolte and Patricia Arquette in *Night Watch*, a remake of the chilling black comedy from Sweden (qv).

Most recently McGregor starred in *The Serpent's Kiss*, in which he played a young craftsman who becomes romantically involved with his wealthy employer's wife (Greta Scacchi) and daughter – under the direction of the Oscar-winning French cinematographer Philippe Rousselot.

FACT FILE:

Born: Crieff, Scotland; 1972
TV: *Lipstick on Your Collar*; *Scarlet and Black*; *Karaoke*
Films: *Being Human*, *Shallow Grave*, *Blue Juice*, *The Pillow Book*, *Trainspotting*, *Emma*, *Brassed Off*, *The Serpent's Kiss*

Guilty secret: He's a chain-smoker
Love of his life: His baby daughter (born 1996)
Fabulous fact: He lost nearly 30 pounds to play Renton in *Trainspotting*
Penetrating quote: 'They're making great films in this country at the moment. I'm lucky to be around right now'

Alicia Silverstone

Who would have thought that the actress who played the surly, psychotic fourteen-year-old child prodigy in *The Crush* would go on to earn $5 million a movie two years later? Following less-than-spectacular roles in *The Babysitter* and *Hideaway*, Silverstone hit her stride as the naive, fashion-wise matchmaker Cher Hamilton in *Clueless*. It was one of those rare instances when a middling actress cast in the right material gelled into celluloid ambrosia.

The youngest child of three, Alicia (pronounced A-lee-see-ah) is the daughter of an English real-estate investor (her father) and a former flight attendant, and grew up in San Francisco. A frequent visitor to England, her parents' native country, she became interested in theatre and decided to become an actress, making her debut in a pizza commercial, followed by her stage initiation in *Carol's Eve* in Los Angeles.

Her appearance in three Aerosmith videos ('Cryin'', 'Amazing' and 'Crazy') made her something of an MTV icon, the first attracting the attention of director Amy Heckerling. Heckerling cast her in *Clueless*, a hip comedy on Californian cool in which Silverstone rose to the material. The film, a true original, was a hit and Silverstone became the babe-to-know of her generation.

Hollywood, forever on the lookout for fresh, accessible talent, jumped. Columbia Pictures, who had already paid $20 million to Jim Carrey to star in *The Cable Guy*, signed Alicia up to a three-year, two-picture deal worth $10m. The actress is now producing her next comedy, *Excess Baggage* (co-starring Christopher Walken), and has signed with Warner Brothers to play Batgirl in *Batman and Robin*.

FACT FILE:

Born: San Francisco; 1977
TV: *The Wonder Years*; *The Cool and the Crazy*
The other movies: *Torch Song* (TV); *Shattered Dreams* (TV); *True Crime*; *Le Nouveau Monde*
Reported squeeze: Comedian Adam Sandler
Claim to fame: Her bungee jump off a bridge in Aerosmith's 'Cryin'', voted Best Video of All Time on MTV
Guilty secret: She sweats more than most
Finest hour?: Voted Outstanding Newcomer by The National Board of Review of Motion Pictures
Penetrating quote: 'I've been so focused on my work, it's like I kind of forgot I was a girl. I feel like a man most of the time'

Mira Sorvino

It is only when you look at her earlier roles that you begin to realise what a stretch *Mighty Aphrodite* was. In danger of being typecast as a latter-day Anthony Quinn, Sorvino played a Brazilian aristocrat in the BBC's *Buccaneers*, a Spanish siren in Whit Stillman's *Barcelona* and a Jewish wife in *Quiz Show*. Then, in Woody Allen's *Mighty Aphrodite*, she portrayed the ultimate dumb blonde, a helium-voiced prostitute who stars in porn movies on the side under the nom-de-plume of Judy Cum. The blonde hair was her idea, and it was a conceit that caught the director's interest. She landed the role – and the reviews – and the Oscar.

The Italian-American daughter of the actor Paul Sorvino (*Reds*, *GoodFellas*, *Nixon*), Mira graduated with honours from Harvard with a degree in East Asian Languages and Civilisations. Following an eight-month stint teaching English in Beijing, she produced a documentary called *Freedom to Hate*, a film about anti-Semitism in the former Soviet Union. But it was when she was working as third assistant director on the $370,000-budgeted *Amongst Friends* that she suggested to the director Rob Weiss that she take the female lead. She got the role after an audition, stayed on as third AD and watched as the film reaped rave

Liv Tyler, in Stealing Beauty

reviews at the Sundance Film Festival.

FACT FILE:

Born: Tenafly, New Jersey; 1970

The other movies: *Parallel Lives* (TV); *NY Cop*; *Blue in the Face*; *Sweet Nothing*; *Tarantella*; *Neil Simon's 'Jake's Women'* (TV); *Beautiful Girls*; *Norma Jean & Marilyn* (TV) (as Marilyn Monroe); *Romy and Michele's High School Reunion*

Reported squeeze: Quentin Tarantino (her Oscar show date)

Vital statistic: Her six-foot build

Finest hour: Winning the Oscar for *Mighty Aphrodite*, whose words at the podium, 'When you give me this award you honour my father,' reduced the latter to uncontrollable sobs

Fabulous fact: She speaks fluent Mandarin

What they say: 'I was very upset when Mira told me she wanted to be an actress. My problem was not that she wouldn't make it, but that she would.' Her father, actor Paul Sorvino

Penetrating quote: 'You can't just be a message actor. You have to take

The helium-voiced hellcat: Mira Sorvino in her Oscar-winning turn as Linda Ash – aka Judy Cum – in Woody Allen's Mighty Aphrodite

roles where you can find them. If you find a great role, it in itself has a message – because there is something about it which communicates to the audience and makes them understand that kind of person better. In its own little way, it makes the world smaller'

Future: The Puerto Rico-set drama *Dreaming of Julia*, with Harvey 'pass that screenplay' Keitel

Liv Tyler

Cannes was the clincher. Journalists had already waxed rhetorical about her endless legs. Trendy magazines had her gushing from their Faces To Watch columns. And she had caused a minor stir in Aerosmith's music video 'Crazy' (alongside Alicia Silverstone). But it was her domination of the 49th Cannes film festival that opened up the eyes of the world.

Liv Tyler is, unquestionably, very, very beautiful. The daughter of rock

Race to the top: Kate Winslet

which she played a college dropout. She was a virginal record shop employee in the endearing *Empire Records*, which, she says, she wished had never been released (a rather strange request, under the circumstances). No, the movie that turned young Liv into an 'overnight' star was Bernardo Bertolucci's *Stealing Beauty*, with Liv as the ultimate virgin pursued by a community of cherry-picking oddballs (including Jeremy Irons). She then joined Julia Roberts and Goldie Hawn in Woody Allen's *Everyone Says You Love Me* and took a starring role in *That Thing You Do*, Tom Hanks's directorial debut.

FACT FILE:

Born: Maine; 1977
Next movie: *Inventing the Abbots*, a drama directed by Pat O'Connor
Love of her life: Her cat, Little Man
Vital statistic: Her six-foot build
Guilty secret: She didn't discover who her real father was until she was nine
Penetrating quote: 'I'd rather be at home with my dog, a book and bed.' What happened to the cat?
What they say: 'I felt immediately that I'd found a miracle.' Director Bernardo Bertolucci on their first meeting

Kate Winslet

Not since the eruption of Julia Ormond has an English rose vaulted from obscurity to stardom with such velocity. From her big-screen debut in a New Zealand film to the lead in one of the most expensive epics ever made, Ms Winslet took just two years. Since then Julia Ormond disappointed her devotees as Sabrina Fairchild, and Kate Winslet moved into prime place on the British map.

Hardly drop-dead beautiful in the tradition of Julie Christie or Charlotte Rampling, Our Kate was pretty enough, and displayed a remarkable talent for one so young.

Following in the footsteps of her grandparents, uncle, father and older sister, Winslet made her acting debut in a Sugar Puffs commercial at thirteen. She then trod on and off the boards for four years until trumping 175 actresses for the lead role of real-life killer Juliet Hulme in *Heavenly Creatures*. A low-budget feature shot by New Zealand's splatter king Peter Jackson (*Bad Taste*, *Meet the Feebles*, *Braindead*), *Creatures* went on to confound the critics and win countless international awards, including a trophy for Winslet as Best British Actress bestowed by the London Film Critics' Circle.

From there, aged eighteen, she won the key role of Marianne Dashwood opposite Emma Thompson in *Sense and Sensibility*, and took home an Oscar nomination and a BAFTA for best supporting actress. She then caused a storm at Cannes for her portrayal of Sue Bridehead in Thomas Hardy's *Jude*, abandoning her petticoat and stays for scenes of full frontal nudity. The Hardy Society and the editor of *Thomas Hardy Journal* threw up their arms in dismay, but Kate countered that the sex scenes were 'perfectly natural', adding, 'The language is so contemporary and what happens is so of today that you could have put us in jeans and T-shirts and it would have been exactly the same.'

She next played Ophelia to Kenneth Branagh's Hamlet, with a supporting cast that included Gerard Depardieu, Robin Williams, Billy Crystal, Jack Lemmon, Julie Christie and Charlton Heston, and was then signed up by James Cameron to star in his $100 million blockbuster *Titanic*, which some insiders predict could end up being the most expensive film ever made (give or take *Waterworld*).

FACT FILE:

Born: Reading, Berkshire; October, 1975
TV: *Get Back*; *Shrinks*; *Anglo-Saxon Attitudes*; *Dark Season*; *Casualty*
The forgettable movie: Disney's *A Kid in King Arthur's Court* (as the Arthurian Princess Sarah)
Guilty secret: Nicknamed 'Blubber' at school (but, then, she was 13 stone)
Love of her life: *Hamlet* co-star Rufus Sewell
What they say: 'Kate impressed me straight away as an actress with enormous range' (award-winning director Peter Jackson); 'Who is this girl? She's one of the most amazing actors I have ever seen!' (Oscar-winning director and executive producer of *Sense and Sensibility* Sydney Pollack)
Penetrating quote: 'I sometimes ask myself, Is this all happening to me?'

god Steven Tyler (of Aerosmith), Liv started modelling at fourteen. 'I had auditioned for several films and had been offered roles in some very popular films, but I felt the characters weren't right for me somehow,' she says. 'I wanted to hold out for something that had it all.'

That something was the role of Sylvie Warden in Bruce Beresford's *Silent Fall*, an eighteen-year-old girl who may or may not have witnessed the horrific slaughter of her parents. 'I saw hundreds of actresses, many of them quite well known,' recalls Beresford. 'But it was hard to find someone who could be mature as well as emotionally child-like. There was a curious mixture about Liv Tyler that could make the part work.'

The film was not a success and neither was the low-budget *Heavy*, in

Film World Diary

James Cameron-Wilson

July 1995 – June 1996

July 1995

Eva Gabor, 74, dies in Los Angeles of respiratory distress. She will of course be best remembered for her role as Lisa Douglas in TV's *Green Acres* ✳ **Hugh Grant** goes on *The Tonight Show with Jay Leno* and faces stiff questions about his misdemeanour with prostitute **Divine Brown**. The audience loves him and forgives him ✳ In Dublin to star in the black comedy *Divine Rapture*, **Marlon Brando** announces that he plans to take up Irish citizenship ✳ **Elizabeth Hurley** accompanies **Hugh Grant** to the Hollywood première of *Nine Months* – and looks none too happy ✳ Disney offers **Mel Gibson** $20 million to star in *Ransom* ✳ *Batman Forever* grosses $150m in the US ✳ **Larry Clark**'s controversial low-budget *Kids*, an everyday story of sex and 12 year olds, is refused an R rating in the US. The film's distributor, Excalibur, will now release the film unrated ✳ *Batman Forever* trounces box-office records in the UK, amassing £1,238,085 on its first day ✳ T-shirts selling outside the Hollywood Municipal Courthouse where **Divine Brown** pleads not guilty to lewd conduct: 'To Err is Hughman … To Forgive is Divine' ✳ The character actor **Harry Guardino**, 69, dies of lung cancer in Palm Springs. His many screen credits included *Houseboat*, *Dirty Harry*, *The Enforcer* and *Any Which Way You Can* ✳ In the US, *Showgirls* becomes the first studio picture in five years to be branded with a dreaded NC-17 rating. The last major picture so rated was Universal's *Henry and June* (1990), a box-office disappointment ✳ *Pocahontas* becomes the second release of 1995 to pass the $100m mark in the US ✳ *Divine Rapture*, the $25m comedy shooting in County Cork starring **Marlon Brando**, **Johnny Depp**, **Debra Winger** and **John Hurt**, is abandoned mid-shoot when the financing collapses ✳ *Apollo 13* grosses $100m in the US ✳ **Miklos Rozsa**, 88, dies of pneumonia in Los Angeles. A versatile and prolific composer, Rozsa was nominated for 17 Oscars and won the

Elizabeth Hurley: none too pleased

Hugh Grant: Tonight, *a speeding ticket and a fat pay cheque*

statuette for *Spellbound*, *A Double Life* and *Ben-Hur* ✳ After seven years of marriage and the recent birth of their son, **Val Kilmer** and **Joanne Whalley-Kilmer** separate ✳ The Walt Disney Company buys a chunk of Times Square in New York to develop into an urban 'theme park' ✳ **Pamela Anderson** suffers a miscarriage ✳ In a controversial interview with *The Sunday Times* **Michael Caine** accuses his colleagues **Peter O'Toole**, **Richard Harris** and **Richard Burton** of being 'drunks,' adding, 'but at least it takes 25 years to kill yourself with it.'

August 1995

The Walt Disney Company buys the major American TV network ABC for $12 billion ✳ **Ida Lupino**, 77, dies of cancer in Burbank, California ✳ In an angry letter to *The Sunday Times* **Richard Harris** accuses **Michael Caine** of being a 'fat, flatulent 62-year-old windbag, a master of inconse-

quence masquerading as a guru.' Caine replied that he was not interested in reading the letter – 'and that's my only comment,' the actor said ✳ Universal Pictures offers **Jim Carrey** $20 million to star in *Liar, Liar* ✳ The actress **Tilda Swinton**, star of Sally Potter's *Orlando*, becomes an art exhibit at London's Serpentine Gallery, where she is to sleep in a glass case for eight hours a day. The work, titled *The Maybe*, is intended to examine 'the unconscious state and the enigma of mortality' ✳ **Don Johnson** denies tabloid rumours that he's having an affair with **Oprah Winfrey** ✳ **Heidi Fleiss**, 'madam to the stars', is found guilty on eight charges of money laundering and tax evasion. She faces a maximum penalty of 120 years in prison ✳ **Phil Harris**, 89, band leader, comic, singer and the voice of Baloo the Bear in *The Jungle Book* and Thomas O'Malley the alley cat in *The Aristocats*, dies of heart failure in Rancho Mirage, California. His wife, **Alice Faye**, 83, was at his side ✳ **Anna Nicole Smith**, 27, fights over the body of her late husband, the multi-millionaire **J. Howard Marshall**, who has died aged 90. She wants him buried in a mausoleum, but Marshall's family want him cremated ✳ **Howard Koch**, 93, who won an Oscar for his screenplay to *Casablanca*, dies of pneumonia in Kingston, New York. His other credits include *The Sea Hawk*, *Sergeant York*, *The Best Years of Our Lives* and *Letter From an Unknown Woman* ✳ **Hugh Grant** is fined £125 (with £25 costs) for speeding down the A38 in Devon at 98mph ✳ CAA superagent **Michael Ovitz** takes over as president of the Walt Disney Company ✳ *Apollo 13* grosses $150 million in the US ✳ In a court hearing in Houston, Texas, a settlement is reached between the actress-model **Anna Nicole Smith** and the family of her late husband, **J. Howard Marshall**, whose ashes will be shared among the opposing parties. There is now the question of Marshall's fortune, estimated to be worth $450 million ... ✳ *Casper* grosses $200 million worldwide ✳ **Elizabeth Taylor**, 63, separates from her eighth husband, former truck driver **Larry Fortensky**, 43. The couple were married in October of 1991 ✳ **Frank Perry**, 65, director of *David and Lisa*, *Diary of a Mad Housewife*, *Mommie Dearest* and *Hello Again*, dies of prostate cancer in New York.

September 1995

Batman Forever grosses $315 million worldwide ✳ Following a prodigious career of womanising, **Charlie Sheen**, 30, finally ties the knot – with model **Donna Peele**, 25 ✳ *Street Fighter* grosses $100m worldwide ✳ **Divine Brown** (aka Stella Marie Thompson), the prostitute caught *in flagrante delicto* with **Hugh Grant** last June, is sentenced to six months in prison for violating an earlier probation and for failing to surrender. 'It's great being famous,' she says ✳ *Apollo 13* grosses $200m worldwide ✳ **Christopher Reeve** is told by doctors that he will never walk again ✳ Castle Rock Entertainment is to pay **Hugh Grant** $6 million to appear in their thriller *Extreme Measures*. **Elizabeth Hurley**, star of such British duds as *Beyond Bedlam* and *Mad Dogs and Englishmen*, will produce ✳ *Bad Boys* grosses $138 million worldwide ✳ One month after losing her eighth husband, **Elizabeth Taylor** is admitted to hospital in Santa Monica, California, suffering from an irregular heart beat ✳ **Martin Lawrence** signs up for a $20 million three-picture contract with Columbia Pictures ✳ Time Warner buys the Turner Broadcasting System for $7.3 billion, providing media mogul **Ted Turner** with ten per cent of the Time Warner pie ✳ *Die Hard With a Vengeance* grosses $245 million worldwide ✳ Britain's National Lottery awards £2.32 million to six indigenous features, including *The Woodlanders*, *Crime Time*, *Love and Death on Long Island* and *Gallivant* ✳ *Casper* grosses $100m in the US ✳ The state of Alabama refuses to show *Showgirls* ✳ **Kenneth Branagh** and **Emma Thompson** separate, with the Oscar-winning actress now 'seeing' **Greg Wise**, her co-star from *Sense and Sensibility*.

October 1995

After 266 days, the jury in the **O.J. Simpson** trial finds the defendant not guilty of the murder of his ex-wife Nicole and her companion Ronald Goldman ✳ *Outbreak* grosses $190m worldwide ✳ DreamWorks SKG signs a five-year 'output deal' with the BBC ✳ **Ted Danson** and **Mary Steenburgen** tie the knot – in the presence of

President Clinton ✻ Six hours before **O.J. Simpson** is due to be questioned by **Tom Brokaw** and **Katie Couric** on *Dateline NBC* – in his first TV interview since his trial – he pulls out ✻ Following the success of *Dangerous Minds*, scripter **Ronald Bass** flogs his *My Best Friend's Wedding* screenplay to TriStar for $2 million upfront ✻ **Pamela Anderson** is hospitalised after collapsing at her home. Insiders hint that the *Baywatch* star may have taken an overdose of sleeping pills following a row with her husband ✻ *Die Hard With a Vengeance* grosses $100 million in the US – after 21 weeks ✻ **Giancarlo Parretti**, former owner of MGM, is arrested in Los Angeles on charges of fraud and embezzlement ✻ *Waterworld* grosses $200 million worldwide ✻ **Clint Eastwood** wins $150,000 in damages from the *National Enquirer* over a fabricated 'exclusive interview' with the magazine ✻ *Die Hard With a Vengeance* grosses $350m worldwide ✻ **Simon Perry**, chief executive of British Screen Finance, announces his imminent resignation ✻ **John Calley**, head of United Artists, marries actress **Meg Tilly** ✻ **Viveca Lindfors**, 74, the Swedish actress, dies of pneumonic complications in Uppsala, Sweden. Her films included *The Adventures of Don Juan* (1948) opposite Errol Flynn, *Dark City*, *Four in a Jeep*, *Welcome to LA* and *Stargate* ✻ **Kim Basinger** and **Alec Baldwin** are the proud parents of a baby girl, Ireland Eliesse ✻ The beloved character actress **Mary Wickes**, 85, dies from post-surgery complications in Los Angeles. Her films included *The Man Who Came to Dinner*, *Now Voyager*, *The Trouble With Angels*, *Sister Act* and *Little Women* ✻ In spite of the dire box-office performance of *Showgirls* and *Jade*, screenwriter **Joe Eszterhas** is getting $2.5 million for his screenplay *Blaze of Glory*. Universal Pictures is handing out the readies ✻ **Roland Joffé**, the acclaimed British director of *The Killing Fields* and *The Mission*, is in talks to direct **Steven Seagal** in *The Glimmer Man*. Sounds crazy, but then Seagal could give Joffé some box-office muscle and, in return, Joffé could give Seagal some class ✻ The character actress **Rosalind Cash**, 56, dies of cancer in Los Angeles. Her credits include the female lead in *The Omega Man* and *Uptown Saturday Night*.

November 1995

Paula Barbieri, the woman expected to marry **O.J. Simpson** soon after his acquittal, announces the end of their relationship. Having remained celibate during her lover's trial, the 28-year-old model says she was shocked when Simpson suggested they pose for photographs for an undisclosed sum ✻ The scenarist and playwright **John Patrick**, aged 90, commits suicide by pulling a plastic bag over his head. His films numbered *Three Coins in the Fountain*, *Love is a Many Splendored Thing* and *High Society*, and his plays included *The Hasty Heart* and *Teahouse of the August Moon* ✻ **Emma Thompson** splits up with her boyfriend **Greg Wise**, the latter reputedly being the reason for her separation from **Kenneth Branagh** ✻ *Pocahontas* grosses $200m worldwide ✻ Carolco Pictures, the film company responsible for such box-office hits as *Terminator 2*, *Total Recall* and *Basic Instinct*, files for Chapter 11 bankruptcy protection ✻ Following the success of *Get Shorty*, **John Travolta**'s agent has hauled the actor's price tag up to $21 million. That would make Travolta the highest paid actor of all time – should any film studio take the bait ✻ Plans are unveiled for a new British film studio – Third Millennium Studios – on the 300-acre site of the Leavesdern Aerodrome, Hertfordshire, where *Goldeneye* was shot ✻ The wife of **Frank Langella** files for divorce after 18 years of marriage. Langella, whose films number *Dracula*, *Dave* and *CutThroat Island*, has been inseparable from **Whoopi Goldberg** since the summer when they made *Eddie* together ✻ **Julia Ormond** signs a two-year first-look production deal with Miramax Films ✻ *Apollo 13* grosses $300m worldwide ✻ *First Knight* grosses $120m worldwide ✻ **Sir Robert Stephens** dies, aged 64 ✻ **Barry Sonnenfeld**, director of *The Addams Family*, *Addams Family Values* and *Get Shorty*, signs a two-year first-look production deal with Walt Disney Pictures ✻ *Goldeneye* breaks box-office records at London's Odeon Leicester Square, where the film amasses £41,986 in only four performances ✻ *Ace Ventura: When Nature Calls* grosses a staggering $45,510,178 in its first week on release in the US. How much will they be paying **Jim Carrey** next

year? ✻ In the US, *Goldeneye* becomes the biggest opening James Bond film yet, grossing $26,205,007 in its first weekend. The figure is also a record opening for MGM/UA ✻ **Louis Malle**, 63, dies of lymphoma complications at his home in Beverly Hills ✻ **Whoopi Goldberg** files for separation from her husband of one year, union leader **Lyle Trachtenberg** ✻ **Michelle Pfeiffer** signs a two-year first-look deal with the Walt Disney Company ✻ **John Singleton**, director of *Boyz N the Hood*, *Poetic Justice* and *Higher Learning*, signs a two-year first-look deal with Universal Pictures ✻ *Species* grosses $100m worldwide.

December 1995

The Ritzy Cinema in Brixton, London, hosts the first **Carole Bouquet** film season in Britain (although the actress's turn in the Bond film *For Your Eyes Only* will not be represented) ✻ **Robert Parrish** dies in Long Island, aged 79. A child actor and Oscar-winning editor, Parrish directed his first picture (*Cry Danger*) in 1951 and went on to make such films as *The San Francisco Story*, *Fire Down Below*, *Casino Royale* and *The Marseille Contract* ✻ *Congo* grosses $150m worldwide ✻ *The Bridges of Madison County* grosses $170m worldwide ✻ *Under Siege 2* grosses $100m worldwide ✻ Following the catastrophic opening of *Cut-Throat Island* in the US, Mario Kassar, the film's spendthrift producer, signs a three-year deal with Paramount Pictures ✻ **Jane Seymour** and **James Keach** are the proud parents of twin boys ✻ *Ace Ventura: When Nature Calls* grosses $100m in the US – in just over five weeks ✻ **Butterfly McQueen**, 84, most famous for playing Prissy in *Gone With the Wind*, dies following a kerosene fire in her home in Augusta, Georgia ✻ *Toy Story* grosses $100m in the US – in just under five weeks ✻ **Dean Martin**, 78, dies of respiratory failure in Beverly Hills on Christmas morning ✻ *Toy Story* passes the $150m mark in the US ✻ The Oscar-nominated costume designer **Richard Hornung**, 45, dies from complications of Aids in Los Angeles. His credits numbered *Raising Arizona*, *Barton Fink*, *City Hall* and *Nixon* ✻ *Goldeneye* grosses $225,000,007 worldwide.

January 1996

Anthony Hopkins leaves his wife of 23 years for American actress **Joyce Ingalls** ✳ **John Hargreaves**, 50, dies in Sydney after a long illness. One of the leading actors of the Australian New Wave, Hargreaves notched up such credits as *Don's Party, Careful, He Might Hear You, My First Wife, Malcolm* and *Country Life* ✳ *Apollo 13* grosses $350 million worldwide ✳ **Patsy Kensit** separates from her husband of four years, Jim Kerr, lead singer of Simple Minds ✳ **Emma Thompson** wins the Golden Globe for her screenplay to *Sense and Sensibility* and delivers an acceptance speech inspired by Jane Austen: 'I can't thank you enough for honouring me in this capacity. It is horribly gratifying. I'm bloated with pride.' ✳ *Dangerous Minds* grosses $100m worldwide ✳ **Marlee Matlin** gives birth to Sarah Rose Grandalski, the same night that her character in *Picket Fences* gives birth on TV. Spooky ✳ **Don Simpson**, 52, dies in Bel-Air, Los Angeles. With his professional partner **Jerry Bruckheimer**, Simpson produced *Flashdance, Beverly Hills Cop, Top Gun, Bad Boys, Crimson Tide* and *Dangerous Minds*, among others ✳ *Goldeneye* grosses $100m in the US ✳ **Jamie Uys**, 74, the South African director of the Golden Globe-winning documentary *Beautiful People* (1974) and the surprise international hit *The Gods Must Be Crazy* (1981) dies of a heart attack in Johannesburg ✳ *Goldeneye* grosses $300m worldwide.

February 1996

Following a series of strokes, **Gene Kelly**, 83, dies at his home in Beverly Hills ✳ *Dangerous Minds* grosses $100m worldwide ✳ **Joan Collins** is sued by her publisher, Random House, for the return of their $1.2 million advance to the actress for writing two novels. Ms Collins, who has counter-sued for the balance of her $4 million contract, argues that she delivered two completed manuscripts as promised. Random House contends that her first novel, *A Ruling Passion*, is unprintable ✳ **Guy Madison**, 74, erstwhile matinee idol, dies of emphysema at the Desert Hospital Hospice in Palm Springs, California ✳ After two

hours of deliberation a Manhattan jury finds **Joan Collins** not guilty of failing to fulfil her contract to write a 600-page manuscript, *A Ruling Passion*, for the publishers Random House. However, the jury felt that Ms Collins' second novel, *Hell Hath No Fury*, was not up to scratch. Anyway, the literary actress will be able to retain her $1.2 million advance and is still owed a substantial sum from her publisher ✳ *Die Hard With a Vengeance* grosses $365m worldwide, making it the highest-grossing picture of 1995 ✳ Miramax Films and director **Michael Caton-Jones** come to blows over the casting of the central role in the London-set *B. Monkey*. Following the audition of 300 actresses, Caton-Jones settled on **Sophie Okenedo** (*Young Soul Rebels*), but was then told Miramax wanted a 'star', like **Drew Barrymore**. The director refused to back down over his choice and was dismissed from the project. Enter **Michael Radford**, fresh from his success with Miramax's *Il Postino*, who admitted he loved the script of *B. Monkey*. But then he also thought Sophie Okenedo would be perfect for the central role. The case continues ... ✳ The character actor **Martin Balsam**, 76, is found dead on the floor of his hotel room in Rome. The winner of an Oscar for *A Thousand Clowns*, Balsam also made appearances in *On the Waterfront, Psycho* and Scorsese's *Cape Fear* ✳ *French Kiss* grosses $100m worldwide ✳ Due to the outrage and disappointment of certain figures in the French cultural establishment, the world première of *The Hunchback of Notre Dame* is switched from Paris to New Orleans ✳ *Seven* grosses $300m worldwide ✳ **Haing S. Ngor**, the Cambodian doctor who won an Oscar for his portrayal of Dith Pran in *The Killing Fields*, is shot dead outside his apartment in Chinatown, Los Angeles. Ngor's film credits also included roles in *My Life* and *Heaven and Earth* ✳ **Katharine Hepburn**, 88, is hospitalised with pneumonia. One source said doctors thought her condition was fatal ✳ *Heat* grosses $100m worldwide.

March 1996

Katharine Hepburn is discharged from Manhattan's Lenox Hill Hospital ✳ Former Wimbledon champion **Andre Agassi**, 25, proposes to

Brooke Shields, 30, under a Hawaiian waterfall. She says 'yea' ✳ **George Burns** dies in Beverly Hills, six weeks after his hundredth birthday. Cause of death is not given ✳ To mark the centenary of the cinema, the Vatican releases a hallowed list of 45 films chosen for their 'religious content, spiritual values and artistic excellence,' including works by Chaplin, Ford, Capra, Bergman, Fellini and, more surprisingly, Bunuel and Pasolini ✳ **Ross Hunter**, 75, dies of lymphoma in Los Angeles. The prolific producer's credits include *Magnificent Obsession, All That Heaven Allows, Pillow Talk, Imitation of Life, Thoroughly Modern Millie* and *Airport* ✳ **Jason Connery** and actress **Mia Sara** (*Ferris Bueller's Day Off, Legend*) tie the knot in a secret ceremony at a drive-in chapel in Las Vegas ✳ **Vince Edwards**, 67, who played the eponymous young doctor in TV's *Ben Casey* (1960-65), dies of pancreatic cancer in Los Angeles. His film credits include *The Killing, City of Fear, Murder by Contract, The Victors* and *The Devil's Brigade* ✳ **Krzysztof Kieslowski**, 54, dies of heart failure in Warsaw. Considered by many to be one of the greatest of contemporary filmmakers, Kieslowski directed *A Short Film About Killing, A Short Film About Love, The Double Life of Veronique, Three Colours: Blue, Three Colours: White* and *Three Colours: Red*, among others ✳ Following the slaughter of 16 young school children in Dunblane, Scotland, Warner Home Video decides to postpone the release of *Natural Born Killers* 'indefinitely' ✳ The French film director **Rene Clement**, 82, dies of heart complications in Monte Carlo. His films included *Les Jeux Interdits, Knave of Hearts, Plein Soleil, Is Paris Burning?* and *The Deadly Trap* ✳ *Babe* grosses $200m worldwide ✳ *Toy Story* grosses $184,205,561 in the US, making it the No.1 film of 1995 ✳ *Heat* grosses $150m worldwide ✳ Robert Dewey Hoskins, of no fixed abode, is sentenced to ten years in prison for stalking **Madonna** ✳ A settlement is reached out of court between TriStar Pictures, who made *Philadelphia*, and the family of Tom Bowers, the lawyer who died of Aids while fighting his firm for unfair dismissal. Not surprisingly, Bowers' family sued the studio for filming their son's story (without permission or financial compensation) ✳

Alec Baldwin is cleared of charges of assault towards a photographer who attempted to take pictures of the actor's new-born daughter. Had the jury found the actor guilty, he could have faced six months in prison ✳ At the 68th Academy Awards, **Emma Thompson** becomes the first Oscar-winning performer to win an additional trophy for best screenwriter (for *Sense and Sensibility*) ✳ Not long after a stroke, **Kirk Douglas** turns up at the Oscars to receive an honorary award for 'fifty years as a creative and moral force in the motion picture community'. Then, shortly after the ceremony, the actor-producer is rushed to hospital for an emergency heart bypass operation.

April 1996

Il Postino grosses $50m worldwide ✳ *Father of the Bride Part II* grosses $100m worldwide ✳ *Toy Story* grosses $250m worldwide ✳ **Clint Eastwood**, 65, marries TV presenter **Dina Ruiz**, 30, in a secret sunset ceremony in Las Vegas. This comes as something of a surprise to many, since the Oscar-winning director became the proud father of a baby girl just two-and-a-half years ago – courtesy of actress **Frances Fisher** ✳ **Greer Garson**, 92, dies of heart failure, in Dallas ✳ *Babe* is banned in China ✳ Following his comments on the CNN chat show *Larry King Live*, **Marlon Brando** is branded 'The Godfather of Hate' by the Jewish lobby. Brando, who turned down his Oscar for *The Godfather* in protest of Hollywood's representation of the American Indian, noted 'Hollywood is run by Jews, it is owned by Jews and they should have a greater sensitivity about the issue of people who are suffering.' He then went on to complain that, in the cinema, 'we never saw the kike.' Besides having a swastika placed on his plaque on the Hollywood Walk of Fame, the actor receives a letter from the chairman of the Jewish Defence League that reads, 'Shame on you and shame on the next Jew responsible for giving you a job. We're going to make the rest of your life a living hell.' Furthermore, the national president of the Coalition for Jewish Concern calls for the actor to be completely boycotted by the cinema and television industry ✳ It's official: **Gre-**

gory Peck, 80, announces his retirement from acting ✳ **Ben Johnson** dies of an apparent heart attack in Mesa, Arizona. Johnson, who was 77, won an Oscar in 1972 for his performance in *The Last Picture Show* and also notched up appearances in *She Wore a Yellow Ribbon*, *Shane*, *The Wild Bunch*, *The Getaway*, *The Sugarland Express* and *The Evening Star* ✳ **Sean Pean** and **Robin Wright** tie the knot ✳ The actress **Alison Steadman** (*Clockwise*, *Life is Sweet*) leaves film director **Mike Leigh**, her husband of 22 years, for **Michael Elwyn**, her co-star from TV's *No Bananas* ✳ *Babe* is given permission to be shown in China. Will sweet and sour pork ever be the same again? ✳ Following 'creative differences,' **Meg Ryan** drops out of New Line's *Easy Women*. Word has it that there's nothing easy about Ms Ryan, who's still due to team up with **Julia Roberts** in (just) *The Women* ✳ **Madonna**, 36, announces her four-month pregnancy from the Budapest set of *Evita*. The proud father-to-be is physical fitness trainer Carlos Leon, 29 ✳ *Jumanji*, starring **Robin**

Dustin Hoffman: complaints to the press

Williams, grosses $100m at the US box-office in 18 weeks ✳ *The Birdcage*, starring **Robin Williams**, grosses $100m at the US box-office in six weeks ✳ **Margot Kidder** is found hiding in the back garden of a house in Glendale, Los Angeles. According to police, the actress was 'frightened and paranoid', and in 'obvious mental distress', with her hair shaved off by a safety razor and her two front teeth knocked out. She is taken to hospital for psychiatric assessment ✳ **Tomas Gutierrez Alea**, 69, the Cuban director of *Strawberry and Chocolate*, dies of lung cancer in Havana ✳ **Donald Cammell**, 62, director of *Performance*, *Demon Seed*, *White of the Eye* and *The Wild Side*, dies from 'a self-inflicted bullet wound' at his home in Los Angeles ✳ **Gerard Depardieu** is presented with the Chevallier de la Legion d'Honneur by Jacques Chirac.

May 1996

In a public tirade at the Cannes film festival, **Dustin Hoffman** accuses Hollywood of promoting violence, citing Dunblane and Port Arthur as typical consequences ✳ *Get Shorty* grosses

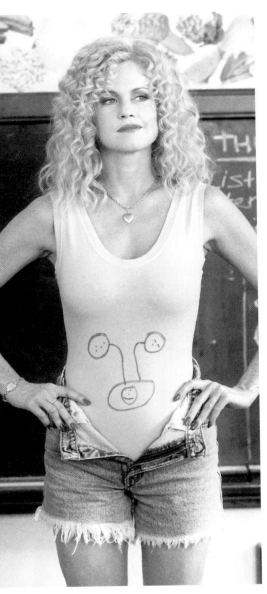

Melanie Griffith: wedding bells

pathetic woman ✳ *Twister* grosses $57,982,084 in its first week in the US ✳ **Melanie Griffith** and **Antonio Banderas** tie the knot in London ✳ Rumours abound that **Richard Gere** and actress **Carey Lowell** (*Licence to Kill*, *The Guardian*) are to get hitched ✳ *Mission: Impossible* grosses a record $56,811,602 in its opening weekend in the US (the previous record holder being *Batman Forever*, with $53.3m) ✳ **Keanu Reeves** crashes his motorcycle ✳ *Twister* grosses a phenomenal $151.7m in three weeks ✳ Following a 17-hour labour, **Pamela Anderson Lee** gives birth to a 7lb 7oz baby boy, Brandon Thomas ✳ **Norman René**, 45, director of the Aids drama *Longtime Companion*, dies from complications of Aids in Manhattan ✳ **Halle Berry** announces that her three-year marriage to baseball star **David Justice** is over ✳ The film producer and former vice president of Universal Pictures, **Jennings Lang**, 81, dies of pneumonia in Palm Desert, California. Besides his championship of Sensurround, the sound system developed in the mid-1970s, Lang will be remembered for such films as *Coogan's Bluff*, *Airport 1975* and *Earthquake* ✳ **John Travolta**, who was to be paid $17m for his part, clashes with director **Roman Polanski** on the Paris set of *The Double* and walks off the film. Apparently, a nude scene had been added to the script which the actor objected to.

June 1996

Jodie Foster clashes with Propaganda Films over her role opposite **Michael Douglas** in the psychological thriller *The Game*. The company turns to **Jeff Bridges** to replace her. Huh? ✳ **Michael Bay**, director of *Bad Boys* and *The Rock*, ties up a staggering two-picture deal with Disney worth $12 million, making him one of the highest paid filmmakers of all time ✳ *Twister* grosses $200 million worldwide – in just five weeks ✳ **Martin Clunes** gets a 'quickie' divorce from his wife, the actress Lucy Aston ✳ **Dudley Moore**, 5'2", files for divorce from his fourth wife, Nicole, 5'10". The 61-year-old comic and pianist was previously married to Suzy Kendall, Tuesday Weld and Brogan Lane ✳ **Arnold**

Schwarzenegger is reportedly to be paid a record $25m (on top of a share of the profits and merchandising revenue) to play Mr Freeze in *Batman and Robin* – for six weeks' work. **George Clooney**, as Batman, will pocket $10m ($8m more than the last Caped Crusader, **Val Kilmer**) ✳ Apprehended by police in Malibu, **Robert Downey Jr** is charged with driving under the influence of alcohol, carrying a handgun and possessing drugs ✳ *Mission: Impossible* grosses $150m in the US ✳ After **Al Pacino**, **Robert De Niro** and **Sean Penn** say 'non', **Steve Martin** is hired as a replacement for **John Travolta** in Roman Polanski's troubled production of *The Double* ✳ **Demi Moore** shows off her new bald look at the New York première of *Striptease*. She has shaved her hair for her role as a navy rating in **Ridley Scott**'s *G.I. Jane* ✳ **Isabella Adjani** walks off **Roman Polanksi**'s *The Double* after **Steve Martin** is hired to replace **John Travolta**. Mlle Adjani maintains that she had casting approval but was not consulted ✳ Following reports in the press that she had walked off **David Fincher**'s *The Game*, **Jodie Foster** hits back with a £36 million lawsuit against PolyGram, stipulating that she was unfairly dismissed from the production ✳ **Phil Alden Robinson**, the director of *Field of Dreams* and *Sneakers*, returns two library books he checked out in June of 1970. With a fine of 10 cents a day, he owed $1,900 – and paid it ✳ **Oliver Stone** and Warner Brothers are sued for $30 million by Patsy Ann Byers for encouraging violence in their film *Natural Born Killers*. According to Sarah Edmondson, the eighteen-year-old daughter of a judge, she and her boyfriend (Benjamin Durrus) went on a cross-country crime spree after seeing the film. Sarah herself shot Patsy Ann in the throat, causing the latter paralysis from the neck down. Under America's 'product liability laws', both Stone and Warner Brothers can be accountable for the crime ✳ After French actress **Carol Bouquet** (*For Your Eyes Only*, *Trop Belle Pour Toi!*) turns down the female lead in *The Double*, **Roman Polanski** abandons the film ✳ *Twister* grosses $200m in the US ✳ **Anthony Quinn**, 81, is rushed into the heart unit of Rhode Island Hospital, New York ✳ *Jumanji* grosses $250m worldwide.

$110m worldwide ✳ **Jack Weston**, 71, dies of cancer in New York. The mournful character actor appeared in such movies as *Wait Until Dark*, *Cactus Flower*, *A New Leaf*, *Fuzz*, *The Ritz*, *The Four Seasons* and *Ishtar* ✳ **Bo Derek** cancels her appearance on ITV's *Tonight with Richard Madeley and Judy Finnigan*, to avoid appearing alongside **O.J. Simpson** ✳ **Brenda Blethyn**, whose last film role was as Brad Pitt's mother in *A River Runs Through It*, is voted Best Actress at Cannes for her performance in *Secrets & Lies* – as England's most

Film
Soundtracks

**James
Cameron-Wilson**

Having exorcised my grievances about film music in last year's annual, I thought I'd concentrate on the positive this time round. So, rather than dissect the commercial success of such soundtracks as *Dangerous Minds*, *Batman Forever* and *Waiting to Exhale*, allow me to introduce a counterpoint to *Time* magazine's Man of the Year: *Film Review*'s Composer of the Year.

Composer of the Year

PATRICK DOYLE

A graduate of the Royal Scottish Academy for Music and Drama, the Scottish-born Doyle wrote music for a number of theatre productions before enlisting with Kenneth Branagh's Renaissance Theatre Company as actor, composer and musical director. It was Branagh who gave Doyle his first chance to score a movie, and the latter's rousing, symphonic composition for *Henry V* heralded the arrival of a major new talent. Indeed, Doyle's 'Non Nobis' theme was awarded the Ivor Novello Award of 1989. He was also commissioned by Prince Charles to write a song cycle for choir and orchestra, 'The Thistle and the Rose,' in honour of the Queen Mother's 90th birthday.

Since then Doyle has written for such films as *Into the West*, *Much Ado About Nothing* and *Carlito's Way*, and has clocked up a Golden Globe nomination for his music to *Dead Again* and a Cesar nomination for *Indochine*.

But this last year the 42-year-old composer has really come into his own.

His scores for *A Little Princess* and *Sense and Sensibility* are two of the best of the year, the latter securing him his first Oscar nomination. Furthermore, Doyle's vibrant, sweeping composition for the romantic French epic *Une Femme Francaise* is about the only living thing in the movie. By the time you read this, Doyle's music for Branagh's four-hour *Hamlet* should already be in the shops.

Not the Composer of the Year

As enthusiastic as I am about the music of Patrick Doyle, I am distressed by the ubiquity of James Newton Howard. Besides his panicked theme tune to *ER* (which rings out in my house every week), there was a period when a Howard score graced a new film each month. Recently, the former husband of Rosanna Arquette and erstwhile boyfriend of Barbra Streisand has composed the soundtracks to *French Kiss*, *Waterworld*, *Eye for an Eye*, *The Juror*, *Primal Fear*, *The Trigger Effect*, and *One Fine Day*.

As is the case with Mark Isham, Howard's music strives too hard to do the acting for the stars. Take a look at *Restoration*. Carried away with his enthusiasm for recreating the spirit of Henry Purcell, Howard whipped up a luxuriant score he couldn't let go of. So, wherever the film goes – into court, the bedroom or the conflagration of London – Howard goes too. Eventually the film is stripped bare of any emotional light and shade and all one is left with is Howard's droning music. Indeed, when the film's key emotional scene finally arrives, the audience barely seems to notice as it sounds just like the one before it.

Original Motion Picture Soundtrack

SENSE AND SENSIBILITY

Music by Patrick Doyle

Soundtracks of the Year

Apollo 13
A comprehensive aural record of one of the year's most successful films, this miraculous album has it all: **James Horner**'s stirring score, a handful of hit songs and Tom Hanks declaring, 'Houston, we have a problem.' Perfect.

Beyond Rangoon
In a career embracing such prestigious titles as *Rain Man*, *Thelma & Louise* and *The Lion King*, **Hans Zimmer** has created one of his most textured, descriptive and moving scores for John Boorman's little-seen epic. Utilising ethnic pipes against a lush symphonic canvas he conjures up an exotic world of enormous emotional range.

Broken Arrow
One of the year's most enjoyable action scores, proving again what a versatile and talented musician the ex-jingles king **Hans Zimmer** has become. Here, he charms his way into John Travolta's charismatic villain with a distinctive phrase provided by Duane Eddy on baritone guitar and then flavours his more frenetic passages with a children's choir. Not to be played while driving the car.

The Brothers McMullen
Blissful, haunting collection of diverse melodies composed by Irish folk musician **Seamus Egan**, performed on guitar, uillean pipes, violin, mandolin, banjo and tin whistle. Possibly the most exquisite soundtrack of the year, capped by the soulful ballad 'I Will Remember You' sung by the incomparable Sarah McLachlan.

Casino
A fabulous treasure trove of golden oldies produced by old Scorsese colleague Robbie Robertson. Besides the customary standards from Dean Martin, Tony Bennett and Cream (the last two featured on *GoodFellas*), there's vintage Ramsey Lewis, Jimmy Smith, Dinah Washington, Lee Dorsey, Eric Burdon and much, much more. The most satisfying compilation since last year's *Forrest Gump*.

Congo
Sterling work from **Jerry Goldsmith**, an epic, vibrant and Afro-centric score, loaded with musical thrills and capped by a rousing ten-and-a-half minute suite, 'Amy's Farewell'/'Spirit of Africa', performed by Lebo M.

Dead Man Walking
A terrific line-up of names and dollops of heartfelt atmosphere make up this intelligent album produced by Tim Robbins. Springsteen, Tom Waits and Michelle Shocked shine, but it is Eddie Vedder and Nusrat Fateh Ali Khan's extraordinary, haunting theme that signs this collection in permanent ink.

Desperado
The best Latino soundtrack of the year, headed by Los Lobos, Dire Straits, Santana and some frenetic electric guitar. Plus a few salient lines from the movie (Banderas: 'Bless me, Father, for I have just killed quite a few men') and a touching ballad from actress Salma Hayek. Finger-clicking good.

Devil in a Blue Dress
Sublimely evocative collection of vintage rhythm 'n' blues, featuring such authentic acts as T-Bone Walker, Jimmy Witherspoon, Pee Wee Crayton and Bull Moose Jackson, as well as the more familiar Duke Ellington and Thelonious Monk. Bliss.

The Englishman Who Went Up a Hill but Came Down a Mountain
Exquisite, textured score from the up-and-coming **Stephen Endelman**, who not only delivers a fine melody, but has created an evocative sound

DESPERADO
THE SOUNDTRACK

that pinpoints the Welsh character. I can't stop playing it.

Farinelli

Every bit as dulcet and addictive as *The Madness of King George* and *Restoration*, this compilation of classical highlights boasts the supplementary distinction of being sung by a eunuch. Well, not quite. Thanks to the technical wizardry of digital recording, the remarkable voice of the castrato Carlo 'Farinelli' Broschi (whose vocal range encompassed three-and-a-half octaves) has been recreated by combining the singing of the counter-tenor Derek Lee Ragin and the soprano Ewa Mallas Godlewska. At times necessitating the fusion to be edited note by note, the initial production took ten months and 3,000 edits. A rare case of art and technology converging to create real magic.

Funny Bones

One of the year's most hybrid albums, stuffed with dialogue, **John Altman**'s incidental score and a raft of tracks never intended to end up on one CD. Thus Charles Trenet's relentlessly jolly 'La Mer' nestles alongside John Lee Hooker's smoky 'Boogie Chillen' and Eartha Kitt's pricelessly camp 'Uska Dara'. Irresistible.

The Hunchback of Notre Dame

Glorious Broadway-style musical from **Menken** and **Schwartz**, every bit as stirring and polished as *Pocahontas*. If the film hadn't been so exceptional, I would have said the score was too good for it. Latin chants courtesy of the Royal Opera Choir, while Tony Jay makes a wonderfully eloquent villain.

Jack and Sarah

Following in the confetti of *Four Weddings and a Funeral*, with chart hits punctuated by snatches of dialogue. Simply Red, East 17, Gabrielle and Annie Lennox lend star power, while the 10.35 minutes of **Simon Boswell**'s incidental composition is most pleasant. Not a great album, but one very successful on its own terms.

A Little Princess

Exquisite score from **Patrick Doyle**, blending Western and Indian themes and capitalising on the magical sound of children's voices (courtesy of the New London Children's Choir).

The Madness of King George

A majestic compilation of melodies by George Frederick Handel, superbly arranged and conducted by the redoubtable **George Fenton**.

Nine Months

When I first listened to this I dismissed it as slight and repetitive. Yet on closer inspection, the delicate, sweet nuances of **Hans Zimmer**'s composition began to emerge. It is in fact a heartfelt, subtle and delightful score, capped by three choice vocals from Little Steven, Marvin Gaye and Tyrone Davis.

Now and Then

Considering the film itself looked like an illustrated greatest hits album, the soundtrack was bound to be good. 'Sugar, Sugar', 'Knock Three Times', 'Band of Gold', 'Daydream Believer', they're all here. Shame about the movie.

Pocahontas

Conveying the complexity and sophistication of a Broadway hit, **Alan Menken** and **Stephen Schwartz**'s rousing, witty score is one of the best ever recorded for a Disney film. Menken, incidentally, won his seventh Oscar for this, and an eighth for the song 'Colors of the Wind'.

Restoration

Opulent, stately and melodious compilation of 17th-century baroque, blending **James Newton Howard**'s contemporary orchestrations with the classical sound of Henry Purcell. For added verisimilitude, there's a wide range of authentic instruments on dis-

SONGS FROM THE FEATURE FILM

Jack & Sarah

Featuring classic tracks & new recordings from

SIMPLY RED · EAST 17 · ANNIE LENNOX · LIGHTHOUSE FAMILY and many more

play, including early cellos and violins and the antiquated theorbo, a large bass lute. A soundtrack to play at your wedding.

Seven

If nothing else, this is the most eclectic soundtrack of the year – and I like that in an album. Besides **Howard Shore**'s menacing suite, the set boasts the driving rock of Gravity Kills, the Country harmony of The Statler Brothers, and Charlie Parker, Thelonious Monk, Marvin Gaye, Haircut 100, Billie Holiday and J.S. Bach. Many sins, indeed, but thankfully not the deadliest of all – rap.

Stonewall

Hyperbole aside, this is the finest set of cuts crammed on to one CD this year (give or take *Casino*). From the gay abandon of The Shangri-Las and The Shirelles to the inspirational Patti La-Belle and her Bluebelles (on 'Down the Aisle') – via the mandatory inclusion of Judy Garland – this soundtrack is ambrosia to the ears, feet and heart.

To Wong Foo, Thanks for Everything! Julie Newmar

The year's most vibrant disco set, with standout turns from Crystal Waters, the rappy Salt-N-Pepa and Patti La-Belle reinventing 'Over the Rainbow' with vitality to spare.

Trainspotting

The 'in' soundtrack of the year, featuring such vital bands as Primal Scream, Sleeper, Blur, Pulp, Elastica, Leftfield, et al. A legend in its own time.

Ulysses' Gaze

An unlikely source of great film music, *Ulysses' Gaze* worked better on the home hi-fi system than in the cinema. Composed by the Greek musician **Eleni Karaindrou**, the music attains enormous emotion through sheer simplicity and subtle phrasing. Ultimately, the most authentic, direct and moving composition since John Williams' *Schindler's List*.

A Walk in the Clouds

Splendid return to form for **Maurice Jarre**, combining his traditional sweep with an exotic Latin air. Includes two vocal tracks written by the film's director, Alfonso Arau.

Bookshelf

James Cameron-Wilson

The Art of Walt Disney, by Christopher Finch; Virgin; £50.00; 456 pages.

I can't help feeling that with all the money at Disney's disposal they could have produced a more generous book than this for the consumer's £50. In spite of its finger-buckling weight and plethora of colourful, bewitching illustrations, it cannot equal the value of, say, Dorling Kindersley's *Chronicle of the Cinema* (a steal at £30) (qv). Having said that, and if money is no obstacle, then this reverent tome is a miracle of production skill and back-slapping bravado. Substantially updated and revised from the previous printing of 1973, *The Art of Walt Disney* takes us on a fascinating voyage from the birth of Walt in 1901 right up to Tokyo Disneyland, Disneyland Paris (previously EuroDisney) and the forthcoming animated features *Hercules* and *Fantasia Continued*.

A Biographical Dictionary of Film, by David Thomson; Andre Deutsch; £14.99; 834 pages.

Yet another biographical dictionary of film, *A Biographical Dictionary of Film* distinguishes itself from sibling volumes by its untethered insight and unabashed wit. In short, it is rather good writing. Thomson describes Woody Allen as 'a Chaplin hero for the chattering classes ... no director works so hard to appear at a loss,' while summarising *Radio Days* as 'a random brainwave in the night'. As for range, the book documents all the great act-ors, producers and directors of the cinema, while periodically embracing other figures, including a hefty three columns devoted to composer Bernard Herrmann and a couple on cinematographer Nestor Almendros. Intriguingly, though, Erich Wolfgang Korngold, Max Steiner, Miklos Rozsa, James Wong Howe, Vittorio Storaro and Sven Nykvist are absent. Updated for the second time in 1994 (previously in 1980), the book, which was originally compiled during the years 1971-75, now includes entries on Demi Moore, Alec Baldwin and even Madeleine Stowe, while scraping shy of Nicolas Cage and Quentin Tarantino. Happily, Thomson is not averse to letting personal favourites rule this meditative, highly individual diary.

Box Office Hits, by Phil Swern; Guinness; £12.99; 447 pages.

Catering to the continuing public hunger for cultural shopping lists, *Box Office Hits* presents a decade-by-decade look at all the films that made the British top ten; then, from 1969, including every film that reached No. 1. Ultimately, however, the book is useless, as it offers no box-office figures. Consequently, there is no way of ascertaining a film's success in relation to another's – a movie placed at No. 1 in February can make a lot less money than one ranked fifth in December. Even the lists of 'Top Male Actors' is pointless, as it fails to reflect the commercial muscle of the stars included. Alec Guinness is listed 11th in the

1969-94 chart, whereas Schwarzenegger comes in at 12th, while Ned Beatty's mighty pulling power puts Kevin Costner in the shade. Beatty may have popped up in more box-office hits, but does that make him a bigger star? A stupid excuse for a book (although the cast lists and synopses may satisfy some fans).

Brando: Songs My Mother Taught Me, by Marlon Brando and Robert Lindsey; Arrow; £6.99; 468 pages.

For students of acting and/or the cinema, the autobiography of Marlon Brando, Hollywood's most enigmatic and charismatic star, should hold some interest. Of course, any autobiography must be filtered through subjective memory and Brando's makes no bones about it. This is no juicy kiss-and-tell disclosure. However, the fact that it is by Brando himself – shaped with an objective hand by Robert Lindsey (collaborator on Ronald Reagan's *An American Life*) – deserves our undivided attention. While refusing to talk about his wives and children, the actor pulls no punches when it comes to other aspects of his remarkable life. Straight off he calls his father 'a card-carrying prick' and the legendary acting guru Lee Strasberg 'a man for whom I had little respect … After I had some success, Lee Strasberg tried to take credit for teaching me how to act. He never taught me anything.' Chaplin suffers worse: 'Chaplin was probably the most sadistic man I'd ever met. He was an egotistical tyrant and a penny-pincher.' Marilyn Monroe, Montgomery Clift and James Dean come off better. There is, none the less, much rambling: Brando pontificating on acting, mythology, Shakespeare, celebrity, racism, psychoanalysis, Native Americans, John Hurt and what-have-you. There's even a whole chapter devoted to his pet raccoon Russell. This is a shame, as much of Brando's stream of consciousness is repetitive and slows down an incredible story.

Brewer's Cinema, edited by Jonathan Law; Cassell; £20.00; 617 pages.

With the market flooded by film reference books it seems foolhardy to join the race at this late stage. Still, with the cinema celebrating its centenary, it was inevitable that publishers would use this as a peg for more titles. Now comes the turn of the venerable Brewer's, whose laudable *Dictionary of Phrase and Fable* has been sitting by my desk since I started writing professionally 20 years ago. Subtitled *A Phrase and Fable Dictionary*, this handsome tome, running to 617 pages, follows in the thumb prints of Halliwell's *Filmgoer's Companion* (qv) and Ephraim Katz's exhaustive *International Film Encyclopaedia*. Authoritative and eminently readable, it is as commendable for its range as it is capricious in its omissions (Keanu Reeves is in, Christian Slater is out; Dan Aykroyd in, Bill Murray out, etc). Covering classic films, themes, terms and personalities, the volume aims for entertainment and essence rather than bulk and comprehension. Mistakes, of course, are inevitable, although there are rather a lot of them. In the Susan Sarandon entry alone it is claimed that the actress married Tim Robbins and received her first Oscar nomination for *Thelma & Louise*. In fact, Sarandon and Robbins have never married and she received her first nomination for *Atlantic City*. Worse, factual statements contradict each other, depending on where you dip: under Dennis Hopper, *Easy Rider*'s gross is cited as 'some $16 million', but under *Easy Rider* itself the figure has climbed to $50m. And what can you say of a reference book that claims 'by 1989 he [Schwarzenegger] was able to command a fee of $25 million for *Twins*'? Phooey! Another quibble: entrants with a popular surname (Howard, Taylor, York, etc) are lumped together and lost in the text. Thus, it's far easier to locate, say, Akira Kurosawa than it is to find Roland Young. Perhaps not a volume one would recommend to film buffs, so much as a diverting distraction for every home with an inquisitive general interest.

Chronicle of the Cinema, edited by Robyn Karney; Dorling Kindersley; £29.95; 920 pages.

The ultimate browse. Weighing in at a shelf-winging six pounds, this mammoth treasure chest of facts and photographs surveys the century of cinema from the first projection of Thomas Edison's films in 1894 (in New York, on 5 February) to the triumph of *Forrest Gump* at the 1995 Oscar ceremony. Divided into 101 colossal chapters that include colourful stills, classic posters, a list of the main Oscar winners for each year, births of future luminaries and news stories, the book captures the imagination and seduces the eye. Beyond this, the substantial index at the back quickly draws the researcher to any relevant passage. By dint of its prodigious range and substantial illustration, the volume's coverage of individual films and artists is limited, but then these are chronicled extensively in other publications. No, the book's true pleasure is experienced by lying it flat out on the carpet, sprawling over it and flicking through all those colourful memories.

Cinemania '96, Microsoft; £29.99.

While this CD-ROM is not a book by any stretch of the imagination, I include it here as a handy companion to the other guides reviewed. The cross-referencing joys of any CD-ROM needs no explanation – suffice it to say that you can find yourself whipping from *It Happened One Night* to a profile and filmography of Clark Gable to *Gone With the Wind* to hearing Vivien Leigh declare 'As God is my witness, I'll never be hungry again!' to Laurence Olivier and, via *Bunny Lake is Missing*, to Keir Dullea – and before you know it you are watching a scene from *2001: A Space Odyssey*: all at the click of your mouse! With cast lists, biographies, reviews, stills, sound bites, film clips and no end of little happy extras (such as a step-by-step guide to help you find your subject of choice, even if you've forgotten the name), this is a cineaste-cum-computer nerd's dream come true. It will cost you weeks of your life. N.B. *Cinemania '96*, unlike *Cinemania '95*, will only run on computers installed with Windows '95.

Classic Film Guide, by Simon Rose; HarperCollins; £5.99; 495 pages.

Concise, witty and action-packed, Simon Rose's literary chaperone to the thousand-plus most important films of all time is a delicious browse. Exceedingly well informed, the book jettisons all the chaff to make way for a readable bedside/TV-top companion which is as useful as it is diverting. Blessed with cast lists, quotes, anecdotes and, at the back of the book, a pithy list of biographies and filmographies, the tome concentrates on just those films worth seeing (again and again). If you're a cinematic purist, this is the only book you need.

The Encyclopedia of the Movies, by Derek Winnert; Virgin; £19.99; 304 pages.

Derek Winnert's glossy and attractive companion to the first century of the cinema does not pretend to compete with the other reference books reviewed here. It is, however, a handy and accessible guide, broken up into sensible sections that provide an entertaining overview of the medium. The main bulk of the book is divided into two segments, 126 pages devoted to 500 biographies (including the likes of Drew Barrymore, Zbigniew Cybulski, Max Linder, Sergei Paradjanov, Victor Sjostrom and Harry Dean Stanton – but no composers, cinematographers or writers), and another 88 pages dedicated to 250 'Landmark Movies', arranged by year. There are also useful chapters on a variety of subjects ignored by most guides, including animation, the publicity machine, censorship and underground cinema, as well as the mandatory table of Oscar winners at the back (and a brief list of Palme d'Or victors). On the downside, there are a *lot* of inaccuracies (Sigourney Weaver was born in 1949, not 1945, and *My New Gun* certainly didn't win the Palme d'Or), while the alphabetical arrangement of names credited to the Landmark Movies is extremely misleading (endowing Ray Collins with top-billing in *Citizen Kane* and Rodney Dangerfield top-billing in *Natural Born Killers*).

Gramophone Film Music Good CD Guide, edited by Mark Walker; £8.95; 256 pages.

This is the book I have been waiting for. A devotee of film music, I have always bewailed the absence of a good guide to feed my passion. But here it is: comprehensive reviews of 400 major soundtracks, biographies of composers, discographies, lists of record companies, dealers and mail order services – and a rear index of film titles. So, if you want to find out who wrote the music to *Wyatt Earp*, check the index, leap to the entry on James Newton Howard and discover that he was once a member of Elton John's band and has also written such scores as *The Fugitive* and *Waterworld* (both reviewed) and *Dying Young* and *Junior* (listed, but not reviewed). To save disappointment to collectors, the CDs included in the book are only those that were available at the time of going to press.

Halliwell's Filmgoer's Companion, edited by John Walker; £14.99; 730 pages.

This is an indispensable, prodigious volume of reference, covering themes, personalities, characters, countries, awards, technical terms – all in an easy-to-read A-to-Z format. Now bulging off the bookshelf at 730 pages, the 11th edition of Halliwell's features an additional 29 pages devoted to 'a brief history of the cinema' from 1873 to *Natural Born Killers*. Yet besides its invaluable, accessible coverage of the cinema, it is the little things that make it such a good browse, from the ad hoc quotes littered throughout the book ('cocaine is God's way of saying you're making too much money' – Robin Williams) to the idiosyncratic lists at the back (including a catalogue of *Guardian* readers' 100 favourite contemporary films). On the downside, the filmographies are on the incomplete side (and several in dire need of updating), the inclusion of Oscar nominations erratic from after 1990 and the range of contemporary character actors wanting (there are no entries on Kevin Dunn, R. Lee Ermey, Dan Hedaya, Oliver Platt, Stephen Tobolowsky or Stanley Tucci). Mistakes, too, are inevitable, with Zhang Yimou alphabetically entered under his given name, Mike Leigh credited as the director of *Four Weddings and a Funeral*, Adam Baldwin entered as the brother of Alec Baldwin (he isn't) and, worst of all, the hyphen left out of James Cameron-Wilson.

Halliwell's Film Guide; edited by John Walker; Harper Collins; £16.99; 1,300 pages.

The 11th edition of this mighty tome, *Halliwell's Film Guide* is now bigger than ever before. Besides its enormous compass of over 21,000 films, the tome is full of little extras that include famous selling lines (from 'Garbo laughs!' to 'In space, no one can hear you scream'), critics' comments, supplementary trivia and Oscar wins and nominations. Not only is Halliwell's guide hard to beat, it keeps on getting better.

Leonard Maltin's Movie and Video Guide 1996; Signet; £7.99; 1,582 pages.

The best value, most comprehensive film guide in the world, Maltin's bible now stretches to 1,582 pages, two more than last year's. This means that with the introduction of 300 new entries, lesser films will have fallen by the wayside, so don't throw away those back numbers (I have a Maltin's in the office, my living room, the loft and one in the garden shed – seriously). Packed with information you won't find anywhere else, the book excels at summarising film plots, detailing blink-and-miss performances and includes video availability, film debuts, uncredited cameos and much, much more – and it's highly accurate and frequently very amusing.

Leonard Maltin's Movie Encyclopedia; Plume/Penguin; £13.00; 981 pages.

Now here's a novel concept. Somebody's come up with the bright idea of compiling a whole book of biogs of movie personalities. OK, enough sarcasm. Adding Maltin's tome to my shelves already creaking with Katz, Halliwell, Quinlan, Thomson and Brewer's, I realised my latest addition was a godsend. Maltin, aided by a team of researchers and contributors, has really done his homework. Cutting through the waffle, his profiles manage to be both concise and encyclopaedic, peppered with brisk and tart opinion, while often setting records straight. Furthermore, the book frequently details actual performances – above and beyond the standard list of credits – and also includes major stage and TV appearances (and even the odd music video). Leaning towards the American mainstream, the book still spreads its net pretty wide, embracing everybody from silent star Colleen Moore to such contemporary, lesser-known actors as Dan Hedaya, Ernie Hudson, Charles Napier and Daphne Zuniga, as well as foreign stars like Nathalie Baye and Bruno Ganz. In addition, it profiles directors, writers, composers, cinematographers, costume designers and so on. Oh, and it passed my major litmus test: it is the first reference book to include both Helen Mirren and Annabella Sciorra's birthdays!

Quinlan's Illustrated Directory of Film Character Actors, by David Quinlan; Batsford; £19.99; 384 pages.

I don't know anybody as thorough and painstaking as David Quinlan, a man who *always* stays till the end of each movie to make sure its copyright date corresponds to the one on his notes. He's also been known to sit through videos just to confirm a brief cameo appearance from an actor. So, apart from anything else, you can rely on Quinlan's latest comprehensive work for accuracy. His invaluable book, now updated to include over 1,100 entries, is a labour of love that pays tribute to those nameless faces that have coloured movies since the advent of the medium. Compiling the *complete* filmographies of such prolific performers as Monte Blue, John Carradine, Elisha Cook Jr, Tully Marshall, ZaSu Pitts, Addison Richards and Marianne Stone is an Olympian feat, particularly as such character actors can turn out four movies to any star's one. Good, too, to see the inclusion of such recent names as Brenda Fricker, David Strathairn, Stephen Tobolowsky and J.T. Walsh (although I challenge Quinlan to include the ubiquitous Mike Starr in his next volume). Mistakes do, inevitably, occur (Richard E. Grant, not Hugh Grant, is credited for *An Awfully Big Adventure*), but these are invariably last-minute ones.

R.E.D. Soundtracks Catalogue; Retail Entertainment Data Publishing Ltd; £14.95; 326 pages.

This is the sort of book that ought to be kept a trade secret. Its wealth of data relating to TV, stage and film soundtracks would give film journalists an unfair advantage on the public had it not been published on the open market. An alphabetical listing of soundtracks from *A Bout de Souffle* to *Zulu Dawn*, the book includes track titles, artists, format, catalogue number, availability, label, release date (month and year) and distributor, with a handy index of 'compilations' and composers in the back. Of course, the catalogue would be even more useful had cast members been credited on the song listings under musicals, so that, say, on *Paint Your Wagon* you would know that it was Clint Eastwood singing 'I Talk To The Trees' and Lee Marvin growling 'Wand'rin' Star'. It should also be pointed out that the book is by no means comprehensive, either in its inclusion of entries or its coverage of track listings. Still, there's enough information here to make it an invaluable addition to any film buff's reference library. What's depressing is seeing the sheer volume of titles that have been deleted from the market, but it's still nice to have them listed here for the record.

Time Out Film Guide; Penguin; £12.99; 999 pages.

At 999 pages, the fourth edition of the *Time Out* guide falls short of Maltin's manual and Halliwell's handbook, but it's the little extras that make it a favourite of mine. The reviews themselves can border on the pretentious (culled from the London listings magazine), and the credits are rudimentary, but the appendices at the back are invaluable (all 160 pages' worth). So, should you wish to see what films Tunisia has served up (at least, those which made it to Britain), or which films were set in Rome, or which films feature bomb disposal, you can look the answers up alphabetically (under bomb disposal, Rome and Tunisia). There are also comprehensive filmographies of actors and directors, and a formidable list of all-time top tens contributed by directors and critics. Thus, you can see who exactly nominated *Citizen Kane* best film of all time (the winner by 111 points), while marvelling at some oddball choices (Adrian Turner includes *Avanti!* in his top ten, Jackie Chan *My Fair Lady* and Richard Linklater *Barry Lyndon*).

Variety Movie Guide '96; edited by Derek Elley; Hamlyn; £14.99; 1,130 pages.

The fifth edition of this exhaustive guide (culled from the trade paper's vaults) now includes foreign 'classics'. But don't get too excited, as only 350 foreign language titles have been squeezed in, a small percentage of the 8,000 films under review. Thus, while such obvious standards as *L'Age d'Or* and *The Seventh Seal* are included (and, commendably, Zhou Xiaowen's 1994 *Ermo*), others – like *Les Visiteurs* (the highest-grossing French film in history) and Jean Vigo's seminal *Zero de Conduite* – are missing. None the less, the reviews remain the most comprehensive available in this format, so if you find what you're looking for (which won't include *The Fiend With the Atomic Brain*), you'll get your money's worth. The other remarkable thing about the book is that even at 1,130 pages it remains surprisingly light. Big, but manageable.

The Virgin Film Guide; edited by James Pallot; Virgin; £14.99; 1,055 pages.

This is a good book. Not because it's published by Virgin, but because it manages to include the best of the other directories without sacrificing its usefulness. Like the Variety guide (above) it excludes lesser titles that buffs (inexplicably) want to read about (like *The Fiend With the Atomic Brain*), but makes up for it by giving you more information on the films you should be interested in. Consequently, the reviews and synopses are more comprehensive, and so are the credits, right down to the costume designer and special effects guy. There are also Oscar nominations and awards, US ratings and British certificates, and other useful bits and pieces, not least an index of directors at the back with their films listed chronologically. Best of all, though, is that the cast lists include the characters' names as well as the actors, so you can work out who's who in each film. Another little extra is that each title is defined by genre. It's a little thing, I know, but you'd be surprised how hard it is to fathom out what some movies are supposed to be from other guides on the market.

With Nails: The Film Diaries of Richard E. Grant, by Richard E. Grant; Picador; £16.99; 310 pages.

For those tired of reverent journals chronicling the halcyon days of Balcon, Powell and Pressburger, Richard E. Grant's zippy autobiography will prove a genuine tonic. Neatly divided into ten chapters which more or less focus on Grant's major pictures – *Withnail & I*, *Warlock*, *Hudson Hawk*, *The Age of Innocence*, etc – the book affectionately takes no prisoners. Although his style reflects the writing of someone who's spent too long subscribing to the *Sun* (with phrases in all caps and others in italics), Grant is not beneath using words like 'explicate', 'obeisant' and 'saturnine'. On a literary level the book may be a dog's dinner, but its zeal is irresistible.

Other notable books:

Burton on Burton, by Mark Salisbury; Faber & Faber.

David Lean, by Kevin Brownlow; Richard Cohen Books.

Derek Jarman: A Portrait Artist, Filmmaker, Designer; Thames and Hudson.

Derek Jarman's Garden, by Derek Jarman, photos by Howard Sooley; Thames & Hudson.

Fellini on Fellini, edited by Costanzo Costantini; Faber & Faber.

Film Noir: An Encyclopaedia Reference to an American Style, edited by Alain Silver and Elizabeth Ward; The Overlook Press.

Flickers, by Gilbert Adair; Faber & Faber.

Frank Sinatra: An American Legend, by Nancy Sinatra; Virgin.

Gaumont British Cinemas, by Allen Eyles; BFI.

Grace, by Robert Lacey; Sidgwick & Jackson.

Hawks on Hawks, by Joseph McBride; Faber & Faber.

Hitchcock on Hitchcock, edited by Sidney Gottlieb; Faber & Faber.

Howard Hughes: The Untold Story, by Peter Harry Brown and Pat H. Broeske; Little Brown.

'If They Move ... Kill 'Em': The Life and Times of Sam Peckinpah, by David Weddle; Grove Press.

Immoral Tales: Sex and Horror Cinema in Europe 1956-1984, by Cathal Tothill and Pete Tombs; Titan.

In the Arena: The Autobiography, by Charlton Heston; HarperCollins.

James Whale, by Mark Gatiss; Cassell.

Jane Austen's Sense and Sensibility: The Screenplay and Diaries, by Emma Thompson; Bloomsbury.

John Wayne: American, by Randy Roberts and James S. Olson; The Free Press.

The Kid Stays in the Picture, by Robert Evans; Aurum Press.

London on Film: 100 Years of Filmmaking in London, by Colin Sorense; Museum of London.

Magic Hour: The Life of a Cameraman, by Jack Cardiff; Faber & Faber.

Magnum Cinema: Photographs From 50 Years of Moviemaking; Phaidon Press.

Making Movies, by Sidney Lumet; Bloomsbury.

The Making of David Lean's Lawrence of Arabia, by Adrian Turner; Dragon's World.

The Monster Show: A Cultural History of Horror, by David J. Skal; Plexus.

Orson Welles: The Road to Xanadu, by Simon Callow; Jonathan Cape.

Past Imperfect: History According to the Movies, edited by Mark C. Carnes; Cassell.

Projections 5, edited by John Boorman and Walter Donohoe; Faber & Faber.

Psycho: Behind the Scenes of the Classic Thriller, by Janet Leigh and Christopher Nickens; Pavilion.

The Queen of Camp – Mae West: Sex and Popular Culture, by Marybeth Hamilton; Pandora.

Rebel Without a Crew, by Robert Rodriguez; Faber & Faber.

Steve McQueen: Portrait of an American Rebel, by Marshall Terrill; Plexus.

Tarantino – Inside Story, by Jeff Dawson; Cassell.

The Unkindest Cut: How a Hatchet-Man Critic Made His Own $7,000 Movie and Put It All On His Credit Card, by Joe Queenan; Picador.

In Memoriam

F. Maurice Speed

Film actor **Martin Balsam**, who died 14 February 1996 at the age 76, enriched many of the films he appeared in as a feature player. He made his screen debut in *On the Waterfront* (1954) and followed that impressive performance with some 50 films of which *Twelve Angry Men* (1957) is considered to have been his most impressive performance. He also appeared in *Al Capone* (1959), *Psycho* (1960), *Breakfast at Tiffanys* (1961), *The Carpetbaggers* (1964), and *Two Evil Eyes* (1989).

In spite of his formidable list of dramatic and musical stage performances, **Jeremy Brett** (born Peter Jeremy William Huggins), who died in October 1995 at the age of 59, will almost certainly be best remembered for his many TV performances as Sherlock Holmes. In addition to four series he made between 1984 and 1994, he appeared in a number of TV films which featured the adventures of the famous sleuth. Trained at the Central School of Speech and Drama, Eton-educated Brett began his theatrical career at the Library Theatre, Manchester, in 1954, and made his London debut the same year in *Troilus and Cressida* at the Old Vic. His versatility was subsequently proved by appearances in such diverse productions as *Macbeth, Romeo and Juliet, Hamlet,* the musicals *Meet Me by Moonlight* and *Marigold,* and Arnold Wesker's *The Kitchen*. His films include *War and Peace* (1956), *The Wild and the Willing*

Jeremy Brett

(1961), *My Fair Lady* (1964), *The Medusa Touch* (1977) and *Mad Dogs and Englishmen* (1995).

George Burns (born Nathan Birnbaum), who died in March 1996 at the age of 100, was the survivor of the famous husband-and-wife vaudeville partnership of Burns and Allen. Well known for his quick wit ('Acting is all about honesty. If you can fake that, you've got it made'), Burns continued to crack jokes while appearing on stage and television right up to his death. He wrote two autobiographies: 1955's *I Love Her, That's Why* and 1976's *Living It Up*. His films with his wife

George Burns
Eva Gabor

Gracie Allen include *The Big Broadcast* (1932), *A Damsel in Distress* (1937), *The Gracie Allen Murder Case* (1939) and *Two Girls and a Sailor* (1944). As a solo performer, he won an Oscar in 1975 for *The Sunshine Boys*, and other successes included *Oh God* (1977) and *Just You and Me Kid* (1979).

Youngest and smallest of the famous Hungarian-born Gabor sisters, **Eva Gabor** died at the age of 74 on 4 July 1995. Married five times (she was credited with saying 'marriage is too interesting an experiment to be tried only once'), Eva began her career as an ice skater and café singer in her native Budapest, before moving to Hollywood in 1939 – the first of the sisters to do so. She made her stage debut in the Broadway show *The Happy Time*, and followed that with brief appearances in several movies. Her first real film role came in *Forced Landing* in 1941, and she continued to make films and TV programmes for over 30 years. When she retired from acting, Eva formed and ran a multi-million dollar wig company, and also managed to build up one of the finest collections of orchids in the United States. Her autobiography *Orchids and Salami* was published in 1954. Her films include: *Paris Model* (1953), *The Last Time I Saw Paris* (1954), *Artists and Models* (1955), the remake of *My Man Godfrey* (1957), *Gigi* (1958) and *Youngblood Hawke* (1963). She also supplied her voice for Disney's *The Aristocats* (1970) and *The Rescuers Down Under* (1990), her final film.

Flame-haired Irish actress **Greer Garson**, who died in June 1996, did not make many films but several of those she did make achieved worldwide success. Born in 1908 in County Down, Northern Ireland, she was educated in London and Grenoble. She gained considerable stage experience before making her first film, *Goodbye, Mr Chips*, in 1939. At her peak in the 1940s, she became one of Hollywood's biggest stars. In 1942 she won an Oscar for her performance in *Mrs Minever*, starring opposite Walter Pidgeon.

After serving in the US Navy during the war, and the Merchant Navy after it, **Harry Guardino** turned up in Hollywood in the 1950s and went on to have a very successful career in the movies. Though never a huge star, Guardino did receive star billing with Cary Grant and Sophia Loren in *Houseboat* (1958). He also appeared in many stage plays and television series, including *Perry Mason*, *Kojak* and *Murder She Wrote*. Guardino died on 17 July 1995 at the age of 69. His films include *Flesh and Fury* (1952), *Pork Chop Hill* (1959), *Madigan* (1968), *Dirty Harry* (1971) and *Any Which Way You Can* (1980).

The popular, much-loved cockney actress **Kathleen Harrison** died at the beginning of December 1995, at the age of 103. Among her many triumphs was beating *Coronation Street* to the top of the TV ratings tree as Mrs Thursday in Ted Willis's comedy about a charlady who comes into a £10 million fortune. It was George Bernard Shaw who coached her to specialise in a cockney dialect when she played Eliza in a production of his play *Pygmalion*. She claimed her desire to be an actress was born the very first time that, as a child, she was taken to a music hall. As soon as she could, she enrolled at RADA, where she won the Du Maurier award. On leaving, she had no trouble finding work with touring companies, but she retired from acting in 1916 when she married. For the next nine years she remained a housewife, moving with her husband to Argentina, Las Palmas and Madeira. But in 1925, the call of the stage became too powerful and she returned to RADA to take a refresher course before returning to the stage and later, the screen. She appeared in more than 70 films, including *Hobson's Choice* (1931), *The Ghoul* (1933), *The Ghost Train* (1941), *In Which We Serve* (1942), *Holiday Camp* (1947), *The Pickwick Papers* (1952), *Cast a Dark Shadow* (1954), *A Cry from the Streets* (1958), *The Fast Lady* (1962) and *West 11* (1963).

One of the cinema's greatest all-round entertainers – dancer, director, actor and choreographer – **Gene Kelly** died on 2 February 1996 at the age of 83. Born Eugene Curran Kelly in Pittsburgh, he originally planned a career in journalism, but switched to economy and law before finally decid-

Greer Garson

Kathleen Harrison

Gene Kelly

ing to become a dancer. With his brother he launched a tap dance act which quickly proved a successful act in clubs. His first big break came when he was hired as dance director for Billy Rose's Diamond Horseshow Revue production of *Pal Joey*. This led to his first film in 1942, *Me and My Girl*, in which he co-starred with Judy Garland. From then on, Kelly had one success after another both on stage and film, and also on TV, notably in the classic dance musical *Singin' in the Rain*. Some of his best remembered roles include those in *Cover Girl* (1944), *The Pirate* (1948), *On the Town* (star and co-director) (1949), *Take Me Out to the Ball Game* (1949), *An American in Paris* (1951), *Singin' in the Rain* (star and co-director) (1952), *Brigadoon* (1954), *Les Girls* (1957), *Hello Dolly* (director only) (1969), *That's Entertainment* (1974) and *Xanadu* (1980).

Patric Knowles, who died at the end of December 1995 at the age of 84, had a career spanning over 40 years during which time he made numerous films, often playing the romantic lead. His early British films include *Abdul the Damned* in 1934, and *Mister Hobo*, which was made the following year. In 1936, Knowles moved to Hollywood, where he enjoyed instant success in films like *The Charge of the Light Brigade* (1936), *How Green Was My Valley* (1941), *The Mystery of Marie Roget* (1942), *Frankenstein Meets the Wolf Man* (1943), *Of Human Bondage* (1946), *Terror in the Wax Museum* and *Arnold* (his final two films, both made in 1973).

The multi-talented Swedish actress/writer **Viveca Lindfors** (born Elsa Viveca Forstendotter) died on 25 October 1995 at the age of 74. Trained at the Royal Stockholm Theatre, she made eight Swedish films, beginning with *The Spinning Family* (1940) before moving to America. Her US screen debut was in the 1947 film *To the Victor*, and she went on to appear in numerous films – including *Night Unto Night* in 1948, in which she starred with Ronald Reagan – and many plays, including the highly praised *Anastasia* and *Miss Julie*, and the production *Brecht on Brecht* in 1961. In addition to her Hollywood film career, she undertook a large amount of television work and also appeared in various foreign films including *Four in a Jeep* (1951) in Switzerland. In 1987 she wrote and directed the film *Unfinished Business*. Her other films include *The Story of Ruth* (1960), *King of Kings* (1961), *The Way We Were* (1973), *Welcome to LA* (1977) and *Summer in New Hampshire*, which at the time of writing has yet to be released.

Ida Lupino, who died on 3 August 1995 at the age of 77, was a significant figure in the history of the cinema and one of the few women directors in the world. A talented actress, her work was seldom given the credit it deserved, and this also applied to her producing, writing and directing. She was also a pianist of some distinction, who wrote

Patric Knowles

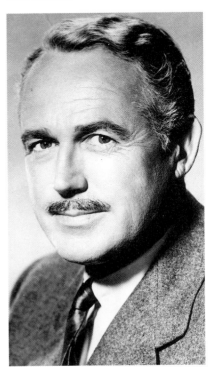

a number of pieces of music, including the scores for some of her own films. Descended from an old and distinguished Italian family of entertainers who emigrated to England in the 17th century, Ida was the daughter of popular musical comedy star Stanley Lupino. Enrolled at RADA by the age of 13, she was playing the ingenue leading role in the film *Her First Affair* by the time she was 14. Her first opportunity to direct came when the director of a film which she had written and was starring in fell ill within a few days of the start of production, and Lupino successfully took over and completed it. It was, however, in *The Young Lovers* (1950) that she made her official directing debut. Lupino became known for tackling difficult and controversial subjects such as rape and bigamy, which featured in her films *Outrage* (1950) and *The Bigamist* (1953). Apart from her considerable work (writing, producing, directing and – less as time passed – acting) in some 60 films, Lupino was involved in a good deal of television work, with her last performance being in an episode of the TV series *Charlie's Angels*. She was working on her next film when she was diagnosed with cancer, and a subsequent stroke ended her career.

Ida Lupino

Louis Malle

A true artist of the cinema, a fine draughtsman, and a man with a deep philosophical understanding of human nature, **Louis Malle** died on 23 November 1995 at the age of 63. Too often undervalued, but a jewel in the crown of the so-called New Wave school of movie makers, Malle was one of their most able and interesting directors. His output proved his versatility and integrity – he was the only director who went to Hollywood and imposed on it his essentially European style. Coming from a wealthy family, Malle attended the Institut des Hautes Etudes Cinematographique, which he left when he was offered a position as assistant to Jacques Cousteau, who was making one of his underwater movies, *The Silent World*. After two years with Cousteau, Malle became Jacques Tati's cameraman on *Mon Oncle*. His first solo direction was on *Lift to the Scaffold*, which he followed with the somewhat controversial *The Lovers*, which brought him his first taste of trouble from the censors. Next

came the crazy comedy *Zazie Dans le Métro*, which, though critically scorned, proved a great success. Brigitte Bardot starred in Malle's next film *Le Privée*, which he followed with *The Fire Within* (*Le Feu Follet*), now seen by many as his most outstanding movie. Tired of making fictional films, Malle set off for India, where he shot some 40 hours of film which he later edited down to eight one-hour movies. Although almost universally acclaimed, the Indians objected to the films' emphasis on the country's poverty and squalor, while the English complained about the anti-colonial bias of the movie. Back in Europe, Malle made a comedy about incest, *Murmur of the Heart*, followed by *Lacombe Lucien*, an ironic story about French collaboration with the Nazis during the war. In 1978, Malle moved to New York to make *Pretty Baby*, set in a New Orleans brothel, and *Atlantic City*, which successfully wedded a con-

Dean Martin

temporary American story to a wholly French style. In the same year Malle made an experimental two-character piece, *My Dinner With Andre*, which boasted exemplary dialogue. In 1987, Malle returned to France to make his largely autobiographical success *Au Revoir les Enfants*, a moving story about Jewish children in a Catholic school in World War II. His final film was an experimental filming of a rehearsal of Chekhov's *Uncle Vanya*, entitled *Vanya on 42nd Street*. Malle's films established him as a great movie maker and his output includes *Lift to the Scaffold* (1957), *The Lovers* (1958), *Calcutta* (1960), *Zazie Dans le Metro* (1960), *Le Privée* (1961), *Vive Le Tour* (1962), *The Fire Within* (1963), *Viva Maria* (1965), *Le Voleur* (1967), *Histoires Extraordinaires* (1968), *Phantom*

India (1969), *Murmur of the Heart* (1971), *Humaine Trop Humaine* (1973), *Place de la République* (1973), *Lacombe Lucien* (1974), *Black Moon* (1975), *Pretty Baby* (1978), *Atlantic City* (1980), *My Dinner With André* (1981), *Crackers* (1984), *Alamo Bay* (1985), *Au Revoir les Enfants* (1987), *Milou en Mai* (1990), *Damage* (1992), *Vanya on 42nd Street* (1994).

The crooked nose and battered features gave it away: actor/crooner **Dean Martin** (born Dino Crocetti) – who died aged 78 on Christmas morning, 1995 – had an earlier career as a boxer. In fact, he was a teenaged fighter who, as an amateur, earned himself $10 a fight. Later, he worked in a steel mill, and then as a croupier while doing various singing jobs. This led to a booking with Sammy Watkins and his band at $50 per week. His first

big break came when, now billed as Dino Martini, he was booked in a New York nighterie to replace Frank Sinatra. In 1946, he appeared with a young comedian named Jerry Lewis, and the success was immediate. They eventually moved into the New York clubs, and in the years that followed they reached the heights of fame, making 16 movies and appearing at America's most prestigious night clubs. When the two split up, Martin was not given much chance by the critics, but they were soon proved wrong and Martin flourished in his own TV show and as the hero of numerous films. They include (with Lewis) *My Friend Irma* (1949), *That's My Boy* (1951), *The Stooge* (1952), *Three Ring Circus* (1954), *Hollywood or Bust* (1956), and (without Lewis) *Ten Thousand Bedrooms* (1957), *The Young Lions* (1958), *Sergeants Three* (1962), *What a Way to Go* (1964), *The Sons of Katie Elder* (1965), *Murderers' Row* (1966), *Bandorlero* (1968), *Mr Ricco* (1975) and *The Cannonball Run* (1980).

Patsy Ruth Miller, who died on 16 July 1995 aged 91, was just 16 years old when she was 'discovered' by the then reigning star of Hollywood, Alla Nazimova, who got her a small part in the film she was then making with Rudolph Valentino, *Camille* (1921). Miller then went on to make a number of films, gaining high praise for her performance in Lon Chaney's *The Hunchback of Notre Dame* (1923). She never achieved major stardom, however, and with the advent of talkies and several less successful films, she decided to retire from acting, and turned to writing with considerable success. Her output included popular radio scripts, short stories, a novel and stage plays. She also wrote the book for the stage musical success *Music in my Heart*.

A true cockney born and bred, **Arthur Mullard**, who died in mid-December 1995 at the age of 85, continued to live in an Islington council flat during his more affluent years. He led a busy and varied life, as an actor, radio interviewer, film star and even pop singer, and appeared in some 50 TV shows, stage plays, and more than a hundred films. His father was a

Vivian Blane

Simon Cadell

labourer, and Mullard began his working life as a butcher boy until he enlisted (under age) in the army, where he soon became a physical instructor and amateur boxer. After three years he returned to civilian life and made a living as a professional fighter, chalking up over 20 fights before he decided to try his hand at acting. He obtained a small part in the Mae West show at the Prince Of Wales theatre, and from there began to get small parts in films. He soon established himself as a reliable cockney character on both stage and screen (and TV commercials), and continued to work until he was in his eighties. His films include *Sparrows Can't Sing* (1962), *The Loneliness of the Long Distance Runner* (1962), *Morgan – A Suitable Case for Treatment* (1966), *The Great St Trinian's Train Robbery* (1966), *Chitty Chitty Bang Bang* (1968), *Crooks and Coronets* (1969) and – voice only – *101 Dalmatians* (1960).

Others who have died

Maxene Andrews, one of the three singing sisters who were popular in the 30s, died on 21 October 1995 at the age of 79. During their career the sisters achieved 19 gold records (in their career they sold in the region of 100 million records), had a regular radio show and appeared in 16 films.

Vivian Blane, who died on 9 December 1995 at the age of 74, was best known for her original stage production and later film of *Guys and Dolls*. The daughter of a theatrical agent, she began her career as a vaudeville singer and vocalist with a number of dance bands. After going to the American Academy of Dramatic Art, she toured as a star of productions such as 'Born Yesterday'. Signed by Fox, she appeared in a number of films including *State Fair* (1945), *It Happened in Flatbush* (1942), *Something for the Boys* (1944), *If I'm Lucky* (1946) and Laurel and Hardy's *Jitterbugs* (1943).

Estelle Brody, who died in June 1995, was a New York born actress who began her career as a dancer and then moved to Britain to make a number of films, including her biggest successes, *Mademoiselle from Armentieres* (1926), *Hindle Wakes* (1927) and *Kitty* (1929). In the 1930s, she returned to Hollywood but found little success there, so she went back to Britain. Her final major screen appearance was in *Never Take Sweets From a Stranger* in 1960. In 1969, she retired to Malta.

Simon Cadell, the British actor who died at the beginning of March 1996 at the age of 45, will be best remembered for his TV work, especially his role as the holiday camp manager in the long-running series *Hi-De-Hi*. Two years ago, he was diagnosed as having an incurable and advanced heart disease. In his remaining years, he wrote a book on wine and completed two final films.

Derek Ford, the British writer/director, died 19 May 1995. His output was mainly sex and horror films, including *The Black Torment* (1964), *The Wife Swappers* (1969), *Suburban Wives* (1971), *Keep It Up Jack!* (1973) and *What's Up Nurse* (1977).

The less famous brother of Leslie Howard, **Arthur Howard** (born Arthur Stainer) who died in July 1995 at the age of 83, was a popular comedian whose greatest success was as Jimmy Edwards' tormented schoolmaster in the radio series 'Whack-O'. His films include *Frieda* (1947), *London Belongs to Me* (1948), *The Passionate Friends* (1948), *The Happiest Days of Your Life* (1950) and several of the *St Trinian's* series.

Jimmy Jewel, who died at the beginning of December 1995 aged 82, was half of the music hall act of Jewel and Warriss, who for 33 years topped the bills. At the break-up of the act, Jewel began a new and highly successful stage, screen and TV career.

Ben Johnson died in April 1996, aged 77. He won an Oscar in 1972 for his performance in *The Last Picture Show*, and also appeared in *She Wore a Yellow*

Arthur Howard

Ribbon, *The Wild Bunch* and *The Getaway*.

Jeffrey Lynn (born Ragnar Godfrey Lind), who died in November 1995 at the age of 89, was the perfect, clean-cut hero. He made his acting debut in repertory in the early 30s, and was signed up by Warner Brothers in 1937, who cast him opposite some of the top stars of his day, including Humphrey Bogart and Bette Davis. After the war, few good parts came his way and he concentrated on stage plays and television roles, until he retired in 1973. His films included *Four Daughters* (1938), *Four Wives* (1939), *All This and Heaven Too* (1940), *Four Mothers* (1940), *A Letter to Three Wives* (1949), and *Tony Rome* (1967).

Esther Muir, who died in late August 1995, at the age of 100, is best remembered for her dumb blonde performance in the Marx Brothers film *A Day at the Races* (1937). Starting in stage musical comedies, her busiest and best film period was in the 30s: *A*

Jeffrey Lynn

Dangerous Affair* (1931), *The Bowery* (1933), *City Girl* (1938), *The Girl and the Gambler* (1939), and her last film *X Marks the Spot* (1942).

Anthony Oliver, who died in November 1995 at the age of 73, was a leading authority on Staffordshire pottery, and combined his acting with running a shop in Kensington Church Street in London. His was a quite familiar figure on television, and was to be seen in many British films in the 1950s and 60s.

Actor-playwright **Joseph Tomelty**, who worked at the Ulster Group Theatre for 20 years, died in 1995 at the age of 84. He appeared in a number of films including *Odd Man Out* (1946), *Bhowani Junction* (1956) and *Moby Dick* (1956) and also wrote novels, plays and short stories.

Mary Wickes, who died on 22 October 1995 at the age of 85, was a popular character actress who appeared in more than 50 films and 27 Broadway shows, as well as numerous radio and TV shows. Her first film was *The Man Who Came to Dinner* (1941), and her last was *Little Women* (1994), and a voice-only contribution to the Disney animated feature *The Hunchback of Notre Dame* (1995).

Awards and Festivals

The 68th American Academy of Motion Picture Arts and Sciences Awards ('The Oscars') and Nominations for 1995, Los Angeles, March 1996

Best Film: *Braveheart*. Nominations: *Apollo 13*; *Babe*; *Il Postino*; *Sense and Sensibility*.

Best Director: Mel Gibson, for *Braveheart*. Nominations: Mike Figgis, for *Leaving Las Vegas*; Chris Noonan, for *Babe*; Michael Radford, for *Il Postino*; Tim Robbins, for *Dead Man Walking*.

Best Actor: Nicolas Cage, for *Leaving Las Vegas*. Nominations: Richard Dreyfuss, for *Mr Holland's Opus*; Anthony Hopkins, for *Nixon*; Sean Penn, for *Dead Man Walking*; Massimo Troisi, for *Il Postino*.

Best Actress: Susan Sarandon, for *Dead Man Walking*. Nominations: Elisabeth Shue, for *Leaving Las Vegas*; Sharon Stone, for *Casino*; Meryl Streep, for *The Bridges of Madison County*; Emma Thompson, for *Sense and Sensibility*.

Best Supporting Actor: Kevin Spacey, for *The Usual Suspects*. Nominations: James Cromwell, for *Babe*; Ed Harris, for *Apollo 13*; Brad Pitt, for *12 Monkeys*; Tim Roth, for *Rob Roy*.

Best Supporting Actress: Mira Sorvino, for *Mighty Aphrodite*. Nominations: Joan Allen, for *Nixon*; Kathleen Quinlan, for *Apollo 13*; Mare Winningham, for *Georgia*; Kate Winslet, for *Sense and Sensibility*.

Best Original Screenplay: Christopher McQuarrie, for *The Usual Suspects*. Nominations: Randall Wallace, for *Braveheart*; Woody Allen, for *Mighty Aphrodite*; Stephen J. Rivele, Christopher Wilkinson and Oliver Stone, for *Nixon*; Joss Whedon, Andrew Stanton, Joel Cohen, Alec Sokolow, from a story by John Lasseter, Andrew Stanton, Pete Docter and Joe Ranft, for *Toy Story*.

Best Screenplay Adaptation: Emma Thompson, for *Sense and Sensibility*. Nominations: William Broyles Jr and Al Reinert, for *Apollo 13*; George Miller and Chris Noonan, for *Babe*; Mike Figgis, for *Leaving Las Vegas*; Anna Pavignano, Michael Radford, Furio Scarpelli, Giacomo Scarpelli and Massimo Troisi, for *Il Postino*.

Best Cinematography: John Toll, for *Braveheart*. Nominations: Stephen Goldblatt, for *Batman Forever*; Emmanuel Lubezki, for *A Little Princess*; Michael Coulter, for *Sense and Sensibility*; Lu Yue, for *Shanghai Triad*.

Best Editing: Mike Hill and Dan Hanley, for *Apollo 13*. Nominations: Marcus D'Arcy and Jay Friedkin, for *Babe*; Steve Rosenblum, for *Braveheart*; Chris Lebenzon, for *Crimson Tide*; Richard Francis-Bruce, for *Seven*.

Best Original Score (musical or comedy): Alan Menken (music and orchestral score) and Stephen Schwartz (lyrics), for *Pocahontas*. Nominations: Marc Shaiman, for *The American President*; John Williams, for *Sabrina*; Randy Newman, for *Toy Story*; Thomas Newman, for *Unstrung Heroes*.

Best Original Score (dramatic): Luis

Three cheers for Mel Gibson! The Scots rally to Mel's Oscar-winning Braveheart

Bacalov, for *Il Postino*. Nominations: James Horner, for *Apollo 13*; James Horner, for *Braveheart*; John Williams, for *Nixon*; Patrick Doyle, for *Sense and Sensibility*.

Best Original Song: 'Colors Of The Wind' from *Pocahontas*, music by Alan Menken, lyrics by Stephen Schwartz. Nominations: 'Dead Man Walking' from *Dead Man Walking*, music and lyrics by Bruce Springsteen; 'Have You Ever Really Loved A Woman' from *Don Juan de Marco*, music and lyrics by Michael Kamen, Bryan Adams and Robert John Lange; 'Moonlight' from *Sabrina*, music by John Williams, lyrics by Alan and Marilyn Bergman; 'You've Got A Friend' from *Toy Story*, music and lyrics by Randy Newman.

Best Art Direction: Eugenio Zanetti, for *Restoration*. Nominations: Michael Corenblith (art) and Merideth Boswell (set), for *Apollo 13*; Roger Ford (art) and Kerrie Brown (set), for *Babe*; Bo Welch (art) and Cheryl Carasik (set), for *A Little Princess*; Tony Burrough, for *Richard III*.

Best Costume Design: James Acheson, for *Restoration*. Nominations: Charles Knode, for *Braveheart*; Shuna Harwood, for *Richard III*;

Jenny Beavan and John Bright, for *Sense and Sensibility*; Julie Weiss, for *12 Monkeys*.

Best Sound: Rick Dior, Steve Pederson, Scott Millan and David MacMillan, for *Apollo 13*. Nominations: Donald O. Mitchell, Frank A. Montano, Michael Herbick and Petur Hliddal, for *Batman Forever*; Andy Nelson, Scott Millan, Anna Behlmer and Brian Simmons, for *Braveheart*; Kevin O'Connell, Rick Kline, Gregory H. Watkins and William B. Kaplan, for *Crimson Tide*; Steve Maslow, Gregg Landaker and Keith A. Wester, for *Waterworld*.

Best Sound Effects Editing: Lon Bender and Per Hallberg, for *Braveheart*. Nominations: John Leveque and Bruce Stambler, for *Batman Forever*; George Watters II, for *Crimson Tide*.

Best Make-Up: Peter Frampton, Paul Pattison and Lois Burwell, for *Braveheart*. Nominations: Ken Diaz and Mark Sanchez, for *My Family*; Greg Cannom, Bob Laden and Colleen Callaghan, for *Roommates*.

Best Visual Effects: Scott E. Anderson, Charles Gibson, Neal Scanlan and John Cox, for *Babe*. Nominations: Robert Legato, Michael Kanfer, Leslie Ekker and Matt Sweeney, for *Apollo 13*.

Best Animated Short Film: *A Close Shave* (UK), by Nick Park. Nominations: *The Chicken From Outer*

Space; *The End*; *Gagarin*; *Runaway Brain*.

Best Live Action Short Film: *Lieberman in Love* (USA), by Christine Lahti and Jana Sue Memel. Nominations: *Brooms*; *Duke of Groove*; *Little Surprises*; *Tuesday Morning Ride*.

Best Documentary Feature: *Anne Frank Remembered*, by Jon Blair. Nominations: *The Battle Over Citizen Kane*; *Fiddlefest – Roberta Guaspari-Tzavara and Her East Harlem Violin Program*; *Hank Aaron: Chasing the Dream*; *Troublesome Creek: A Midwestern*.

Best Documentary Short: *One Survivor Remembers*. Nominations: *Jim Dine: A Self-Portrait on the Walls*; *The Living Sea*; *Never Give Up: The 20th Century Odyssey of Herbert Zipper*; *The Shadow of Hate*.

Best Foreign-Language Film: *Antonia's Line* (The Netherlands). Nominations: *All Things Fair* (Denmark-Sweden); *Dust of Life* (Algeria); *O Quatrilho* (Brazil); *The Star Maker* (Italy).

Honorary Academy Awards: Kirk Douglas, Chuck Jones.

Special Achievement Award: John Lasseter ('for the development and application of techniques that made possible the first feature-length computer-animated film').

Host: Whoopi Goldberg.

Australian Film Critics' Circle Awards, Sydney, 14 December 1995

Best Film: *Angel Baby*.

Best Actor: Aden Young, for *Metal Skin*.

Best Actress: Jacqueline McKenzie, for *Angel Baby*.

Best Director: Michael Rymer, for *Angel Baby*.

Best Original Screenplay: Michael Rymer, for *Angel Baby*.

Best Cinematography: Ellery Ryan, for *That Eye, the Sky*.

Best English-Language Foreign Film: *Heavenly Creatures*, by Peter Jackson (New Zealand); and *Once Were Warriors*, by Lee Tamahori (New Zealand).

Best Foreign-Language Film: *Burnt by the Sun*, by Nikita Mikhalkov (Russia); *La Reine Margot* (France), by Patrice Chereau; *Three Colours: Red*, by Krzysztof Kieslowski (France/Switzerland/Poland).

The 37th Australian Film Institute Awards, 9 November 1995

Best Film: *Angel Baby*.

Best Actor: John Lynch, for *Angel Baby*.

Best Actress: Jacqueline McKenzie, for *Angel Baby*.

Best Supporting Actor: Ray Barrett, for *Hotel Sorrento*.

Best Supporting Actress: Amanda Douge, for *That Eye, the Sky*.

Best Young Actor: Jamie Croft, for *That Eye, the Sky*.

Best Director: Michael Rymer, for *Angel Baby*.

Best Original Screenplay: Michael Rymer, for *Angel Baby*.

Best Screenplay Adaptation: Richard Franklin and Peter Fitzpatrick, for *Hotel Sorrento*.

Best Cinematography: Ellery Ryan, for *Angel Baby*.

Best Editing: Dany Cooper, for *Angel Baby*.

Best Foreign Film: *Once Were Warriors*, by Lee Tamahori (New Zealand).

The Byron Kennedy Award: editor Jill Billcock.

The Raymond Longford Award: George Miller (producer and co-writer of *Babe*).

The 46th Berlin International Film Festival, 26 February 1996

Golden Bear for Best Film: *Sense and Sensibility*, by Ang Lee (UK).

Special Jury Prize: *All Things Fair*, by Bo Widerberg (Denmark-Sweden).

Silver Bear for Best Director: Yim Ho, for *The Sun Has Ears* (China-Hong Kong); and Richard Loncraine, for *Richard III* (UK-US).

Best Actor: Sean Penn, for *Dead Man Walking* (USA).

Best Actress: Anouk Grinberg, for *Mon Homme* (France).

Silver Bear for Single Achievement: *Village of Dreams*, by Yoichi Higashi (Japan).

Blue Angel Prize: *All Things Fair*.

Golden Bear for Best Short Film: *The Arrival of the Train*, by Andrej Sheleznjakov (Russia).

Silver Bear for Best Short Film: *A Country Doctor*, by Katariina Lillqvist (Finland-Czech Republic).

Ecumenical Jury: *Dead Man Walking* (US); *To Have (Or Not)*.

Special Mentions: *Mahjong* (Taiwan); *Sun Valley* (Hong Kong); *Silent Night* (Germany).

Wolfgang Staudte Prize: *Okaeri* (Japan).

International Film Critics' Jury: Best Film: *The Sun Has Ears*.

German Art House Cinemas: *Dead Man Walking*.

Berliner Morgenpost Reader's Jury: *Dead Man Walking*.

Kinderfest Jury: *The Boy Who Stopped Talking* (Netherlands).

CICAE (international confederation of art cinemas) Jury: *Welcome to the Dollhouse* (US); *Chinese Chocolate* (Canada).

Gay Teddy Bear Awards:
Best Feature: *The Watermelon Woman* (US).
Best Documentary: *The Celluloid Closet* (US).

Peace Film Prize: *Devils Don't Dream* (Switzerland).

Mionetto Film Award (for International Forum): *A Drop in the Ocean* (Greece).

Caligari Film Prize (for International Forum): *Charms' Incidents* (Austria).

Berliner Zeitung Readers' Jury (for International Forum): *Picnic* (Japan).

NETPAC (network for the promotion of Asian cinema) Award: *... And the Moon Dances*.

The 1995 British Academy of Film and Television Arts Awards ('BAFTAs'), 21 April 1996

Best Film: *Sense and Sensibility*, by Ang Lee.

Best Film (public vote): *Four Weddings and a Funeral*.

David Lean Award for Best Direction: Mike Newell, for *Four Weddings and a Funeral*.

Best Original Screenplay: Christopher McQuarrie, for *The Usual Suspects*.

Best Adapted Screenplay: John Hodge, for *Trainspotting*.

Best Actor: Nigel Hawthorne, for *The Madness of King George*.

Best Actress: Emma Thompson, for *Sense and Sensibility*.

Best Supporting Actor: Tim Roth, for *Rob Roy*.

Best Supporting Actress: Kate Winslet, for *Sense and Sensibility*.

Best Cinematography: John Toll, for *Braveheart*.

Best Editing: John Ottman, for *The Usual Suspects*.

Best Production Design: Michael Corenblith, for *Apollo 13*.

The Anthony Asquith Award for Best Music: Luis Bacalov, for *Il Postino*.

Best Costumes: Charles Knode, for *Braveheart*.

Alexander Korda Award for Best British Film: *The Madness of King George*, by Nicholas Hytner.

Best Foreign Film: *Il Postino*, by Michael Radford (Italy-France).

Lifetime Achievement: John Schlesinger.

The 16th Canadian Film Awards ('Genies'), Montreal, 14 January 1996

Best Film: *The Confessional*.

Best Director: Robert Lepage, for *The Confessional*.

Best Actor: David La Haye, for *L'Enfant d'Eau*.

Best Actress: Helena Bonham Carter, for *Margaret's Museum*.

Best Supporting Actor: Kenneth Welsh, for *Margaret's Museum*.

Best Supporting Actress: Kate Nelligan, for *Margaret's Museum*.

Best Screenplay: Gerald Wexler and Mort Ransen, for *Margaret's Museum*.

Best Cinematography: Tom Burstyn, for *Magic in the Water*.

Best Editing: Michael Pacek, for *Dance Me Outside*.

Best Art Direction/Production Design: Francois Laplante, for *The Confessional*.

Best Music: Milan Kymlicka, for *Margaret's Museum*.

Best Costumes: Nicoletta Massone, for *Margaret's Museum*.

Best Sound Editing: Andy Malcolm, Steve Munro, Michael Pacek, Michael Worth and Peter Winninger, for *Dance Me Outside*.

Best Overall Sound: Kelly Cole, Dean Giammarco, Michael McGee and Paul Sharpe, for *Magic in the Water*.

Best Feature-Length Documentary: *The Champagne Safari*, by George Ungar.

Best Short Documentary: *Fiction and Other Truths: A Film About Jane Rule*, by Lynne Fernle and Aerlyn Weissman.

Best Short Film: *Les Fleures Magiques*, by Jean Marc Vallee.

Best Live-Action Short Drama: *Arrowhead*, by Peter Lynch and Emmet Sheil.

Claude Jutra Award for First Feature: Robert Lepage, for *The Confessional*.

The Golden Reel Award for Box-Office Performance: *Johnny Mnemonic*.

The 49th Cannes Film Festival Awards, 20 May 1996

Palme d'Or for Best Film: *Secrets and Lies*, by Mike Leigh (UK-France).

Grand Prix du Jury: *Breaking the Waves*, by Lars von Trier (Denmark-France).

Best Actor: Daniel Auteuil and Pascal Duquenne, for *The Eighth Day* (France-Belgium).

Best Actress: Brenda Blethyn, for *Secrets and Lies*.

Best Director: Joel Coen, for *Fargo* (USA).

Best Screenplay: Jacques Audiard, for *A Self-Made Hero* (France).

Palme d'Or for Best Short: *The Wind*, by Marcell Ivanyi (Hungary).

Jury Prize for Best Short: *Small Deaths*, by Lynne Ramsay (Scotland).

Camera d'Or for First Feature: *Love Serenade*, by Shirley Barrett (Australia).

Grand Prix Technique: *Microcosmos*.

Special Award: *Crash*, by David

Isabelle Huppert, winner of the César for best actress, in Claude Chabrol's La Cérémonie

Cronenberg (Canada) for its 'originality, audacity and daring'.

Chevalier of the Legion of Honor: Robert Altman.

Jury: Francis Ford Coppola (president), Nathalie Baye (France), Michael Ballhaus (Germany), Henry Chapier (France), Atom Agoyan (Canada), Eiko Ishioka (Japan), Krzysztof Piesiewicz (Poland), Greta Scacchi (UK), Antonio Tabucchi (Italy), Tran Anh Hung (France)

The 40th David di Donatello Awards ('Davids'), Rome, 8 June 1996

Best Film: *August Vacation*, by Paolo Virzi.

Best First Feature: *The Metre Reader*, by Stefano Incerti.

Best Director: Giuseppe Tornatore, for *The Star Maker*.

Best Actor: Giancarlo Giannini, for *Celluloid*.

Best Actress: Valeria Bruni Tedeschi, for *The Second Time*.

Best Supporting Actor: Leopoldo Trieste, for *The Star Maker*.

Best Producer: Pietro Innocenzi and Roberto Di Girolamo, for *Palermo Milan – No Return*.

Best Screenplay: *Celluloid*, by Furio Scarpelli, Ugo Pirro and Carlo Lizzani.

Best Cinematography: Alfio Contini, for *Beyond the Clouds*.

Best Production Design: Francesco Bronzi, for *The Star Maker*.

Best Foreign Film: *Nelly and Mr Arnaud* (France).

Best Foreign Actor: Harvey Keitel, for *Pulp Fiction*.

Best Foreign Actress: Susan Sarandon, for *Dead Man Walking*.

Luchino Visconti Career Achievement Award: Vittorio Gassman and Gina Lollobrigida.

Special David Award: Virna Lisi.

Special 40th Anniversary Awards: The producers Rita Cecchi Gori, Aurelio De Laurentiis and Giovanni Di Clemente.

The 'Evening Standard' 1995 Film Awards, London, 29 January 1996

Best Film: *The Madness of King George*.

Best Actor: Jonathan Pryce, for *Carrington*.

Best Actress: Kristin Scott Thomas, for *Angels and Insects*.

Best Screenplay: Alan Bennett, for *The Madness of King George*.

Best Technical Achievement: Andrew Dunn, cinematographer of *The Madness of King George*.

Most Promising Newcomer: Danny Boyle, director, for *Shallow Grave*.

The Peter Sellers Comedy Award: Peter Chelsom, writer-director, for *Funny Bones*.

Special Award: Director Lewis Gilbert.

The 21st French Academy ('César') Awards, 2 March 1996

Best Film: *La Haine*.

Best Director: Claude Sautet, for *Nelly et Mr Arnaud*.

Best Actor: Michel Serrault, for *Nelly et Mr Arnaud* (his third Cesar).

Best Actress: Isabelle Huppert, for *La Cérémonie*.

Best Supporting Actor: Eddy Mitchell, for *Le Bonheur et Dans Le Pre*.

Best Supporting Actress: Annie Girardot, for *Les Miserables*.

Most Promising Young Actor: Guillaume Depardieu, for *Les Apprentis*.

Most Promising Young Actress: Sandrine Kiberlain, for *Au Revoir (Ou Pas)*.

Best First Film: *Les Trois Freres*, by Bernard Campan and Didier Bourdon.

Best Original Screenplay: Josiane Balasko, for *Gazon Maudit* (aka *French Twist*).

Best Photography: Thierry Arbogast, for *The Horseman on the Roof*.

Best Editing: Mathieu Kassovitz and Scott Stevenson, for *La Haine*.

Best Production Design: Jean Rabasse, for *The City of Lost Children*.

Best Music: Zbigniew Preisner, Serge Gainsbourg and Michel Colombier, for *Elisa*.

Best Costumes: Christian Gasc, for *Madame Butterfly*.

Best Sound: Pierre Gamet and Dominique Hennequin, for *The Horseman on the Roof*.

Best Foreign Film: *Land and Freedom* (UK-Spain-Germany).

Best Short: *Le Moine et le Poisson*, by Michael Dudock De Wit.

Best Producer: Christophe Rossignon (Lazennec Productions).

The 53rd Hollywood Foreign Press Association ('Golden Globes') Awards, 21 January 1996

Best Film – Drama: *Sense and Sensibility*.

Best Film – Comedy or Musical: *Babe*.

Best Actor – Drama: Nicolas Cage, for *Leaving Las Vegas*.

Best Actress – Drama: Sharon Stone, for *Casino*.

Best Actor – Comedy or Musical: John Travolta, for *Get Shorty*.

Best Actress – Comedy or Musical: Nicole Kidman, for *To Die For*.

Best Supporting Actor: Brad Pitt, for *12 Monkeys*.

Best Supporting Actress: Mira Sorvino, for *Mighty Aphrodite*.

Best Director: Mel Gibson, for *Braveheart*.

Best Screenplay: Emma Thompson, for *Sense and Sensibility*.

Best Original Score: Maurice Jarre, for *A Walk in the Clouds*.

Best Original Song: 'Colors Of The Wind,' music by Alan Menken, lyrics by Stephen Schwartz, from *Pocahontas*.

Best Foreign Language Film: *Les Miserables* (France).

Best TV Film: *Indictment: The McMartin Trial*, by Mick Jackson.

Cecil B. De Mille Award for Lifetime Achievement: Sean Connery.

The 11th Independent Spirit Awards, Los Angeles, 23 March 1996

Best Film: *Leaving Las Vegas*.

Best First Film: *The Brothers McMullen*, by Edward Burns.

Best Director: Mike Figgis, for *Leaving Las Vegas*.

Best Actor: Sean Penn, for *Dead Man Walking*.

Best Actress: Elisabeth Shue, for *Leaving Las Vegas*.

Best Supporting Actor: Benicio Del Toro, for *The Usual Suspects*.

Best Supporting Actress: Mare Winningham, for *Georgia*.

Best Debut Performance: Justin Pierce, for *Kids*.

Best Screenplay: Christopher McQuarrie, for *The Usual Suspects*.

Best First Screenplay: Paul Auster, for *Smoke*.

Best Cinematography: Declan Quinn, for *Leaving Las Vegas*.

Best Foreign Film: *Before the Rain* (Macedonia), by Milcho Manchevski.

Host: Samuel L. Jackson

The 17th London Film Critics' Awards ('The Alfs'), The Savoy, London, 8 March 1996

Best Film: *Babe*.

Best Actor: Johnny Depp, for *Ed Wood* and *Don Juan de Marco*.

Best Actress: Nicole Kidman, for *To Die For*.

Best Director: Peter Jackson, for *Heavenly Creatures*.

Best Screenwriter: Paul Attanasio, for *Quiz Show* and *Disclosure*.

Best British Film: *The Madness of King George*.

Best British Producer: Simon Fields and Peter Chelsom, for *Funny Bones*.

Best British Director: Michael Radford, for *The Madness of King George*.

Best British Screenwriter: Alan Bennett, for *The Madness of King George*.

Best British Actor: Nigel Hawthorne, for *The Madness of King George*.

Best British Actress: Kate Winslet, for *Heavenly Creatures*.

Best British Newcomer: Director Danny Boyle, writer John Hodge and producer Andrew Macdonald, for *Shallow Grave*.

Best British Technical Achievement:

Kate Winslet as Marianne Dashwood in Ang Lee's Sense and Sensibility, *voted best supporting actress in the BAFTAs, best British actress by the London Film Critics' Circle and nominated for an Oscar*

Ken Adam, production designer of *The Madness of King George*.

Best Foreign Language Film: *Il Postino* (Italy-France).

Dilys Powell Award: Dame Wendy Hiller.

Special Award: Peter Rogers, producer of the *Carry On* films.

Presenters: Christopher Tookey, James Cameron-Wilson, Quentin Falk, Marianne Gray, Karen Krizanovich, George Perry, Simon Rose, etc.

The Los Angeles Film Critics' Association Awards, 23 December 1995

Best Film: *Leaving Las Vegas*.

Best Actor: Nicolas Cage, for *Leaving Las Vegas*.

Best Actress: Elisabeth Shue, for *Leaving Las Vegas*.

Best Supporting Actor: Don Cheadle, for *Devil in a Blue Dress*.

Best Supporting Actress: Joan Allen, for *Nixon*.

Best Director: Mike Figgis, for *Leaving Las Vegas*.

Best Screenplay: Emma Thompson, for *Sense and Sensibility*.
Best Cinematography: Lu Yue, for *Shanghai Triad*.
Best Production Design: Bo Welch, for *A Little Princess*.
Best Score: Patrick Doyle, for *A Little Princess*.
Best Foreign Film: *Wild Reeds* (France), by Andre Techine.
Best Documentary: *Crumb*, by Terry Zwigoff.
Best Animation: *Toy Story*.
New Generation Award: Alfonso Cuaron, director, for *A Little Princess*.
Career Achievement Award: Andre de Toth, director.
Douglas Edwards Award for Independent/Experimental Film & Video: *From the Journals of Jean Seberg* (USA), by Mark Rappaport.

The National Board of Review of Motion Pictures, New York, 13 December 1995

Best Film: *Sense and Sensibility*.
Best Actor: Nicolas Cage, for *Leaving Las Vegas*.
Best Actress: Emma Thompson, for *Carrington* and *Sense and Sensibility*.
Best Supporting Actor: Kevin Spacey, for *Outbreak*, *Seven*, *Swimming With Sharks* and *The Usual Suspects*.
Best Supporting Actress: Mira Sorvino, for *Mighty Aphrodite*.
Best Director: Ang Lee, for *Sense and Sensibility*.
Best Screenplay: Emma Thompson, for *Sense and Sensibility*.
Best Documentary: *Crumb*, by Terry Zwigoff.
Best Foreign Film: *Shanghai Triad* (China-France), by Zhang Yimou.
Freedom of Expression Award: Zhang Yimou.
Career Achievement Award: James Earl Jones.
Best TV Movie: *The Boys of St Vincents* (Canada), by John N. Smith.
Special Awards: *The Usual Suspects*, for its ensemble cast; Betty Comden and Adolph Green.
The Billy Wilder Award for Direction: Stanley Donen.
Outstanding Newcomer: Alicia Silverstone.
Special Achievement in Filmmaking Award: Mel Gibson.

The 30th National Society of Film Critics, New York, 3 January 1996

Best Film: *Babe*.
Best Actor: Nicolas Cage, for *Leaving Las Vegas*.
Best Actress: Elisabeth Shue, for *Leaving Las Vegas*.
Best Director: Mike Figgis, for *Leaving Las Vegas*.
Best Supporting Actor: Don Cheadle, for *Devil in a Blue Dress*.
Best Supporting Actress: Joan Allen, for *Nixon*.

The 61st New York Film Critics' Circle Awards, 14 December 1995

Best Film: *Leaving Las Vegas*.
Best Actor: Nicolas Cage, for *Leaving Las Vegas*.
Best Actress: Jennifer Jason Leigh, for *Georgia*.
Best Supporting Actor: Kevin Spacey, for *Outbreak*, *Seven*, *Swimming With Sharks* and *The Usual Suspects*.
Best Supporting Actress: Mira Sorvino, for *Mighty Aphrodite*.
Best Director: Ang Lee, for *Sense and Sensibility*.
Best Screenplay: Emma Thompson, for *Sense and Sensibility*.
Best Cinematography: Lu Yue, for *Shanghai Triad*.
Best Foreign Film: *Wild Reeds* (France), by Andre Techine.
Best Non-Fiction Film: *Crumb*, by Terry Zwigoff.
Best Directorial Debut: Chris Noonan, for *Babe*.
Special Award: Fabiano Canosa, programme founder and director of Film at the Public Theater.

The 18th Sundance Film Festival, Utah, 27 January 1996

The Grand Jury Prize (best feature): *Welcome to the Dollhouse*.
The Grand Jury Prize (best documentary): *Troublesome Creek*.
Special Jury Award: *When We Were Kings*; *Girls Town*.
Best Performance: Lili Taylor, for *I Shot Andy Warhol*.
Best Cinematography: Rob Sweeney, for *Color of a Brisk and Leaping Day*.

Best Cinematography (documentary): Andrew Young, for *Cutting Loose*.
Audience Award (best feature): *Care of the Spitfire Grill*.
Audience Award (best documentary): *Troublesome Creek*.
Filmmakers' Trophy (best feature): Jim McKay, for *Girls Town*.
Filmmakers' Trophy (best documentary): Andrew Young and Susan Todd, for *Cutting Loose*.
Waldo Scott Screenwriting Award: Stanley Tucci and Joseph Tropiano, for *The Big Night*.
Freedom of Expression Award: Rob Epstein and Jeffrey Friedman, for *The Celluloid Closet*.
Latin American Cinema Award: Fernando Perez, for *Madagascar*.
Short Filmmaking Award: Britta Sjogren, for *A Special Domain*.

The 52nd Venice International Film Festival Awards, September 1995

Golden Lion for Best Film: *Cyclo*, by Tran Anh Hung (France-Vietnam).
Special Jury Prize shared by: *God's Comedy*, by Joao Cesar Monteiro (Portugal); and *The Star Man*, by Giuseppe Tornatore (Italy).
Silver Lion shared by: *In the Bleak Midwinter*, by Kenneth Branagh (UK); *Maborosi no Hikari*, by Hirokazu Koreeda (Japan); and *Det Yani Dokhtar*, by Abdolfazl Jalili (Iran).
Best Actor: Goetz George, for *The Deathmaker* (Germany).
Best Actress shared by: Sandrine Bonnaire and Isabelle Huppert, both for *La Cérémonie* (France).
Best Supporting Actor: Ian Hart, for *Nothing Personal* (Ireland).
Best Supporting Actress: Isabella Ferrari, for *Diary of a Poor Young Man* (Italy).
Fipresci International Critics' Jury Prize shared by: *Cyclo* and *Beyond the Clouds*, by Michelangelo Antonioni and Wim Wenders (France-Italy-Germany).
Gold Medal of the Senate: Marco Tullio Giordana, for *Pasolini: An Italian Crime* (Italy).
Golden Lion for Career Achievement: Alberto Sordi, Monica Vitti, director Giuseppe De Santis, producer Goffredo Lombardi and composer Ennio Morricone.

Index

Page numbers in italic refer to illustrations only

Video releases are listed separately between pages 135 and 146

A Bout de Souffle 171
Abdul the Damned 176
Ace Ventura: When Nature Calls 8, 13, 161
Addams Family, The 161
Addams Family Values 161
Adventures of Don Juan, The 161
Adventures of Priscilla Queen of the Desert, The 24, 121
Age d'Or L' 171
Age of Innocence, The 30, 172
Airport 162
Airport 1975 164
Al Capone 173
Alamo Bay 178
Alien 115, 134
Alien 3 109
All About Eve 111
All Men Are Mortal 13
All That Heaven Allows 162
All the President's Men 127
All Things Fair 182, 183
All This and Heaven Too 180
Amateur 91
American in Paris, An 176
American President, The 13–14, 147, 181
American Trail, An 19
Amongst Friends 157
... And the Moon Dances 183
Angel Baby 14–15, 182, 183
Angels and Insects 15, 184
Angus 15–16
Anne Frank Remembered 182
Antonia's Line 182
Any Which Way You Can 159, 175
Apollo 13 8, 16, 147, 159, 160, 161, 162, 166, 181, 182, 183
Appat, L' 18
Apprentis, Les 184

Arachnophobia 120
Aristocats, The 160, 174
Arizona Dream 125
Arnold 176
Arrival of the Train, The 183
Arrowhead 184
Artists and Models 174
Assassins 17
Asterix Conquers America 17
Atlantic City 169, 178
Au Revoir (Ou Pas) 184
Au Revoir les Enfants 178
August Vacation 184
Aunt Julia and the Scriptwriter 37
Avanti! 171
Awfully Big Adventure, An 80, 171

B. Monkey 162
Babe 8, 9, 17–18, 147, 163, 181, 182, 183, 185, 186
Baby's Day Out 15
Babysitter, The 156
Bad Boy Bubby 72
Bad Boys 10, 79, 102, 160, 162, 164
Bad Taste 158
Bait, The 18, 46
Balto 18–19
Bandorlero 178
Barb Wire 19, 150, 152, *153*
Barcelona 82, 157
Barnabo Delle Montagne 19–20
Barnabo of the Mountains 19–20
Barry Lyndon 171
Barton Fink 161
Basic Instinct 161
Basketball Diaries, The 20, 147
Batailles, Les 69
Batman and Robin 154, 156, 164

Batman Forever 8, 9, 21, 71, 83, 120, 154, 159, 160, 164, 165, 181, 182
Battle Over Citizen Kane, The 182
Beautiful Girls 157
Beautiful Thing 21–2, 147
Bed of Roses 22–3, 147, 150
Before and After 23
Before the Rain 23–4, 185
Being Human 155, 156
Ben–Hur 160
Best Years of Our Lives, The 160
Beverly Hills Cop 162 154, 155
Bewegte Mann, Der 86
Beyond Bedlam 160
Beyond Rangoon 166
Beyond the Clouds 184, 186
Bhowani Junction 180
Big Broadcast, The 174
Big Night, The 186
Big Picture, The 78
Big Sleep, The 43
Bigamist, The 177
Birdcage, The 10, 24, 147, 163
Birds of a Feather 24
Black Moon 178
Black Rain 134
Black Sheep 155
Black Torment, The 179
Blackboard Jungle 41
Blade Runner 71, 134
Blaze of Glory 161
Blood Simple 50
Blue in the Face 24–5, 157
Blue Juice 25, 156
Bonheur et Dans Le Pré, Le 184
Bowery, The 180
Boy Who Stopped Talking, The 183
Boys of St Vincents, The 186

Boyz N the Hood 63, 161
Braindead 158
Bram Stoker's Dracula 89
Brassed Off 156
Braveheart 8, 25–6, 53, 69,
    181, 182, 183, 185
Brazil 123
Breakfast at Tiffanys 173
Breaking the Waves 184
Bridges of Madison County, The
    26–7, 127, 147, *151*, 161,
    181
Brigadoon 176
Broadcast News 127
Broken Arrow 27, 147, 166
Brooms 182
Brothers McMullen, The 27–8,
    150, 166, 185
Buddy Factor, The 118
Bugsy Malone 53, 152
Bull Durham 35
Bullets Over Broadway 82
Bunny Lake is Missing 169
Burnt by the Sun 28, 182
Bushwhacked 28, 56
Butch Cassidy 116
Butterfield 8 180
Butterfly Kiss 28–9, 112
Bye Bye Baby 153

Cable Guy, The 10, 147, 156
Cactus Flower 164
Cage Aux Folles, La 24
Calcutta 178
Call of the Wild 127
Camille 178
Canadian Bacon 29
Candidate, The 127
*Candyman 2: Farewell to the
    Flesh* 29
Cannonball Run, The 178
Cape Fear 120, 162
Capricious Summer 77
Captain Blood 40
Care of the Spitfire Grill 186
Careful, He Might Hear You
    162
Carlito's Way 165
Carmen Jones 58
Carpetbaggers, The 173
Carrington 29–30, 184, 186
Casablanca 19, 160
Casino 30–31, 147, 166, 167,
    181, 185
Casino Royale 161
Casper 8, 31–2, 160
Cast a Dark Shadow 175
Celluloid 184
Celluloid Closet, The 147, 183,
    186
Cérémonie, La 32, 60, 184
Chain of Desire 45
Champagne Safari, The 183
Charge of the Light Brigade, The
    176

Charms' Incidents 183
Chasing the Dream 182
Chicken From Outer Space, The
    182
Chinese Chocolate 183
Chitty Chitty Bang Bang 179
Chongqing Senlin 32, *33*
Chungking Express 32, *33*
Circle of Friends 103
Cité des Enfants Perdus, La
    33–4
Citizen Kane 170, 171
City Girl 180
City Hall 33–4, 148, 161
City of Fear 162
City of Joy 106
City of Lost Children, The 10,
    33–4, 185
Clean Slate 102
Cliffhanger 13
Clockers 34
Clockwise 163
Clockwork Orange, A 123, 155
Close Shave, A 182
Closely Observed Trains 76
Clueless 34–5, 148, 156
Cobb 35–6
Cobra 50
Coeur en Hiver, Un 91
Cold Fever 36, 86
*Color of a Brisk and Leaping
    Day* 186
Coneheads 155
Confessional, The 36, *37*, 183,
    184
Congo 161, 166
Coogan's Bluff 164
Cool Runnings 133
Copycat 36–7, 148
Country Doctor, A 183
Country Life 37–8, 162
Cousin Cousine 80
Cover Girl 176
Crackers 178
Crash 184
Crime Time 160
Crimson Tide 10, 38–9, 45,
    148, 162, 181, 182
Crooks and Coronets 179
Crumb 186
Crush, The 156
Cry Danger 161
Cry from the Streets, A 175
Cure, The 39
CutThroat Island 39–40, 88,
    161
Cutting Loose 186
Cyclo 40–41, 186
Cyrano de Bergerac 64

D'Artagnan's Daughter 41–2
Damage 178
Damsel in Distress, A 174
Dance Me Outside 183
Dangerous Affair, A 180

Dangerous Liaisons 81
Dangerous Minds 10, 41, 127,
    161, 162, 165
Dark City 161
Dave 161
David and Lisa 160
Day at the Races, A 180
Day of Reckoning 17
Days of Being Wild 32
Dead Again 165
Dead Drop 166
Dead Man Walking 42, 166,
    181, 182, 183, 184, 185
Dead Poets Society 41
Deadly Trap, The 162
Dear God 155
Death in Venice 86
Deathmaker, The 186
Def By Temptation 91, 128
Delicatessen 34
Demolition Man 71, 116
Demon Seed 163
Denise Calls Up 148
Desperado 42–3, 148, 166
Det Yani Dokhtar 186
Devil in a Blue Dress 43–4, 166,
    185, 186
Devil's Brigade, The 162
Devils Don't Dream 183
Diary of a Mad Housewife 160
Diary of a Poor Young Man 186
Die Hard 48
Die Hard With a Vengeance 8,
    44, 160, 161, 162
Dirty Harry 159, 175
Disclosure 185
Divine Rapture 159
Dolores Claiborne 44–5
Don Juan De Marco 182, 185
Don's Party 162
Double, The 164
Double Indemnity 6
Double Life, A 160
Double Life of Veronique, The
    162
Down by Law 36
Down Periscope 45
Dr Jekyll & Ms Hyde 45
Dracula 161
Dragnet 110
Dreaming of Julia 157
Drop Dead Fred 13
Drop in the Ocean, A 183
Duke of Groove 182
Dumb and Dumber 23
Dunston Checks In 45
Dust of Life 182
Dying Young 170

E.T. 31, 66, 116
Earthquake 164
Easy Rider 169
Easy Women 163
Eclipse 45–6
Ed Wood 78

Eddie 161
Edwards and Hunt 155
Eighth Day, The 184
Elisa 46–7, 148, 185
Emma 156
Emmanuelle 7
Empire Records 46, 47, 158
*En Compagnie d'Antonin
    Artaud* 90–91
End, The 182
Enfant D'eau, L' 183
Enfer, L' 53
Enforcer, The 159
*Englishman Who Went Up a
    Hill, but Came Down a
    Mountain, The* 47, 166
ER 49
Eraser 148
Ermo 171
Escape from New York 48
Evening Star, The 163
Evita 163
Excess Baggage 156
Executive Decision 48
Exit to Eden 48
Exquisite Tenderness 49
Extreme Measures 160
Eye for an Eye 49, 166

Fair Game 49–50, 148
Fall Time 50, 148
Fantasia Continued 168
Fargo 50–51, 184
Farinelli Il Castrato 51–2, 167
Fast Lady, The 175
Father of the Bride Part II 52,
    163
Father's Little Dividend 52
Feast of July 84, 152
Femme Française, Une 53, 166
Feu Follet, Le 177
*Fiction and Other Truths: A
    Film About Jane Rule* 183
*Fiddlefest – Roberta
    Guaspari–Tzavara and Her
    East Harlem Violin Program*
    182
Field of Dreams 164
*Fiend With the Atomic Brain,
    The* 171
Final Analysis 120
Fire Down Below 161
Fire Within, The 177, 178
First Knight 52, 53, 148, 161
Fisher King, The 123, 127
Fistful of Fingers, A 53, 150
Flashdance 111, 162
Flesh and Fury 175
Fleures Magiques, Les 184
Flintstones, The 110
Flor De Mi Secreto, La 53
Flower of My Secret, The 53
For Me and My Girl 176
For Your Eyes Only 161, 164
Forced Landing 174

Forget Paris 53–4, 148
Forrest Gump 87, 166, 169
Four Daughters 180
Four in a Jeep 161, 176
Four Mothers 180
Four Rooms 54
Four Seasons, The 164
Four Steps in the Clouds 130
Four Weddings and a Funeral
   167, 170, 183
Four Wives 180
Foxy Brown 58
Frankenstein Meets the Wolf
   Man 176
Frankie Starlight 54–5
Free Willy 2 55
French Kiss 55–6, 162, 166
French Twist 56, 185
Fresh 113
Frieda 180
From Dusk Till Dawn 56–7,
   154
From the Journals of Jean Seberg
   186
Fugitive, The 170
Fun 112
Funny Bones 56, 57, 148, 167,
   184, 185
Fuzz 164

G. I. Jane 164
Gagarin 182
Gallivant 160
Game, The 164
Gaslight Addition, The 95
Gazon Maudit 56, 57, 185
Georgia 185, 186
Get Shorty 10, 57–8, 161,
   163–4, 185
Getaway, The 163
Ghost in the Shell 58
Ghost Train, The 175
Ghostbusters, The 31
Ghoul, The 175
Gigi 174
Girl and the Gambler, The 180
Girl 6 58–9
Girls Town 186
Glimmer Man, The 161
God's Comedy 186
Godfather, The 163
Gods Must Be Crazy, The 162
Goldeneye 8, 9, 59, 148, 161,
   162
Gone With the Wind 161, 169
Good Cop, Bad Cop 152
Goodbye, Mr Chips 174
GoodFellas 30, 32, 157, 166
Gorillas in the Mist 75
Grace Under Pressure 114
Gracie Allen Murder Case, The
   174
Great Muppet Caper, The 88
Great St. Trinian's Train Rob-
   bery, The 179

Green Hornet, The 154
Grotesque, The 60
Grown Ups 107
Guardian, The 164
Guiltrip 60
Guys and Dolls 179

Hackers 60, 148
Haine, La 61, 184, 185
Halloween 49
Hamlet 166
Hand That Rocks the Cradle,
   The 120
Hank Aaron 182
Happiest Days of Your Life, The
   180
Hate 61
Haunted 61–2
Hearts of Fire 151
Heat 8, 62–3, 162
Heaven and Earth 162
Heaven's Prisoners 63
Heavenly Creatures 28, 112,
   182, 185
Heavy 63, 158
Hello Again 160
Hello Dolly 176
Henry and June 159
Henry V 95, 165
Her First Affair 177
Hercules 168
Hidden, The 115
Hidden Agenda 74
Hideaway 156
High Society 161
Higher Learning 63–4, 161
Highway to Hell 13
Hindle Wakes 179
Histoires Extraordinaires 178
Hobson's Choice 175
Hold Me, Thrill Me, Kiss Me
   64, 148
Holiday Camp 175
Hollywood or Bust 178
Home Alone 116
Homme dans Ma Vie, L' 80
Horseman on the Roof, The 10,
   64, 65, 185
Hotel Sorrento 183
Houseboat 159, 175
How Green Was My Valley 176
How to Make an American Quilt
   64–5
Hudson Hawk 172
Humaine Trop Humaine 178
Hunchback of Notre Dame, The
   (1923) 178
Hunchback of Notre Dame, The
   (1995) 75, 162, 167, 180
Hunt For Red October, The 39,
   45
Hussard Sur le Toit, Le 64, 65

I Confess 36
I Married a Ghoul From Outer

Space 57
I Shot Andy Warhol 186
I've Heard the Mermaids
   Singing 132, 151
If I'm Lucky 179
Imaginary Crimes 65–6
Imitation of Life 162
In the Bleak Midwinter 67–8,
   186
In the Line of Fire 116, 151
In the Soup 78
In Which We Serve 175
Independence Day 150
Indian in the Cupboard, The 66
Indochine 165
Innocent Blood 91
Innocent Sleep, The 66–7
Institute Benjamenta 67
Intimate With a Stranger 68
Into the West 165
Is Paris Burning? 162
Ishtar 164
It Happened in Flatbush 179
It Happened One Night 169
It's a Wonderful Life 120

Jack and Sarah 93, 167
Jade 68, 151, 161
Jake's Women 157
Jason's Lyric 68–9
Jeanne La Pucelle 69
Jeffrey 24, 69–70, 148, 150
Jeux Interdits, Les 162
Jim Dine: A Self–Portrait on the
   Walls 182
Jitterbugs 179
Joan of Arc 69
Johnny Mnemonic 70–71, 148,
   184
Johnny Suede 78
Joyriders 60
Jude 158
Judge Dredd 8, 10, 70, 71, 83,
   148
Judgement in Stone, A 186
Jumanji 8, 71–2, 163, 164
Jungle Book, The 160
Junior 170
Jurassic Park 79
Juror, The 32, 72, 166
Just You and Me Kid 174

Kafka 126
Kaspar Hauser 72
Katia Ismailova 72–3
Keep It Up Jack! 179
Kes 134
Kid in King Arthur's Court, A
   158
Kids 73–4, 159, 185
Killing, The 162
Killing Fields, The 106, 161,
   162
King of Kings 176
King of the Hill 126

Kitty 179
Knave of Hearts 162
Kokaku Kidotai 58
Krays, The 134

Lace Ladies 80
Lacombe Lucien 177, 178
Land and Freedom 74, 185
Land Before Time, The 19
Landscape in the Mist 125
Last of the Dogmen 74–5
Last Picture Show, The 163
Last Supper, The 148
Last Time I Saw Paris, The 174
Lawnmower Man, The 75
Lawnmower Man 2, The: Be-
   yond Cyberspace 75–6
Lawrence of Arabia 172
Lean On Me 41
Leaving Las Vegas 76, 181,
   185, 186
Les Girls 176
Let Him Have It 134
Letter From an Unknown
   Woman 160
Letter to Three Wives, A 180
Liar, Liar 160
Licence to Kill 164
Lieberman in Love 182
Life and Extraordinary Adven-
   tures of Private Ivan Chonkin,
   The 76–7
Life is Sweet 163
Lift to the Scaffold 177, 178
Like Water for Chocolate 130
Lion King, The 118, 166
Little Princess, A 77–8, 166,
   167, 181, 182, 186
Little Surprises 182
Little Women 161, 180
Living in Oblivion 78–9
Living Sea, The 182
Local Hero 79, 155
Loch Ness , 78, 79, 150
London Belongs to Me 180
Loneliness of the Long Distance
   Runner, The 179
Long Day Closes, The 91
Longtime Companion 70, 164
Love and Death on Long Island
   160
Love is a Many Splendored
   Thing 161
Love Serenade 184
Lovers, The 177, 178
Low Down Dirty Shame, A 79

Maborosi no Hikari 186
Mad Dogs and Englishmen 160,
   173
Madagascar 186
Madagascar Skin 79
Madame Butterfly 185
Mademoiselle from Armentieres
   179

Madigan 175
Madness of King George, The 167, 183, 184, 185
Madre Muerta, La 79–80
Magic in the Water 183
Magnificent Obsession 162
Mahjong 183
Malcom 162
Man in My Life, The 80
Man of No Importance, A 80
Man of the Year 80–81
Man Who Came to Dinner, The 161, 180
Man With No Name 53
Margaret's Museum 183
Mariachi, El 42
Marseille Contract, The 161
Martha & Ethel 81
Mary Reilly 81–2, 149
Mask, The 19
McMartin Trial, The 185
Mean Streets 40
Medusa Touch, The 173
Meet Me in St Louis 6
Meet the Feebles 158
Metal Skin 182
Metre Reader, The 184
Mi Familia 89–90
Microcosmos 184
Midnight Cowboy 113
Mighty Aphrodite 82, 149, 156, 157, 181, 185, 186
Mighty Morphin Power Rangers: The Movie 82–3
Milou en Mai 178
Miracle on 34th Street 151
Miserables, Les 83–4, 125, 184, 185
Misery 45
Mission, The 106, 161
Mission: Impossible 164
Mister Hobo 176
Mistress 78
Moby Dick 180
Moine et le Poisson, Le 185
Mommie Dearest 160
Mon Homme 183
Mon Oncle 177
Mon Père, Ce Héros 18
Money Train 84
Month By the Lake, A 84
Moonlight and Valentino 84–5
Morgan – A Suitable Case for Treatment 179
Mortal Kombat 85–6
Moscow Nights 73, 86
Most Desired Man, The 86
Most Terrible Time in My Life, The 86–7
Mr Holland's Opus 87, 149, 181
Mr Ricco 178
Mrs Minever 174
Much Ado About Nothing 95, 165

Mulholland Falls 149
Muppet Christmas Carol, The 88
Muppet Movie, The 88
Muppet Treasure Island 87–8
Muppets Take Manhattan, The 88
Murder By Contract 162
Murder in Mississippi 155
Murder in the First 88–9
Murderers' Row 178
Muriel's Wedding 8
Murmur of the Heart 177, 178
Music of Chance, The 15
My Best Friend's Wedding 161
My Dinner With André 178
My Fair Lady 171, 173
My Family 89–90, 182
My First Wife 162
My Friend Irma 178
My Left Foot 103, 134
My Life 162
My Life and Times With Antonin Artaud 90–91
My Life as a Dog 114
My Man Godfrey 174
My New Gun 170
My Posse Don't Do Homework 41
My Sweet Little Village 77
Mystery Of Marie Roget, The 176
Mystery Train 36, 86

Nadja 90, 91, 149
Nanook of the North 127
National Velvet 6
Natural Born Killers 162, 164, 170
Nelly and Mr Arnaud 91, 184
Neon Bible, The 91
Net, The 92, 152
Never Give Up: The 20th Century Odyssey of Herbert Zipper 182
Never Take Sweets From a Stranger 179
New Leaf, A 164
Night On Earth 36
Night Unto Night 176
Night Watch 156
Nightwatch 92, *93*
Nine Months 92–4, 159, 167
Nixon 94, 149, 157, 161, 181, 182, 185, 186
Norma Jean & Marilyn 157
Normal Heart, The 70
Norte, El 90
Nothing Personal 186
Nouveau Monde, Le 156
Now and Then 94–5, 167
Now Voyager 161
NY Cop 157

O Quatrilho 182
Odd Man Out 180

Of Human Bondage 176
Oh God 174
Okaeri 183
Old Dark House, The 60
Omega Man, The 161
On the Town 176
On the Waterfront 162, 173
Once Were Warriors 182, 183
One Fine Day 154, 166
One Flew Over the Cuckoo's Nest 32
101 Dalmations 179
One Survivor Remembers 182
Only You 55
Orlando 160
Othello 95, 101, 151
Outbreak 123, 160, 186
Outrage 177

Paint Your Wagon 171
Palermo Milan – No Return 184
Panther 95–6
Paoda Shuang Deng 100
Parallel Lives 157
Paris Model 174
Pasolini: An Italian Crime 186
Passion of Darkly Noon, The 96
Passionate Friends, The 180
Peacemaker, The 154
Pebble and the Penguin, The 96
Performance 163
Persuasion 96–7
Petite Voleuse, La 46
Phantom India 178
Phenomenon 149
Philadelphia 162
Pickwick Papers, The 175
Picnic 183
Pillow Book, The 156
Pillow Talk 162
Pint O'Bitter, A 132
Pirate, The 176
Place de la République 178
Platoon 130
Playboys, The 103, 113
Player, The 78
Plein Soleil 162
Pocahontas 8, 97–8, 149, 159, 161, 167, 181, 182, 185
Podmoskovnye Vechera 72–3
Poetic Justice 63, 161
Poison 104
Pork Chop Hill 175
Postino, Il 98–9, 162, 163, 181, 182, 183, 185
Postman, The 98–9
Pretty Baby 178
Pretty Woman 48, 155
Primal Fear 99, 149, 166
Prisons, Les 69
Privée, Le 177, 178
Proof 64
Psycho 162, 172, 173
Pulp Fiction 116, 184

Quick and the Dead, The 99–100
Quiz Show 127, 157, 185

Radio Days 168
Raging Bull 35
Rain Man 166
Raining Stones 74
Raising Arizona 50, 161
Rambling Rose 120
Ransom 159
Raw Justice 152
Red Balloon, The 134
Red Firecracker, Green Firecracker 100
Red Surf 154
Reds 157
Reflecting Skin, The 96
Regard d'Ulysse 124–5
Reine Margot, La 182
Remains of the Day, The 153
Renaissance Man 41
Rendez–vous in Paris 100
Rescuers Down Under, The 174
Reservoir Dogs 50, 57, 154
Restoration 100–101, 166, 167, 182
Return of the Killer Tomatoes! 154
Richard III 101, 182, 183
Ritz, The 164
River Runs Through It, A 164
Rob Roy 53, 181, 183
Robin Hood 26
Rock, The 101–2, 164
Romy and Michele's High School Reunion 157
Ronde, La 45
Roommates 182
Rough Magic 102
Rudy 103
Run of the Country, The 103
Runaway Brain 182
Ryan's Daughter 103

Sabrina 103–4, 155, 181, 182
Safe 104
Safe Passage 104–5
San Francisco Story, The 161
Santa Clause, The 8, 10, 105–6
Scarlet Letter, The 106
Scent of Green Papaya, The 40
Schindler's List 82, 167
Screamers 107
Sea Hawk, The 40, 160
Second Time, The 184
Secret Garden, The 77
Secrets and Lies 107, 164, 184
Self–Made Hero, A 184
Sense and Sensibility 8, 97, 108, 158, 160, 162, 163, 166, 172, 181, 182, 183, 185, 186
Separation, La 108, *109*
Sergeant York 160

Sergeants Three 178
Serpent's Kiss, The 156
Servant, The 32, 60
Seven 8, 9, 109–10, 149, 162, 167, 181, 186
Seventh Seal, The 171
sex, lies and videotape 68, 125
Sgt. Bilko 110, 149
Shadow of Hate, The 182
Shallow Grave 123, 155, 156, 184, 185
Shane 163
Shanghai Triad 110–11, 181, 186
Shattered Dreams 156
She Wore a Yellow Ribbon 163
Shining, The 89
Shooter, The 111
Short Cuts 58
Short Film About Killing, A 162
Short Film About Love, A 162
Showgirls 111, 149, 151, 159, 160, 161
Silence of the Lambs, The 23, 72
Silent Fall 158
Silent Night 183
Silent World, The 177
Simple Men 91
Simple Twist of Fate, A 113
Singin' in the Rain 176
Sister Act 116, 161
Sister My Sister 112–13
Slime Creatures II 57
Small Deaths 184
Small Faces 113
Smile Like Yours, A 155
Smoke 24, 113–14, 185
Snapdragon 152
Sneakers 164
Something for the Boys 179
Something To Talk About 114–15, 149
Sommersby 37
Sons of Katie Elder, The 178
Spanking the Monkey 114, 115
Sparrows Can't Sing 179
Special Domain, A 186
Species 115, 161
Speed 27, 116
Spellbound 160
Spinning Family, The 176
Spiral Staircase, The 89
Split Second 115
Spy Hard 116
Stand and Deliver 41
Stand by Me 94, 130
Stanley's Cup 155
Star Maker, The 182, 184
Star Man, The 186
Star Wars 122
Stargate 48, 161
State Fair 179
Stealing Beauty 157
Stolen Hearts 116, 150, 152
Stonewall 24, 116–17, 167

Stooge, The 178
Story of Ruth, The 176
Strange Days 117
Strawberry and Chocolate 163
Street Fighter 160
Strictly Ballroom 48
Striptease 164
Stunt Man, The 89
Suburban Wives 179
Sudden Death 117–18
Sugarland Express, The 163
Suite 16 118
Summer in New Hampshire 176
Sun Has Ears, The 183
Sun Valley 183
Sunshine Boys, The 174
Superman 21
Superstar: The Karen Carpenter Story 104
Swan Princess, The 118
Sweet Nothing 157
Swimming With Sharks 118, 149, 186

Take Me Out to the Ball Game 176
Tango & Cash 48
Tarantella 157
Taxi Driver 32
Ten Thousand Bedrooms 178
Terminator, The 123
Terminator 2 161
Terror in the Wax Museum 176
That Eye, the Sky 182, 183
That's Entertainment 176
That's My Boy 178
Thelma & Louise 28, 114, 154, 166, 169
Thin Line Between Love and Hate, A 119
Thing, The 48
Things To Do in Denver When You're Dead 119, 149
This Boy's Life 102
This Dream People Call Human Life 67
This Sporting Life 132
Thoroughly Modern Millie 162
Thousand Clowns, A 162
Three Coins in the Fountain 161
Three Colours: Blue 162
Three Colours: Red 162, 182
Three Colours: White 162
Three Musketeers, The 134
Three Ring Circus 178
Three Wishes 119–20
Tie That Binds, The 120
Time of Destiny, A 90
Time of the Gypsies 125
Titanic 158
To Die For 120–21, 127, 185
To Have (Or Not) 183
To Live 111
To Sir, With Love 41, 87
To the Victor 176

To Vlemma Tou Odyssea 124–5
To Wong Foo, Thanks for Everything! Julie Newmar 24, 121–2, 150, 167
Tommy Boy 121, 155
Tony Rome 180
Top Gun 162
Torch Song 156
Total Recall 161
Toy Story 8, 9, 122–3, 150, 161, 162, 163, 181, 182, 186
Trainspotting 8, 123, 150, 155, 156, 167, 183
Travelling Players, The 125
Trial By Jury 72
Trigger Effect, The 166
Trois Frères, Les 184
Trop Belle Pour Toi! 56, 164
Trouble With Angels, The 161
Troublesome Creek: A Midwestern 182, 186
True Crime 156
True Lies 59, 116
Truth About Cats and Dogs, The 152, 153
Tuesday Morning Ride 182
Twelve Angry Men 173
Twelve Monkeys 123–4, 150, 181, 182, 185
Twins 169
Twister 164
Two Deaths 124
Two Evil Eyes 173
Two Girls and a Sailor 174
Two If By Sea 116, 124
2001: A Space Odyssey 122, 169

Ulysses' Gaze 124–5, 167
Under Siege 126
Under Siege 2 126–7, 161
Underground 125
Underneath, The 125–6
Unfinished Business 176
Unstrung Heroes 127, 150, 181
Unzipped 127
Up Close and Personal 127–8
Uptown Saturday Night 161
Usual Suspects, The 128, 150, 181, 183, 185, 186
Utomlennye Solntsem 28

Vampire in Brooklyn 91, 128–9, 150
Vanya On 42nd Street 178
Verbrechen am Seelenleben eines Menschens 72
Victors, The 162
Village of Dreams 183
Visiteurs, Les 171
Viva Maria 178
Vive Le Tour 178

Voleur, Le 178

Waga Jinsei Saiaku No Toki 86–7
Wait Until Dark 164
Waiting to Exhale 129, 150, 165
Walk in the Clouds, A 129–30, 167, 185
War, The 130–31, 150
War and Peace 173
Warlock 172
Washington Square 153
Watermelon Woman, The 183
Waterworld 8, 40, 53, 131, 150, 151, 158, 161, 166, 170, 182
Way We Were, The 176
Welcome to LA 161, 176
Welcome to the Dollhouse 183, 186
West 11 175
What a Way to Go 178
What's Eating Gilbert Grape? 114
What's Up Nurse 179
When Night is Falling 131–2, 151
When Saturday Comes 132
When We Were Kings 186
While You Were Sleeping 8, 55, 132–3
White Balloon, The 133–4
White Men Can't Jump 35, 84
White of the Eye 163
White Room 132
White Squall 134
Who Framed Roger Rabbit 19
Wife Swappers, The 179
Wild and the Willing, The 173
Wild Bunch, The 163
Wild Reeds 186
Wild Side, The 163
Wind, The 184
Withnail & I 172
Wolf 120
Women, The 163
Woodlanders, The 160
Wyatt Earp 170

X Marks the Spot 180
Xanadu 176
Xich Lo 40–41

Young Lions, The 178
Young Lovers, The 177
Young Poisoner's Handbook, The 134
Young Soul Rebels 162
Youngblood Hawke 174

Zazie Dans le Métro 177, 178
Zero de Conduite 171
Zulu Dawn 171